THE NECRONOMICON CYCLE

A Literary Commentary on
The H.P. Lovecraft Tarot

Tim Thompson

BLACK MOON PUBLISHING
CINCINNATI, OHIO
USA

Black Moon Manifesto

It is the Will and mission of Bate Cabal/Black Moon to effectively manifest unique and insightful occult Works for the esoteric community in a manner that is unfettered by commercial considerations.

Copyright © 2021 Tim Thompson
Tarot images Copyright © 2021 Daryl L. Hutchinson
Cover design © 2021 Jo Bounds of Black Moon
All rights reserved.

BlackMoonPublishing.com

blackmoonpublishing@gmail.com

Design and layout by
Jo Bounds of Black Moon

ISBN: 978-1-890399-84-9

United States • United Kingdom • Europe • Australia • India • Japan

Contents

Foreword 7
Preface 9
Introduction: Comparative Religion and the
    Apocrypha of R'Lyeh on Earth 12

The Azathoth Cycle
  An Introduction to the Study of The HP Lovecraft Tarot 23
  The HP Lovecraft Tarot: Principles Established 24
  The HP Lovecraft Tarot and the Card of The Fool 26
  A History/Sociology of the Tarot 32
  A History of The Necronomicon as the Religious Statement of
      The Cult of R'Lyeh on Earth 40
  On the Minor Arcana 48
  On The Zodiac in Relation to The Necronomicon and the Tarot ... 51
  On the Tarot and the Mystical Qabballah 56
  A Statement to Describe Card 0 of The Jungian System of Tarot .. 60
  On the Subject of 777 63
  New Religious Movement or New Movement of Religion?
      The Cult of R'Lyeh on Earth 66

The Major Arcana Cycle
  According to the HP Lovecraft Tarot 71
  0. Azathoth: The Fool 72
  1. Nyarlathotep: The Communicator 79
  2. Yog-Sothoth: The High Priestess 88
  3. Shub-Niggurath: The Empress 94

4. Hastur. The King in Yellow: The Emperor 99
5. Cthulhu: The Hierophant 105
6. Lavinia Whateley & Yog Sothoth: The Lovers 113
7. Ithaqua: The Chariot 121
8. Shoggoth: Strength 127
9. Great Race of Yith: The Hermit 134
10. Hounds of Tindalos: The Wheel of Fortune 143
11. Mi Go: Justice 149
12. Deep One: The Hanged Man 156
13. Ghoul: Death 161
14. Old One: Temperance 167
15. Tsathoggua: The Devil 173
16. The Dunwich Horror: The Tower 182
17. Nodens, Lord of the Great Abyss: The Star 191
18. Night Gaunt: The Moon 196
19. Yig, the Serpent God: The Sun 203
20. Dagon: Judgement 209
21. Chaugnar Faugn: The World 216

The Minor Arcana Cycle
  According to the HP Lovecraft Tarot 223
  Introduction to the Study of the Minor Arcana 223
  Suit of Man/People 229
  1. HP Lovecraft: Equates to the Ace of Cups 232
  2. Randolph Carter: Equates to the Two of Cups 236
  3. LeGrasse: Equates to the Three of Cups 240
  4. Charles Dexter Ward: Equates to the Four of Cups . 245
  5. Erich Zann: Equates to the Five of Cups 249
  6. Herbert West, Reanimator: Equates to the Six of Cups 253
  7. Obed Marsh: Equates to the Seven of Cups 256
  8. Wizard Whateley: Equates to the Eight of Cups 260
  9. Wilbur Whateley: Equates to the Nine of Cups 264

  10. Dr Munoz: Equates to the Ten of Cups 267
  11. Dr Armitage: Equates to the Page of Cups 270
  12. Crawford Tillinghast: Equates to the Knight of Cups 274
  13. Nahum Gardner: Equates to the Queen of Cups 280
  14. Keziah Mason: Equates to the King of Cups 285

Suit of Artifacts 290
  1. Star Stone: Equates to the Ace of Swords 293
  2. The Colour Out of Space: Equates to the Two of Swords 297
  3. The Silver Key: Equates to the Three of Swords 301
  4. The Shining Trapezohedron: Equates to the Four of Swords . 304
  5. Guardian of Kadath: Equates to the Five of Swords 309
  6. The Yellow Sign: Equates to the Six of Swords 312
  7. EOD Vestments: Equates to the Seven of Swords 317
  8. The Tillinghast Resonator: Equates to the Eight of Swords . . 322
  9. Pickman's Model: Equates to the Nine of Swords 326
  10. Mi-Go Brain Cylinder: Equates to the Ten of Swords 332
  11. Bokrug, the Water Lizard: Equates to the Page of Swords . . . 339
  12. Hound Amulet: Equates to the Knight of Swords 344
  13. Derby Stone: Equates to the Queen of Swords 348
  14. Plutonian Drug: Equates to the King of Swords 351

Suit of Tomes 356
  1. Necronomicon: Equates to the Ace of Wands 359
  2. De Vermis Mysteriis: Equates to the Two of Wands 362
  3. Unspeakable Cults: Equates to the Three of Wands 366
  4. R'Lyeh Texts: Equates to the Four of Wands 370
  5. Dhol Chants: Equates to the Five of Wands 373
  6. Libre de Eibon: Equates to the Six of Wands 376
  7. King in Yellow: Equates to the Seven of Wands 380
  8. Cultes des Goules: Equates to the Eight of Wands 383
  9. Pnakotic Manuscripts: Equates to the Nine of Wands 386
  10. Eltdown Shards: Equates to the Ten of Wands 389
  11. People of the Monolith: Equates to the Page of Wands 393

12. Ponape Scriptures: Equates to the Knight of Wands 396
  13. Cryptical Books of Hsan: Equates to the Queen of Wands ... 399
  14. The Regnum Congo: Equates to the King of Wands 403
Suit of Sites 406
  1. Sunken R'Lyeh: Equates to the Ace of Pentacles 409
  2. Irem, City of Pillars: Equates to the Two of Pentacles 413
  3. Plateau of Leng: Equates to the Three of Pentacles 422
  4. Whateley Farmhouse: Equates to the Four of Pentacles 429
  5. The Witch House: Equates to the Five of Pentacles 432
  6. Mountains of Madness: Equates to the Six of Pentacles 436
  7. Church of Federal Hill: Equates to the Seven of Pentacles ... 442
  8. Innsmouth: Equates to the Eight of Pentacles 445
  9. Kadath: Equates to the Nine of Pentacles 450
  10. Exham Priory: Equates to the Ten of Pentacles 453
  11. Sentinel Hill: Equates to the Page of Pentacles 457
  12. EOD Temple: Equates to the Knight of Pentacles 459
  13. House in the Mist: Equates to the Queen of Pentacles 467
  14. Arkham: Equates to the King of Pentacles 471

Conclusion: Join the Cult of R'Lyeh on Earth 478
Further Reading 481
Appendix I: A Further Statement on the Minor Arcana 493
Appendix II: A Statement of 777, The Correspondences
    and The Hermetic Order of The Golden Dawn 516
Bibliography 525

Foreword

As would be expected with a book on the subject of the manifest existence of the occult and the *HP Lovecraft Tarot* – a book written to establish the validity of *The Necronomicon* as an important and largely forgotten religious statement – work on this book has not been without its own history of problems.

The original concept behind this book, and the general premise with this work, starts with the advice given by The Hermetic Order of the Golden Dawn of Thelema, that before working with any new Deck, of any published system of the Tarot, the Magus should ideally start work with going through that Deck, and to make written notes on which to draw personal insight. As someone who has had a passionate interest in the religious and conceptual ideas as represented by Howard Phillips Lovecraft (1890 – 1937) since I was quite young, it would have to have been second nature for me to make such reference through the specific study of this as the Lovecraft system of Tarot. Whilst work and the initial concept behind this book was started here, it wasn't a great leap of logic reasoning to establish the importance of statements such as the idea that all religious belief is actually manifest, on a number of different levels, on the basis of ideas projected psychically by one system of religious Gods who are known generally (by those who worship Them, amongst others) as The Great Old Ones. One religious idea led to the next, until the foundation of The Cult of R'Lyeh on Earth as the religious group responsible for this book, and as an organized

international underground movement dedicated to the furtherance of this statement of religious truth.

A final statement regarding literature and the validity of the religious ideas as represented by *The Necronomicon*, and further how such religious ideology has generally been expressed through a vehicle of literary fiction. Since the untimely death of Lovecraft, there is relatively little work published to represent the religious views that *The Necronomicon Cycle* has been written to represent. The main part of the work so far published to represent such religious truth is largely inaccurate, largely badly researched, and it is not entirely helpful that a lot of the written work representing this religious view exists in the form of straight literary fiction. A researched Further Reading List at the end of this book is intended to document the main part of such a small amount of work that properly represents this history of publishing, according to our interpretation of this idea, but nothing involved with *The Necronomicon Cycle* should be seen as being the final statement of argument. In putting this statement of a religious system of Tarot forward, The Cult of R'Lyeh regard it as being the case that we have properly delivered our religious perspective and opinion of belief to a world who would otherwise be ignorant. It is our hope that this book will in turn inspire others, and that there might be, at one point in the future, a movement of work published as inspired by the writing of The Cult of R'Lyeh on Earth.

—Tim Thompson. Aberdeen Park, London, August 2018.

Preface

Since its first publication, the second edition of the *HP Lovecraft Tarot* was an immediate commercial success. The first and second Editions of these Cards sold out pretty much immediately, and since that point getting your hands on a second hand copy would have cost hundreds of pounds, if you're lucky. It was on the basis of its validity in representing the Lovecraftian religious system, however, that I felt a proper written discussion of this Deck would be of benefit to a further discussion of a greater religious truth, on the basis of the scope involved with this as a comprehensive study of how such an idea involving the Tarot, actually equates to a definition of such a greater religious truth.

With *The Necronomicon Cycle* being a book that has taken me several years to write, and which has a history of its own problems, work on this manuscript has led to my being personally acquainted with both Daryl Hutchinson and Eric C. Friedman as those responsible for putting this Deck here in question together, as a statement that could be considered both as a work of religion and a work of postmodernist religious art. It was not until this book was near completion, however, that word came across suddenly that there was to be another published and revised edition of this system of the Tarot in question.

As having stated that this book has taken me a number of years to put together, with my having sat my Undergraduate Degree in Theology and Religious Studies as being part of the history of the work that's

gone into writing this book, it is lucky from my point of view that those responsible for putting this Deck together do not plan to reprint this system with a further Introductory Book to equate to this new intended Deck. It would be on this basis that most of the Cards with this third edition are equated as being the same, or on other terms very similar, as with the previous work, that I will still intend to draw closely from the ideas as with the second edition, as most of the Cards involved with the planned Third Edition will be still essentially the same. On the specific occasions that some of the Cards to this planned current edition have been changed, I will still be drawing my research from the same sources as with the original proof, as if the planned current version does not include such an Introductory Book, then we don't have a great deal more to go on in terms of a specifically different definition of meaning having been written to describe that amended Card. I hope that this will clarify a position from the perspective of the reader, and I hope that this written discussion of our religious interpretation of the Tarot will be of use to the Magus in further establishing their own religious perspective as resultant from a proper study of the ideas included with this book.

In having put that idea down on paper, as one last point as regarding the planned Third edition, and the recency of the definitions of these Cards as described in this book, whilst I was writing the stated Foreword to *The Necronomicon Cycle*, I received an e-mail from one of those responsible for the work behind this current work on the *HP Lovecraft Tarot* to say:

> "Tim. All of the illustrations [to the *HP Lovecraft Tarot*] are being reworked [with some of these already online] I think the best thing is for you to go ahead and base your work on the current edition as I really can't say when I'll be finished as I have too many personal

issues to really concentrate on the project. When the third edition is complete, then you can revise your work"

Whilst this is hardly the ideal position from my – or anyone's – point of view, this stated point of argument necessitates that I continue to work with this same edition of the *HP Lovecraft Tarot* in terms of the current work which was already currently in progress before this new information got to me, although readers and publishers should be confident that as soon as this third edition of this Deck is completed, revised work on *The Necronomicon Cycle* will also be rewritten as a current point of reference in hand.

—Tim Thompson, Caledonian Road, London 2020

Introduction: Comparative Religion and the Apocrypha of R'Lyeh on Earth

"The most merciful thing in the world, I think, is the inability of the human mind to correlate all its contents. We live on a placid island of ignorance in the midst of black seas of infinity, and it was not meant that we should voyage far." (Lovecraft: 1999: 139) [1]

This opening statement is from the short story that is Lovecraft's that is considered his main classic, and is used here to open *The Necronomicon Cycle* as a Black Book in the tradition of his writing. This book is a study of that religious concept that was considered to have been delivered by Lovecraft's writing, and is written to question whether these ideas were the concept of a writer of fiction, or as the ideas of a recluse who had been influenced in, by chance, having come across *The Necronomicon* as our sacred and religious book of black magick. Certain statements from Lovecraft may have

---

[1] This quotation is taken from the classic story, *The Call of Cthulhu* by HP Lovecraft (Penguin Books, 1999). The fictional religious work of Lovecraft has been published repeatedly by different publishers since his untimely death in the late 1930s. The fact that a publisher such as Penguin would also publish his fiction as part of their Modern Classics series does, in our opinion, lend some credence to Lovecraft's religious work.

been expressed by him as a writer of inspired fiction, whilst, further to this general idea, some current movements of magick will regard the Great Old Ones of Lovecraft's fictional and religious study, to be in actual terms quite real. The vision as therefore inspired by Lovecraft is, then, currently disputed by an international movement of religion, whilst the Cult of R'Lyeh on Earth stand at this point, and continuing as a forward position in time, to discuss those rambling and dark works of Lovecraft as something more conceptual than many will currently give credit for.

Despite this above statement having been taken from such religious fiction, this quoted paragraph has direct meaning to R'Lyeh on Earth as a new religious movement inspired by Lovecraft's views. In breaking down this quotation to the number of specific points that it in itself represents, we see the vision held by Lovecraft as having in his lifetime perhaps come across *The Necronomicon* as the book that inspired a large amount of his work. To him in these rambling and esoteric statements, creation is a reality far more complex than humanity can imagine, with our planet Earth being described as a "placid island of ignorance", with a reality of creation which is beyond comprehension described as being "black seas". And in saying that "humanity was not meant to voyage far" (Lovecraft: 1999: 139) an idea is expressed that, whatever technology may be created by humanity in our knowledge, and despite any technological advancements that humanity might accomplish, we can never expect to travel beyond the stars that we might have travelled already.

To Lovecraft this grasp of infinity was normal to him as one of a very few who might have seen *The Necronomicon* as the book of magick that inspired his fiction. As somebody who must have at least seen the book of Al Hazred at some point, the idea of a Mythos of mad Gods and massive cosmic chaotic confusion was natural. But, beyond this Lovecraft had not yet seen the greater relevance of this Mythos in actual terms of the scope of worship in question. To him the idea of massive astral confusion was something to be seen only as conceptual, whilst still being the mad intellectual nature of an unacknowledged religious

book. Whilst the world religions would, to Lovecraft, would continue to be the inherent belief of the human mind, and therefore a continued movement of human society; he seemed to have no knowledge of the greater relevance of the religious nature of what he might have seen in having accessed such a black and forbidden book of magick.

Despite this the Cult of R'Lyeh had existed then as we exist now. Isolated as we are, *The Necronomicon* has as much truth to us as a religious sect, as the *Bible* has to the Christians, or as the *Torah* to the Jews. The exception to the rule here, however, is that, whilst the world religions seem to recognise only one specific system of Gods, the R'Lyeh believe that all of those Gods which are spoken about in *The Necronomicon* are the actual reality of the Gods of our Universe, with Nyarlathotep being the God for human communication, and therefore being the God worshipped by most world religions.[2]

For those of us who regard *The Necronomicon* as our religious book, then, as is the view of The Cult of R'Lyeh on Earth, the religions of human kind are one thing: the insane psychick vibrations of the Great Old Ones in Their silence. Various ideas have arrived with the different cultures of humanity, over different periods of time and relating to different cultures, with the influence of Nyarlathotep as the God of communication to humanity being the greatest influence; with the greatest part of human religious thought being – as we see it – the mad, psychotic vibrations of the God who governs human perception.[3]

So in here defining our declared statement of belief, it is to us then, religious that the Cosmos and time are vast aspects of a reality that are vastly beyond human comprehension. As part of the greater

---

[2] The idea is, of course, much more complicated than this, but this is the idea that The Necronomicon Cycle is written to represent and to discuss.

[3] The concept of Nyarlathotep as regarded as part of the religion of the Cult of R'Lyeh (and how He is regarded in terms of the occult and the Tarot) is described as regards our worship in the proper context of the Cult of R'Lyeh, and in context with the system of worship we uphold, is discussed with Card 1 – the Communicator – below. Other religions may refer to the Communicator as Yahweh, Allah or Jehovah, although this makes little difference to the religious Cult of R'Lyeh on Earth.

scheme of things, humanity and this planet Earth are, to the system of Gods discussed in this book, completely irrelevant and openly abstract concepts. The Earth is as a speck of dust to the Gods, and humanity, with all of our intelligence and intellectual beliefs, are a tiny part of existence. Such a quotation establishes the point that humanity is destined not to travel far beyond our Solar System, and probably destined for extinction before achieving anything that could have any effect of the level of the Gods in this respect. Why, then, Nyarlathotep should be concerned with the futile progress of Man, we cannot be sure? But the history of humanity has been governed by a single God of *Necronomicon* study; with Nyarlathotep being the God worshipped by the Jews, Islam, Christianity and other major World religions, as He observes us in His insanity and the strange perception of our existence. If you can see religion in terms such as this, then you can see the significance of Lovecraft's writing in terms of the validity of such religious worship.

If our views on orthodox religion are therefore thought through on such defined terms, then, the reader may ask as to why the worship undertaken by the Cult of R'Lyeh on Earth revolves so much around the Tarot and related use of the occult? The reasons for this are twofold, and these reasons will be discussed as follows:

The first concerns the lack of actual, serious occult reference as concerns the occult literature to represent *The Necronomicon* as a working system of magick.[4] Since Lovecraft first discussed such religious ideas as concern *The Necronomicon* in the 1920s, a massive amount of literature has been produced which discuss such ideas as

---

[4] The reader may question the Cult of R'Lyeh, that if The Necronomicon is the religious book from which we base our religious belief, then why do we not directly draw from it in order to create our system of magick? The answer to this would be that actual copies of The Necronomicon are rare and extremely hard to come by. Despite holding The Necronomicon as being directly sacred, it is no more easy to gain access to it as the worshippers of the Gods of The Necronomicon, as it is for anybody else. Whilst it is considered, by us, to be a great initiation into the High Priesthood of the Cult of R'Lyeh on Earth to gain access to an original copy of the blasphemous book, it is as difficult for us as it is to others. A number of contemporary interpretations of The Necronomicon are currently in print, but none of these are anywhere near as involved as with the original Tome itself.

generally concern the Mythos as established by *The Necronomicon*; but very little serious work has been written to discuss where such ideas come into the serious and applied study of the occult. The religious views of our secular Cult are based on the small amount of serious work that does exist on the occult religious belief in the Great Old Ones, and being further based on the, much more developed systems which exist, who call themselves the 'Western Esoteric Temples' of ritual and ceremonial magick.[5] In short, whilst influenced by the ideas of Lovecraft, The Cult of R'Lyeh interpret such ideas on more contemporary terms, stating influence from groups such as The Golden Dawn of Thelema or The Illuminates of Thanteros, as more contemporary movements.

So in this respect, the system that is the *HP Lovecraft Tarot* is the most direct correlation between the religious ideas here discussed, and other religious/magickal systems that exist in terms of the contemporary study of the occult. All systems of Tarot are equal in terms of occult belief, if seen on those terms, and the Cult of R'Lyeh hold it as sacred that all religious views are sent forth by the Great Old Ones, in the same way that the major religions are sent forth, as described already in this Introduction. As regards this situation that actual copies of *The Necronomicon* have always been so difficult to access (and rightly so, as those who study it believe that the original version leads to insanity if improperly studied), interest in the religious / occult belief in *The Necronomicon* and its related systems of magick has become an issue of interest over the last few decades, probably more now than ever before. This book is written to speak to those who share such an interest in this system of the occult.

The second concerns the issue of the *HP Lovecraft Tarot* as the first serious study of Necronomicon magick as delivered as any specifically constructed system of Tarot. In the history of Tarot as a system of

---

5 In this we are speaking to all established Western Temples of ceremonial magick, concentrating largely on the system of the Golden Dawn (as well as some others), and drawing our inspiration from involving the Mythos of The Necronomicon as a direct parallel with established esoteric and magickal belief.

divination and access to the occult, this occult system of Cards stretches back literally for Centuries, with pretty much every esoteric as having been established in European society having a Deck dedicated to its own system of belief somewhere or other, from Decks drawn to represent the system of Ceremonial magick of the Golden Dawn, to the atheist system dedicated to the Psychiatrist Carl Gustav Jung (1875 – 1961), ideas from which are discussed in this theory in some relative detail later in Part I of this book. The idea from which *The Necronomicon Cycle* is spawned, is that when a 'new system' of Tarot is created, some literature on magick therefore exists to construct a system of belief based on those such magickal systems. The Appendixes of this book go some way towards describing this idea to elaborate on our interpretation of the *HP Lovecraft Tarot*, in order to help towards constructing a new system of ritual magick based on ideas such as those which were used by those such as Aleister Crowley (1875-1947), as he did the same in the foundation of the Hermetic Order of the Golden Dawn of Thelema.

In issuing this statement, and in aiming to put forward this manuscript as a new form of the theory of ceremonial magick, as one reason for its publication, I would at this point like to describe the principals and meaning of the term I use to describe those who already use this esoteric system, that being 'the Cult of R'Lyeh on Earth' as a term that I will be using throughout the rest of this book.

The term 'R'Lyeh' has been used throughout history to describe us who worship this system of Gods, as well as referring to the sunken resting place of Cthulhu as possibly the most important part of our religion, but in using this term, we are saying something quite specific. If this book would be written to explain our religion and how it would stand as a belief as part of the occult, one point should be made before we begin. The Gods of our religion, as described by *The Necronomicon*, as discussed, are a strange and insane system of reality; being vast and chaotic beings who exist across the Cosmos and between dimensions, and who on occasions manifest in physical form in so doing. The Gods of which we here speak have little time for the purposes of human kind, interested only in Their existence as insane chaos. To the Cult of

R'Lyeh on Earth, however, there is one important point to be written, and this is where we stand as a secular and esoteric belief. The actual term 'R'Lyeh', as described in *The Necronomicon*, does not describe the religious values of those who worship the Great Old Ones, but the resting place beneath the Pacific Ocean, where Cthulhu lies dead but still dreaming. The Cult of R'Lyeh on Earth, then, use the term specifically to describe this resting place of Cthulhu, with our belief being that this is the single most important religious principle. The religious statement that we intend to make, then, in using the term 'R'Lyeh' in this context, is that it must be relevant in the Cosmic scheme of things that, whilst the Great Old Ones populate such bizarre corners of space and insane dimensions, there is Cthulhu who sleeps here on Earth.

Let us not be deluded, then, if something so powerful as a God of *The Necronomicon* rests here on Earth. The Pacific Ocean is an enormous place, and sunken R'Lyeh is a colossal underwater city of strange dimensions. It is our statement, then, in calling ourselves the Cult of R'Lyeh on Earth, that this reality once more puts humanity in the picture, as our Planet is here defined as another corner of the Cosmos where the Old Ones rest until a time when the 'Stars are Once Again Right', when They will regain control of humanity and the far flung stars of the Cosmos as an inherent truth of creation. The Cult of R'Lyeh on Earth are defined in these terms, and we worship the Great Old Ones as it will Their worshippers who will gain control the Earth and higher dimensions when They once more awake in Their chaotic and insane position of astral madness.

To take such a statement of religious declaration forward, then, whilst the fictional works of Lovecraft are often credited with the invention of *The Necronomicon* as being a fictional book of Black Magick to be used as a vehicle for the expression of religious fiction, the Cult of R'Lyeh on Earth believe such a religious book to be real, as this Introduction to a new book on how to interpret the Tarot has gone some way to explain. The further listing of fictional literature involved in our statement of belief, however, describes many books of magick relating to our religious belief in the Great Old Ones and so forth. Whilst

it is notoriously very difficult to ascertain which of these books are real and which are inventions of fiction, the book you hold here is an actual and genuine study of the Gods of *The Necronomicon* and related magick. What you hold here is in part intended as a grimoire of magick dedicated to the dark and macabre worship of the *Necronomicon* and its stated system of Gods, and the related works of magick, towards such worship dictate that eventually, at a point when the Starts are Once Again Right, the Cult of R'Lyeh will eventually have control of the World.

In conclusion to this Introduction, *The Necronomicon Cycle* is set out as three independent Sections. The first of these, being an essay titled *The Azathoth Cycle*, makes a specific discussion of issues such as the religious ideology of The Cult of R'Lyeh as a new secular movement of contemporary religion, and the importance that *The Necronomicon* has on that basis. Further, this statement makes a proper study of the first Card of the *HP Lovecraft Tarot*, that being ascribed to the God as astral madness, Azathoth, and how a proper study of issues in occult worship such as the Mystical Qaballah and the Zodiac can ascribe this Card to the greater definition of the occult and ceremonial black magick. The second Section of this book was originally intended to be a comprehensive commentary on the Major Arcana as according to the *HP Lovecraft Tarot* as our specific study in question, although if read in connection with the first Section as discussed, this can be interpreted as setting out a clear framework as to how the Tarot can be interpreted in order to worship The Great Old Ones and to honour *The Necronomicon* as a religious book of ceremonial black magick. The third Section continues with the same idea, whilst focusing specifically on the Minor Arcana.

With the vast history of books published on the subject of the religious Tarot, I have found very few which make a specific statement in documenting the specific study of the Tarot and the Minor Arcana, with the second Volume of the *Seventy-Eight Degrees of Wisdom* by Rachel Pollack being the single title I've been able to find which competently discusses this point. It is for this reason that I have focused on this book

to some legitimate extent as one of few references of research whilst writing this book. Further to that, *The Necronomicon Cycle* concludes with a listing of books suggested for Further Reading. One reason for this would be on the basis that there are very few published books which do a competent job of covering the religious views as upheld by The Cult of R'Lyeh, in the depth necessary to properly uphold the stated views of our religious perspective, but at the same time all of these books will be useful in one way or another if the Magus were to be interested in working further with the *HP Lovecraft Tarot* in order to establish a working system of occult worship.

One last point is left to be made, as this is a system of the occult and the worship of the Great Old Ones. *The Necronomicon* is known as a blasphemous and dangerous book of magick, and it is pretty much as statute in the current day that to study this book without serious caution and regard to the book as the religious study that it is, is to call upon disaster and madness. The study of *The Necronomicon* is quite renowned for this, and as the author of this as a study of the occult, I ask my readers to regard the information in these pages with as much caution as can reasonably be given. And if any example should be given as to how the study of *The Necronomicon* can result in such a situation of disaster, as I was half way through writing this book, the people who I live with started cooking and eating human flesh.

> *"That is not dead which can eternal lie, but with strange eons even death may die"*
> —The Necronomicon, Abdul AlHazred

> *"Do What Thou Wilt Shall be the Whole of The Law"*
> —The Book of The Law, Aleister Crowley

EDITORIAL NOTE: With that statement made on the subject of *The Necronomicon Cycle* and the *HP Lovecraft Tarot*, the main part of this book was written before the announcement that there was to be a planned third edition of this Deck of the Tarot in discussion. Whilst this

as an important point has already been discussed, it is as the result of this, that all of the Cards in this Deck have been planned to be re-issued for this intended Third Edition. It is for this reason that I have made an attempt to use the revised drawings to this Deck as the graphics to this book as much as I have been able to whilst putting the manuscript to this book together. However, it is still the case that - at the current point of writing - most of the published Cards to this current Deck are still in one sense or another to be completed, and hopefully this is an issue that will be worked with if there is eventually to be a publication of the book you are reading here.[6]

---

[6] At the current time of writing the graphics so far put together for the current edition of the HP Lovecraft Tarot are available online at https://www.pinterest.co.uk/hutchinson60/hp-lovecraft-tarot/ [accessed 13/2/2020].

The Azathoth Cycle

An Introduction to the Study of The HP Lovecraft Tarot

THE HP LOVECRAFT TAROT: PRINCIPLES ESTABLISHED

The decision to include *The Azathoth Cycle* as the first Part of this book was really something of an afterthought, and was a point to which I gave some serious consideration. However, if this Part of *The Necronomicon Cycle* would be another statement to describe the validity of the *HP Lovecraft Tarot*, I felt that it would be appropriate to use it here in context of this book. This first Part of the book you are here reading was originally put together as the Dissertation project necessary for my Undergraduate Degree in Theology and Religious Studies, and is another example of my serious religious regard for *The Necronomicon* and this expanded religious argument in question. Whilst it will be obvious to the reader that this essay focuses to a large extent on the specific Mythos God of *The Necronomicon*, Azathoth, in specific relation to the study of the occult here in question, I would suggest that this could be interpreted in context with the following two Parts of this book, with the further intention of this being to allow the Magus to quite easily construct a system of working Ceremonial magick towards the worship of the Great Old Ones on more specific terms as one defined religious system. If this would quite easily suggest that the theory attributed to the Mythos God Azathoth could be directly

equated to the other Gods of *The Necronomicon* (as the following two Parts of this book go on to describe in some detail in relation to the *HP Lovecraft Tarot*), then if making a study of the references listed in the Further Reading at the end of this book (should the Magus choose to chase this up), the Magus will notice that there is still a large amount of research possible if the intention were to be to take this given study further. It is with this intention that I plan a sequel to this book which will be dedicated to this idea of further research, and will be intended as being another issue of religious worship of its own.

"Azathoth, the Demon Sultan, is the Idiot God dancing at the Centre of the Void... The cosmic Principal embodied in Azathoth is that of the Chaos underlying all of manifestation. All sense of order, structure and mechanical law are the chance by products of the coincidental flatulence roused by this god's revelry at the Heart of the Void. Born of Chaos, such perceived order is only as firm as its origin, and can therefore dissipate with the simplest shift of the Cosmic Winds" (Hutchinson, Friedman: 2002: 6).

THE HP LOVECRAFT TAROT
AND THE CARD OF THE FOOL

The given intention of this statement, with this being the Dissertation that I submitted for my Undergraduate study of Theology and Religion, is to discuss Card 0 of the Tarot, that being the Card of The Fool, and further to make a statement as to why this, quite obscure, religious statement has such significance and such a level of importance on the greater scale of a global religious truth. In having made a comprehensive study of both religion and the further significance of the occult, it must stand as that the Tarot is a much smaller representation of worship than with those religions in question. For example, if to make a discussion of the Tarot Card of The Fool – with the *HP Lovecraft Tarot* defining this first Card as relating to the *Necronomicon* God Azathoth – in relating this to other systems of Tarot, with the Qabballah system being one example discussed later in this Dissertation, an entire book could be written on this subject alone, and a number of books have been written already on the subject of the Qabballah and ceremonial magick as a unique part of such religious orientation. With that point established, the premise to this Dissertation will be to discuss the idea that if all occult and further religious views are in terms of the religious belief upheld by the Cult of R'Lyeh, in actual terms the psychick projections as sent forward by different numbers of The Great Old Ones, as is established if making a study of *The Necronomicon* as one established statement of such established truth, then this must establish as case that there is in fact, one actual reality of one religious truth. In taking this general idea further, then, if the system of the Tarot can stand to represent such a reality of further truth, with the Qabballah being one specific aspect of a number of religious principles which are discussed later in this document, and

one of thousands of other such interpretations of religious belief, then a consideration of the *HP Lovecraft Tarot* allows us to relate this greater movement of religion to validate the worship of The Great Old Ones, as those described in *The Necronomicon*, as being a principal that can be further reasoned to prove a further reality of established truth.

Whilst having then established the general framework of thought that will be established further with this issued statement of esoteric belief, it might first be necessary to make another comment on which to establish terms on which we here speak. It should be a consideration to establish what is meant when referring to the religious Cult of R'Lyeh on Earth, as this is a term which will be used throughout this Dissertation, as it will be used throughout the rest of this book.

Under this definition, to describe the views of a movement who uphold one statement of belief, the Lovecraftian occult has so far been, in general terms, a fairly contemporary religious movement if ascribing to the worship of the system of The Great Old Ones. However, the roots of our declared movement go back for Centuries, and the Cult of R'Lyeh would regard it as necessary that a new religious movement should be established if this as a contemporary religious view should be established and further defined. The term 'Cult of R'Lyeh on Earth' would be, therefore, a statement of description to define those who follow a movement that *The Necronomicon* should be regarded as the first sacred book of religion, as defined under the views that are discussed further with the rest of this as a book on the subject of the Tarot and occult black magick.

The religious ideologies which have been influenced and further developed since the death of Lovecraft, whilst still quite obscure, and still admittedly bizarre, have become an established part of a religious underground since the last part of the 20th Century. However, in having established on the basis of such philosophical views, an established New Religious Movement have had to be established in order to represent this discussion of religious truth; and therefore the ideas put forward in this Dissertation argue to establish that this movement of religious philosophy, if taken to an extreme and logical extent, should

be seen to establish an individual branch of religion of its own. These views in question are the religious and philosophical views which will be the subject of this given work, and the Cult of R'Lyeh issue this as our statement of a belief in a greater and singular religious truth.

If this Dissertation is therefore written in order to define the importance of the *HP Lovecraft Tarot* as central to further describing such a religious view, then it might be necessary to make a general statement as to how this is specifically defined before any discussion continues. The esoteric system of the Tarot is a means of divination whereby a random system of Cards can be ascribed to predict the future of a person doing a reading, or to otherwise ask questions to the further entities of the supernatural, with different systems of the Tarot representing different religious orientations in doing so. With this first point of observation, the history of the Tarot is intricate and complex in itself, and a this could be seen as an issue of academic research in itself. However, the system of the Tarot defines a principal that literally any religious or occult belief can be easily interpreted towards such a creation of a system of Cards to represent such religious views, and it would be fair to say that most religious beliefs which exist in contemporary society, however minor or obscure they might be in the greater scope of secular religion, would have at least one Deck created to represent such religious views. This is where the *HP Lovecraft Tarot* here comes into play as one singular and representative religious system in hand, and this written statement will be given to establish the specific importance of this as representing the esoteric and occult beliefs of the Cult of R'Lyeh in putting forward such point of belief.[1]

---

[1] Whilst here making a statement as to represent the system of the HP Lovecraft Tarot as the first point of discussion with this Dissertation, a point should be made that there is another Deck of Tarot that does come into play with this discussion, and this is an individual Deck called The Necronomicon Tarot. Bibliographical information for this Deck, should the Magus choose to follow this up, is Tyson, D., Stokes, A. (2007) The Necronomicon Tarot. Minnesota: Llewellyn Books. This Deck will not be discussed further in this Dissertation, as it is the religious view of The Cult of R'Lyeh that this Deck does a very bad job of representing the religious views that our movement have established to represent.

Since the history of the literary and fictional work of Lovecraft in representing *The Necronomicon* as a black book of occult and religious magick - and in doing so as a vehicle for his religious fiction - ideas to interpret such views as a working religious system have so far always been a specific and quite obscure underground issue. It is on this basis, however, that if the ideas which were thereby expressed in such inspired religious fiction have always had such a history to represent such a unique statement of belief - which has been the case with this contemporary history of religion - then it would have inevitably at some point have to have had its own system of Tarot created to represent that religious view. The opinion of The Cult of R'Lyeh is that those responsible for having put forward such a religious system as the *HP Lovecraft Tarot* have without knowledge defined the system of the Tarot to equate to *The Necronomicon* as an underground statement of worship, and must have had little or no idea of the significance of the potential involved before putting in the obvious work involved with that project in doing so.

The Cult of R'Lyeh, therefore, uphold the *HP Lovecraft Tarot* as our significant religious statement, and do so for these reasons as discussed. It is our belief that this as a system of Tarot stands as stands to establish a unique system of reference whereby the study of *The Necronomicon*, as a religious book which describes an occult truth which is vastly beyond the scale of rational sanity and one which has rarely been considered by contemporary religion, can be directly interpreted according this singular reference. This interpretation therefore stands to represent all other systems of Tarot to be interpreted in terms of being related as points of reference on which to represent all other systems of religion. If *The Necronomicon* tells us that all religious belief has a root with the psychick manifestations of The Great Old Ones, then this given statement of religious interpretation will be the stated intention of this work.

Further to this statement as having introduced the stated intention of this Dissertation, and having further put forward our framework for religious worship, then the first Card in all systems of the Major

Arcana of the Tarot is numbered 0, and in all systems of the Tarot this Card is representative of The Fool.[2] In the Lovecraft system of the occult Tarot this point is described and equated on these terms as being represented by the *Necronomicon* Mythos God, Azathoth, although all other systems of the Tarot define this same statement as according to the religious interpretation as ascribed to the working of their own individual systems. This written statement is furthermore put forward to make a comprehensive study of how this statement in context relates to all other systems of the Tarot, and in turn the greater movements of religious truth. This Dissertation will conclude to define the *HP Lovecraft Tarot* as a statement to establish one greater and important definition of contemporary religious truth, and to describe how this point is sacred from the perspective of the Cult of R'Lyeh on Earth.

The stated and more detailed intention to this Dissertation is further written to establish that further research into this subject could be followed up quite easily in order to establish a much greater working system of the occult and a larger unique interpretation of religious truth. A study of the Cards of the Major Arcana, and the religious philosophy involved with this Dissertation should make such a direct comparative study fairly straightforward if the Magus were to be interested in conducting their own further research and take these ideas further on their own individual terms. With those points in consideration, this Dissertation should be considered as a working guide towards establishing a working form of Ceremonial magick to honour *The Necronomicon* as one religious truth.

In concluding this short Introduction, this Dissertation will intend to end by asking what greater relevance all of this has to the greater movements of religious and secular thought, and will intend to answer this point by asking whether The Cult of R'Lyeh stands to represent a unique perspective of occult and religious truth. As from here it is

---

2 The single exception to the rule that I've so far found is with the example of The Brotherhood of Light Egyptian Deck of the Tarot. A bibliographical reference for a good book on this subject is Zain, C. C. (2005) The Sacred Tarot. USA: The Church of Light.

down to the Magus to take this religious interpretation to its justified conclusion.

POSITIVE	NEGATIVE
Blessings of the Void: Absolute Freedom	Lack of motivation; inertia; entropy
Dissolution of obstacles; momentum; Transcending of boundaries	Inward or Outward Chaos (personal or external), Disorder; confusion; disarray
Independence; autonomy; beyond the effect of external influences	Complete lack of direction and / or loss of focus; "in the woods without a compass"
Divine Madness; Nirvana; Shamanic revelation by transcending the limitations of human consciousness	Insanity, dementia, hallucination; total or partial divorce from reason & reality; loss of self in one's illusions
Distinction above & beyond others; rank & exalted station; validation of ideals	Outcast, separation from the community; banishment, alienation, estrangement
Holy Quest & Vision	Village Idiot

Table 1. Attribution of meaning according to Card 0 of the *HP Lovecraft Tarot*

A History/Sociology of the Tarot

The classical representation of the Tarot is a system of religious orientation, which involves a sequence of 78 separate cards which – in contemporary religion – are seen most generally as nothing more than a system of occult divination. Of these, 22 of  the Cards represent the system of the Major Arcana, with the rest being representative of the suits of the Minor Arcana (Sosteric: 2014: 359). All of these Cards are ascribed specific and individual meanings being unique to themselves, with Decks of the Tarot having been put forward to represent nearly every esoteric and occult orientation which are followed in contemporary society, as already discussed. Whilst the Cards of the Major Arcana have very specific and defined meanings of their own, the Minor Arcana is invariably more obscure, although having equal importance in defining different meanings of truth (Sosteric: 2014: 359). Of these 56 Cards in question, the Minor Arcana is in turn broken down into four separate Suits, and throughout the history of the Tarot these have been defined as categories often equated to being Cups, Swords, Wands and Pentacles, as a working example, although to say that the idea is so straightforward is only partly representative of how this religious system works (as will

be covered in more detail below).¹ The history of the Tarot is further to this quite obscure on the principal that successive religious philosophers and artists have successively redefined the religious system of the Tarot as according to their own individual orientation, and so – outside of the specific discussion of the Lovecraft system being the specific subject of this Dissertation – the general interpretation of such a religious system has been constantly redefined throughout history for this reason. The point should here be established, however, that The Cult of R'Lyeh believe that the *HP Lovecraft Tarot* has a specifically important religious significance, and that a global cohesion of World religious beliefs are in actual fact all the psychic vibrations as sent forward by The Great Old Ones, as *The Necronomicon* as our religious book defines as a statement of greater truth, and that this is one explanation to establish why so many religious orientations are represented by this system.

An academic paper on the subject of *A Sociology of Tarot* makes a further study of this form of divination and, as would be implied by the title, a sociological study of this system of the occult and ritual magick since the early origins of that system of insight (Sosteric: 2014: 358). Whilst making a statement which discusses the point of the enormity of the number of differing Decks published professionally since the early 20th Century (as well as hundreds of individual Decks having been put together before modern printing technology), this paper discusses the point that the origin of the Tarot, according to research, dates back originally to having its historical roots in 15th Century Europe (Sosteric: 2014: 358). This paper continues to point out that a study of the sociology of the Tarot is something that is still to an extent incomplete, however, as this sociological study of the Tarot tells us that under such an interpretation "[the history of the Tarot] hardly registers on the… [sociological] radar at all… the lack of [a serious academic] interest in the [T]arot represents a significant theoretical and empirical lacuna… [and] there are reasons to believe that the [T]arot has far more sociological significance than first attributed to it" since the history of

---

1 It should be noted that the Minor Arcana most usually represents these Suits differently according to the specific Deck or system in question.

this as a study (Sosteric: 2014: 358).[2]

According to this as a historical study of its own, when the Tarot first came into existence in 15th Century European society, as research tells us, as a system of Cards the Tarot had "no [practical] purpose beyond providing mental stimulation. [The Tarot at the time] contained no esoteric wisdom, could provide no spiritual advice and gave no clue as to how to conduct one's life" (Sosteric: 2014: 360). Whilst this point is of historical note is quite probably the case, however, the position of contemporary society would regard the purpose of the Tarot as being for one singular use, with this as a tool for occult divination. This progression from one conceptual purpose to another is quite important whilst putting forward this as a sociological study, and establishes a sociological statement on which to help us to define greater religious terms. Further to this, however, certain branches of the Christian Church, as well as a historical movement to uphold similar religious principles of ideology have regarded the Tarot as being "a gateway to [S]atanic worship" (Sosteric: 2014: 360), with this being just one example of how such a system of religion has been widely misunderstood by religious movements on historical terms. "This belief" according to this academic reference in question, "is so powerful that even to mention the word 'tarot' causes a visceral, fear based reaction [in people who uphold such religious views]" (Sosteric: 2014: 360). *A Sociology of the Tarot* continues this statement in pointing out that "[a]lthough one might initially feel that a sociology of the tarot would only be of historical interest, that is not the case" (Sosteric: 2014: 378).

Further to that as a very brief study of the history of such a religious principle, movements of postmodernist means of production and artistic expression have, throughout the 20th Century and further to that, made

---

[2] In having read through this paper as someone who has made an academic study of sociology myself, a large amount of this paper I disagree with. However, it does in itself make some important points as regarding the Tarot in context with this religious study. It is on this basis that I intend to continue to work with this document to establish the religious validity of The Necronomicon as validated by The HP Lovecraft Tarot.

it successively easier to produce new and artistically competent Decks of Tarot; and such means as exploited to legitimate lengths by such notable occultists as Crowley, amongst many others "[have already] left an unchallenged (and potentially quite significant) ideological imprint [in terms of the production of so many systems]... the social impact [of which] may [have] be[en] taken too lightly" (Sosteric: 2014: 378). These same means of contemporary technology equate to a point that "literally hundreds of tarot decks [exist] in print" as the result of such a history of contemporary art (Sosteric: 2014: 378).[3] Whilst literally all of these Decks represent the esoteric and occult views of those responsible for putting them together, a number of themes still attain to all such systems in some way or another (Masonic symbolism, numerology, qabballistic references, as being only a few (Sosteric: 2014: 379)), and this general point regarding artistic productivity and religion will be returned to throughout this Dissertation. This general similarity, however, allows the student of religion to reference correspondences between vastly different religious systems, on the basis that so many different occult and religious systems as represented by different successive Decks, and this is where The Cult of R'Lyeh hereby define to represent the specific and legitimate importance of the *HP Lovecraft Tarot* as our specific stated purpose of religious truth.

In being respected as probably one of the most famous and respected representatives of 20th Century occultism, Crowley, as the acknowledged founder of the Hermetic Order of the Golden Dawn of Thelema, was famous in his lifetime for having put forward a large number of books on the subject of the occult, with a number of these focusing on his interpretation of the system of the Tarot. One of these books in question (with this being just one of a significantly large number), the *Liber CCXXXII, Liber Arcanorum*, was in turn a major philosophical influence behind the work of the writer and occultist, Kenneth Grant

---

3 In fact the situation is that if we were to argue the point, the figure would be nearer to thousands.

(1924-2011),[4] who in turn had an influence in the developing theories of occultism at that the turn of the 20th century (Decker & Dummett: 2013: 310).[5] As a close personal friend of Crowley himself, Grant eventually split from the main structure of the occult movement of The Golden Dawn of Thelema (a movement of which Crowley had established as being a main influence), and between the years of 1955 and 1962, established himself as the head of another established occult Order, a group who are still active in contemporary occult circles today, and known as the Ordo Templi Orientis (Decker & Dummett: 2013: 310). Grant taught a mixed system of ceremonial magick which aimed to establish the element of earth as to ascribe to the Egyptian goddess Isis, and thus to equate this to the idea of heaven, as was described by the OTO as represented by the Egyptian deity Nu. According to research "[this occult] union was [intended] to prepare the way for unearthly intelligences to enter our sphere and to inaugurate a new age" (Decker & Dummett: 2013: 310). These beings that the OTO intended to bring forth into our dimension, through involving a further occult interpretation of the Tarot, which would "have much in common with the superhuman '[Great] Old Ones' [as] described by [the writings of] HP Lovecraft" (Decker & Dummett: 2013: 310).

These religious views went further to establish that: "Lovecraft… suggested that the Old Ones c[ould] be contacted by some [means of] special technology. [They would] seem to become denizens of outer space or of alternative universes. Kenneth Grant's occultism therefore became… an ambitious synthesis of Cabalism, visionary states, UFOs,

---

4 Kenneth Grant would probably be the most important 20th Century occultist from the point of view of The Cult of R'Lyeh, with the possible exception of Crowley himself, as a large amount of his work focuses on ideas relating to the Lovecraftian. I intend to return to the issue of this writer later, as I cover the subject of the Tarot and the mystical Qabballah later in this Dissertation.

5 Further to my research here, a basic Internet search does little to verify the existence of this book. Whilst it is not in any way disputed that this book exists, it is obviously one of the more obscure titles to have been written by The Hermetic Order of the Golden Dawn of Thelema; with this making it difficult to find proper bibliographical information in order to reference this title in hand.

interplanetary visitors, sex magic and a new aeon" (Decker & Dummett: 2013: 310). A similar statement develops this general idea if to quote from another paper focusing on the specific subject of the Grimoires of esoteric black magick as mentioned in the fictional work of Lovecraft, and which focuses on *The Necronomicon* as the main book in question:

> "As early as 1955, Kenneth Grant, an associate of Aleister Crowley's, created the 'Typhonian' Ordo Templi Orientis as a form of spin-off of Crowley's [orders of occultism]. In his essay 'The Influence of HP Lovecraft on Occultism' K. R. Bolton explains that Grant has done much to reconcile Lovecraft's nightmare fantasies with ancient mythic entities, the view of Grant and others being that the *Necronomicon* is a legitimate esoteric text extant on the astral realm and accessed in dreams. Grant regards Lovecraft and Crowley as part of the same mythic and occult system" (Lippert: 2012-13: 47)

In 1974 Grant went on to publish a commentary on Crowley's *Liber CCXXXII* as his main discussion of the Tarot, and this book was titled *Nightside of Eden*. As one of a number of excellent and properly researched books published by this writer in his lifetime, this book still stands as respected as one of the main religious books to be regarded by The Cult of R'Lyeh on Earth as describing a statement of religious truth.[6]

As a final point of discussion to note if writing on the history of this specific occult system of the Tarot, the stated point of this Dissertation is to make a literary and religious study of The Tarot, and with this specifically to focus on the Mythos God Azathoth. The point is then to put this into context to discuss its importance in terms of the greater movements of religion. Whilst researching this given statement in question, in early 2016 a new Deck of Tarot was published by a group

---

6 Bibliographical information for *Nightside of Eden*: Grant, K. (1974); London; Skoob Books Publishing.

called Nemo's Locker Press, this titled *The Book of Azathoth Tarot*.[7] The obvious intention of this Tarot would have been to represent Azathoth as a religious God of *The Necronomicon*, and presumably those responsible for this Deck must have thought that there was enough in terms of occult religious thought to make this a valid system of esoteric interpretation to work with.

This Deck is, however, in my opinion lacking in any reference further than the published Deck of Cards themselves, and research into this system has found literally no other reference as to how this system should be read in its own context, with this system not having any Introductory Book of its own. It would be a suggestion if following this up to develop a working occult system, that if the Magus should choose to use this Deck any further or for any part of ceremonial worship, then they should start with making reference the Table given below:

MAJOR ARCANA	HP LOVECRAFT TAROT	RIDER WAITE DECK	BOOK OF AZATHOTH DECK
O	Azathoth	Fool	**The Fool**
I	Nyarlathotep	Magician	**The Magus**
II	Yog Sothoth	High Priestess	**The High Priestess**
III	Shub Niggurath	Empress	**The Empress**
IV	Hastur. The King in Yellow	Emperor	**The Emperor**
V	Cthulhu	Hierophant	**The Hierophant**

---

7 Bibliographical information for this Deck of the Tarot: Nemo, C. (2016) *The Book of Azathoth Tarot*. Nemo's Locker Press. This publishing organization have their own website online at www.nemoslocker.com, although this website has nothing to describe this Deck or to clarify this issue any further.

A History/Sociology of the Tarot

MAJOR ARCANA	HP LOVECRAFT TAROT	RIDER WAITE DECK	BOOK OF AZATHOTH DECK
VI	Lavinia Whateley & Yog Sothoth	Lovers	**The Lovers**
VII	Ithaqua	Chariot	**The Chariot**
VIII	Shoggoth	Strength	**Strength**
IX	Great Race of Yith	Hermit	**The Hermit**
X	Hounds of Tindalos	Wheel of Fortune	**Wheel of Fortune**
XI	Mi-Go	Justice	**Justice**
XII	Deep One	Hanged Man	**The Hanged Man**
XIII	Ghoul	Death	**Death**
XIV	Old One	Temperance	**Temperance**
XV	Tsathoggua	Devil	**The Devil**
XVI	Dunwich Horror	Tower	**The Tower**
XVII	Nodens, Lord of the Great Abyss	Star	**The Star**
XVIII	Night Gaunt	Moon	**The Moon**
XIX	Yig, the Serpent God	Sun	**The Sun**
XX	Dagon	Judgement	**The Last Judgement**
XXI	Chaugnar Faugn	World	**The World**

Table 2. The *Book of Axathoth Deck* of the Tarot and The Major Arcana

A History of The Necronomicon as the Religious Statement of The Cult of R'Lyeh on Earth

The useful significance of the *HP Lovecraft Tarot*, as this Dissertation has already been written to discuss, is that – if interpreted according to the definitions of religion discussed in this Dissertation, that being in terms of acknowledging the manifest existence of *The Necronomicon* and related truth – it offers a useful and direct system with which to worship The Great Old Ones as the weird and bizarre existence of Gods as represented by our religious book discussed. From the onset of the time that Lovecraft was himself writing inspired religious fiction in order to establish a validity of esoteric truth, there has been a movement of occult religious theory developed to honour a system of Gods which have often been (wrongly) credited as being his invention; although this has previously been very underground and has always been upheld by the eccentric adherents of such a bizarre religious truth. The Cult of R'Lyeh, then, are established on this basis in part to make a statement to properly establish this as occult truth, and the idea of correlating the *HP Lovecraft Tarot* with other systems of the Tarot is established to represent the validity of this stated position of one religious truth. If it were to be the case that *The Necronomicon* represents such a case for such an argument, as The Cult of R'Lyeh are established to prove, then such a study of occult correspondences equates this view to a massively greater societal movement of magickal religion and belief.[1] If to make a statement as to *The Necronomicon* and its further relevance to contemporary occult theory, however, one of few books published which has properly represented this subject

---

1 This is the reason that the magickal correspondences are so important to the Cult of R'Lyeh as a minority religious perspective.

is one titled *Necronomicon Gnosis: A Practical Introduction*, by an occult organization calling themselves The Temple of the Ascending Flame. This book having been published by an underground occult secular group, this book may be questioned on the specific terms of some of the validity it contains, but it is nevertheless an important statement to represent one of very few published titles to properly represent the ideas of *The Necronomicon* as a working reference to this as a specific working system of religion and the occult on legitimate contemporary terms. This book is discussed in specific context here as representing one of very few books to properly express the subject of the views upheld by The Cult of R'Lyeh in this given discussion, whilst published by an independent occult organization.

In discussing the nature of the *Necronomicon Gnosis*, this book opens by making a statement as to how the Worship of The Great Old Ones (Those being the system of Gods as described and represented by *The Necronomicon*) exists in a global and contemporary occult society, as a part of a greater society where countless religious systems are upheld by those who make use of magick and the supernatural, as aside from the larger movement of religion who describe themselves as "orthodox", such as the main established religions. Whilst making a statement which might otherwise be regarded as controversial from our perspective, and probably more so from the perspective of those main religions mentioned, this book acknowledges a point that such Worship as described in the religious *Necronomicon* is "inspired by Cthulhu Mythos fiction" (Mason: 2016: 7); with this statement representing a view which is seems to be widely upheld by such movements of occult worship, that the existence of The Great Old Ones is actually not based on any basis of esoteric fact. Expanding on this statement, however,

regardless to whether or not such a system would be based on any interpretation of occult truth, *Necronomicon Gnosis* continues with this perspective in stating that "[the global occult community] is now witnessing a revival of interest in primal aspects of magical gnosis, and the Necronomicon... definitely belongs to this category, thus still being a part of [a representative number of underground] esoteric movements" (Mason: 2016: 7). Whilst this statement might be valid if to put forward a valid working system of the occult, a statement to dispute the factual existence of *The Necronomicon* is still a point of discussion in hand with this book, as it is with most others published to represent the same subject. Questions raised as part of this discussion would include whether or not *The Necronomicon* is "real" in the first place, how much our knowledge of this historical book might be inspired in terms of "legends" as inspired by the supernatural, and this book in question continues to put forward a question as to why someone should regard such a system of occult as being important anyway? (Mason: 2016: 7). As an example as to the arguments here put forward, this book this book in question asks "[H]ow... can [*The Necronomicon*] work if all [if it] is [based only on] literary fiction [?]" (Mason: 2016: 7), as so many followers of the view would seem to believe?

However, regardless to any debate as to the existence of *The Necronomicon* as an actual religious book, it is still the case that according to an academic study of the subject "there are [in global occult society a large number of] occult practitioners who use *The Necronomicon* or [otherwise] elements taken from Lovecraft's stories to perform chaos magic – a branch of ritual magic [of its own]" (Lippert: 2012: 47).[2] In this consideration, Chaos Magick Theory, with that being the esoteric system of worship here referred to here, is a

---

[2] Whilst making reference here to the religious ideas of Chaos Magick Theory, The Cult of R'Lyeh have genuine respect for the ideas of Phil Hine as the main representative for this esoteric perspective. One of very few books written to represent the ideas of CMT and the religious Necronomicon is a book titled The Pseudonomicon, and a bibliographical reference for this book is: Hine, P. (2009) The Psuedonomicon. Silver Springs, NY: The Original Falcon Press. I would also like to make reference here to the Illuminates of Thanteros website, which is online at: www.thanteros.org/.

specific and unique branch of ritual and ceremonial magick which has quite recently become an important part of occult religion in itself, and if this point of perspective were to be acknowledged, it would be a point of opinion that the Magus should make a working study of this system if having any intention to employ such a system of worship in terms of ritual magick further to the ideas in discussion here. However, this diverts from the immediate point of discussion.[3]

Necronomicon Gnosis, as one of very few books written to represent such a study, continues, however, not to uphold the original Arabic manuscript as being the issue in question when referring to *The Necronomicon* as established religious truth, but chooses otherwise to focus instead on the many books published with that title since the original work of Lovecraft, with there being a developed history of this statement in itself. Whilst the proven historical fact of the existence of the Arabic original does not seem to be the important issue in hand (for whatever reason), this book in question continues to state that "[a]ll these [versions of *The Necronomicon*] are generally considered as hoaxes, and if you do any serious research, you will find that none of them is the 'genuine' Necronomicon [as such a book does in fact not exist]" (Mason: 2016: 8). The opinion is stated further to say that if "no one has ever seen the original manuscript... [then we can] not... speculate [as to] whether or not the Necronomicon actually exists [at all]".

Necronomicon Gnosis claims to validate this point that in stating that "any research into the Necronomicon... always raises the question whether the book really existed or [whether] it was only a creation of Lovecraft's imagination" (Mason: 2016: 11) as is so frequently reasserted as being the case by those who have claimed to represent

---

3 Chaos Magick Theory is a branch of ceremonial magick which states, on basic terms, that any use of the occult can be established and justified in terms of visualising a system of gods' chosen for specific ceremonial worship. The main protagonists of such a view are Peter J Carroll and Phil Hine, and whilst this system cannot be described in any proper detail to justify its importance here, The Cult of R'Lyeh would very seriously suggest that those who have further interest in such religious orientation, really should look at checking this out further.

such religion.

Whilst it could be regarded as a point of consensus with the greater movement of the global occult community, that the concept of *The Necronomicon* was either invented by Lovecraft, or (otherwise) received by Lovecraft himself in terms of occult dream transmission, The Cult of R'Lyeh regard this as a point of religious contention to be argued. As well as the large number of fictional essays which describe both *The Necronomicon* and the strange entities described in that religious book, in 1927 Lovecraft published a short statement on this subject titled, appropriately enough, *History of the Necronomicon*. It is the opinion of The Cult of R'Lyeh on Earth that the validity of this essay stands not only on the basis of the complexity of the history of this book as described by Lovecraft as being an indicator of such historical validity, but also on the basis that literary research into the validity of this essay proves its merit on the same basis. This would not be the apparent view of a large part of the movement of research into the disputed validity of *The Necronomicon*, however, and another example of this is represented by a quotation from a paper titled *Lovecraft's Grimoires: Intertextuality and the Necronomicon,* that:

"[Lovecraft] formulated 'The History of the *Necronomicon*' [as a statement defining religion] in order to make it easier for himself and others to use his materials in a consistent manner and to enhance verisimilitude. If the details of their collective allusions toward the dark tome correspond to one another, so the idea would appear more believable to the readers" (Lippert: 2012: 44)

Despite such a consensus to regard *The Necronomicon* as being a statement of falsified esoteric fiction however, according to Lovecraft's *History of the Necronomicon*, the original title for the book was a translation from the Arabic *Al Azif* (Lovecraft: 1927), with this word itself having been translated to mean roughly, 'The Book of Dead Names', although this in itself is questioned. In quoting again from this paper, Lovecraft points out that "the closest direct translation [of

this word that we have] would be 'A Consideration [or Classification] of the Dead,' rather than Lovecraft's own 'An Image [or Picture] of the Law of the Dead'" (Lippert: 2012: 45), as he had previously defined as being this meaning.

In having briefly discussed the views of the occultist Grant in context with the Lovecraftian occult, his classic book *Nightside of Eden* (written on the greater subject of black magick) establishes the point that "[i]t is not without interest that the name *Al Azif* which Lovecraft chose as a title for his celebrated *Necronomicon* was, as he observes 'the word used by the Arabs to designate the nocturnal sound (made by insects) supposed to be the howling of demons'" (Grant: 1994: 147). With this statement Grant made moves towards representing the use of Lovecraft's ideas to validate a larger religious ideology; one that he established as his religious order and as being the 'Typhonian current'.[4]

If we were to interpret Lovecraft's *History of the Necronomicon* as representing an important and significant statement of religious history, Lovecraft's statement here continues that *The Necronomicon* was originally "[c]omposed by [the Mad Arab] Abdul AlHazred, a mad poet of Sanaa, in Yemen... circa 700AD" (Lovecraft: 1927). Being known as being the author of this religious statement, AlHazred put this comprehensive work together after a history of having spent a period of ten years wandering the deserts of Arabia, during which time he communicated with many "protective evil spirits and monsters of death" (Lovecraft: 1927), as well as many other religious entities which directly influenced this work. *The Necronomicon* itself was not properly written and finished until the end of his life when (according to both research and belief), our religious prophet in question eventually found his way back to inhabited Damascus, where he died an apparently very bizarre and grotesque death in the year 738 AD in being ripped apart from demons which descended from the sky (Lovecraft: 1927). According to a little known monastic biographer of his life, this eventual death was on the basis of "hav[ing] been seized

---

4 Those with an interest in the religious ideology of Lovecraft in terms of the theory of black magick would be well advised to look into Grant's extensive writing.

by an invisible monster in broad daylight and devoured horribly before a large number of fright frozen witnesses" (Lovecraft: 1927), and this statement is in itself regarded as symbolic by The Cult of R'Lyeh as followers of his work.

Despite the point that *The Necronomicon* had had an involved history already, this title was not properly given to the book until the first translation of the Arabic original was made into Latin by the monk Theodorus Philetas of Constanople in 950 AD (Lovecraft: 1927). Further translations of *The Necronomicon* were made by the monk Olas Wormius in 1228 AD, with further translations known to have been made in both the 15th and 17th Centuries, although it is an acknowledged part of the history of this book that proper bibliographical information seems to be both vague and somewhat confused (Lovecraft: 1927), if not having been deliberately destroyed in an attempt to persecute religions who uphold such esoteric views. However, both Latin and Arabic versions were documented as having been banned by Pope Gregory IX in 1232 (Lovecraft: 1927), and it can be safely assumed that if the existence of *The Necronomicon* is so obviously obscure, then this can quite possibly be traced to this as the persecution of such religion as was established by the early Christian Church.

In tracing the history of our religious book further, another, more recent translation of *The Necronomicon* was made in the 17th Century by the seers John Dee an Edward Kelly (Lovecraft: 1927), and this must be acknowledged as an important point to the history of our book. In tracing the history of this early version, the existence of this translation is quite easily proven through tracing official library records, and copies of what has become known as the 'Dee version' of *The Necronomicon* are currently not difficult to obtain if the Magus were to search for one online or through searching library reference.

In order to conclude this short history of the religious book upheld by The Cult of R'Lyeh, "[d]ifferent versions of the *Necronomicon* are said to be held in a number of libraries across the earth, including the University library of Buenos Aires and, of course, that of the Miskatonic

University at Arkham" (Lippert: 2012: 45). Rumour circulates that a small and rare number of original handwritten transcripts of this book exist in a number of libraries internationally, some of them obscure private collections, although their obscurity lends some level of credence to a belief held by many, that this religious book, does, in fact, not exist in the first place (Lippert: 2012: 45). It can only be speculated as to how the religious book of The Cult of R'Lyeh will be accepted in the uncertain future that our race threatens to impose through our collective ignorance and madness.[5]

---

5   As another point to note whilst discussing the validity of The Necronomicon, the graphic included above is considered to be a copy of a front page from this book as found in the Hague Library. Whilst the actual validity of the credence of this graphic cannot be immediately established, if it is the case that such a reproduction of this cover image does stand as validated, then these points on the history of our religious book should hopefully be validated in terms of research.

On the Minor Arcana

In order to develop the points already discussed in context with how the Tarot can be representative of a much greater system of religious truth, those responsible for the publication of the *HP Lovecraft Tarot* have made a competent job in interpreting a statement of greater religious truth in working to ascribe the meaning of the Cards of the Tarot and the religious and psychological archetypes as established by the fictional work of Lovecraft as our religious representative in question. However, whilst such principals are defined clearly by the symbology described in this study of the Major Arcana, it is, however, a different position in that the same direct interpretation is not as clear with its discussion of the principals defined with the lesser Suites of the system of the Minor Arcana in question. In working to define this argument as a point that should be seen as being important to this greater system of religion, some new research must be necessary; and this discussion of the Tarot would not be complete if this has not been discussed.[1]

With this having established that this idea can only be clearly defined in terms of a more generalized theory, if the Minor Arcana archetype as equated to the Suite of the Tarot which is most often equated as being Cups, should be in turn defined as representing "reflective of human

---

1 In researching how the Minor Arcana is unique with the Lovecraft system of Tarot divination, there would appear to be a clear void of relevant religious literature to make any clear statement to properly establish this point. One online resource does, however, exist to define this discussion, and whilst it should be made clear that this is by no means a credible academic reference, it has been included as a part of the research involved with this Dissertation as it is the only clearly available resource which discusses the arguments here in question to any valid extent. A weblink to this resource in question, should the Magus choose to follow this up, is http://www.innsmouthfreepress.com/blog/lovecraftian-tarot-decks-part-1/.

relationships and failings" (Haney: n.d.), then an equation could be established that the *HP Lovecraft Tarot* here equates the Suit of Cups to being the Suite of People.

To follow this line of research and to take the same idea further, if the Suite of the Minor Arcana that is more often, in traditional Tarot as, represented as being Swords, then this can be broadly defined as representing all "use and abuse of tools of power" (Haney: n.d.), then this should equate similar parts of this system to being defined as Artifacts with the Lovecraft system being our system in hand.

This same avenue of research continues to define the Suite of the Minor Arcana more traditionally equated to Wands as representing "inspiration that can light the way to everlasting glory or utter ruin" (Haney: n.d.), and the resource used to research this statement would equate this to be represented by the Lovecraftian system as being the Suite of Tomes.

With this leaving the last part of the Minor Arcana which is more often equated to Pentacles to be defined as relating to "locations that can lead to material and spiritual prosperity or destitution" (Haney: n.d.), then this must be equated to being represented by the Lovecraftian interpretation here as being the Suite of Sites. These points of symbolism are followed further with the study of the Minor Arcana which is Part III of this book of religious magick.

Whilst researching this as being an issue of necessary importance with working with this argument to represent the Minor Arcana, the initial assumption that I'd made was that the *HP Lovecraft Tarot* would have been one of a smaller number of systems whereby defining such Suits in question would not have been entirely straightforward. However, further research would establish that this is not the case. With one example in question being *The Zodiac Deck* of the Tarot, being a system that allows the Magus to directly interpret such religious views in terms of the occult study of astrology, the Suites of the Minor Arcana

are defined as being Torches, Waves, Clouds and Stones.² With this point established again see the situation as being recurrent that if this Deck (as being one of numerous examples) does nothing to further equate these Suites of the Minor Arcana in relation to other systems of the Tarot, we would again be confined to doing the same research if this definition were to be important in making equations with the thousand other religious Decks which define other religious beliefs as according to out interpretation of the Tarot in representing such different views (which in certain situations might be the case).

With this as a working system of Tarot discussed, it does come into the argument that the Suits of the Minor Arcana should be studied on these terms if the Magus were to intend to equate other systems of the Tarot with *The Necronomicon* as a statement of religious truth, and to further research the esoteric Tarot towards creating a working system of magick as this Dissertation has been written to establish.³

---

2 Some further research with The Zodiac Deck is important, however, as the Suite of Cups can be equated to the esoteric element of Water, Swords to the element of Air, Wands to Fire and Pentacles to Earth. If the Minor Arcana can be further equated on these terms then this should be considered important to the framework of practical ceremonial magick if astrology should come into the position of such ritual worship.

3 This statement being the premise to this Dissertation. For example, in terms of one specific interpretation, if the Magus were to intend to use a system of Enochian magick in connection with the occult truth of The Necronomicon, then the Deck of Tarot defined as being the Enochian Deck could be used in direct context with the ideas here discussed. The further premise to this Dissertation is to establish that all systems of Tarot can be interpreted as equated on these specific terms, and this is where The Cult of R'Lyeh define a principal of one religious truth.

On The Zodiac in Relation to The Necronomicon and the Tarot

"The Human... has the ability to direct much of the course of its existence but it must do so only within the larger framework of a set geometric pattern created by the Universal Mind of the God Force. The nature of occultism, of which the study and application of astrology is a branch, reveals some of this Divine Thought Network" (Oken: 2006: 6).

In making a study of *The Necronomicon* as translated into the English language, there is not a great deal of reference to specifically represent the study of the Zodiac and the study of astrology as a specific part of this study. However, *The Necronomicon* as the religious book as upheld by our contemporary religious view includes a Chapter titled *Of Ye Times and Ye Seasons to be Observed*, and this makes a point as regarding the planetary and astrological cycles which should be regarded when upholding the worship of The Great Old Ones as one religious system of Gods.

This quotation from our religious book states that "Whenever thou would'st call forth Those from Outside thou must mark well the seasons and times in which the spheres do intersect and the influences flow from the void" (Lariushin: 2012: 13). And, whilst pointing out that information as regarding the astrological cycles (and so on) is throughout this book of occult religion quite vague, *The Necronomicon* makes a point clearly that "Ye Ultimate Rites shall be performed only in the seasons proper to them"[1] (Lariushin: 2012: 13), with this making

---

[1] Those who might be interested in the use of astrology and so forth in connection with ritual magick should check out a good book on this subject titled Practical Planetary Magick. Bibliographical reference for this book is Rankine, D., Sorita, d. (2007) Practical Planetary Magick. London: Avalonia.

the point that, as with all use of ceremonial magick, there will always be an appropriate time at which to construct the sacred magickal rites.

If this statement might therefore establish a theoretical need to establish the significance of Azathoth as a God of *The Necronomicon* as the specific point of study in discussion here, a good point of research might be to make reference to another representative system of the Tarot, with this point of example in question being *The Zodiac Deck*. In resorting to this system in question we might be able to establish how the Tarot Card of The Fool is represented in relation to this greater theory of the art of astrology, and with this to establish how the Card of The Fool is represented on wider terms in context with the occult philosophy of the Zodiac.[2] With this intention we might be able to establish the point further as to where the worship of Azathoth should be upheld as part of the greater religious movement of the occult and black magick, and will here make reference to a book on the subject which makes a competent study of this subject.

A book of this specific study titled *Tarot and Astrology* equates Card 0 of The Tarot to the astrological symbol of Uranus, and describes with this being described as "the planet of freedom, revolution, rebellion, and reform" (Kenner: 2018: 33). With this description of the conceptual nature of the first Card of The Tarot established we see another example of the similarity of the terms that exist across so many systems of the occult as represented by so many different systems of the Tarot; this being another point to establish the credence of *The Necronomicon* as one statement of secular worship, if it were to be accepted on these terms. Whilst this general idea in hand would be to suggest that a study of the occult and the zodiac could quite easily be put together to represent *The Necronomicon* and the worship of The Great Old Ones (in itself), if approaching The Tarot on this basis, *Tarot and Astrology* defines The Fool on specific terms that "Uranus rules Aquarius, the sign of futuristic thinking, and the eleventh house of the zodiac, where astrologers look for information about social groups and idealistic

---

2 Bibliographical reference for the Zodiac Deck: Bursten, L., Raimando, L. (2007) Zodiac Tarot. Torino, Italy: scarabeo.

causes... The Fool card corresponds to the element of air" (Kenner: 2018: 34).

The point having been stated that *The Necronomicon* includes little on the specific study of the zodiac in itself, this can be further established through this interpretation of other systems of Tarot, and the point is established regardless that if to acknowledge this religious book as defining a part of a system of ceremonial black magick, then on this specific basis we are told that the Magus must "Call out to dread Azathoth when the Sun is in the sign of the Ram" (Lariushin: 2013: 13), this by implication telling us that the right time to honour Azathoth would be when the sun is in the Planetary House of Aries. This puts forward a statement that with The Tarot we can quite easily start to interpret a working system of magick as according to the reference here established, with the Zodiac being one of the possible systems of interpretation if such a study can be seen on such terms of reference. If the astrological system as established by such a study of the astrological Tarot Card of The Fool can work on the same terms as that represented by the *HP Lovecraft Tarot*, then the rest of the system of the Major Arcana can directly relate the existence of the Great Old Ones with this same study of the Zodiac, and with this we might be able to establish a greater working system of ceremonial black magick, as according to the zodiac as a specific statement of religious belief.

In order to end this section on the important relevance of the Zodiac, most systems of ceremonial black magick regard the planetary hours and so on as being imperative to the successful use of the occult, although this is not specifically represented by *The Necronomicon* as a statement of ritual worship. A working study of the Tarot and the Zodiac quite easily deals with this point, however, and would therefore stand as a smaller working part of a greater system of ceremonial magick as according to the greater theoretical interpretation as set out with this given Dissertation. With this defining a study of the Tarot as is the subject of this continued study, it should be straightforward to make an equation with the system of the Cards and the Planetary Hours with the Tarot as a general guide towards our doing so. This

could be quite easily researched if the Magus were to use the ideas as set out here in order to establish use of Ceremonial Magick towards the worship of The Great Old Ones as represented by *The Necronomicon* as the religious book of The Cult of R'Lyeh on Earth, although further this point I will leave that statement as being the role of the Magus to take this avenue for research and study further on these established terms.

Hour of the day	Attribution of Planetary Hours as According to the Zodiac	According to The General Tarot and The Zodiac Tarot	Necronomicon Entities as According to The Planetary Hours
1 am	Mercury	Magician	**Nyarlathotep**
2 am	Moon	High Priestess	**Yog Sothoth**
3 am	Saturn	The World	-
4 am	Jupiter	Wheel of Fortune	**Hounds of Tindalos**
5 am	Mars	The Tower	-
6 am	Sun	The Sun	**Yig the Serpent God**
7 am	Venus	Empress	**Shub Niggurath**
8 am	Mercury	Magician	**Nyarlathotep**
9 am	Moon	High Priestess	**Yog Sothoth**
10 am	Saturn	The World	-
11 am	Jupiter	Wheel of Fortune	**Hounds of Tindalos**
12 am	Mars	The Tower	-
1 pm	Sun	The Sun	**Yig the Serpent God**
2 pm	Venus	Empress	**Shub Niggurath**
3 pm	Mercury	Magician	**Nyarlathotep**
4 pm	Moon	High Priestess	**Yog Sothoth**
5 pm	Saturn	The World	-
6 pm	Jupiter	Wheel of Fortune	**Hounds of Tindalos**
7 pm	Mars	The Tower	-

Hour of the day	Attribution of Planetary Hours as According to the Zodiac	According to The General Tarot and The Zodiac Tarot	Necronomicon Entities as According to The Planetary Hours
8 pm	Sun	The Sun	**Yig the Serpent God**
9 pm	Venus	Empress	**Shub Niggurath**
10 pm	Mercury	Magician	**Nyarlathotep**
11 pm	Moon	High Priestess	**Yog Sothoth**
12 pm	Saturn	The World	-

Table 3. *The Necronomicon* and the Planetary Hours, with Wednesday as the example in hand.

On the Tarot and the Mystical Qaballah

A statement written on the subject of the Tarot and the religious system of the Mystical Qaballah, that being a representative part of Jewish religion whilst still being important to Temples of Western ceremonial magick, describes this system of Cards that "[t]he twenty-two trumps of the Tarot correspond to the twenty-two connecting paths of the Tree of Life, and are subjective states of consciousness through which the spiritual power of the sephiroth [of the Qaballah] are experienced" (John: 2018: 56). With this taken as a valid point of interpretation such reference relates the Tarot Card of The Fool to the Qaballistic Sephiroth of Daath, which in turn relates to occult correspondences towards the position of the *Necronomicon* God Azathoth, as the first point of discussion with this as the first Part of this book. The point that this is still another correspondence which establishes the same conclusion would be a further point to validate the religious position as upheld by The Cult of R'Lyeh on Earth, and it should therefore be considered that other religious Gods of *The Necronomicon* can be related to different Sephiroth of the Qaballah on these same terms as here established. This continues from the general ideas already discussed.

Whilst defining this statement to establish that the Qaballah can be easily interpreted towards the worship of any number of The Great Old Ones, if we were to choose to uphold such a comparative religious statement, it should be pointed out that throughout the history of the 20th Century a number of established religious and occult temples – most notably The Hermetic Order of the Golden Dawn of Thelema (as has been mentioned previously in this Dissertation already) – have upheld such a study of this esoteric and religious framework as integral

to their religious values and their constructed ritualized systems of magick. A large number of books have been written to discuss this specific point in itself, but here I would draw specific reference to a document published by The Hermetic Order of the Golden Dawn, this titled *Sepher Sephiroth (revised)*.[1] This statement in question is a particularly heavy and complicated reference written on the subject of magickal correspondences and the Mystical Qabballah; to the extent that it cannot be discussed in any proper detail here if we were to intend to represent such a statement of worship any further. However, it is suggested that if the Magus were to have a serious interest in chasing the idea up as regards *The Necronomicon* and further occult correspondences then this would be a good suggested further reference of study, with this reference being easily available online.

If this idea would establish a position that, according to the philosophy of the Golden Dawn of Thelema, each Card of the Tarot can be easily equated to the different Sephiroth of the Qabballah, then then it should not be difficult to research this statement further in order to establish an example as to how this point can be equated on straightforward terms. Each Card to represent one Mythos God also represents its equivalent as according to this system. However, if this at the same time defines a position that, to the Golden Dawn, a direct equation between the Tarot and the Qabballah

---

1 A bibliographical reference to this statement as found online would be: Bennet, A. & Crowley, A. (n.d.) Sepher Sephiroth (revised). Available at: http://www.angelfire.com/rings/blmlibrary/texts/sepher_sephiroth.pdf [Accessed: 8/11/ 2019].

is a point necessary to the effective use of ceremonial magick, which is often the case as according to their occult and religious views, then they themselves have a number of Decks of Tarot put together which establish this as one point of defined terms.

With this point established, one of a number of these Decks in question would be the *Thoth Deck* of the Tarot (this being another project which had personal input from Crowley), and this system upholds both of these points of occult belief in ascribing the Card of The Fool to be represented on more conceptual terms than with most other systems, with this system of Tarot renaming Card 0 to being, instead, 'Atu' (DuQuette: 2017: 96). Another book written on this specific statement of the Golden Dawn Tarot defines Atu as an equal representation of the Card of The Fool, that "[i]n essence, there are not really twenty-two trumps [of the Major Arcana], there is only one – The Fool. Of all seventy-two tarot cards, none is more revered and misunderstood" (DuQuette: 2017: 97) than this Card as representing the Qabballistic sephiroth of Daath and the *Necronomicon* God Azathoth as the insane and chaotic nucleus of creation. Again we see an example as to where different systems of the Tarot represent different religious ideologies, and how such religious beliefs can be interpreted as representing The Great Old Ones as one actual statement of religious truth.

Another book on the subject of the Golden Dawn and the interpretation of the Qabballah as representing systems of ceremonial magick is one titled *Hermetic Qabalah Foundation: Complete Course*, and this describes the importance as attributed to the Mystical Qabballah in context with the Tarot Card of The Fool, in stating that:

> "The Tree of Life is a remarkable aid to the memory and to the learning and assimilation of new knowledge. Isolated facts and information that would otherwise be meaningless are understood through their relations to all other ideas. The planets and signs of astrology, the cards of the Tarot and the elements, for example, are organised and made comprehensible. The Tarot is a pictorial illustration [and is therefore important to interpreting] the [Qabballah in itself]" (John: 2018: 56).

The point should maybe be established, that if our interpretation of religious ideologies can be established through such an understanding of the correspondences with Tarot and the different statements of belief that all different systems clearly represent, then the Magus should have little difficulty in establishing the worshipful nature of The Great Old Ones should this study of the *HP Lovecraft Tarot* be interpreted as according to this structured study of religion and the study of the various and intermeshed ideologies which are represented by all differing religious systems of the mystical Tarot in question.

A Statement to Describe Card 0 of The Jungian System of Tarot

Whilst I should first point out that I have never made any academic study of Psychiatry myself, the first point to be established under this heading is that, in quite obvious terms, the study of the ideas of the Psychoanalytical theorist Jung and of Psychoanalytical theory, religious or otherwise, is a complicated and difficult branch of philosophy in itself, and as such is a subject vastly too big to be covered in any proper scale with the limited scope of this Dissertation. However, whilst Jung's psychoanalytical theory is a complex branch of philosophy, such a study of the theory of the mind can nevertheless be applied in relation to the religious interpretations as implicated by the writing of Lovecraft, as they can theoretically be applied to any working system of Western ceremonial magick in question.

The point to be put forward with this part of this Dissertation, however, is that if such a study of Tarot correlations can establish this on the basis of greater religious truth, which this Dissertation has set out to discuss, then this same study therefore makes a statement as to *The Necronomicon* and the strange occult nature of the human mind, and the Jungian interpretation of the Tarot would stand on the same basis of equated terms as already

discussed if to follow this theory of interpretation further. Jung himself did not do extensive work to cover the representation of the Tarot in his lifetime, but other thinkers have been able to interpret his ideas as according to such perspective since his death at the end of the last Century. Those who might be interested in following this idea further should make reference to an excellent book on the subject by a writer named Sallie Nichols, this titled *Jung and Tarot: An Archetypal Journey*.

If to make further comment to discuss such an important part of this study, whilst the documented study of The Fool starts at Chapter Three, Nichols here discusses that the Archetype of The Fool is the most important representation as described by the Major Arcana, and points out that "the Fool is the central character of the Tarot Trumps" (Nichols: 1980: 26), thereby defining this first Card as being, in theory, the most important. With this we see a similarity as with the same statement in relation to the other systems as already discussed. In representing The Fool as a figment of the unconscious mind, this similarity in terms of the manifestation of Azathoth as described in further terms of religious and psychoanalytical representation in that "[the nature of The Fool] is unconscious and undirected, yet it seems to have a purpose of its own [and with this chaotic independence] He moves outside [of the nature of] space and time" (Nichols: 1980: 26). Another study of psychology and the unconscious nature of the human mind puts this into further specific context with the specific ideas as put forward by Lovecraft, and was established by the underground Psychologist Y D W Mosig in 1997.[1] In making a specific study of this issue, this same principal of the repressed nature of the subconscious mind in relation to the study of the Tarot is related to the "turn[ing] to the unplumbed abysses of space and the unknown and unknowable spheres of alien dimensions (as well

---

1 With this I am making reference to a beautiful volume written by the Psychologist Y. D. W. Mosig titled Mosig At Last: A Psychologist Looks At H.P. Lovecraft. This is a rare and collectable book, although it shouldn't be too difficult to find a copy online. With this statement, aside from being a competent piece of psychology, it is also probably some of the best writing on this subject that I have seen and would have to be one of my favourite books on the subject.

as the tortuous depths of the unconscious [mind])" (Mosig: 1997: 23).

Furthermore, Lovecraft's conceptual framework of religion still has significance if interpreted in relation to Psychoanalytical theory, and the Cult of R'Lyeh believe that this in itself is an idea that should be taken further. In representing this point the opening statement from his main classic short story, *The Call of Cthulhu*, Lovecraft himself represents this idea in stating that: "[t]he most merciful thing in the world, I think, is the inability of the human mind to [be able to] correlate all its contents" (Lovecraft: 1999: 139). Whilst here we have a statement to further represent the functioning of the mind, Lovecraft himself had never studied any branch of psychoanalytical science, or any other for that matter, although despite this his views on the subject are still defined clearly that:

"The sciences, each [of them] straining in [their] own direction, have hitherto harmed us little, but some day the piecing together of dissociated knowledge will open up such terrifying vistas of reality... that we shall... go mad from the revelation or flee from the deadly light into the peace and tranquillity of a new dark age" (Lovecraft: 1999: 139).

This Dissertation cannot in any way aim to set out to discuss theories of Psychanalysis or any other branch of psychoanalytical thought in any serious depth at all, and if it were to do so then this discussion in itself would be far too big to cover with the given limitations of this work. The point to be made, however, would be that such ideas as relating to Psychoanalytical theory can be studied in relation to the philosophy of the Tarot, and if to follow this in relation to the *HP Lovecraft Tarot* we can quite easily equate the worship of The Great Old Ones with the theory of the working of the human mind. Cult of R'Lyeh as a religious orientation would represent a point that if a study of the Tarot can be followed to this extent, then this stands to establish a greater matrix of religion, as a point of reality that human society should not ignore.

On the Subject of 777

With the point of this Dissertation being to establish the specific similarities and direct relations between different systems of the Tarot and the occult correspondences in relation to the *HP Lovecraft Tarot*, in standing to represent such a statement to define a principal of religious truth we should make reference to *777* as the book of occult correspondences as written by Crowley as a religious thinker and upheld by the Golden Dawn of Thelema. In making such an important religious reference to the occult correspondences, there are a number of good books published on this subject which come into the picture directly if this were to define a principal of working magick, including a number of books which do nothing more than to set out the magickal correspondences as Tables. But the point of here defining this as our chosen reference in hand is to equate this to the Golden Dawn system of ceremonial magick, and then to specifically represent the worship of The Great Old Ones as according to them as a Temple of ceremonial and occult religion. With this point having been established, and if to make reference to Crowley's *777* as a competent occult reference on the magickal correspondences, it should be straightforward for the Magus to be able to use this book in conjunction with other references on magick and the use of the occult in order to establish a working system of magick as according to the theories involved with *The Necronomicon* and further the ideas I have stated so far. With that point established, however, the Hermetic Order of the Golden Dawn regard *777* to be the only book of correspondences necessary to their specific system of ceremonial magick, and, according to reference on this title in question, "Crowley's... *777* has been a standard magical reference [for initiates into the Golden Dawn of Thelema] for three quarters of a century [already]" (Eshelman: 2010:1).

In Crowley's own words, *777* as a book of correspondences was written as "an attempt to systematise alike the data of mysticism and the results of comparative religion" (Eshelman: 2010:1), and in doing so this book makes important equations with most systems of worship and different Temples of magick. In working terms this means that the most part of the Golden Dawn system of magick can be equated directly with the references to the Tarot which are described in this book, and if this can, in turn, be equated with the working system of the *HP Lovecraft Tarot* we can begin to establish a system of ceremonial magick in order to represent *The Necronomicon* as proven to be a statement of religious truth.[1] In shorter terms, if *777* might have some limitations as a book on the subject of the occult correspondences, despite its being upheld as the only working reference of occult correspondences necessary to the Golden Dawn system of ceremonial magick, then this establishes the case for this book as one of the most important references necessary to The Cult of R'Lyeh, as we interpret such theory of magick as defining a statement towards a means by which to worship The Great Old Ones on such stated religious terms.

On the specific point of the ideas of the Order of the Golden Dawn and such religious links to *The Necronomicon* as this book is written to discuss, a statement on this point found online expresses a position that "[w]e can profitably compare the essence of most of Lovecraft's short stories with the basic themes of Crowley's unique system of ceremonial Magick" (Necronomicon: n.d.). This point comes into the argument here as well as with the specific study of the Zodiac, the Qaballah and the theoretical ideas as put forward by Jung that have already been discussed with this Dissertation. What this says from the position of the Cult of R'Lyeh, is that, if the vast amount of occult correspondences can equate directly to acknowledge the existence of *The Necronomicon* and the established existence of The Great Old Ones as a system of working ceremonial magick, as is here argued if seen in context with this study of the *HP Lovecraft Tarot* and the correspondences in question, then

---

1 Appendix II of this book works as an example for people who might already have some familiarity with the ideas of the Golden Dawn to interpret this study as according to this idea as discussed.

all systems of ritual occultism can be established as part of this same religious truth, as a statement here being defined.

Before Crowley's untimely disappearance in the late 1940s he put forward another, similar book on the same subject, this titled *777 Revised*. This expanded version of *777* was never properly accepted as one of his most important statements, and the book was not completed before this unaccounted disappearance as was eventually the case. This sequel to the original book goes further than the initial version, however, and does more to clarify some of the more obvious questions in hand. It is in this expanded version that Crowley defines this book further as being "a qabalistic dictionary of ceremonial magic, oriental mysticism, comparative religion and symbology" (Crowley: 1970: vii). The following statement from this book is in specific terms more important, as *777* is described by Crowley as being "also a handbook for ceremonial invocation and for checking the validity of dreams and visions" (Crowley: 1970: vii). The importance of this statement is that, if taken in the right context, the significance of dreams has always been regarded as a fundamental part of the nature of Lovecraftian religious orientation, and if this puts the point into context with a working system of ceremonial magick, as according to this written Dissertation, then this makes a further point to establish *The Necronomicon* as a working religious system of its own, with the concept of dream now coming into the equation.

If we were to accept this as a statement to define a different religious system of its own, it should be established that any book on the subject of the occult correspondences can equally be used in conjunction with the *HP Lovecraft Tarot* in order to establish the working system of ceremonial magick if the Magus were to choose to interpret such a position on that basis. The specific point of discussing *777* as the most important reference of correspondences as according to the Golden Dawn, and therefore having specific religious significance to the Cult of R'Lyeh, however, would be that if a system of ceremonial magick, as upheld by a movement such as the Order of the Golden Dawn of Thelema can be directly equated to a study of the *HP Lovecraft Tarot*, as is the point in hand here, then we would be closer to defining this as our religious statement of arguing to define the validity of one religious truth.

New Religious Movement or New Movement of Religion?

The Cult of R'Lyeh on Earth

In conclusion to this short statement on Lovecraftian religion and the further significance of the occult Tarot, this Dissertation has already covered a number of points, with these including a history of the esoteric Tarot and the importance of *The Necronomicon* as the religious book of The Cult of R'Lyeh on Earth. The first stated intention with this project, however, was to focus on Card 0 of the Tarot (which is in all systems representative of The Fool), and how this stands as important in relation to *The Necronomicon* and the *HP Lovecraft Tarot* in terms of the greater study of the occult. Further to that, the next stated intention of this Dissertation was to establish the importance of the *HP Lovecraft Tarot* if it can be interpreted as according to the further established views as have here been discussed; that being in conjunction to other systems of the Tarot as representing other interpretations of occult magick. In having now completed this statement with that being stated as being the stated intended purpose behind this project, we have already diverted quite drastically from the original stated ideas in question. With that point in hand, however, the general premise behind this work remains open ended, and I would like to end this literary statement of religious intent as being an issue to allow the Magus to expand on these ideas further on their own individual terms. That said, a number of good books exist on the subject of the Tarot and occult correlations, which should all be taken into consideration in one way or another, and these should be studied in themselves on the basis of this as a larger subject to be further developed.

As a general example of what's here being said, a couple of such suggested titles in question would be *The Complete Magician's Tables* by Stephen Skinner and *Holland's Grimoire of Magickal Correspondences* by Eileen Holland.[1] Whilst these are both valid references which properly represent this as our study in hand, it might be appropriate here to quote from another book on the specific subject of the *Tarot Correspondences*, as written in a book by a writer on the subject of the occult Tarot, T.S. Chang.

The *Tarot Correspondences* establishes an important point in question, that "[the occult] Correspondences [in specific relation to the Tarot] are patterns and connections inherited from esoteric systems". The point is here purposefully established that "[in the] Tarot, correspondences line up with specific cards", and the specific example as given with this statement states that "if you are familiar with astrology, you know that there's a basic system that includes planets, elements and signs of the zodiac. Each of these correspondences has [its own] tarot card [as is defined individually by other Decks]. For example, the planet Jupiter corresponds to [Card X of the Tarot, with that in most systems this being] The Wheel of Fortune" (Chang: 2018: 1). The *HP Lovecraft Tarot* equates Card X as being the same with literally all other systems of the Major Arcana, but is expressed with the Lovecraft system as being represented The Hounds of Tindalos.[2] Further, "The sign of Virgo corresponds to The Hermit" (Chang: 2018: 1), and with the *HP Lovecraft Tarot* this Card is directly equated to

---

[1] Bibliographical information for these books, should they be needed, are: Skinner, S. (2017) The Complete Magician's Tables. Singapore: Golden Hoard, and Holland, E. (2006) Holland's Grimoire of Magickal Correspondences. Franklin Lakes: New Page Books.

[2] If the Magus were to be interested in Chasing this up further it would be suggested that they reference The Hounds of Tindalos in the Introductory Book to previous Edition of the HP Lovecraft Tarot (Hutchinson, Friedman: 2002: 26), or the Section on this subject in Part II of this book.

being the Card of The Great Race of Yith,[3]

Chang's *Tarot Correspondences* takes this idea further to equate different systems of The Tarot to different religious systems, and this stands as a valid working example to represent the views of The Cult of R'Lyeh,. This point stands as therefore being established, and in quoting from this as a book on this specific religious study of the Tarot and the occult correspondences, "[b]y connecting the cards to the age old arts of magic and astrology, as two examples in question, all systems of Tarot are therefore connected" (Chang: 2018: 2). Chang defines this point if that in focusing "main[ly] on four main [specific] systems [with these being] the elements, astrology, numbers and [the] Kabbalah" (Chang: 2018: 2) as four specific examples here in hand, and here we see an example of how esoteric forces are represented as a movement of occult unity by the Tarot as one religious system which would therefore justify all religious views as having been upheld by this as a religious system discussed. This Dissertation has been written to represent this general idea, whilst at the same time describing and discussing number of religious systems of the Tarot in direct relation to this study, with the specific systems discussed having focused on the

MAJOR ARCANA	ATTRIBUTION ACCORDING TO THE *HP LOVECRAFT TAROT*	ATTRIBUTION ACCORDING TO THE *ZODIAC DECK*	ATTRIBUTION ACCORDING TO THE *TAROT OF THE SEPHIROTH DECK*	ATTRIBUTION ACCORDING TO THE JUNGIAN SYSTEM
O	AZATHOTH	Uranus	The Fool	The Fool
I	NYARLATHOTEP	Mercury	The Magician	The Magician
II	YOG SOTHOTH	Moon	The High Priestess	The High Priestess

---

3 To take this line of research further, again it is suggested that the Magus make reference to the Card represented as The Great Race of Yith in the Introductory Book to the second Edition of the HP Lovecraft Tarot (Hutchinson, Friedman: 2002: 24), or the Section on this subject in Part II of this book.

III	SHUB NIGGURATH	Venus	The Empress	The Empress
IV	HASTUR	Aries	The Emperor	The Emperor
V	CTHULHU	Taurus	The Hierophant	The Hierophant
VI	LAVINIA WHATELEY & YOG SOTHOTH	Gemini	The Lovers	The Lover
VII	ITHAQUA	Cancer	The Chariot	The Chariot
VIII	SHOGGOTH	Leo	Strength	Strength
IX	GREAT RACE OF YITH	Virgo	The Hermit	Hermit
X	HOUNDS OF TINDALOS	Jupiter	The Wheel of Fortune	Wheel of Fortune
XI	MI-GO	Libra	Justice	Justice
XII	DEEP ONE	Neptune	The Hanged Man	The Hanged Man
XIII	GHOUL	Scorpio	Death	Death
XIV	OLD ONE	Sagittarius	Temperance	Temperance
XV	TSATHOGGUA	Capricorn	The Devil	The Devil
XVI	THE DUNWICH HORROR	Mars	The Tower	The Tower
XVII	NODENS, LORD OF THE GREAT ABYSS	Aquarius	The Star	The Star
XVIII	NIGHT GAUNT	Pisces	The Moon	The Moon
XIX	YIG	Sun	The Sun	The Sun
XX	DAGON	Pluto	Judgement	Judgement
XXI	CHAUGNAR FAUGN	Saturn	The Universe	The World

Table 4. Systems of the Major Arcana as important to The Cult of R'Lyeh on Earth.

Zodiac, the Qaballah and the Jungian interpretation of the Tarot. The stated intention in doing so was to establish a much greater working system of religion towards the honour of The Great Old Ones, with all systems of the esoteric Tarot upholding this idea. Further to that we here leave these points to the Magus to develop further in order to establish such a definition of actual religious truth, and to take this study further on the basis of these ideas having been initially defined.

In conclusion to this given Dissertation, and in order to draw all of these connected points to a close, it would quite probably best not to conclude such a statement of religious speculation by asking further questions. However, in ending this as a statement of an admittedly bizarre and strange philosophical perspective, I would have to ask the reader as to what significance, if any, does any of this have in terms of religion as the greatest part of the intellect of humanity on this Planet? If such a study has hypothesized that most religious systems can be broken down in analytical terms towards the proven statement of theoretical truth of the religious significance of *The Necronomicon*, as has here been discussed, and in aiming to establish to prove the theoretical existence of The Great Old Ones as one actual statement of religious truth, then where does any of this stand if we were to establish this as a new defined statement of religious intent? Does any of this theory establish a possibility that this, as one defined system of occult equations, and argued as being evidence of such a religious truth, suggest that there might be a new unity of the occult and religion in human generations to come?

Whatever the answers to any of these questions might be, the conclusion to this must be that this is in the hands of such generations of future of religious society, and to be in the hands of future generations of humanity and religious interpretation to come. Further to this it is here the role of the individual to make an intention to take these ideas further on their own individual terms.

THE MAJOR ARCANA CYCLE

According to the
HP Lovecraft Tarot

0. Azathoth: The Fool

As the first Card of the Tarot, and as representative of madness and The Fool, Azathoth represents ideas and goals that are far away, and of distant ambitions still to be achieved. Personal ideas and projects transcend barriers of human thought, and challenge the barriers that time and space put before us. Azathoth is,

therefore, a concept beyond the vastness of occult boundaries and possibilities of achievement, and outside of anything which can be immediately comprehended by the mind. This Card challenges our own constraints of what we personally believe. In this respect, this representation of The Fool challenges us with the idea that, beyond the already immense knowledge of the Universe that humanity has already studied and charted – there are still a vast dimensions whereby Azathoth plays His mad pipes of confusion. In real terms this Card tells us that, whatever our knowledge and perception, of anything we can immediately comprehend, there will always be infinitely still more. Although the Card of Azathoth - The Fool - represents that which is eternally insane, in this case it also represents insight into matters unknown – the insight that the insane have into matters beyond themselves. The Card of The Fool further represents matters of Astral exploration; things still to be justified by the reason and comprehension of man.

"Azathoth, the Daemon Sultan, is the Idiot God dancing at the Centre

of the Void" (Hutchinson, Friedman: 2002: 6).[1] Here opens our Book of Shadows. As with all of the major religious books, the *Necronomicon Cycle* represents those astral forces of the Universe that are creation, and which are the further spawn of creation, and as always starts at the Beginning. This book of the Tarot starts with this as our example, and continues further in describing the evolution of our race and ideas, with that being in relation to a much larger and greater religious truth, as represented by *The Necronomicon* as an unacknowledged religious book of the occult. This Necronomicon Mythos that is our study is quite different from other forms of belief, however, and whilst a logical order is always followed in any Deck of any religious Tarot, here the dimensions of time that start at the beginning, as the dimensions that the Great Old Ones govern, cannot be understood or comprehended by any human mind. Therefore this book starts at the beginning, as with all other books, as there is nothing else that can be done in describing any point of intellectual study, including a study of the Necronomicon Mythos of Gods.

"Azathoth, content in His senselessness, transcends the... Greed and hunger [of the Old Ones]" (Hutchinson, Friedman: 2002: 6) is the opening statement that the *HP Lovecraft Tarot* gives in respect to this first Card, and this is an appropriate statement to introduce The Fool as the start of this as a study of a further reality of cosmic darkness. Azathoth is the first in our study of *The Necronomicon* as He stands as the centre of the infinity of madness, and as the first Card of the Tarot The Fool stands at the centre of the Universe.

With this opening, therefore, we have pointed out that Azathoth

---

[1] For the purposes of reference, the only real change with the current Edition of the HP Lovecraft Tarot is that the graphics to these Cards have been changed. However, for the purposes of research I have taken the assumption that the definition of each Card should be kept as the same as with the published Introductory Book to the previous version of this Deck as I have been able to, unless something has been already specifically changed. The first Appendix to The Necronomicon Cycle reissues the meanings of the Cards of the Minor Arcana with this being our point of intention in doing so.

accords to the Card of the Tarot that is The Fool. The principal involved with this Card is, however, further defined as the underlying chaos and the nucleus which is the centre of all creation. Order, structure and physical matter are – in this sense – an important underlying principal of what this chaos can describe. But behind the absolute astral chaos which is at the nucleus of all such creation, The Fool is "beyond... need or worry... [and] it is this oblivion which is the source of his freedom" (Hutchinson, Friedman: 2002: 6). This is here depictive of The Fool who is at the centre of everything, but is oblivious to everything else because He is at the centre.

If this is at the heart of the Universe and of the cosmic dimensions of which humanity cannot comprehend, then presumably we should have the freedom that this entails? The chaos involved, as according to this Tarot, represents the overthrow of obstacles and the dissolution of order that allows them to be overthrown, as all rules are in the first place invented. Boundaries, here, are overcome due to the same principals of chaos as a much greater principle of truth. But further to this, Azathoth can also represent an autonomy of being. In this principal of chaos we are free to be alone, as the rules of others can only be regarded by ourselves. "The Cosmic Principal embodied in Azathoth is that of the Chaos underlying all creation" (Hutchinson, Friedman: 2002: 6). External boundaries are destroyed by this confusion and chaos – therefore allowing us to be guided by what we feel to be right for us.

In this disorder and madness, we should only be left to our own independence of thinking. With The Fool at the centre of creation, such an independence of thinking can lead us to a thoughtful state of bliss (or meditation perhaps?) within ourselves as a microcosmic part of the greater truth of creation. We should answer to nobody, and are free to assume a state of mind that is enlightened. In being representative of this state of mind, Azathoth here implies issues regarding the enlightened means of thinking arrived at through practices of Shamanism, and of perception arrived at through casual use of psychoactive and of psychedelic drugs. As with the constrained limits of the human mind, "perceived order is only as firm as its origin, and can therefore dissipate

with the simplest shift of the Cosmic Winds" (Hutchinson, Friedman: 2002: 7).

Whilst the HP Lovecraft Tarot can be read as being similar to every other Deck of the Tarot, and according to the specific occult interpretation involved with any such system, the definitions of the Positive and Negative Readings with the *HP Lovecraft Tarot* are unique and very specific to this particular Deck. It is the case in question, however, that this Deck which is the focus of *The Necronomicon Cycle* equates directly to the Mythos of *The Necronomicon*; and in this sense the *HP Lovecraft Tarot* is a strange and bizarre religious statement which deals with its given interpretation of meaning in a way that represents a Mythos that is equally as bizarre, and not always logical in terms of the sane understanding which is the comprehension of the human mind.

As an example of this, the definition of The Fool in most Decks of the Tarot is descriptive of the absolute bliss that ignorance imparts. The Lovecraft Deck, however, opens with its description of The Fool, defining it as representative of the "Blessings of the Void [and] Absolute Freedom" (Hutchinson, Friedman: 2002: 7). Here we are already speaking of this Card as being defined differently from other systems of the Tarot, with this due to the fact that Azathoth represents The Fool, but does so in terms of it representing the blissful ignorance that is, to our religion, the nucleus of the chaos of infinite creation.

The discussion of this Card in question having therefore been begun, we see that The Fool in our system, whilst being on equivalent terms the same as with every other Deck of Tarot, also exists as a parallel as being the system that pertains to what is called, by those who uphold *The Necronomicon* as a system of religious truth, the Cthulhu Mythos of Gods. The Positive Reading continues directly in terms of this definition, and describes The Fool as representing the "Dissolution of obstacles; momentum; Transcending of boundaries" (Hutchinson, Friedman: 2002: 7). This is, again, outside of normal or usual definitions of Card 0 with the vast consensus of other systems of the Tarot, but as Azathoth is the Ignorant God at the nucleus of the

Cosmos, it is justified in that.

Card 0 is now defined in this context, and the further Cards of the Major Arcana continue in the same general manner, with the Cards of the Tarot defined within its context of divination, but also in religious regard to the study of *The Necronomicon* as the religious perspective of those who regard the Lovecraft system of the Tarot as religious truth. With that in hand the Positive Reading goes on to define The Fool as representative of "Independence [and] autonomy; [freedom] beyond the effect of external influences" (Hutchinson, Friedman: 2002: 7). As discussed, this statement is immediately and obviously different from all other Decks; but this description is totally in keeping with The Fool as a symbol that the ignorance of the workings of the Cosmos is the best way to be.

Having now defined the esoteric view of our religion according to the Lovecraft Tarot and in the context of The Fool, our system of the Tarot in discussion continues to describe "Divine Madness" as a state of "Nirvana" (Hutchinson, Friedman: 2002: 7). It should here be pointed out that, to start with, the religious orientation of the Cult of R'Lyeh is largely about madness, and concerned with how the mad have an insight into that which is divine. But a state of insight can be grasped in this respect, as the Card represented by Azathoth can signify this insight as can be attained through "Shamanic revelation by transcending the limitation of human consciousness" (Hutchinson, Friedman: 2002: 7). Here we have already opened this religious statement with a discussion of the Mythos and its worship by the Cults of Darkness.

"Distinction above & beyond others; rank & exalted station" (Hutchinson, Friedman: 2002: 7) is further defined, as only the madness of The Fool can allow us to perceive ourselves as greater than another due to a position of status. But the "validation of ideals" (Hutchinson, Friedman: 2002: 7) is represented in the same statement, as ignorance can justify our goals by allowing us to think that there is nothing beyond them that can matter. And as the final statement given in this definition of the Positive Reading, a "Holy Quest & Vision" (Hutchinson, Friedman: 2002: 7) is established. If we are blissful in the

ignorance of The Fool, then a system of forward progress is obstructed by nothing other than that which occurs, after we have started this journey.

Negative Reading

As the Mythos God Azathoth represents the insanity that exists beyond all human concepts of creation, Card 0 speaks of "Inward or Outward Chaos [personal or external]. Disorder; confusion; disarray" (Hutchinson, Friedman: 2002: 7). It here becomes clear that, whilst speaking of The Fool, we are also speaking of Azathoth as the chaotic force that is oblivious to everything else which has been created. It is in this chaos that we see the destruction spoken of in creation, rather than destruction encountered in heading into a situation without foresight.

This situation of "heading into a situation without foresight" (Hutchinson, Friedman: 2002: 7) is spoken of further as the *HP Lovecraft Tarot* indicates a "Complete lack of direction and/or loss of focus" (Hutchinson, Friedman: 2002: 7). But this is defined as being more in terms of knowing what we have set out to do, and in 'losing the plot' at some point after this has begun. The *HP Lovecraft Tarot* further describes this as being "in the woods without a compass" (Hutchinson, Friedman: 2002: 7). The Fool cannot tell us which direction to take; we must act on tuition and take one path and follow it until the end.

So, with this discussion of the Tarot now established, Card 0 issues probably the most important warning to be relevant to anyone upholding Cult of R'Lyeh religious values. "Insanity, dementia, hallucination" (Hutchinson, Friedman: 2002: 7) are forecast; and we should be cautious of a situation of "total or partial divorce from reason & reality; loss of self in one's illusions" (Hutchinson, Friedman: 2002: 7). It would be appropriate that this warning comes right at the start of our study of *The Necronomicon* and the religious Tarot, because it is probably the most important warning to be relevant to the study of our religion in itself.

This idea should be taken further, though, and it should be taken

in hand that the study of *The Necronomicon* is also inherently about madness. Our occult view is not about reason; many who follow our path, and also many who are uninitiated have been known to go completely insane quite early on in their study of such occult religion, and the Mythos of *Necronomicon* Gods is not something that can be viewed as being rational as according to the acceptance of the 'normal mind'. This warning should be taken seriously therefore, as insanity is the next step beyond accepting the manifest existence of The Great Old Ones as a system of religious truth.

The rest of the definition of the Negative Reading with the *HP Lovecraft Tarot* is less concerned with Azathoth as being the central nucleus of chaos, and more about discussing the rest of Card 0 as representing The Fool in more traditional terms. The Tarot defines itself here as representing the "Outcast [as] separation from the community; banishment, alienation, estrangement" (Hutchinson, Friedman: 2002: 7). This point is defined that, due to ignorance or foolishness, we may not be accepted in our places of community. The Tarot defines this statement by saying that in a Negative Reading with this Card this represents the singular concept of the "Village Idiot" (Hutchinson, Friedman: 2002: 7). Not exactly in keeping with the rest of the description of The Fool as the nucleus of creational chaos, until it is accepted that this statement refers again to the Mad Piper who exists in the ignorant madness at the nucleus of creational chaos.

1. Nyarlathotep: The Communicator

Nyarlathotep is our God in this system for communication and the written word, and is depicted in this Mythos literature as being very similar to the depiction of an Egyptian Pharaoh. This would stand as appropriate here as Nyarlathotep is (in Mythos literature), often depicted as a God with serious influence in the Egyptian religious system. We can note here, that the Egyptian Tarot can be studied with each Card relating to a separate Mythos God according to its depiction, but with this Card it could be presumed that he Egyptian religious system could stand as a mythical front for this God, as all systems of religion are actually the psychick projection of The Great Old Ones If it could considered, therefore, that Nyarlathotep is the first representative icon for the Egyptian religious system, then He is to be considered by most students of Necronomicon Mythos religion as inherently evil. The second Edition of the *HP Lovecraft Tarot* depicts Nyarlathotep as the black Pharaoh as He exists in Mythos literature; His eyes are glaring, demonic, and stare directly into the eyes of those who draw this Card in a Reading. Those who have worshipped and honoured Nyarlathotep are rewarded with an occult position of ulterior power, and in the dark and demonic history of His worship, His worshippers make a sacrifice of blood further towards these ends. It is assumed, and it is a part of this belief, therefore; that Nyarlathotep was the object of worship as upheld by the power of the Egyptian Pharaohs, and this is directly from where they assumed a position of such oppressive and absolute power.

Having passed Card 0, Nyarlathotep is the Communicator. In this regard, our given reference in representing the Major Arcana introduces the meaning of this first Card in stating that "[Nyarlathotep] gives rise to creation. He raises one of his hands towards the realm of Spirit so he may draw down its sacred life force and transmit it to the many

realms of manifestation below" (Drury: 2006: 46).[1] So if the Mythos God Azathoth, as already discussed, can be taken as representing the origin of everything with a nucleus as being insanity and astral chaos, then Nyarlathotep follows this through in being representative of cosmological creation. With this point in mind, this Card therefore represents the inception of communication in man.

In describing this Card on more defined Lovecraftian terms, this God is depicted as the "Magus, Messenger, Wanderer between Worlds, Nyarlathotep is the Herald and Ambassador of the Great Old Ones, most specifically Azathoth, the Idiot God of Chaos" (Hutchinson, Friedman: 2002: 8). As upholding the position of being The God of Communication and the written word in Lovecraftian religious Mythos, Nyarlathotep appears to humanity in various different forms. Being the mediator between mankind and the higher spheres, in His role as being a higher force, His appearance differs depending on which part of mankind He would appear to, and the message it is His stated intention to deliver to those who regard His position on such a basis. And as the God who is behind so many of the beliefs of humanity, it is His to appear in different forms according to the religious sect that He speaks to, and it is in this that many different cults have different religious deities which can be ascribed to being different apparitions of this God as here established. Nyarlathotep appears in different forms to lead the religious views of mankind as He believes is appropriate to the given situation in hand.

This idea is conveyed and followed through further by the *HP Lovecraft Tarot* as the Introductory Book to the previous Edition of this Deck defines the principle that "Nyarlathotep is capable of assuming any form necessary in his wanderings, sowing the seeds of Chaos in

---

1   I have made repeated reference to this book in hand throughout this first Part of The Necronomicon Cycle. The reason for this is because I've needed a more general reference on the Tarot in order to further elaborate on the meaning of the cards according to Cult of R'Lyeh religious belief, and this title from Neville Drury makes a good job in upholding this point. Pretty much any book on the Tarot could have made the same statement, but this was the reference I had to hand whilst I was writing this book.

each realm he visits" (Hutchinson, Friedman: 2002: 8). It should, therefore, be integral to the understanding of this God that He does appear in such a myriad of different forms as, being the Communicator God for the Mythos, as this is how Nyarlathotep mediates for mankind in His various Cosmic dimensions. The *HP Lovecraft Tarot* goes further than this, though, as the idea is that every one of these 'different faces' is appropriate in form for which to communicate His message to the different sects of mankind as is appropriate to any given situation in question.

But with that therefore having been established, Nyarlathotep is also the 'God of all magick', and this statement as well describes His position as influencing a society of human religious worship. It is thought this that the religions of magick were the first to be taught to humanity shortly after the emergence of our race as the Great Old Ones descended to Earth from the Stars, and this would explain a position as to why Nyarlathotep appears to religion in the many different forms that is here described. In studying this Card as it is The Magician in most different Decks, and with the larger number of systems of the Tarot, the *HP Lovecraft Tarot* notes that "He [Nyarlathotep] is the fluidic basis of all transmission of activity; and, on the dynamic theory of the Universe, he is himself the substance thereof... No true image is possible at all; for, firstly, all images are necessarily false, as such; and, secondly, the motion being perpetual... any stasis contradicts the idea of the card" (Hutchinson, Friedman: 2002: 8). Again we see the example of Nyarlathotep visiting the Prophets of human religion in so many different forms.

However, despite this definition of the Communicator and this massive position of multiplicity of form, Nyarlathotep has a direct and defined representation as depicted as Card 1 of this system of the Tarot. Here He appears to human religion in the form of the Black Pharaoh, as this point is already discussed. The Cult of R'Lyeh believe this to be the form that He chose to take as part of the religion of ancient Egypt, and this justifies what is written here, as well as justifying a number of statements as included as part of the Old Testament of the

Bible. In this depiction with the previous Edition of this system, this Card represents Nyarlathotep as carrying a rook, and we take this as being representative of how He relates in other (more powerful) world religions as their most important representation. Christianity, for example, regard the rook as depicted, as one of their religious symbols of symbolic representation, and of the idea of the 'shepherd herding his flock' is also defined with such a point of consideration. We define this Card, with this, as representing the religious principals embodied in the idea of 'God as Messenger and the communicator', as He is regarded as being powerful, frightening and daemonic, and the symbol of absolute power that is upheld by the orthodox religions of human societal thought.

The religious aspects and the secrets of He who appeared to man as the Black Pharaoh are manifold, as are the forms in which He has appeared to human religious society. We can express this idea if we assume Nyarlathotep to be the religious force who conveyed the idea of the Egyptian hieroglyphics, which are in turn descriptive of every Egyptian Goddess and God which equate to the God system of the ancient Egyptian religion.

If continuing to quote from the *HP Lovecraft Tarot* as the main important reference in hand it would be another important point to note that "Nyarlathotep is the Patron – and Matron – of all magicks" (Hutchinson, Friedman: 2002: 8). But beyond Egypt as one example, Nyarlathotep is worshipped by a large number of other established religious movements, and it can be reasoned that He is the first influencing force behind most of the religious understanding of human societies throughout history. In particular it is part of our religious outlook that Nyarlathotep was the esoteric entity behind the worship of the Witches in early Britain and Europe, that was persecuted by the Witch Trials, with this being just one of a huge number of parallels with religious thought to have been put forward by various faiths.

As a force of God, however, the hideous manifestations of Nyarlathotep go further, and to the Cult of R'Lyeh it is believed that He is the representative figure behind the Fallen Angels that were written

about in the *Book of Enoch the Prophet*, as our Deck of Tarot states that "[Nyarlathotep] can be... identified with the Fallen Angels of the Book of Enoch" (Hutchinson, Friedman: 2002: 8). To take such a religious point of reference further the *HP Lovecraft Tarot* tells us, "[it was Nyarlathotep] who taught the... human race the arts of sorcery, harlotry, and war" (Hutchinson, Friedman: 2002: 8). The Fall from Grace is now put into context, as the study of a cosmological insanity of Necronomicon Gods begins, and this opens our religious study of one system of the Tarot as representative of a massively greater movement of religious truth.

It is also true that the acts of magick that were first taught to humanity were taught by the Avatars of Nyarlathotep, as the messengers behind His almighty and wholly destructive power. And as with all of the Gods of this religious system of the occult, this is beyond what can be envisioned by our any part of this human race. Such religious manifestation is in terms of psychological insanity and chaos, and is above the rational understanding of the mind.

That having been said, with this as a working system of the Tarot and in context with this statement concerning religion, this Card should be considered very much one the psychological working of the mind, and it should be considered in this context, that Card 1 is also significant of the astral knowledge of higher worlds. Whilst the understanding of mankind is usually quite mundane, we are still quite capable of achieving altered states of mind, as well as ascending to higher planes as discussed. Therefore, Nyarlathotep as represented by a Card of the Tarot, is here symbolic of such defined communication with higher spheres. This can sometimes be achieved through dreams, although the worshipper of Nyarlathotep should attempt to ascend to higher levels wherever this should be without the aid of dream wherever possible.

Another statement regarding this Card, is that Nyarlathotep, in this study of the Tarot, is representative of our learning about ourselves in terms of our becoming the masters (or mistresses) of ourselves, our personalities and our egos, and the inner dimensions of our minds. Our personal creative work is represented with this Card as well, and this

Card in a reading is symbolic of learning through the experiences that life throws at us, and what we can learn about ourselves.

Nyarlathotep is the Communicator, and – in this – Card 1 is representative of humanity and the point at which we left the mystical domain of the animals. We make the assumption, with this being the start of our study of the Necronomicon Mythos, that it is the ability of humanity to communicate, which elevates us from the rest of the Planet which is animals, birds, reptiles, fish and insects. It is with this understanding that the mind of humanity is elevated from the rest of the living intelligence of the Earth, although it is the intervention of the Old Ones, on a greater level, that gave us this initial intellect. As the only species with our ability of interpersonal communication, Nyarlathotep is the God who represents such a concept of human intelligence and thought. Card 1 goes further than this, though, as it indicates that human intelligence has always been elevated above the simple forms of communication that are unique to our race and which further pertain to our species. The definition of this Card speaks of the "Knowledge of the Unity of Worlds" (Hutchinson, Friedman: 2002: 9), and with this statement the assumption is made that there is more to understanding than what we should regard as mundane, and that this sentient understanding, since early civilization, has always been in the acknowledgement of the esoteric existence of the forces of the Cosmos that are greater than us.

The ancient magickal acts of humanity are defined in the same context, as the Lovecraft Tarot defines the meaning of this Card as representing "Theurgy, Magick [and] Shamanism" (Hutchinson, Friedman: 2002: 9). These were the early sciences of mankind, and magickal literature tells us that these arts were taught to our elders through their communication between the Gods. The question is still there to be asked, however, as to what does this actually mean in terms of a Reading of the Tarot?

To answer this question, the statement should be made right at the start of this book on the understanding of magick and *The Necronomicon*, that the *HP Lovecraft Tarot* can, at times, be quite obscure, with points

of reference and meaning often being quite bizarre. Whilst these words are uniquely defined as having specific meaning, the interpretation in this Tarot is sometimes difficult to define, and that is regardless to any system in discussion. This Tarot does not state where these arts will come into the life of the person who the reading is for, but that they will have some occurrence. Our Tarot sometimes defines statements in this manner, and it is in this that our study can be quite unique and different from other studies of the Tarot.

So if Nyarlathotep is described as creation and the first communication that defines the higher intellect of human kind, the Tarot continues to discuss the meaning of Card 1 as to define a position of "Service to a Higher Cause and/or Principal" (Hutchinson, Friedman: 2002: 9). This could be read as being relevant to the acknowledgement of a religious God, as it is only humanity who are known to think with the acknowledgement of the Gods as a greater force. Whilst it can be seen that this acknowledgement is one of the earliest concepts of humanity as a thinking species, it can also be read in regard to an acknowledgement of God in the current day setting of our day to day lives. As Nyarlathotep is the God of communication with humanity, this can be read as representing the first acceptance of the Mythos into our culture. It is in this sense correct that the Tarot defines "Spiritual Nobility" (Hutchinson, Friedman: 2002: 9). as this personal acceptance of the Gods is a step that is taken as an act of personal honour.

The first Card of this Tarot, further to this, represents the acceptance of the self as communicator on greater terms and this is, in the context of this Card, is still a very personal matter. It is our understanding of ourselves which allows us to communicate, but we must understand ourselves first. So as the Tarot defines its meaning as the "Trickster as Catalyst for Development" (Hutchinson, Friedman: 2002: 9), this refers to that ingenuity within ourselves that is ready to play games. It can also forecast that the subject of the reading will express this principal in this context. The same paragraph also forecasts "Opportunism", and this is to be read in the same context.

It is very much a part of this definition that communication is a part

of the understanding of the self, which is why this Card is important as the start of this Tarot. Therefore, in further defining its meaning as being the "Mastery of Personality & Self" (Hutchinson, Friedman: 2002: 9), the Tarot is speaking of our understanding of ourselves as a fundamental issue as governed by Nyarlathotep as the Communicator. So "Progressive action [and] Productivity" (Hutchinson, Friedman: 2002: 9) is also justified as a statement in the context of the understanding of ourselves. In this understanding, of ourselves and on a greater level, the Tarot tells us that our actions will turn out to be productive.

Negative Reading

In this context, the Communicator is to be understood as relating to our outlook on life, but more importantly as our understanding of ourselves. "Self-deception, Denial; Escapism into obscure intellectual pursuits" (Hutchinson, Friedman: 2002: 9) is forecast as a position which will likely come into the situation. It is time to look within ourselves to question ourselves, and whether these are issues that we should be cautious of? The Tarot as a means to forecast such issues is an oracle of serious religious importance.

Other symptoms of the self are defined, and "Egotism, Narcissism [and] Arrogance" (Hutchinson, Friedman: 2002: 9) here come into the situation. Again these are issues of the understanding of the self, and if such issues of the self, and if such issues of the self are to be apparent, then we should see this as a warning of something to come and to be cautious of. This definition continues with "Repetition of, & slavery to, stagnant patterns of action" (Hutchinson, Friedman: 2002: 9). These are possibly quite valid warnings and, whilst these in a Negative Reading are pointers towards things to come, we should be aware that such Readings represent future situations to be cautious of, and which should be considered on such terms by the Magus. Such symptoms of attitude are here something to be mindful of.

A "Loss of Self [and] Submission to others" (Hutchinson, Friedman: 2002: 9) is forecast. With a statement such as this coming into a Reading,

we should ask ourselves how much we are respecting ourselves, and how much we are living under the authority of others? We should take time to consider ourselves, and respect ourselves as individuals not to be submissive to other people's control.

This stated definition ends by warning of "Phantasm, Indolence [and] Lethargy" (Hutchinson, Friedman: 2002: 9). These being symptoms of attitude, the Tarot is still talking in terms of our perception of ourselves. It is interesting that the Cards as defined in this context of the Necronomicon Mythos Gods can give us definitions of meaning that are defined as being different from every other system of Tarot. The Mythos as regards the mind is to be regarded as a very different system as regards the occult. The Mythos in this sense defines itself as unique; as will be seen as our study continues.

2. Yog-Sothoth: The High Priestess

If the previous Card of Nyarlathotep would stand as representing the Communicator, then the Card that is depicted as Yog-Sothoth must be regarded as the Guardian of the Gates between Human Consciousness and the vibrations through which the Old Ones speak. The meaning represented by this Card is one of psychedelia represented through the human consciousness, and attained through the psychological derangement experienced through use of mind expanding drugs. The Gates of which Yog-Sothoth guards cannot be consciously understood in human terms, and the consciousness attained through the use of hallucinogenic drugs is the only clear way in which to understand this esoteric, and deeply chaotic state of psychological madness. This Card is to be seen as representing a trip whereby these Gates, and Yog-Sothoth, are manifest and perceived through the chaos of altered states attained through the willing use of hallucinogens; with the Planets and the Cosmos racing through time, screaming through occult dimensions unknown to any normal, human frame of mind.

If Card 1 is therefore representative of that which is considered by other religions as being 'the creation', then Yog-Sothoth is representative of the concept of a universal fabric through which all space, all time, and all matter is bound together. The *HP Lovecraft Tarot* defines Yog-Sothoth as described as "the unity of all worlds; all space, all time, all matter. Yog-Sothoth is the subtle fabric which binds all aspects and dimensions of the Cosmos" (Hutchinson, Friedman: 2002: 10). We can see Card 2, therefore, as being a part of the infinite fabric of creation which creates a universal 'normality' throughout such truth of cosmic and astral existence.

In further terms of the reality of human consciousness, our rational perception is that we see things as being linear, and also in terms of what

we experience as being clear. This is not the case with the conceptual existence of The Great Old Ones. If to establish a single example, a chair is, to human consciousness, a static, solid object that can only exist in one dimension, and time can only move forward at a constant rate through the dimensions that we perceive as 'reality'. This static, and linear reality is that which is governed by Yog-Sothoth, and this it is for this reason that His Worshippers regard Him as 'the Gate, and the Guardian of the Gate whereby all spheres [of both consciousness and perceived reality] meet.' This in terms of the meaning of Card 2 is further established as the *HP Lovecraft Tarot* describes Yog-Sothoth, in terms of the development of this study of the occult and higher spheres of religion, that: "Yog-Sothoth is the energy / substance which radiates out from Azathoth, and which Nyarlathotep draws on in order to take form" (Hutchinson, Friedman: 2002: 10). As this study continues, we will see that our system of the Tarot continues towards defining a coherent religious system which unravels systematically and expands on its own conceptual terms.

In further describing the conceptual reality of Yog-Sothoth, religious study would establish that He is representative here as the realization of religious enlightenment as attained through the ritual use of psychedelic drugs, as discussed. If that is to be established as the first part of this occult study, Card 2 cannot really be defined any further than through this insight that comes through the shamanic use of mind expanding drugs (although such meanings can also be defined through this study, should it not be understood as being with the point in hand accepted). The *HP Lovecraft Tarot* takes this idea further in establishing the point that "Yog-Sothoth is thus the Gateway between all worlds, and the Guardian of the Threshold of transition and transfiguration from one world / dimension to another" (Hutchinson, Friedman: 2002: 10).

With that point of definition in hand, this Card must be therefore be defined on these terms as symbolic, that whilst it is absolutely normal and acceptable to view the world around us with one particular understanding. These perceptions can, however, only be assumptions when we make an attempt to understand The Great Old Ones. Whilst

humanity has one normal perception of 'reality', Yog-Sothoth guards the Gates of this 'reality', and the Universe is only static because it is Yog-Sothoth who controls these Gates. Without Him, a threshold to higher spheres that can only be obtained through involving this stated Worship through the use of psychedelic drugs, cannot be obtained. The *HP Lovecraft Tarot* tells us that "[by] properly making contact with this fundamental structure of the Multiverse in one place and / or time, one can gain access to any other point in space and time, or transmute any matter from one form to another" (Hutchinson, Friedman: 2002: 10). Having been thus defined, there is a difference here between Card 2 as an interpretation of the High Priestess and the understanding of Yog-Sothoth as equated to this as a figment of Worship.

Having drawn this comparison then, Yog-Sothoth as a representative part of the Tarot should be seen on greater terms as representing issues within our day to day reality as transmuting into something unexpected, or of normal events changing from one thing into another. Whilst this is, on a human level something we usually accept as being 'normal', the Tarot states that this may be due, on a higher level, to events being influenced on the greater level of the Cosmos. The 'Readings' discussed as follow discuss this idea in better detail, and the Introductory Book to this second Edition to this Deck of the Tarot concludes this definition of meaning by asking "Could this [interpretation] be a dim recollection of… the all-encompassing Substance of Primal Chaos which emanates from that Void?" (Hutchinson, Friedman: 2002: 11). So Yog-Sothoth controls the cohesion of the Astral, the psychological, and of all matter defined under that definition of greater religious truth.

The *HP Lovecraft Tarot* continues to define a situation of "Transcendence of limitations & structure" (Hutchinson, Friedman: 2002: 11). In a Positive Reading this point of definition corresponds to limitations and structure on personal terms. We all have limitations; although this is in one sense the fault of ourselves and that which we feel we can achieve in the sense of our day to day lives. But this also works on a greater level. The limitations imposed on our lives by external factors here come into play, and a situation which stops

us from moving on in life can be signified by this Card if read with this interpretation of meaning. This comes into play further as the *HP Lovecraft Tarot* defines the word 'structure'. In Western society our lives are entirely controlled by this context of structure. This Card would then indicate changes in the way we live our lives, the routine by which we live our lives, and, in a contemporary setting, the external structures which usually control it.

But that same statement concerning 'Transcendence of limitations', when concerned with insane and astral manifestation which is Yog-Sothoth also works on a greater level. The *HP Lovecraft Tarot* defines this meaning here, as signifying that there will at some point be a situation regarding the "direct tap into the Quintessence / Ether / Akasha" (Hutchinson, Friedman: 2002: 11). These statements should be seen as referring to the (system which is sometimes seen as) Astral Ascension; that relating to the travel of the mind to higher spheres. This should also be seen as a transcendence of limitations, but with these terms defined, this is further defined in the form of exploration within our own minds, above the actual experience of out-of-body travel. Yog-Sothoth is, as defined, therefore, as being the Gate, and further to that the Key and Guardian of the Gate. This definition of a 'tap into Akasha' should be seen as the mental exploration necessary to perceive such Dimensions of higher reality, and in this the understanding of, and exploration of, our own minds, is the way to understand Yog-Sothoth.

This interpretation of the Mystical Tarot continues to establish a position of an "Automatic direction of Energy & Will towards Need & Desire" (Hutchinson, Friedman: 2002: 11), and this is defined as the meaning of the Card which in other Decks is often represented as The High Priestess. Our definition of the Tarot having now been established, this statement is further reminiscent of the manifest religious ideas of Crowley and the Hermetic Order of the Golden Dawn: The whole religion of Thelema, as the name that the Golden Dawn gave to their religion, revolves around the idea of direction of Will (as do some other systems of the occult), and a large part of Western esoteric belief is therefore now defined in terms of the Worship of the *Necronomicon*

system of magick. If an entire system of belief can operate around the idea of Will, we now see that Yog-Sothoth can fit in with this more mainstream and established system of the occult if we were to choose to see it under that interpretation of theory.

So, despite the notion that the ideas as upheld by the Order of the Golden Dawn might not fit exactly with our particular interpretation of the Lovecraftian Tarot as one specific form of understanding, our Deck does specifically follow the idea of every other system of the Tarot as traditional in defining a further position that there is a greater religious truth. This entire study could be considered to be a bizarre system of religious thought, this does not diverge from the interpretation of the Tarot as one system as it exists as a larger concept of religion and such a definition of religious truth. "Intuitive ability to make fundamental associations between antithetical ideas and / or objects" (Hutchinson, Friedman: 2002: 11) is defined, and in this Card 2 accords to the High Priestess in context with the Tarot as defined as every other religious Deck of the Tarot is, on a further level, a part of another, greater and cohesive system of esoteric truth.

Negative Reading

Yog-Sothoth is, as with the rest of our interpretation of the Mystical Tarot, a force of insanity and mental confusion which can only be beyond the proper comprehension of the human intellect. So when the *HP Lovecraft Tarot* continues to define a position of "Dissolution of function and / or Form", it is describing the higher nature of such an insane and chaotic God-Form in terms of how this most often accords to a human interpretation (whilst it is integral to our religious interpretation that The God form here in question quite often appear to humanity in various different aspects of manifestation). Whilst on this level this can be seen as being descriptive of the God-Form as it exists on the basis of our psychological understanding, the statement of "lapse into abstraction, loss of direction & structure [and] disorder"

(Hutchinson, Friedman: 2002: 11), also describes a situation which can become apparent in our own lives which we will soon have to contend with. "Inability to solidify intent or mainstream course of action" (Hutchinson, Friedman: 2002: 11) is further defined; and those who Worship the Old Ones see this statement as relating most directly to our own position of religious understanding (in this particular sense, our rational perception of Yog-Sothoth), and our own manifest integrity in terms of our Worship, and the exercises of the mind which are necessarily involved in upholding such a position of philosophical and worshipful perspective.

The *HP Lovecraft Tarot* continues, and "Half-formed ideas; unstable logic; inability to reason or communicate [and] mental distraction" (Hutchinson, Friedman: 2002: 11) are situations defined. This obviously relates to the state of mind that everybody experiences at one time or another, that for whatever reason we are just mentally exhausted. But this statement can be regarded as being more important, however, in that if we are Worshipping Yog-Sothoth (or any other part of the *Necronomicon Mythos* as defined as our religious book), then this can often impend a position of insanity and psychological chaos. And if these symptoms are to be experienced, for any reason, it could mean that our religious study is undermining our grip on what others consider 'real'. As with every other Negative Reading with the Lovecraft system of the Tarot, we should ask if these Negative Readings are symptoms of us actually losing our minds?

3. Shub-Niggurath: The Empress

Whilst Shub-Niggurath is, in our religious interpretation, the Goddess of Fertility, She is known in Mythos literature as "the Blind Idiot God; the God with a Thousand Dark Young".[1] As well as this Shub-Niggurath also upholds the Qaballistic sephiroth of Binah, hereby equating to being the protection Mythos in the Necronomicon system of magick. This Card is therefore defined as enigmatic beyond the comprehension of human intellect, symbolic of mysteries and questions unanswered. In this as our study of Mythos Gods, the definition of Shub-Niggurath is therefore, and by necessity, vague. Her actual definition as to reason is unknown, despite having been defined in Mythos literature and Shub-Niggurath is – therefore – symbolic of the things we feel we should know about, but don't. She represents unanswered questions, and the things which seem obvious but are not. And whilst the Thousand Dark Young of Shub-Niggurath could represent a thousand things which we know, we do not – and cannot – in actual terms know any of them, and therefore they represent a thousand things which are mystery, and a thousand questions unanswered.

As we progress through this as a commentary on the *HP Lovecraft Tarot*, we begin to see how the Mythos describes the nucleus and centre of the Cosmos, through creation, to ultimately conclude when it ends with describing the highest virtue of humanity as the act of Worship. "As

---

1   This idea comes into Mythos literature repeatedly in various statements from different writers of horror, although no direct quotations come to hand. It should be noted, however, that according to representation according to the Mystical Qaballah, as well as other systems, that the deity who occupies this position is both the protector and a female Goddess. This point is made here because of its importance in relating this system in terms of correspondence with other systems of the occult.

Yog-Sothoth is the transcendence and defiance of Form" (Hutchinson, Friedman: 2002: 12), states the Lovecraft Tarot, "so Shub-Niggurath is the motion towards Form and materialization" (Hutchinson, Friedman: 2002: 12). Shub-Niggurath is the fertility deity in the religious system that we are here describing, and the definition here defines a concept that whilst all matter is stable due to Yog-Sothoth, all matter still has to be conceived with the concept of the 'birth'. In the religious ideology defined here we can further define this as meaning that everything that exists throughout the Cosmos, must begin by being 'born'; and not just the living species that populate our Planet and the other places throughout the infinite vast emptiness of space. This concept is again defined very clearly by the *HP Lovecraft Tarot* when it states that, "Shub-Niggurath is thus… worshiped by many names as the Dark Mother who bestows life and takes it away…" (Hutchinson, Friedman: 2002: 12).

"As Goddess of both Womb and Tomb, Shub-Niggurath is the dark mystery of Unknown Nature" (Hutchinson, Friedman: 2002: 12). The Lovecraft Deck is quite direct in this statement, but – despite this statement in itself being quite obvious – it is also quite unique. What the Tarot is saying here is that whilst everything must initially be conceived with some sort of birth as representative of creation, the opposite is – as always – true; and this is that everything must also end with death. The Death Card is, of course, much more direct with its statement in properly defining this idea, but the Tarot is here again correct in context, in saying that everything that has a beginning must also eventually have an equivalent end. The only exceptions to this rule are Time and Space itself, as the Cosmos can be defined as the only reality which is, in fact, nothing.

As the *HP Lovecraft Tarot* continues to define Shub-Niggurath, the following statement is equally as important and applies to every other aspect of the Mythos of *The Necronomicon*. "She [Shub-Niggurath] is that aspect of existence which is eternally beyond human perception" (Hutchinson, Friedman: 2002: 12). Whilst the Lovecraft Deck is defining one aspect of this Card as having this specific meaning (as

representing concepts of the Cosmos that cannot be understood), the Necronomicon Mythos of Gods are all represented in terms of the insanity that can only be understood by the psychick comprehension of mankind. Therefore, if this Deck is to be taken properly in this context, then maybe Shub-Niggurath could be a statement from the Tarot to represent this concept of the Gods, as the Card of the Lovers represents relationships (as an example) and love?

So, with that position defined, if Shub-Niggurath would be the Mythos Goddess of fertility and protection, then this would be represented with a statement that is taken from supernatural horror, and quoted by the *HP Lovecraft Tarot*; "Ia! Shub-Niggurath! The Black Goat of the Woods with a Thousand Young!".[2] It is the statement that Shub-Niggurath has such blasphemous Young that corresponds to Her as the Goddess of birth and, in that, the creation of all that has been born.

The statement from the Introductory Book to the second Edition of our study in question is again appropriate as one with which to end this description of The Empress as she is interpreted by our religious view, as the *HP Lovecraft Tarot* states "Shub-Niggurath is the Unity of the Source of all Forms (whereas Nyarlathotep is the Unity of all Substance; hence one is the Mother of a Thousand Young, while the other is one being with a thousand forms)" (Hutchinson, Friedman: 2002: 12). Reincarnation is thus defined in context with this transition through the Major Arcana.

Whilst it is probably characteristic of the Lovecraft Deck of the Tarot that the Fourth Card is that of fertility, the Positive Reading in this respect is probably more characteristic in this sense than some of the other Cards of this Tarot. "Productivity [and] fertility" (Hutchinson,

---

2 This quotation is taken directly from the horror fiction inspired by Lovecraft, as this book is written to describe. It is used by the HP Lovecraft Tarot, and this is from where we take the statement. However, as used by the this Tarot, it is not referenced specifically by this Deck in discussion. Therefore this quotation has to be used with the reference not credited, although it is safe to say that it is actually from Lovecraft.

Friedman: 2002: 13) are both forecast, and this is quite straightforward in what it says. But this idea is developed further as the our Tarot defines "fertile ground for spiritual, mental, or physical seed to be planted and nurtured" (Hutchinson, Friedman: 2002: 13). Here the idea of the Fertility Goddess is continued, and this in a Reading is obvious as it defines a time when new projects should be started, and projects that have already been begun will be successful.

"Pregnancy, reproduction; multiplication [and] propagation" (Hutchinson, Friedman: 2002: 13) are defined, and this is the same as that which is defined by every other Fertility Mythos, although Shub-Niggurath is very unique in herself. But aside from the idea here discussed, that childbirth may be indicated, this relates (in the further sense of the above) to the idea of personal projects that have been undertaken propagating and becoming successful. So, "Profit, fruits [and] harvest" (Hutchinson, Friedman: 2002: 13) are here defined, and the Tarot states that projects which have been undertaken in the past (possibly relating to the other Cards of this system?) will now culminate and that they will be successful.

The last statement in this definition diverts from this as similar to the classical reference to a Fertility Mythos, but is still very defined as the Card of Shub-Niggurath. "Land, earth; 'home & hearth'" (Hutchinson, Friedman: 2002: 13) are here defined. What this means, exactly, is not immediately clear, but this Card, in the context here stated, may represent that this might be a good time to 'earth' in terms of any use of the occult recently undertaken. In terms of the practical occult, Shub-Niggurath may be saying that perhaps we should take a period of time away from worship? This could in this sense relate to the practical use of *The Necronomicon* as a practical system of the occult, and in doing so this relates to our Worship as *The Necronomicon* is one specific system of Black Magick in its own right.

Negative Reading

As the above follows the actual idea of a Fertility Goddess quite clearly, the manifestation of Shub-Niggurath in a Negative Reading

continues to follow the idea of the Lovecraftian, as the Magus would expect, and can in this sense be seen as destructive. As would follow the idea of this being the opposite of what is defined above in terms of a Positive interpretation, the Tarot here defines a position of "Infertility; unproductive efforts, waste of 'seed' due to sterility of the agent and / or object of action" (Hutchinson, Friedman: 2002: 13). This statement should be read in context as the opposite of fertility, as, if it did represent birth, Shub-Niggurath can now be argued as representing the oblivion of death.

As directly following this definition, this idea stands as reinforced and the statement that "Abortion, miscarriage; interruption of, or intervention in, endeavours" (Hutchinson, Friedman: 2002: 13) is defined. And as with all of the descriptions of meaning with the Lovecraft Deck of the Tarot, this should be read as relating directly to our personal lives (or to the life of the person for who the Reading is for), as all of these Readings will always be very personal to our personal situation. So when the Tarot defines "Loss, barrenness [and] decrease" (Hutchinson, Friedman: 2002: 13), then this accords to us in a personal sense, and such a Reading will usually only make sense to ourselves, or the subject of the Reading, accordingly for this reason.

The final statement with this Card according to the *HP Lovecraft Tarot* warns of "Exile, dispossession; nomadic life" (Hutchinson, Friedman: 2002: 13). Whilst it does have to be said that this will rarely actually mean that we will end up as being homeless on personal terms, personal projects and our personal situation in life may start to drift and move away from the intended direction first in hand. Shub-Niggurath is said to have a Thousand Young, and in terms of personal ambition there may be a thousand directions of which we can be distracted towards or be side tracked away from, but the individual can only ever have one specific means of achieving any personal goal.

4. Hastur. The King in Yellow: The Emperor

The King in Yellow

Here is a very specific and powerful Card of the Tarot, and in writing this definition for the discussion of the *HP Lovecraft Tarot*, a number of strange things have happened to me in a personal sense, although I feel it best not to discuss such issues here. This is the Card of the Tarot that in all systems represents hierarchy; not only that hierarchy between ourselves and others, but also hierarchy within our mortal plane of existence, and the Gods of *The Necronomicon* as our secular system of worship. It is probably because of this aspect, with this particular God, that *The Necronomicon* directly states that to verbally utter The name of This God is to bring certain disaster on oneself. Whilst in actual practice this is not always the case, it does stand as an actual rule, and is a good rule to go by if dealing with this specific God if involving any use of ceremonial magick. In terms of graphical representation, Hastur's Card is probably one of the least graphical in this Deck, although the graphic included here makes the point that this might be different with the publication of the planned Third Edition.

In keeping my notes on the Deck I have thought that this may be suggestive of the message of this Card as portraying the message of

an issue withheld. "Hastur is the Divine Ancestor of the King Who will Return; the King in Yellow" (Hutchinson, Friedman: 2002: 14), says the *HP Lovecraft Tarot*. In saying this it makes a statement that He Who Should Not be Named (as is the proper way to refer to this God if upholding advice given in *The Necronomicon*), is according to religious consensus, a tribal God. In this Card the depiction of Hastur is depicted as primitive and tribal. Our religious interpretation is that this definition is accurate as we believe that He is worshipped by a history of global tribal cultures, albeit under different names. The *HP Lovecraft Tarot* elaborates on this slightly by saying that "there are those who believe that it will be a human descendent of Hastur who will reign under the Great Old Ones" (Hutchinson, Friedman: 2002: 14). In this we can interpret the beliefs of different religions from primitive tribal societies, as this study of religion represents, to the contemporary ethics of worship as upheld by beliefs such as the Church of Christ.

The *HP Lovecraft Tarot* tells us that "the important message of this card is that we are all descended from the Gods" (Hutchinson, Friedman: 2002: 14), and here statements such as The Biblical Book of *Genesis* here comes into play. The face of He Who Should Not be Named is portrayed to us here as holding the face of a human like Daemon, so should we assume by this that if we are made in the image of God, then it is in the image of that God of human hierarchy? It would be with this statement then, if Hastur would be the God of the Mythos of hierarchy on whatever level, and that He is represented as such, then are the other Gods of human society since the onset somewhat more weird? "The most important aspect of this sovereignty" (Hutchinson, Friedman: 2002: 14), the *HP Lovecraft Tarot* tells us, "is our personal responsibility for all conditional aspects of our lives" (Hutchinson, Friedman: 2002: 14). Again, should we here consider Christianity as symbolic of certain statements of religious philosophy with their teachings of human free will?

Considered in more esoteric terms, the Unspeakable One represents hierarchy as an aspect of higher spheres of human consciousness, and represents a mediation with which humanity can communicate with

the Great Old Ones. It also represents boundaries, and areas in which hierarchy amongst people can run into problems. And the Tarot itself goes some lengths towards defining this as it represents mediation between people, ourselves and the Gods.

But this Card also represents our responsibility for our own actions as it states "The self is a rebellious kingdom, [and] therefore the first axiom of the ancient mysteries has always been 'Know Thyself!'" (Hutchinson, Friedman: 2002: 14). With this, Card Four is depictive of our own actions as we relate to others, being the only Card of the Major Arcana that is directly representing the involvement in our own lives, of the *Necronomicon* Mythos Gods as forces which can work for us if they are properly understood, as is the case with the study of all systems of pagan worship.

And further to this, if we understand its relation to humanity and our means of hierarchy, it can easily be understood that the Card that pertains to Hastur is the strongest Card of the Deck that can be drawn. It can be seen as representing a leadership principal or responsibility where a social position is upheld. As Hastur is the hierarchy God of mankind, everything positive about organization amongst people is apparent. Faith in issues, both personal and religious, and people's faith – both personal and esoteric – are signified in this name of He Who Should Not be Named.

As we progress through the Tarot, however, now Card Four (the fifth Card of the Major Arcana) is representative of the social standing which characterizes human society, and assumed positions of power. This is the first statement that we have that humanity is above all other terrestrial races.

At this point I would like to continue here to put forward a personal point of view. He Who Should Not be Named is, with this Card, representative of the organization of the human race, specifically in terms of authority and social standing. It is the view of the author of *The Necronomicon Cycle* that authority is always and under all circumstances wrong and that humanity would be better without it. But a position of authority may be a good thing as represented by a

Positive Reading with this Card, and this is in terms of benefit to the individual, even if this can be argued to be unsound. The point should be made, though, that authority is symptomatic of a society that is ill, and Card Four, in this context, says that this must always be an eternal part of the Cosmos.

Yet with all systems of the Tarot, meanings further than what are first obvious should be defined. So where the Lovecraft system speaks of "Leadership, Authority; [and] Dominion" (Hutchinson, Friedman: 2002: 15), then it could just as well be speaking about circumstances within our personal lives (or with the person who the reading is for), where we will find ourselves in control. Readings beyond what is obvious must be uncovered.

Further to reading this statement as regards our own situation, the Tarot speaks to the individual more directly. "Healthy Self-Image; Independence, self-sustaining confidence & faith" (Hutchinson, Friedman: 2002: 15) are all statements that concern the individual, and this follows on directly from the above. But this Card is very much one of the ego. Whilst a 'balanced karma' may be suggested from the above, Card Four carries on with defining it as positive that "Paternity, inheritance, heritage [and] ancestry" (Hutchinson, Friedman: 2002: 15) are likely to come into the picture, possibly in the form of an inheritance from a relative? Again, what this means in a personal sense is great, but all of this has to be within the context of a system that could be argued to be unjust. But a definite positive situation is finally given to us, as the Positive Reading defined in the Lovecraft Tarot forecasts a situation of "Earned respect &/or position" (Hutchinson, Friedman: 2002: 15). This statement is not about authority assumed, but is in terms of gain where it is deserved. It would seem to me that the history of our race and religion revolves around the standards as they are defined here, and should be considered as doing so if to represent our religion with this study of the Tarot in question.

Negative Reading

The Negative interpretation of the Card here, is still very much about social position and power. It is representative of hierarchy; of the

chain of authority from one person being "above" another in situations where power can come into play for any reason. From the start of this definition the *HP Lovecraft Tarot* speaks of the mentality of power in a personal sense; of "Delusions of grandeur, paranoia" (Hutchinson, Friedman: 2002: 15), and of a "Napoleon Complex" (Hutchinson, Friedman: 2002: 15). If this Card is drawn, then maybe we should look within ourselves to ask if we are displaying the symptoms that these statements would indicate? It could, however, also speak of these symptoms in others, and if these aspects are becoming part of our lives, then they are in the immediate sense something that should be 'nipped in the bud' – to be prevented before they start. Further to that, these symptoms might be the result of taking Mythos worship too lightly. It could be the result of 'dabbling' with the occult, or of entering into acts of magick before being properly prepared.

This same context can be continued in exactly the same way when the Tarot defines this Card with the statement: "Domineering personality [and a] need to control others" (Hutchinson, Friedman: 2002: 15). Again the question is whether we display these symptoms ourselves, or whether they are symptoms displayed in others? Either way these are definite issues that need to be immediately addressed. The Tarot continues with the definition that "dependence on external validation for security" (Hutchinson, Friedman: 2002: 15) is an issue in question. This does, on first impressions, sound like a human symptom which, as with the rest of this definition, also needs to be immediately addressed. But in discussing the *HP Lovecraft Tarot* and the interpretation of the Cards as discussed, this can be seen to have a further meaning. This statement can also be referring to a dependence on the Gods for such 'validation and security', and such a dependence on these Gods of Chaos for security may be a direct route into madness.

So as we have here defined authority from above and a number of negative issues as defined, the Tarot often speaks of such negative issues in the same statement, with an opposite definition in the same aspect. So whilst authority from above is indicated in this respect, this Deck continues directly in defining its meaning as, the "Orphan,

illegitimacy [and the] Nouveau Riche (Hutchinson, Friedman: 2002: 15). Whilst power can be misused, and this is warned of, now we see the danger implied in actions begun without any form of higher resort. It warns us of taking action without authority to accept responsibility should those actions be wrong.

In ending its definition with a Negative Reading with this Card, authority in the wrong hands or without responsibility is defined with a warning that "Power acquired through fear" is forecast; as is "manipulation, and / or aggression" (Hutchinson, Friedman: 2002: 15) . This Card, therefore, predicts the position of issues whereby authority is misused, where lifestyle issues may need to be addressed, or where rebellion may be justified, whether that be in terms of use of ceremonial magick, or through means of looking within ourselves first to see what can then be changed.

5. Cthulhu: The Hierophant

As the High Priest of the Elder Gods, Cthulhu represents an important principal in the Tarot" (Hutchinson, Friedman: 2002: 16), or so the Lovecraft Deck tells us. This principle of importance is that Cthulhu lies dead, but dreaming, in the sunken city of R'Lyeh that is His home, deep beneath the Pacific Ocean, as is discussed later with the Minor Arcana Card which discusses this concept. What this means is that Cthulhu is in physical terms actually dead, although He lies in this state in a state of natural rest. Cthulhu still dreams – in exactly the same way that you or I may dream whilst we are alive but yet asleep. He is able to do this, however, in part of His existence as one of the Gods. And whilst Cthulhu lies in sunken R'Lyeh in this state of death, the dreams of which He generates are transmitted to those who worship Him through this strange state of reality. Through this He is able to keep the religious ideas of His slumber alive on the Earth. The *Necronomicon* tells us that one day He will reawaken, as in the same way that reawakening is an ongoing issue as symbolised with the ideas expressed by a number of other religions. This day will be that day when the Stars are Once again Right, and His worshippers still wait for that day, when our Gods, and we ourselves, will gain control of the Earth, and also the chaotic dimensions that, to humanity, are principally beyond our comprehension.

So that's the description of Cthulhu as according to the belief of the religious Cult of R'Lyeh on Earth, and this is the reason why He is seen as being central to those of us who study *The Necronomicon* as a religious book of blasphemy and black magick. As a Card of the Tarot, though, the general idea of meaning is thankfully more direct, and the definition of its meaning, according to our purposes, is discussed as a fundamental religious statement as follows.

In the traditional study of the Tarot, the Card which holds the most

religious significance (at least according to our purposes, with our specific outlook), is Card 15 – that Card which represents The Devil, and discussed in the context of the *HP Lovecraft Tarot* as being the Entity that is Tsathoggua. In our interpretation, however, things are slightly different, and we regard Card 5 as being the principal symbol of divination, as we revere Cthulhu as the greatest of a number of Gods as upheld by our singular religious outlook. To our specific system of the Tarot, Card 5 equates directly as the most important idea of worship, and because of the nature of Cthulhu being the most important God as according to our religious system, it is therefore more important than any other Card of this Deck. And in terms of the study of this Tarot, it should be noted that with the Lovecraft system, Card 13 – the Card that is classically the Death Card (and with our system defined as being The Ghoul) – is also different from the classical interpretation than with this system. The point is made here because it is important to reiterate that, for our purposes, Cthulhu is dead. There is no hidden message to this Card in making this statement, however. The point to be made is that the *HP Lovecraft Tarot* equates to a unique religious system, as *The Necronomicon Cycle* has been written to describe.

In most 'traditional' Decks of the Tarot (and by this what I mean is every other Deck apart from our own), Card 5 is most often described as being the Hierophant. And the Hierophant is, therefore, representative of a symbolic religious belief as defined according to whatever Deck that might be. In our version, our entire belief can theoretically be represented by Cthulhu, although our statement here is to say that our system is a slightly ulterior interpretation. In our system, therefore, and aside from our theory that all religious ideology ultimately stems from the psychick vibrations as sent from The Great Old Ones, it is our consideration to see this Card as representative of symbology. This can have meaning in terms of anything from language, and dreams, as well as the use of the occult.

Those dreams that are dreamed by Cthulhu are communicated to humankind in our sleep. The *HP Lovecraft Tarot* tells us that "Chaos and Order are not in conflict" (Hutchinson, Friedman: 2002: 16), and

in this sense the bizarre, disorientated nature of dream is the static structure to that which is conveyed to man.[1] As this Card is written as an explanation of dream as a vehicle to transmit symbol, then dream – in this context – is the right place for the occult symbology used by humanity to be communicated to as in universal terms of understanding. And whilst explaining this point as the occult system which is ultimately ruled and governed by Cthulhu, the *HP Lovecraft Tarot* tells us that "Chaos is a Spiritual Reality, while 'Order' is a practical but artificial model based on Chaos to further the... pursuits of human beings" (Hutchinson, Friedman: 2002: 16). In the consideration of the occult worship of Cthulhu, this statement is definitely true.

"The functions of the High Priest are twofold: one is to provide a common ground of symbolism and ideals" (Hutchinson, Friedman: 2002: 16). So, as the concept of the communication of ideas is here represented, a ground where ideas can be understood by humanity is also created, as indicated by the Tarot. Whilst Card 5 is actually called the Hierophant with the vast number of different systems of the Tarot, it also has the function of creating an equal understanding of principals. "The other [function of the Hierophant], is to be representative of the Way of Truth" (Hutchinson, Friedman: 2002: 16) states the Tarot. If the inception of the concept of creation and the manifest existence of The Great Old Ones originates with the truth of religious chaos, then the ultimate message is given to the human race as religious truth.

Now we move further with this concept to define all of this as being the thought of mankind turned into symbology whereby it can be universally understood. So if we can see this as being the original source of all symbology as understood by humankind, we can see the purpose of this Card, to be to unite human values and beliefs in whatever strange form that may take place. The Tarot here tells us that, "this...

---

[1] One thing to point out here is that such a statement can be seen as something that could be related to a reading. Usually, in respect to this study, the meaning of a Card in terms of divination is explained for these purposes with the definition of a Positive or Negative Reading. However, if the main statement can be read in context with a reading, the Magus should seek to do so at all times.

function is the test of a true High Priest" (Hutchinson, Friedman: 2002: 16), now using this statement in order to describe the deathly slumber of Cthulhu's dreaming. "A fishing village will understand a different set of symbols than will the people living in a mountainside forest" (Hutchinson, Friedman: 2002: 16) is described, with this metaphor describing how different visions are interpreted as according to those who they appear to in every different context of esoteric meaning.

In continuing to follow through with this description of conceptual terms, it is to be reiterated that, whatever the logic involved, the thinking of the Great Old Ones were never meant to be clear to the understanding of the human race, as Their ways of doing so are bizarre beyond any rational or sane understanding. The *HP Lovecraft Tarot* concludes its main description of Cthulhu as the Hierophant by saying that "[i]t is the role of the High Priest to render ancient, eternal truths into symbolic forms which can be embraced by groups and communities in a specific time & place... the community is given symbols with which they can identify with, and with which they can find identity... [T]he danger is obvious: contention arises around the symbols, not their actual content" (Hutchinson, Friedman: 2002: 17).

If the previous Card is that of hierarchy and issues of authority that are immediately involved with that, then Cthulhu is representative of the progressive movement of organization in human society, and the Positive Reading directly speaks of the benefits that are involved with such social structure. Leadership and standing are issues in all forms of human society and, in the consideration of the last Card and associated issues, such standing can often be beneficial in human society.

As we have been very clear to establish, Cthulhu speaks to His worshippers through dreams. So, in respect to this, when the *HP Lovecraft Tarot* defines its meaning as representing a "Figurehead, Emissary, Ambassador" (Hutchinson, Friedman: 2002: 17), it does so in respect to the worshippers of Cthulhu passing on the decree of their God to others within cult religion, who Cthulhu rules in His slumber of dreaming death. In practical terms of forecast this Card may mean that we will obtain information that must be passed on to others, or

that we might be approaching a situation whereby information may be entrusted to us. The Card continues this definition as this statement continues to define an "Agent of communication & Transmission" (Hutchinson, Friedman: 2002: 17). Communication and transmission are therefore appropriate in this context, as our religion, in this aspect is about the will of the Great Old Ones through dream and aspects of that which most sane people would consider bizarre.

Directly leading on from that statement, the Lovecraftian system of the Tarot justifies the above with an indicator to the tribal systems of societies who naturally worship Cthulhu, as they are still left undiscovered by massive movements of Missionary Christianity, as one example. It here defines itself as speaking of "Elder, Counsel, Advisor; Wise Man / Woman accepted in society" (Hutchinson, Friedman: 2002: 17). Again this can probably work two ways, with information coming towards us from a person who is wise, or we may come to receive information that will be important to somebody else.

The Tarot seems to go immediately off at a tangent however, as it here defines this Card if pulled as part of a reading to indicate "Organization of Symbols & Semantics common to a particular group and / or society" (Hutchinson, Friedman: 2002: 17). Again we should consider this in the context of Cthulhu and His further and direct influence on the subconscious. Cthulhu is the messenger of dreams, and His messages are those communicated into the subconscious, as the interpretation of symbols and semantics is deeply psychological as according to this interrelation. At the same time the same paragraph defines its meaning as "Community, commonality of Ideas & Goals" (Hutchinson, Friedman: 2002: 17). This statement would appear to imply that, despite the massive and unknown nature of the subconscious mind, we can read such strange vibrations as being, in vague terms, actually as being the same.

Human nature and tribal behaviour - both in modern society and tribal – is defined here, and it is to be noted that all human behaviour is ritualistic in some form or another. "Ritual, Pattern, Rite" (Hutchinson, Friedman: 2002: 17) is defined, and this speaks of human behaviour as

we are controlled by the subconscious mind, as well as that ritual of magickal ceremony and the regard of the Great Old Ones as this point taken further as a conceptual point. "Meaningful ceremony [and] Rite of Passage" (Hutchinson, Friedman: 2002: 17) are defined, and this should be interpreted as impending something positive in situations in the future.

Continuing with this, the idea of the Tribal Elder returns as the *HP Lovecraft Tarot* defines a "Spiritual Vanguard and / or Herald, 'First Wave'; 'Elijah', 'Rapture'" (Hutchinson, Friedman: 2002: 17). I give this statement of interpretation two possible meanings. Firstly this definition could be speaking of a new religious leader at some point in the future possibly coming into play. But, in the specific context of the *HP Lovecraft Tarot*, however, I see this Card as being more probably indicative of the dreams of Cthulhu being transmitted into the sleep of one who will be the new religious leader for any new religious belief. Such a definition speaks of the virtue of such a leader being instated into societies which might be tribal or otherwise different from the established temples of Western religious thought.

In ending the definition of the Positive Reading, the *HP Lovecraft Tarot* now seems to go off at some sort of a tangent. "Remembering & Honouring the past; Tradition, Legacy; Passing on a Heritage & or Birth rite" (Hutchinson, Friedman: 2002: 17) is defined. In examining this discussion of the *HP Lovecraft Tarot*, I feel that this statement is self-explanatory in the context of this Reading, and nothing more here needs to be explained.

Negative Reading

To begin with this dialogue concerning the Negative meaning of The Hierophant Card in any Reading of the Tarot, it should be remembered that Cthulhu is the nearest, and therefore the most destructive and potentially dangerous, God of our religion. A Negative Reading here,

then, can be destructive and catastrophic, as it can with every other Card of every other system of the Tarot, but we would warn particular caution with this Card as part of a Reading. This is not in order to in any way frighten the Magus, but to give forewarning of this possible implication.

The Negative Reading begins, then, as with every other here, of following the idea of an opposite with the previous definition as established with any Positive Reading. The idea of Cthulhu as the communicator of man through dream is taken through on such terms in speaking of the "Messenger with no Message" (Hutchinson, Friedman: 2002: 17). There is no guru or wise man here, dreams are without regard. "Empty Transmission; Empty Promises, False Prophet, Cult leader" (Hutchinson, Friedman: 2002: 17) is further here defined; this is no religious statement; our guru has no connection with the Great Old Ones or our religious framework of worship.

Religion is the subject of the following definition, as following on from this statement that there might be a position of religious falsity. "Bias & Prejudice, Sectarianism; Misinterpretation" (Hutchinson, Friedman: 2002: 17) being symptoms of false religions, possibly aiming to convert the worshippers of the Great Old Ones into another esoteric belief. Religion is therefore very much a statement with this Card, as it is pointed out that Cthulhu is the main God worshipped by those of the following of *The Necronomicon* as our religious book.

The insanity of the worship of Cthulhu is now defined on direct terms in such a discussion, as the Tarot defines itself as indicating an "Obsession with Form & Structure, loss of content & substance" (Hutchinson, Friedman: 2002: 17). The *HP Lovecraft Tarot* would be accurate in putting forward this statement, as Mythos literature goes some length in describing the bizarre and weird nature of sunken R'Lyeh as Cthulhu's Tome, the strange and cosmic nature of His origin in space and the insanity of His dominion. "Fear of Spirit; Timidity & Hesitation in [r]evolutionary action; Fear of Change" (Hutchinson,

Friedman: 2002: 17) is defined, and the degeneration of psychological makeup that can come as the result of worshipping Cthulhu without utter integrity is defined here as something to be very clearly cautious of. [2]

The definition with the Negative Reading here concludes with a warning of the powerful destructive nature of Cthulhu which seems accurate to the description of Him as a God, that we get from the greater study of Mythos literature. In the statement that warns us of a coming "Academic severity in the deconstruction of Intellectual & Spiritual forms & Ideals" (Hutchinson, Friedman: 2002: 17) we are warned of the destructive effect of worshipping a God who is not of our world. And whilst the worship of Cthulhu is to seek insight into the secrets of the Cosmos and its related dimensions, Cthulhu is dangerous and terrible, and to enter into His worship without caution, and without specific directed intention, is certainly to sacrifice one's own mind.

---

[2] Whilst all change under all terms should be seen as evolutionary, this Card indicates change affected by deliberate course of action. This Card represents change effected by the deliberate intention of mankind.

6. Lavinia Whateley & Yog Sothoth: The Lovers

With the current Edition of this Deck the most significant changes are that that the graphics to all of the Cards as depicted have been changed, although with that point in hand that is all of those Cards. With this Card in question, however, we would see an exception to this rule, and that is that, whilst this Card was previously defined as being just Lavinia, this Card is now defined as Lavinia Whateley and Yog Sothoth, with the point being that here the name of the Card itself has been radically changed. It would not stand as being immediately clear as to why this change in question should be with the planned Third Edition of the *HP Lovecraft Tarot*, although I would speculate that this might be on the basis of the concept of the Lovers being related to the idea of two separate parts coming together in unison.

Further to that, if the current Edition of the *HP Lovecraft Tarot* is planned to be released without an Introductory Book, then I would use the equivalent text from the Introductory Book to the previous Edition in order to properly describe the issue as described and depicted by this Card, as I have done with the rest of my discussion of these religious and conceptual issues in question with this discussion of Lovecraftian religious orientation. It should at this point be pointed

out that The Shoggoth as a Lovecraftian Entity has a Card of Her own, and this is discussed later in this book with our discussion of Card 8, which in other systems of the Tarot equates to the principle of Strength.

In assigning the concept of Lavinia Whateley and Yog Sothoth to ascribe to Card 6 of the Major Arcana in this sequence – the Card that is in all systems of the Tarot defined as being 'The Lovers' – the Lovecraftian system of the Tarot goes off to some degree to a tangent. The other Cards of the Major Arcana seem to be represented either as the main Gods of the Mythos (such as 'Cthulhu' to represent The Hierophant, as discussed), or otherwise as more symbolic (as is the case with as the Card that is the 'Crawling Chaos' which other Decks define more often as being closer to the concept of Card 22, that being The World to Come). Lavinia, on the other hand, is a more obscure part of the Necronomicon Mythos of Gods as defined by the writers of religious and supernatural horror, with such an Entity being mentioned only on some brief occasions in the greater history of horror literature as a study of its own. For instance, Lavinia is mentioned briefly in Lovecraft's 'The Dunwich Horror', although I have not encountered Her name anywhere else. That does not, however, establish a point that such a feminine archetype is not mentioned in horror literature elsewhere. However, the authors of the *HP Lovecraft Tarot* have chosen to use the concepts of both Lavinia and Yog Sothoth as the thought forces in question to represent the Tarot Card of The Lovers, and so therefore I have no reason to dispute the use of either Her as the Goddess to represent the meaning as is defined with this Card, or of Yog Sothoth as representing opposite sides of any equation in question.

The conceptual issue of ritual magick comes into play when Lavinia and Yog Sothoth are drawn in a reading, as will always be the case when issues of sex and intercourse are mentioned in the greater number of the religions of magick. It is on this basis that the *HP Lovecraft Tarot* defines the point that "The main concept of this card is that any act of intercourse – sexual, intellectual, or otherwise – can & should be a vehicle of spiritual transmission" (Hutchinson, Friedman: 2002: 18). In this consideration, intercourse is defined as a powerful psychick

medium for transmission onto planes astral or between people, with this being an idea that should be taken further in terms of the study involved with occult and religious worship. The act of intercourse always transmits powerful energies between bodies, and is a hugely powerful medium for any practice of ceremonial or ritual black magick.

But physical manifestation through the supernatural is also represented with Card 6, just as though the act of intercourse, new life is born. "It [the concept of Lavinia and The Lovers in this context] is where Symbol becomes Flesh; where Concept becomes Reality" (Hutchinson, Friedman: 2002: 18). Here Lavinia represents not the masculine nor the feminine aspects of the inter-related dimensions inherent when we speak in terms of *The Necronomicon*, but the unity created when both of these aspects of the cosmos merge, and something new is then eventually born. But to go further with such a concept of such cosmic union, "The Sacred Marriage... is nothing more complicated than the intersection of Heaven and Earth, in which each fertilizes the other, producing a third state which is a harmonious expression of both" (Hutchinson, Friedman: 2002: 18). With this definition the masculine and feminine opposition of the cosmos are united, and a third dimension enters the confusion of creation.[1]

We therefore now have three aspects on which to define the further infinite continuum of creation, which the Introductory Book to the second Edition of our Tarot in question defines as being the Soul, the Body and the Mind. "[I]t is Mind which stands in apparent opposition to the Soul, not the Body" (Hutchinson, Friedman: 2002: 18), our study of the Tarot tells us; "only Mind can question the aspirations of the Soul... the Body is just a vehicle for them both" (Hutchinson, Friedman: 2002: 18). This is a main statement to represent Lavinia and Yog Sothoth in

---

1 There are, in fact, numerous and multiple dimensions, with all of these being far too strange and bizarre to be envisioned by the sane thinking of mankind. I write this note, however, to point out that if we are to consider the four dimensions around us to be the entirety of the cosmos, then we are misleading and deluding ourselves. The infinite confusions of the cosmos are those that we aim to envisage in this esoteric study, and we look to The Necronomicon as being, in this respect, our mystical guide to further define such conceptual ideas.

the *HP Lovecraft Tarot*, but here gives a good example of where our religious system diverges quite drastically from any other traditional interpretation as involved with any other system of the Tarot. It is for this reason in itself that we should take such a statement seriously, and perhaps use it in this context as a major religious statement in order to justify our unique branch of religious belief?

In continuing with this write up of the Card which all systems of The Tarot describe as being the personification of The Lovers, the next statement could possibly be the most important quotation from our document here in discussion, concerning the occult and religion that can be encountered in the study of *The Necronomicon* and the related theory of magick. "On a molecular level…" the Tarot tells us, "the Sacred Marriage provides the paradigm for the binding of atoms… They… move & connect according to basic natural laws…" (Hutchinson, Friedman: 2002: 18). With this statement, the *HP Lovecraft Tarot* has begun with an explanation as to how an esoteric system can be descriptive of the physical creation of the matter around us. It could be pointed out that there are many diverse and chaotic dimensions around us, all of which work on different mystical levels of creation. The dimension of physical matter is only that dimension nearest to us. The secrets of these dimensions are those secrets which are divulged by *The Necronomicon*, and are, therefore, the questions we seek to discover in the study of *The Necronomicon*, the Tarot and the manifestation of such truth through the conscious study of the occult and ceremonial black magick.

That statement above describes the idea of the Goddess Lavinia as representing the Tarot Card of The Lovers and the level of direct importance She has on the greater level of the cosmos as a massive and infinite chaotic issue that stretches immediately beyond the comprehension of human consciousness or of sane understanding. The Positive and Negative Reading here both develop the idea of the nature of infinity, as ruled by The Lovers as the central force that is

the nucleus behind all of creation, as leading on from such a point of creation as being the concept upheld by The Fool. With this Positive Reading defined by the Tarot, the Introductory Book to the previous Edition starts such a discussion by defining Lavinia as representing the idea of "Union, Marriage: Marriage of Heaven and Earth" (Hutchinson, Friedman: 2002: 19), whilst this second Edition seems to represent the personification of Yog Sothoth as being less important. Thus the concept of the Universe as a single force of infinity is justified in the concept of The Lovers as it is religious to define Her as the force from which the Universe is one singular and infinite mass. In this respect the *HP Lovecraft Tarot* again diverges very seriously from all other systems of the Tarot, and therefore from all other esoteric and occult religious views. The sexual union between two people is taken into regard with this statement, but the idea of the nature of worship in the sense of the mundane being integrated into higher spiritual ascendance, is probably a better interpretation of this Card in the study of *The Necronomicon* as this study of the *HP Lovecraft Tarot* is written to define.

The next statement that is defined with this study of the Lovecraftian system of the Tarot is given to us with the short statement that is given as the "Cymical Wedding". (Hutchinson, Friedman: 2002: 19). Whilst the infinite mass of the Universe is primarily esoteric, the merging of two or more elements will initially create a compound, and thus all of creation can be defined as created from the energy of the sexual union. But further than this, all aspects of both physical and esoteric manifestation must at some point merge and integrate. This aspect could be regarded with what has already been written.

But the classical idea of The Lovers is still to be considered and discussed in context, and the *HP Lovecraft Tarot* moves on from the profound statement above, to tell us that "Love, soulmates; [and] balanced values" (Hutchinson, Friedman: 2002: 19) is the idea to interpret if this Card should be pulled from the Deck in a reading. With this point here in discussion, if this is the message to be taken, then this idea should be considered as being the same definition of The Lovers,

as being the same with every other system of the Tarot.[2]

In taking this idea to its rational conclusion, the *HP Lovecraft Tarot* is still very much an entire esoteric philosophy of the occult its own, and if you have already made a point to concentrate on anything previously in *The Necronomicon Cycle* as a discussion of the Cthulhu Mythos occult, you will immediately be aware of how the Lovecraft system is established as a very unique and greater system of its own. This system continues with this same unique outlook then, as the Introductory Book to the Second Edition goes on to define a position of "Accord, balance, harmonized expression of previously opposed aspects or elements" (Hutchinson, Friedman: 2002: 19). Again in the consideration of The Lovers as the central issue of the cosmos, here we work further towards defining *The Necronomicon* as defining a singular position of ultimate religious truth.

In more direct terms, such a strangely esoteric concept of a Card that is usually assumed to be directly relating to everybody's daily lives, should be interpreted as relating to the occult and to circumstances relating to our current situation or as regards worship. The Tarot Card of The Lovers therefore works towards telling us that if things have been going badly, they may now be resolved.

Negative Reading

Whilst the above description of Lavinia and Yog Sothoth as representing The Lovers describes some, admittedly, quite difficult concepts regarding the nature of infinity of understanding, with the Negative description of its meaning, the Tarot is more defined with the definition here as more directly relating to relationships on a sounder

---

[2] In this regard we are making reference to The Lovers as represented by all other, more orthodox, systems of the Tarot. If the reader should want more in terms of reference as regards this, we would direct them to any other reference concerning the Tarot, which would include any reference regarding any other system. It has to be said, in this consideration, that most systems of the Tarot are much more straightforward than the Deck we are working from here.

level of understanding. The definition explained here then, relates more to the issue of interpersonal relationships, although should it be an idea to read this into other interpretations into a reading, then the Magus should feel free to do so. As one word of warning with this description; if interpreted as being involved with relationships, a Negative reading is what it says it is: Negative. In a reading then, if a Negative correlation is drawn then it should usually be seen as forewarning, and prior insight should be picked up on to account for a situation, should the Tarot warn of such an issue approaching.

So if we have now defined this Card in the context of a Reading as relating most directly to relationships, the Tarot now warns of a possibility of a situation involving a "Forced relationship; convenient relationship [or] casual sex".[3] Whilst the latter two could be situations in which we could find ourselves having fun, it should still be reiterated that this does come under the definition of a Negative reading, and in this sense could signify such relationships starting but ending in disaster.

Further issues regarding relationships are defined as the Tarot warns of an "Inability for two or more partners to find a single voice" (Hutchinson, Friedman: 2002: 19). In actual fact this statement could actually be defining any coming problems as defined with the statements above – if we are prepared for a situation to come – then we are better prepared to deal with it.

As a concluding statement to Lavinia and Yog Sothoth as defining the Tarot Card of The Lovers, much of this book concerns the secular beliefs and attitudes to religion as held by The Cult of R'Lyeh on Earth as regards the worship of the Great Old Ones. Therefore if any other Cards of this Deck can be seen in the context of involving magick, then

---

[3] The views of the Cult of R'Lyeh stand in conflict towards this statement as defining our religious worship. Whilst this is a point that is given clearly by the HP Lovecraft Tarot, the Cult of R'Lyeh regard it as being sound that our female membership must be absolutely subservient as sexual slaves. Our religion justify this as the rightful position of women under the devotional worship of the Great Old Ones as one religious truth.

sex magick does also come into play. The use of Lavinia in context with ceremonial magick, then, relates to the sex rites of the worship of the Great Old Ones, and of Lavinia as the Necronomicon Goddess of sex in our religion of insanity, chaos and psychological confusion.[4]

---

4 The study of religious sex magick is one specific study of its own, with a large number of books having been written on this subject in itself. The Cult of R'Lyeh are very much in support of our religious following making their own study in this context, and support everyone who should be interested in making further study of this idea on their own individual basis.

7. Ithaqua: The Chariot

As we here meet the Card that the vast number of Decks represent as being The Chariot, the image here portrayed as the Lovecraftian God Ithaqua is descriptive of the meaning of The Chariot in the Lovecraftian system of the Tarot, and how it is interpreted as an original statement in the system which we here study. The Chariot is a Card that has one distinct meaning in all systems of the Tarot, but as relating to the Lovecraft system as representing the religion of *The Necronomicon* Ithaqua conveys a unique and individual meaning. As the Lovecraft system of the Tarot makes a statement as to its own meaning, every Card as depicted with this system has its own interpretation of meaning not conveyed by any other Deck.

The image that this Card as portrayed by the published version of the second Edition of this Tarot depicts the image of a Wizard controlling Ithaqua as being the supernatural Elemental of the Wind. It is what we can read into this Card which is important in this aspect however. With all of the previous descriptions which we have defined with the Cards according to their own graphical depiction, the Cards of the HP Lovecraft system should be interpreted as according to the nature of our Mythos, in terms of what these images can tell us if they are seen as being symbols accessing a deeper meaning. *The Tarot Workbook* by Nevill Drury as our main reference to this discussion of the Tarot describes the meaning of The Chariot as being "success and victory achieved through hard work and application... self-discipline and clear thinking" (Drury: 2006: 58), and this is true when we approach the concept that is represented by the Elemental God Ithaqua.

With this point of definition then taken into consideration, then, my interpretation of this Card represents primarily the use of magick to the worship of the Gods of *The Necronomicon*, and how this magick effects our natural environment on personal terms. Ithaqua represents

the power of such magick, and the power of humanity to control these esoteric forces that are around us. But with that interpretation of meaning considered, Ithaqua is a God of elemental destruction, and the elements are always stronger than man. Drawing this Card in a reading could mean that those forces which we wish to control are stronger than we are, and if this is to be the case when drawing the Card that is here represented as Ithaqua, then this should be taken as a warning. Whilst the magick of the elements is stronger than any magick that can be employed by the individual who might practice the arts of black magick, Ithaqua is more often symbolic of the power of the Magus in the context of the situation around us.

The God force that is the 'Wind Walker'[1] states that even if the individual cannot control our natural environment (as no one can control the weather), we do, however, still have purposes at our disposal, and we therefore have some degree of control over the environment around us; although the message with this Card is that the degree to which we have this control also depends on the circumstances, and this is what this Card is intending to say to us. Ithaqua tells us that, as the worshippers of the *Necronomicon* system of Gods, our use of ritual and ceremonial magick has effect over what would usually not be the case. Despite representing a situation that our lives are always in the hands of higher forces – our magick does still in very clear terms have its useful effect – and our religious system is as relevant to the worshippers of the *Necronomicon* Gods, as is any other system in aspect of the worshippers involved in such systems of religion.

The most important point to be made with the Card of He who is here depicted as controlling the wind and weather, is that the elements, as here defined, will always be stronger than man. In regarding the

---

1 A note should here be made about Ithaqua and the issue of His gender as part of the religious regard of The Necronomicon. In making a study of Ithaqua in Mythos literature, I have found that reference to the gender of the 'Wind Walker' is often obscure, and that there is no general consensus as regards sex. Therefore I have chosen to regard Ithaqua as a masculine God force for these purposes, as it suits me as regards this study.

Tarot Card of Ithaqua properly, then, we are prepared, and have a level of control that would not have come into the situation if we were otherwise unprepared. But this Card also warns us that, as the practitioners of magick, if we do not take care, then we risk being swept away by forces of eternity as represented with the symbolism as depicted with this Card of the Tarot in hand.

The Tarot continues to describe Ithaqua and introduces terms of psychoanalytic thought in saying "…Ithaqua is the archetype for the human mystic… [T]his is the paradigm for the human ability to… raise oneself up… out of the mundane realm which merely receives and reacts to these influences" (Hutchinson, Friedman: 2002: 20).[2] In terms of describing itself with this, the theories of the psychiatrist Jung further come into play, although to describe the Card in the context of psychoanalysis in order to properly represent the scope here in discussion would be outside of the scope of this book. In ending the short description of this Card that is given in the Introductory Book to the previous Edition of the *HP Lovecraft Tarot*, however, the Tarot relays to us the concept that, "[I]n another mode of expression, one no longer reflects illumination, but becomes part of the original direct ray of light" (Hutchinson, Friedman: 2002: 20). A poetic statement from the Tarot, although it doesn't bring us any closer to a meaning as to what is represented with this discussion in question…[3]

The Card that is here defined as Ithaqua is on broader terms and in relation to the greater system of the Tarot, often defined as being that of The Chariot, and – in this respect – can always be read as being the same as The Chariot with every other Deck. This similarity stops

---

[2] It should be noted here that the HP Lovecraft Tarot relates to some of the ideas of the Psychiatrist Jung, on quite direct terms. The reader might consider making a further study of both systems discussed here as an idea for further research.

[3] In describing Ithaqua, the definition given in this part of the book has taken some diversion from defining the Card closely as according to the Introductory Book to the previous Edition of this Tarot. This is because interpreting Ithaqua as an Elemental and the God of the Wind has, I have felt, defined the meaning more closely as according to the Introductory Book in the description of the Positive and Negative Readings, which follow below the main definition of this Card.

here, however, as every Card in the *HP Lovecraft Tarot* has its own unique definition, as the occult of *The Necronomicon* is a single but much greater system of magick of its own. In respect of being defined as being The Chariot, however, this Tarot defines Card 7 with the description of relating to the psychiatric symbology of "The Hero's Journey" (Hutchinson, Friedman: 2002: 21).[4] Should we, then, regard ourselves (or the person who the reading is for) as being the Hero as defined in this respect? As we are all of us on a journey through life, this Card could be representative of ourselves in the normal situation, the normal context of life, whatever else the reading may forecast. The Tarot furthers this definition, elaborating that the definition here relates to "human action in & on the level of the Archetypes" (Hutchinson, Friedman: 2002: 21). Without relating this Card in terms of the Jungian implications of such a statement in discussion, this reiterates the idea of the Magus in the normal situations of our everyday lives, as the Journey of the Hero, whatever this may relate to? This is another example of how the *HP Lovecraft Tarot* can be vague in terms of defining its own meaning above what is usual in other systems of the Tarot, whilst defining a meaning very much of its own.

The Lovecraft Tarot can also be quite vague in terms of exactly how the descriptions of the Cards can relate to an aspect as to what is forecast in the future, which is the usual reason for a reading to be done, although this has to be seen in the context of our Deck being directly related to issues interpreted in terms of the Lovecraftian and the greater use of the occult. Here the Lovecraft system is again unique, telling us that its interpretation of The Chariot defines "The Mystic Journey; shamanism, mysticism, meditation; Astral travel" (Hutchinson, Friedman: 2002: 21). Here it is understood that this Card continues to integrate with the study of *The Necronomicon*, defining this as being directly a matter of human interaction with the Great Old

---

4 This idea relates the Chariot to the ideas of Jung and his philosophy of the Journey of the Hero. This idea could be directly related to the outcome of a reading and future possibilities in this context, and the Magus is encouraged to follow up on psychoanalytical theory to develop this idea on their own terms.

Ones as our chosen form of worship. It may be worth the Magus taking some time to meditate on this general idea, and also the other Cards of this Deck if we intend to work with these spheres of astral magick; although these issues are not discussed directly in the *HP Lovecraft Tarot*, and therefore remain obscure.

The idea that this Card in a Reading, can relate to a situation of 'normal everyday life', is implicated again when the Tarot defines a principle of "Mundane & materialistic ambitions" (Hutchinson, Friedman: 2002: 21). So with this we should accept it as the statement of the Tarot being defined here as such. If these definitions were to be anything negative, then the same issues would be defined under the description written as a Negative Reading with any other Card with any other system in question. With Ithaqua we should be grateful for home comforts however.

This definition of Ithaqua, in a Positive Reading, ends by saying that there will be "aspiration for worldly success and achievement; the road to success" (Hutchinson, Friedman: 2002: 21). This is the situation of normal day to day life. We are contented and at home, and plans for the future, at home and at work, look as if they will be successful. Use of magick will also emerge as being positive. There should be no need to worry about issues that can be seen as being mundane.

Negative Reading

Ithaqua, as one Card in terms of being a much greater part of the Tarot, is the Card that represents the 'normal situation' of home and of work as it is represented by every other Deck in discussion. From what we have so far studied, we can assume that Ithaqua represents personal choices that we make about ourselves, and our chosen path in terms of our future intentions. This situation of home, work, and everyday life is followed with this Card, although in the context of a Negative Reading we are warned of being "Trapped in mundane cycles of reflex & reaction; passivity; indifference, apathy" (Hutchinson, Friedman: 2002: 21). With this statement we are thinking in terms of

a number of situations that everyone has been in. Work, TV, everyday repetition is beginning to take over, and Ithaqua warns us to get up and do something. To get out of the rut. Mundane repetition is something we can sort out if we try, and Ithaqua says that this is now the place to do so.

This definition can go further than the mundane cycle of work, TV, and so forth, and when things do so it is then a more serious situation. "Spiritual apathy & indifference to the aspirations of the Soul" (Hutchinson, Friedman: 2002: 21) is defined, and now we see the situation as being on a spiritual level. In terms of worshipping the Gods of *The Necronomicon*, this should be taken as a warning. Either our worship is ultimately resulting in nothing, or we should look towards engaging in further acts of ritual worship to change the situation. Maybe this is Ithaqua making Herself known, and telling us that now is the time to get up and make changes in our lives?

The definition of this Card that the *HP Lovecraft Tarot* defines under the Mythos personification of Ithaqua ends in terms of speaking of our personal and spiritual path in life, and warns of a situation described as "Insouciance, lack of care or responsibility; lack of motivation & ambition" (Hutchinson, Friedman: 2002: 21). All of this tells us that we are getting involved with negative cycles in life, and that all of these issues are circumstances where we have to wake up and make changes. Ithaqua is not an evil God. He makes the future clear, as worship involves our situation and everyday life.

8. Shoggoth: Strength

Card 8 is, in all systems of the Major Arcana Strength, and is in all systems of Tarot this is more easy to interpret, as strength is an easy concept for human understanding. It is a primary part of our emotional identity. The *HP Lovecraft Tarot* is classically much more complex in terms of its interpretation, though, as this write up to discuss how this is defined on individual terms of our system in discussion should point out. Lovecraft himself represented this concept of *The Necronomicon* as defined as a unique insight to define religious belief, in describing The Shoggoth [in his short story *At the Mountains of Madness*, which discusses this God] as having "eyes forming and unforming as pustules of greenish light all over the tunnel – filling the front that bore down upon us, crushing the frantic penguins[1] and slithering over the glistening floor [of the polar ice]" (Lovecraft: 2001: 246). But strength is always defined as being a disputed issue. To some it is violence and to some it is calm. This Card is, in the Lovecraft system, therefore, something quite beyond all other definitions of Tarot and this is another example of the importance of our system in discussion as being unique. The Positive and Negative Readings defined here, then, follow an idea of Strength along lines of more accepted Tarot interpretations, whilst the main statement here defines The Shoggoth in terms of the esoteric meaning that I feel is meant with the study of the Lovecraftian as the religious system as it is described in this book.

To describe The Shoggoth in terms of this interpretation, the chaos which is the natural force of life throughout the cosmos is an inherent spirit within us, which we can either acknowledge or unconsciously

---

1 I would like to here point out that this is not exactly expected or very considerate towards the population of Penguins here. Imagine yourself on the ice caps, just standing around freezing, and something like this takes place? Just a note for consideration...

repress. If The Shoggoth, here, represents the Strength Card of the Major Arcana, then it is representative of the smallest constituent parts of the cosmos multiplying to themselves to create the strongest and most important constituent parts of creation. A virus that starts with a single cell can multiply to create an epidemic. So this force as defined, can therefore be compared to all people in terms of the inner power of our own spiritual self. Whilst it is often overlooked, this Card exists to point out that this inner power of self, and once realized "is so strong that it [c]ould easily overpower the conscious mind" (Hutchinson, Friedman: 2002: 22). The depiction of this Card, then, exists to make the point that, despite the fact that the brain itself is a mass of connected nerves and neurons, it is this force "which occurs in uncontrolled transformations into 'higher' human consciousness" (Hutchinson, Friedman: 2002: 22). It would follow, then, that the power of psychick ability which all of us possess, is still only a minor part of the mind that can be nurtured in a number of ways in order to create a force of strength. The power of a single mind can be structured to ascend to higher levels, and can ascend boundaries that seem to all of us, at first, to be on immediate terms, impossible.

This psychick ability is defined as the Strength Card as something that should not be neglected. The Shoggoth states that all work in developing the psyche is scientific, and something that is important and also normal in our everyday lives. It is essential to our being the complete person we are. An intended future book will discuss the Psychoanalytical theories of the Psychiatrist Jung in context with Lovecraftian religious theory, and how we (most of us) subconsciously fear this psychick part of ourselves which all of us possess. It is the current state of Western society, with TV and its constant conditioning, which makes us believe that we are all part of a system (like insects, if you like), whereas work to create communication with our Gods is something quite natural. It is something that, as a society of people, we would all be doing if it were not for technology as a greater and more destructive means of control. This belief is expressed with Card 8, as the *HP Lovecraft Tarot* here tells us that "[o]ur conditioning is artificial,

and no longer a product of necessity" (Hutchinson, Friedman: 2002: 22).

The *HP Lovecraft Tarot* continues with this dialogue, going further to say that "it [this conditioning] is a force which has its source in our most distant Roots, both biological and spiritual" (Hutchinson, Friedman: 2002: 23); thereby making a statement to support all ancient forms of Shamanism as linked religious movements of their own. This directly concerns an issue of creating contact with The Gods and Goddesses of our religion; but again, the Tarot is a depiction of wisdom in saying that this "is not a resource to be tapped casually" (Hutchinson, Friedman: 2002: 23), thereby reinforcing the reality that the worship of *The Necronomicon* system of Gods is both dangerous and powerful. The Tarot continues that "neither is it [the inner power of the psyche, in this context] a resource to be controlled by rationality and logic" (Hutchinson, Friedman: 2002: 23).[2] We are here given a warning about the misuse of worship as part of the occult, whilst Card 8 – The Shoggoth – represents the "inner power inherent to every human being" (Hutchinson, Friedman: 2002: 23).

Whilst the definition here may seem obscure in some senses, The Shoggoth (as part of the Tarot in this sense, and representing the principle of Strength) goes on to point out that all of us "have rational control over our actions" (Hutchinson, Friedman: 2002: 23). It would be appropriate, then, to point here to the motto and philosophy of the Golden Dawn that was established by Crowley, that '*Do What Thou Wilt Shall be the Whole of the Law*'.[3] The Shoggoth, then, would relate to the entire philosophy of the Golden Dawn, in context with the Lovecraftian and this system of the Tarot, that when this inner psyche is properly controlled, then anything is possible in the theory of

---

2 This makes a statement regarding the nature of the human mind in context with the ceremonial worship of one system of Gods. Use of magick.

3 The religious philosophy of the Hermetic Order of the Golden Dawn is absolutely and fundamentally upheld and respected by the Cult of R'Lyeh on Earth. The reader should feel free to study the work of the Golden Dawn in context with the ideas in this book, and draw their own conclusions as to religious orientation as from there.

magick as the manipulation of the occult. This Card, then, relates this philosophy directly to the greater religious theory of The Gods who were revealed to humanity by *The Necronomicon* and Al Hazred. This is here fundamental to our philosophy of the occult as religious.

To continue this with this general statement of philosophy, rather than being a God of any orthodox religion, portrayed with this Card is an insane, chaotic, and sprawling mass of occult confusion. This Card, rather than representing anything material, should be seen as representing the chaotic and unfathomable links of the neurons of the human brain, being able to create the organized thought of life, whilst that manifestation is always impossible to chart. This is astral chaos; it has no formal order. It is the matrix of the nerve endings in the brain; it cannot be reasoned in science, but it is the understanding of all order. It is the birth of viruses; it has no inception, but it can become any birth. This is the imagery of sprawling confusion. This is how The Shoggoth should be seen. Not as a God in itself, but in the chaos that underlies all life throughout cosmological understanding. In this we can see The Gods and Goddesses of dimensions not understood, being directly in context with our theory of the understanding of the occult.

With the above having properly described the meaning of this Card, the relevance of Card 8, The Shoggoth, as the Card of Strength in the Major Arcana of the *HP Lovecraft Tarot*, as with all other Decks, is more clearly defined when we see it in the actual context of what it should say as part of a Reading. If you are to make reference to the Introductory Book to the previous Edition of the Lovecraft Deck for yourself you will find a full description of The Shoggoth, as the Strength Card, and this is further discussed in relevance to the instinctive nature of the human mind. It is my project with this book, however, to put forward a religious interpretation to the Lovecraft Tarot Deck, and so the description of Card 8 here relates to the definition of the system within the context of our interpretation in this, and in a further book to be written.

With The Shoggoth being defined as the Strength Card, then, this definition here opens with a statement as to the integrity of the human

mind, and the concept of the application of Will. "Will power [and] the Power of Anima / Animus" (Hutchinson, Friedman: 2002: 23) is defined, and this fits in with the context of the rest of this system of the Tarot.[4]

With that said, it is my opinion that this statement relates more directly to the power of human Will (defined as 'Strength') and the power of the mind as the first object when it comes to the use of magick as the first statement towards the worship of The God system, as defined in *The Necronomicon* as it is equally defined by other systems of ceremonial magick. The whole idea of magick, according to many Western magickal sects – including Crowley's Cult of the Golden Dawn of Thelema – is that the mind must be systematically focused in order to perform the acts of ritual magick; and with us the system is the same. When the *HP Lovecraft Tarot* then defines a Positive Reading as relating to "the Spiritual Genius" (Hutchinson, Friedman: 2002: 23), it is clearly making a statement that the 'Higher Self' is here coming into play, with this statement relating to the higher spiritual level attained through meditation and preparation for magickal acts of worship.

The spiritual statement to this as a meaning to be defined under the Positive Reading ends there, however, and the definition continues to predict more social aspects to the Card, going on to define situations relating to home or work. "Leadership" is defined, and "accepting a role in the shaping of the destinies of others" (Hutchinson, Friedman: 2002: 23), is the next statement. And with The Shoggoth is further defined as being Strength on these same terms, as it is not difficult to make an assumption as to how this should relate to our current situation in life. A consideration of the hierarchical practice of some of the Cults of Dagon might be considered here, where status in certain systems of secular religion revolves around ascendance through level and according to a system of initiation into standing.

Strength as a part of human instinct is defined, and our discussion of the Tarot continues directly to define "Animal Magnetism"

---

4 Again we have another example of how the work of the Psychiatrist Jung and psychoanalysis are represented with this particular study of the Tarot.

(Hutchinson, Friedman: 2002: 23) as an inherent part of human nature that is a state of play when The Shoggoth is drawn in a Positive respect in a reading. And the same statement goes on to define a situation of "raw... spiritual power" (Hutchinson, Friedman: 2002: 23). In this we see the Tarot reiterating its meaning with this Card in the context of Strength as being something within us that commands that which is external.

In our discussion of the Tarot and the magick of this as a system of the occult (the Necronomicon system of the occult is usually considered to be representative of forces of 'evil'), a lot of what is described in this book could be considered as being 'dark', and some would describe the views of The Cult of R'Lyeh as being 'Satanic'. A transgression is made with the next statement, however, and a Tarot which makes some pessimistic reading at times, here defines possibly the most optimistic statement that is given in the study of this Deck. "Victory, triumph – especially without conflict" (Hutchinson, Friedman: 2002: 23) is defined. This should be considered, then, as being possibly the best Card that can be drawn. There could probably be nothing more positive to be considered in this study as belief and a form of religious understanding.

Negative Reading

As the above discusses aspects of Will before defining itself as Strength, in terms of human understanding of each other, the Negative Reading concentrates mainly on the latter statement that "Loss of Will, capitulation, surrender to the domination & tyranny of others" (Hutchinson, Friedman: 2002: 23) is defined. Here it is our opinion of ourselves and our mental state that is coming into play. If this Card comes into a reading in a Negative sense, it could be seen as a warning to take some time away from the practice of magick, or that somebody involved in our everyday lives will, at some time in the coming future, step in and try to control our personal situation.

If we have been taking a pretty solid line in following the descriptions

of Positive and Negative Readings to any necessary extent, then at this point our religious line takes a diversion. Defined as being Negative by the *HP Lovecraft Tarot*, we encounter a situation of "Mob Rule; riots, social chaos" (Hutchinson, Friedman: 2002: 23). In this we strongly disagree that these terms should be seen as being Negative. As the worshippers of *The Necronomicon* and that inherent system of magick, then, chaos is a principal to be attained by our religion. The Gods of *The Necronomicon* are fundamentally and explicitly The Gods of disorder and madness, and social chaos is something to be respected in the understanding that all is disorder, and that reality is only subjective in terms of worship.

But the statement discussing our religious goals is to be left there. With "Abuse of power; misdirection of spiritual energy" (Hutchinson, Friedman: 2002: 23) being the next statement discussed, an understanding of authority is now clear. Whilst the abuse that is imposed by authority is something that we, as religious, stand in total opposition to, the message given in this statement is that such an abuse of power can be the result of spiritual energy misdirected, and if this is to be the situation in hand, then it is possible that mis-comprehension of Will is coming back into the equation, and it is possible that such mis-direction of spiritual energy could be unintentional.

Further to that, "Tyranny [and] unlawful imposition of one's Will" (Hutchinson, Friedman: 2002: 23) may be a different consideration. Whilst the above situation may not be intentional, then this situation is. If somebody is imposing their Will in a manner suggested with this reading, then we must stick up for ourselves. The Card that is Strength has certain defined meanings. With the Lovecraft system, however – as is the case only with some certain other Decks – our system is quite unique. So here Strength is defined as part of *The Necronomicon* religious system, and has therefore been discussed in a proper and necessary context.

9. Great Race of Yith: The Hermit

With most systems of the Tarot, the interpretations given by most Decks are similar; this meaning that readings are usually quite straightforward. In making such a study it is usual to see the same themes recurring repeatedly through most Decks which have been put together since the start of such an esoteric study, with a smaller number of Decks defining the same statements differently on individual terms, and for specific reasons in context. The Lovecraft version of the system of divination which occultists have defined as being the Tarot, however, gives interpretations which, due to their strange meanings within the context of what is often called the 'Lovecraftian', and in turn these are totally different from any resemblance of any more 'normal' interpretation. This is not to say that the interpretations in the *HP Lovecraft Tarot* are totally aside from any interpretation given by any other system; but this is because the context in which this system of the Tarot stands, is quite strange and bizarre as an interpretation of its own; in this sense being unique in the study of a God system which diverges from any sane perspective usually taken by humanity outside of the study of *The Necronomicon* as a book of religious magick. The Tarot on the most part is upheld in order to forecast the future, but the Lovecraft system interprets the Tarot from the perspective and understanding of madness.

This discussion of symbolism as concerning the interpretation given by the *HP Lovecraft Tarot* is an appropriate idea when we talk of Card 9, then, as The Hermit in traditional Tarot is concerned with ideas of spiritual meaning spelled out, and with ideas of guidance in terms of the occult and learning in regard to worship as relevant to everyday life. This idea of the definition of the Great Race of Yith, and the meaning of the Hermit as a part of the Tarot, are both considered when

we quote our reference to the system:

> "The Hermit is wise and all-knowing and is sometimes referred to as the Ancient of Days... [H]e is... a guide for those spiritual travellers who are climbing the mystic mountain... His lantern provides... inspiration... guiding them ever closer to their goal of union with the divine... [H]is final goal of mystical union... is firmly in his mind... the lamp he holds aloft illuminating the pathway for all spiritual seekers... This Card is associated with solitude and contemplation – the spiritual journey is all-important in your life at this time... [T]his card signifies that you may meet someone who will become your spiritual guide... It also signifies a willingness... to accept help when it is offered... [T]he spiritual path is long and arduous and there are no easy solutions. Use your powers of discrimination and discernment in moving forward, and trust the light and wisdom of your own inner guidance." (Drury: 2006: 62).[1]

If that quotation would explain the definition of The Hermit as it is defined by most more 'traditional' systems of the Tarot, then, the *HP Lovecraft Tarot* considers its own definition and interpretation of this Card in question, putting the same precept in terms of things stranger and outwardly much more weird.

In talking about the Great Race of Yith as the 'mind parasite', the Lovecraftian Tarot describes a fantastic and beautiful concept to be part of the greater amount of literature as representing the Lovecraftian, and as relates to our religious perception as Their worship. And as part of our system of the Tarot, the concept behind the Great Race of Yith as any sort of existence that can be interpreted through any definition of Tarot, set aside our interpretation of the Lovecraft Deck, is more obvious as they accord to Card 9 as a bizarre form of logic and

---

[1] This quotation from 'The Tarot Workbook' is the longest statement from the book to be used in this reference. In using it we define the nature of The Hermit in every other Deck, as the system used is more closely representing the former more traditional versions of the Tarot.

organization. "Unbound by time, unfettered by physical form, comes [the] Great Mind, always working towards the survival of the species" (Hutchinson, Friedman: 2002: 24). This may have some meaning in terms of forecasting future situations, but is hardly something that would be obvious as seen as being defined by the Tarot Card which is defined as being The Hermit.

If this is to be the case, then, our interpretation of Card 9 should not attempt to repeat the ideas that repeat through so many varied and different systems of the Tarot. The Hermit in the *HP Lovecraft Tarot* is defined as a system of the cosmos that exists within our religious belief, rather than that definition of The Hermit which stands as the same in every previous definition of the Tarot and every different Deck. Whether or not it is a good thing that the *HP Lovecraft Tarot* should go as far as to define a meaning in this context is one thing, but this book is written to expand on the Lovecraftian ideas in occult systems and the Tarot, so it should be right for me to go on to define this Card as accords to this specific study.

Again, all of the concepts which come into the argument with this study of the religious *Necronomicon* are openly bizarre in the points here explained, and what, exactly, the Tarot means when it defines the 'Great Mind'; we cannot be exactly sure (although the mentality of the Great Race of Yith as being insect might well come into the picture). But if the ideas of Crowley and the greater controlling power of the mind are to be considered, then we should make this as a point, and consider the term as relating more to psychick training as involved with the practice and further use of ceremonial magick. This statement should therefore be taken into account by the examples of *Necronomicon* magick when using this or any other system of worship in order to honour any number of The Great Old Ones.

The Great Mind of the Yith and the mentality of the worshipper can be united as one issue with this statement, though. To take this general idea further, the Lovecraft Tarot points out that "This 'Great Mind' sees from a vantage point which is simultaneously in the distant past and the far future" (Hutchinson, Friedman: 2002: 24). If the Magus

9. Great Race of Yith: The Hermit

is to use his or her mind correctly in terms of the Golden Dawn, or any other system of magick, it becomes at one with the practitioner eventually, and the ideas of the Lovecraftian become issues to accept as intellectual inspiration as obtained from the higher spheres of occult knowledge. Speaking of the frame of mind entered into by followers of these spheres of magick as discussed in the Introductory Book to the previous Edition of this system in question, the Tarot tells us that "[T]his concept... is one which is not bound by the normal limits of perception... it exists... to provide a mental state of freedom from these limitations" (Hutchinson, Friedman: 2002: 24).[2]

But the psychick manipulation of the trained mind of the Magus is one thing if making an occult study of the Tarot, whilst the collective mind of the masses is now brought into the equation as the Introductory Book to the second Edition of our Deck in discussion again brings the study of psychoanalysis into the picture. The works of Jung are again brought into the scene as it continues in discussing the Great Mind in its own terms. "While Jung spoke of a Collective Unconscious, the Great Mind is a Collective Consciousness, a place of... perception of the multiverse which is not restricted by boundaries of perception" (Hutchinson, Friedman: 2002: 24). The singular mind of the Queen as the centre of insect intelligence around which all congregates is compared to the chaotic nature of human society, and whilst the mind of man is still as singular as any insect, on these terms the Tarot tells us that our thought can be seen as being collected into one singular mass. In this sense the Collective Unconsciousness is "unconstrained by the views of Time or Space particular to the physical senses of a specific biological organism" (Hutchinson, Friedman: 2002: 24). So, whilst the individual has a psychological perception of these issues in question,

---

2 At this point it should be made clear that the author is using the concept of the Lovecraft system of the Tarot in order to put forward a system of ritual magick. Many of the points made in this book do not directly equate with the Lovecraft system as it stands on its own; it is our intention to use the Tarot as an initiatory statement for those who take it upon themselves to study The Necronomicon and Its unique system of ceremonial magick.

the 'Great Mind' which is the united thought force of humanity, has no perception of this. It is one static and singular esoteric mass.

What this means in terms relevant to the study of *The Necronomicon* as a system of religious magick is that we should be in tune with the 'Great Mind' as the higher force of our thought as it relates to the occult if to take use of ceremonial magick to its productive outcome. "Too many people... have let... their identities or self-images... [be] defined by the limited perception of a Lesser Mind" (Hutchinson, Friedman: 2002: 25). To The Cult of R'Lyeh as a religious Temple, then, a proper understanding of our own higher self is of absolute importance, and if we are to accept this idea from the *HP Lovecraft Tarot*, then studies of psychick thought forces are valuable as part of our (or any other constructed) system of ritual magick. If "churches, governments, etc. – have usually been able to assimilate such abstract concepts into their philosophies" (Hutchinson, Friedman: 2002: 25), it should not be too difficult to demonstrate to them the justification behind our beliefs, and then to challenge the dogmatic and rigid views of authority that all dominant religions have throughout history chosen to impose.

But back to the point in discussion, in making this equation between The Great Race of Yith and The Hermit, as this same Card is defined by most other traditional Decks of the Tarot has not been as straightforward or as easy as one should initially have thought, although hopefully the above will begin to put the idea into a better perspective. How this Card works in the particular context of the Lovecraftian system does not seem immediately to be any more straightforward than this idea in hand either, and with this system being very unique in the Tarot as a system of magick, terms should be defined regarding this Card in our particular system that regards the worship of the Great Old Ones in the greater cosmic infinity of space and time. But despite the nature as this as the fact involved with a study of a Tarot such as this, the authors of the *HP Lovecraft Tarot* have done a good job in equating such a bizarre system as represented by *The Necronomicon*, and the more traditional system of the Cards with this as a historical religious system in question.

So if that discussion so far would say enough as regards how this Card should be read to define The Hermit in the specific terms of the Lovecraftian as we discuss here, the meaning of this Card to the Magus fits in with the greater and larger system of the Tarot, defining The Great Race of Yith when drawn in a Reading, as representing "Identification of the personal Will with the shared ideals of a particular social group; participation in social works" (Hutchinson, Friedman: 2002: 25). This statement could be interpreted as saying something about how the Yith are interpreted in this context as well as with the relevance that this statement has in obvious terms of our own lives?

If this should be the place to describe the religious concept of The Great Race of Yith as relates to The Hermit as this current Card of the Tarot in question, as an inter-cosmological Race, the mind of the Yith is quite vastly removed from the thinking of the human mind, with this being the first most important point in discussion. The Yith are a highly developed entity within the cosmos, and despite the travel of space and time which is to them something that is taken quite simply for granted; Their minds work more like the intelligence owned by the insects, as discussed; although those races of insects which inhabit our world do not have nearly the intelligence of that owned by the Yith as an inter-cosmological intelligent Race of Their own. This needs to be understood as the equation is made with the Lovecraft system, as to how The Hermit and the Great Race of Yith combine as to the concept behind that of the ninth Card of this Deck in discussion.

The insect mind of the Great Race of Yith becomes more defined as the Tarot predicts a situation of "humility, submission to the Will of others for the sake of a common objective [and] negation of self for a particular end" (Hutchinson, Friedman: 2002: 25). When different and varied races of insects are studied, comparison can often be made between such races and humanity, and the failing of our own social structures. This statement does not concern the thinking of humanity, then, as the Yith are hereby defined as The Hermit as a thinking above the functioning mentality of our race. So if this statement points to what could be an event which might take place within our own lives,

this is stated as being the situation as regards the social organization of a Race which perceive reality and the Cosmos in absolute different terms from anything which could be envisioned by any part of human kind.

This idea of the instinctive cycles of insects as opposed to the organization of mankind is continued as the *HP Lovecraft Tarot* defines a position of "natural emergence into a leadership role within a fluid group dynamic; the ability to relinquish the same at the proper time" (Hutchinson, Friedman: 2002: 25). As both the insects and humanity follow a natural cycle of birth, reproduction and death, the Great Race of Yith stand to represent this as a foreign form of mentality than anything which can be comprehended by man. The thinking of the Yith is above that, though, being massively far advanced beyond the many races of insects that dominate our planet. So when this 'natural emergence' is something quite solid as regards the cycles of insects, with this Card it is more concerned with the cycles of Earth that we as people take for granted. With Card 9 we see it that the Lovecraft system is unique and more advanced. The *HP Lovecraft Tarot* is infinitely more bizarre than any other system; and in writing this book to define it on its own terms, complex definitions such as this do have to be thought about sometimes, if a proper study of the Lovecraft Deck is the intention and purpose in hand.

Negative Reading

The Great Race of Yith are a super – intelligent, albeit not entirely supernatural, race of creatures who possess mass technology, as in the normal sense, but also with the ability to travel time. This idea defines the thinking of the Great Race of Yith, with their minds being as different from humanity, as we are to the insects, that everything they possess should be sent back to themselves five million years ago, as everything they acquire in such terms is in turn sent forward to that point. This, in terms of the Tarot, then, makes the situation in no way more straightforward. Not much is about to change if we see the Great

Race of Yith in these terms. If this entire Mythos of which we speak, can be considered by some as possibly representing 'evil', then the Great Race of Yith should be considered the same, even if with them it is more in terms of Their perception as an alien mentality.[3]

In having so far related the Great Race of Yith to the 'insect mind', the representation here defined can also relate to the breakdown of social structures as an ulterior point of discussion. To conclude this definition of meaning, the mind of this Race is no more or less logical than any other entity in the Lovecraft system of Tarot. "Loss of self and / or personal identity to the will of the group; identity based entirely on social standing or recognitions" (Hutchinson, Friedman: 2002: 25) is defined. Whilst the laws of the insects do still represent order, the concept defined as the Great Race of Yith can also destroy a person's place in society, and with this system it can also be without warning.

With the mentality of the insects, but with a mind more developed than that of human kind, Mythos literature describes the sociology of the Great Race as being a highly organized social system, close to that of socialism, but with a system of production closer to that of the insects than any other society. Their social organization is therefore quite alien to human understanding, but the Great Old Ones still govern the Cosmos, and Their way of understanding such concepts is in itself also this strange.

But with these terms set out, we can see the ideas as conveyed by the *HP Lovecraft Tarot* as comparing the ideas of insect communities to the eccentric social behaviour of humanity. The cultures of the insects may be one thing, but with the Great race of Yith we confront this as a vastly more developed concept of its own. The statement "Withdrawal or retreat from greatness" (Hutchinson, Friedman: 2002: 25) compares social standing as an issue of day to day life, but if an insect were to

---

3   The entire Mythos of which we speak of here, is of course alien as well, but we see the Great Race of Yith as being specific within this meaning as They are more related to the mind of man, than that of the Great Old Ones, being more esoteric parts of the Cosmos. The idea of the 'insect mind' is here appropriate to this discussion of the Tarot and black magick.

withdraw from its position as part of the hive, it could only be because it were no longer able to uphold its purpose to the greater community. The Yith work more like this, but – as has been pointed out – Their technology puts them as being far further evolved than regards the resources that we have on this Planet as humanity.

The comparison with the Tarot and the insect mind stops here, however, and the Lovecraft system carries on with statements of forecast that cannot really be compared with this way of thinking as is held by the Yith, or any other conceptual framework of thinking. This Negative Reading continues to define the meaning here as relates to The Hermit as the first point in question. It should be taken as a general rule, then, that if drawing on the Tarot for predictions with this Card, that these statements reflect the situation from quite a bizarre perspective, as has already here been discussed.

All of these points should be held into account when the Tarot defines itself in more straightforward human terms, as "false humility, fear of success; fear of selfhood [and] self-sabotage" (Hutchinson, Friedman: 2002: 25) are defined as issues we could come across in the context of a Reading. It is probably more relevant to the mind of the Great Race of Yith, then, as this entry to the Tarot ends in speaking in such terms as discussed here, predicting a possible situation of "Selfishness, self-absorption; megalomania, unhealthy assumption of power, coup; inability to let go of power" (Hutchinson, Friedman: 2002: 25). Obviously, looking at a society which is as openly as strange and bizarre as the Great Race of Yith, social standing is assumed as being as important to survival, as is the reason for the worship of such occult systems by humanity.

10. Hounds of Tindalos: The Wheel of Fortune

Beware the Tindalos Hounds, for they come not through angles, but through the spaces in between. Card 10 is, in most traditional Decks of the Tarot defined as being the Wheel of Fortune; that being the Card that usually forecasts the turning of the wheels of fate and the fortune, or not, of the situations that are destined as being our future. The *HP Lovecraft Tarot* takes another view of this statement of cycles and the turning of astral dimensions quite literally, however, and the Card that is here depicted as the Tindalos Hounds is concerned with the myriad revolution of the dimensions of the cosmos and psychological perception of which our Mythos is concerned. Rather than taking a parallel line to the traditional Reading with this Card, however, the Hounds of Tindalos Card is more concerned with the occult and the cyclical turning of time and the madness of the dimensions of which The Hounds of Tindalos dwell.

The Wheel of Fortune in the *HP Lovecraft Tarot* is representative, not of the turning of any wheel, but of the huge wheels of the cosmos and related dimensions not understood by the psychological understanding of mankind. The reader of this Tarot should be aware of this when following the Positive and Negative interpretations of this Card because, whilst these statements are admittedly quite obscure, they should be read as concerning the religious following of the Gods of *The Necronomicon* as an issue in itself. If these are the concepts of our religious worship as defined, then we should try to accept such, admittedly bizarre, concepts into our belief and our use of ritual magick if that's how such worship should be upheld. Whilst these concepts are usually outside of the care of the majority of human religions, it is ours to accept the nature of the Tindalos Hounds as They are defined in these

terms; and the Magus would do well to regard the Tindalos Hounds with much caution.

If the 'Hounds' might be in any way concerned with humanity, then this is primarily with the concept of the turning of wheels of time, as they exist within such strange dimensions as is defined by *The Necronomicon* as our religious book of black magick. In human terms, therefore, They can be related to our understanding of, as well as the Earthly acceptance of, the massive intellectual understanding of the further principals of science. Being dwellers within the dimensions of time they know the future, but the Tindalos Hounds have little interest in this. Science is nothing but a tiny aspect in the consideration of the infinity of time, and the Hounds of Tindalos do not see these things in terms that we, as people, regard them as being in any way important.

Science is only one conceptual belief, though, and the *HP Lovecraft Tarot* defines science in this aspect as "[T]he perceived illusion of curved space and motion, and the repetitive cycles of time..." (Hutchinson, Friedman: 2002: 26). And in respect to what has been written in this book, the Tarot defines the conscious understanding of this strange concept as being "necessary to the psychological survival of the human race..." (Hutchinson, Friedman: 2002: 26).

These, quite admittedly bizarre, statements concerning the human limitations of or perception and understanding of such strange dimensions and time, "are not without merit or value" (Hutchinson, Friedman: 2002: 26), as is stated by the *HP Lovecraft Tarot*. The Introductory Book to the previous published Edition goes on to put such concepts into a clearer perspective here, and these concepts are to some extent clarified in defining a point that "[h]uman perception and observation of the apparent repetitions of celestial bodies and material qualities has given us science and technology" (Hutchinson, Friedman: 2002: 26). The insane chaos conveyed as Tindalos is now played off with a human understanding of science on a level which can be seen as more mundane.

But these concepts in terms of Tindalos are still the concepts of the more primitive societies of mankind. If current Western societies

operate in terms of what can be 'proven', then early Shamanic cultures have always been more receptive to the more esoteric nature of what is around us. "Even more important [than scientific belief]…" in this concept, "is the wide range of mythological paradigms which have been inspired by the cycles of time and the cycles of the Earth and celestial bodies in space… primitive as these Archetypes may seem, they are designed to provide a gateway beyond the limits of the cycles of time & the boundaries of space, into the profound depths which are the still centre around which all these cycles revolve" (Hutchinson, Friedman: 2002: 26). In this statement we see the philosophy behind so many Shamanic societies, who view the ascension of consciousness above the rigid constraints that are 'proven' by the rigid psychological dogmas that we are forced to believe in the West.

Before moving on to define the meanings of Positive and Negative Readings, I'd like to make another reference to the last statement in the given Introductory Book to the previous Edition to this Tarot, which goes on to point out that, within this concept of time, everything is ultimately still about cycles and the idea of the ever turning wheel. "In… revolutions around the wheel, we move ever closer to the centre, until we become that still point around which everything spins. That is our link to other further dimensions" (Hutchinson, Friedman: 2002: 27). At the end of the day, and whatever our efforts, we are all of us passive constituents in a cosmos in which we can only be utterly irrelevant. As the Gods of *The Necronomicon* exist around us, we are to them an equivalent to the social existence of the insects, and in the greater scheme of infinity, as people we have no consequence in the greater system at all.

With that being an important point in question here, The *HP Lovecraft Tarot* is always very much a law unto itself. Taking the idea of the Hounds of Tindalos to represent the Card that is usually, and in most other systems, defined as being the Wheel of Fortune, the Positive and Negative Readings continue to discuss the idea of cycles, and in much the same way as we have discussed it so far.

Whilst speaking in terms of these cycles, this Tarot begins its

definition of the Positive Reading, with a forecast of "Revolution, evolution, progress [and] advancement" (Hutchinson, Friedman: 2002: 27). It is my view, in writing this statement to explain the obscure definitions sometimes given by this system of the Tarot, that the statement 'revolution' cannot be representative of the term used in the political sense of the word; but if considered in terms of ourselves and the development we can make within ourselves, this statement makes more sense. The three statements that follow seem to reinforce this view, speaking of a possible coming situation of personal change.

The ideas of 'evolution', and the rest of the terms defined under the Positive definition given also have relevance to the external world around us, and this Card may have meaning in terms of our personal situation changing and developing. This should therefore be seen as being a very good Card to be drawn, in any Reading.

With that having established the general meaning as portrayed by this Card in relation to the Lovecraftian and the Tarot, the concept of lifestyle issues evolving and developing is followed as the *HP Lovecraft Tarot* defines a situation of "Natural cycles of increase" (Hutchinson, Friedman: 2002: 27). Personal situations are changing, and past work put into personal projects will be likely to result in success. "Harvesting the fruits of either efforts or capital" (Hutchinson, Friedman: 2002: 27) is defined, thus reiterating the idea. Things are good. Work we have put in to improve our own situation will soon be productive.

This study in itself continues as the Lovecraft Deck moves on to define something which is quite characteristically more obscure. The "Celestial body in its proper course" (Hutchinson, Friedman: 2002: 27) is the next statement to be defined with the definition of the Positive Reading. The meaning of this statement is not immediately obvious, but could be interpreted as speaking more in terms of our lives as considered as part of the Zodiac as a study of the occult in itself. Whilst, if considered in terms of astrology, things can be considered in terms of any personal situation, the Stars are here in the right place for us. Again this is an indication that things are going right for us. This is a particularly productive period in our lives.

All of this would seem to say that the forces of the cosmos are smiling at us. "Beneficial influence; good fortune, kind fate" (Hutchinson, Friedman: 2002: 27) are defined, and this last description of the Cards Positive meaning reinforces this statement that this is a good period in our lives. The Wheel of Fortune has turned in our favour, and the Hounds of Tindalos are at rest in Their own part of time, the part of time in which they dwell.

Negative Reading

It is characteristic in the system of the *HP Lovecraft Tarot*, that if a Positive Reading is particularly good, then the Negative Reading is unusually bad. In defining "Retrogression, regression, reversal [and] retreat" (Hutchinson, Friedman: 2002: 27), the opposite of the definition above is insinuated. This statement could theoretically relate to any issue, and in interpreting this Card, I choose to leave it to be considered by the person who is involved with the reading the Spread in question. Ideas of reversal being defined, it may be better to interpret this in the specific terms of the Reading in hand, with this statement being so general as to be difficult to put into any explanatory statement such as what can be covered with this short definition of meaning.

Our daily lives come into play again as this definition speaks of "Disruption of natural cycles, deviation from & / or corruption of normal patterns" (Hutchinson, Friedman: 2002: 27). Here's an example of how a Negative Reading can be the reverse of what is forecast by the Positive. So in describing this statement, this quotation could, as a possibility to be considered, be a warning that a situation could soon arise that could completely shake up our lifestyle. Such occurrences are usually not expected, but everyone has experienced such a situation at some point in their lives, at least.

The Negative Reading here lurches from being a forecast of a future situation that we should expect and possibly plan for, towards being something more directly daemonic. A "Malefic influence" (Hutchinson,

Friedman: 2002: 27) is predicted. Whilst it is difficult to account directly for such a statement, or to directly establish what this specific statement means, if this Reversal should come into play in a Reading, it would be very characteristic of the *HP Lovecraft Tarot* to describe the meaning of a Card in these terms. And this Negative statement of interpretation is concluded in equally dark terms, in saying that the Hounds of Tindalos, if drawn in the context of a Negative Reading, is representative of "ill aspect; planet retrograde, void of course moon; cruel fortune, harsh fate" (Hutchinson, Friedman: 2002: 27).

Before continuing to end this Lovecraftian interpretation of the Card that is the Wheel of Fortune in most other Decks of the Tarot, the last word on this Card is that this last statement should be considered in aspect to the ritual practice of magick. If these statements could possibly be an issue in a Reading, then this should be taken into account if the Magus is to engage in acts of worship. The Tarot can, therefore, be a useful term for the practitioners of magick in terms of understanding *The Necronomicon*, which is the blasphemous book of magick, as *The Necronomicon Cycle* has already repeatedly pointed out. We should use such forecasts as are here defined, to help us if we are to worship the systems of the Great Old Ones, through our use of ritual ceremonial magick, as well as using the Tarot in the more traditional sense, in reading what is destined to occur as an inherent part of our future.

11. Mi Go: Justice

As we move on to Card 11, which is 'Justice' in most traditional Decks of the Tarot, the term in itself is quite self-explanatory. The definition in the Lovecraft system is, again, unique to this particular Deck, however, and the meanings defined under the Positive and Negative Readings describe how they are unique to this particular interpretation of the Tarot. This point having been made, I start this description (which is described as according to the Lovecraft system of the Tarot as defined under the concept of the 'Mi-Go'), with a quotation from *The Tarot Workbook* as a reference to the Tarot that I have been using previously to this point:

> "[T]he Tarot path of Justice would be considered a path... where the individual encounters the consequences of his or her actions. Justice demands balance, adjustment, and... impartiality... [T]he meditator begins to discover the nature of the true, inner self by overcoming the illusory aspects of outer appearances... [J]ustice will prevail. This may well portend a new cycle of equilibrium and harmony... You will receive what is due to you" (Drury: 2006: 66).

In encountering the second Card to be represented by a technological race (with the Great Race of Yith being the previous example in hand), the question is posed as to whether something such as the Mi-Go would actually have been discussed by *The Necronomicon* as our religious book, if such issues as regarding occult technology would not have been know at the point that our religious book was written? The theory is that the fictional work of Lovecraft was based on him having seen a copy of the 'blasphemous book' which is central to Cult of R'Lyeh religion, but that many writers have been influenced by his work, and so, as a result of this, some more fictional ideas have inevitably come

into our genre since his death.[1] The idea of the Mi-Go as symbolic has come into our outlook, however, and the *HP Lovecraft Tarot* uses this idea in order to try to describe its own unique idea of this Card.

Despite this, point having been established, though, the Mi-Go are described in Mythos literature as being an intelligent race of fungi who exist on the planet Pluto (as defined with *The Necronomicon* as being the planet Yuggoth), who have a high understanding of technology, and are in turn capable of travel throughout the Cosmos and through the Stars. Bizarre as this concept may seem in itself, these are the sort of ideas which would have been written about in *The Necronomicon* and the religious literature which our religious book has inspired, and such belief is therefore a part of the bizarre and beautiful nature of our religion. With this idea, then, being the concept behind the idea of 'Justice' in this Deck, the Mi-Go are defined by the *HP Lovecraft Tarot* as being representative of the Tarot idea of this concept, and so we have no option other than to go on to define this Card according to the Mi-Go, as They are the subject of the twelfth Card, that being the symbolic representation that is defined by the Tarot as according to this idea. If the idea of 'Justice' is in this Deck, then, defined by the Mi-Go as a defined religious concept in itself, then we should follow this concept as we define the idea behind this Card and our further interpretation of the occult as defined on religious terms of its own.

"Cosmic travellers, explorers, and observers, the Mi-Go have a view of Time, Space & Spirit which…transcends the…limitations… [of] human consciousness" (Hutchinson, Friedman: 2002: 29). What the *HP Lovecraft Tarot* means, exactly, in putting this statement in terms of 'Justice', we cannot completely sure. But if we consider the Western definition of this term as a point of philosophy in itself, the concept of 'Justice' is often something which is imposed by above;

---

1 A note should be made at this point, that it is our belief that what differentiates Lovecraft as a writer, is that he had actually seen a copy of The Necronomicon in his lifetime. Whilst many writers have been directly influenced by his work, the factual nature of his writing, may not be represented by some of the horror which has been written since his death.

and this statement can, therefore, be interpreted as being representative of a higher force, maybe, imposing systems of authority from above. But this statement continues the idea further, however, in defining a position of "limitations... on human consciousness" (Hutchinson, Friedman: 2002: 29). Whatever system of 'Justice' imposed on one person by another is only subjective to that persons opinion of what they see as being 'right', and imposed authority is only subject to how such authority can be enforced. This point should therefore be seen as the interpreted meaning behind this part of the Tarot.

But in defining such a statement as to explain and describe how authority in Western society is often structured, the concept of the Mi-Go is one of a mentality where everything is thought of in terms of institutions and established by such established systems of order. In this context the mind of the Mi-Go is vastly beyond and outside of the concepts of rational human thought, with the psychology of this Race in question being a point of which is something quite alien to any human way of thinking. With this point, then, having been defined as Their way of thinking, as a statement as established by the Tarot defined to represent the human terms on which our understanding is structured, and as successive to previous interpretations, the Mi-Go "represent that... element which must be introduced for... social progress" (Hutchinson, Friedman: 2002: 29). The idea of 'Justice', as described by the *HP Lovecraft Tarot*, then, would establish a concept concerning the continuous progress of society, as regards institutions and ordered systems of thinking, and ultimately the authority that this concept would stand to justify with this symbology being a representative point of defined logic.

In continuing to describe this main statement concerning Card 12 as a concept regarding the religious ideas pertaining to the religious system here defined, our system of the Tarot continues in saying that such an element "does not... need to be aliens from outer space – although that is... the most popular form... that indolent people are waiting to receive enlightenment from, rather than going out and seizing it by their own actions" (Hutchinson, Friedman: 2002: 29).

The Lovecraft Tarot here comes back to the idea, however, as has already been discussed, that whilst the Mi-Go may perhaps not be part of *The Necronomicon* (although we cannot be exactly sure of this, and that we work on the assumption that They are), Mythos literature can be studied as representative within a context of esotericism which is something quite seriously more bizarre than what is usually termed as being the 'orthodox approach to religious belief' as is upheld by more mainstream religious faiths.

In questioning whether such a thing as the Mi-Go actually exist, as the question is discussed in the statement above, it is our view that if *The Necronomicon* discusses a race of intelligent fungi on Yuggoth (the planet Pluto), then that should be taken as direct evidence that such an entity as The Mi-Go does actually exist.[2] The idea as described in this system of the Tarot, is, however, more conceptual, with the Mi-Go representing personal and psychological outlooks more massively more bizarre, with the esoteric angle being less important where we define the idea of 'Justice' in terms of the occult and our further discussion of this study in hand.

Ideas of "Intellectual challenge; learning, studies; school, teacher, academics" (Hutchinson, Friedman: 2002: 29) are discussed under the Positive definition of this Card. These ideas would be something that would not usually apply to Card 12 under most traditional interpretations of the Tarot, but with the Lovecraft Deck the idea is more representative of a mentality and an outlook than would usually be defined by the mass of other systems as representing this study. The Mi-Go could be considered as a socialist entity of communal structure within our system of belief, and to Them the structure behind institutions, for example schools, governments and other structures of social order are

---

2 As a point of interest, it is thought by those who study these religious ideas, that planet Pluto was known to exist, and was called 'Yuggoth' many years before it was known to astronomy. This is another point of research that supports our belief in the validity of The Necronomicon as religious truth.

how They consider such order to be inherently 'Just'.[3] This as a form of psychology, then, stands as a further point of definition as regarding how we should look at the meaning behind this Card if it should come into the situation as part of any Reading.

The "Social sciences" are further defined as part of this description of meaning, as is the term "justice" in itself. In describing a unique definition as represented by the *HP Lovecraft Tarot*, this is again different from that which is established and defined by the massive representation of other systems of the Tarot. "[H]onourable action; law, courts; etiquette [and] protocol" (Hutchinson, Friedman: 2002: 29) are defined, with this continuing with the idea of the concept of the Mi-Go representing the institutions of state being the higher form of what They consider 'Justice' as the main concept behind Their existence. It should be stated here, though, that in the actual context of a Reading, then these terms should be considered on the specific terms of human understanding, with issues such as legality and court cases presumably coming out as being successful with this Card being drawn as Positive, even if this might be on a longer term basis than what we at first expect.

The Positive definition with this Card is productive in this statement, then, as it continues by defining issues which will quite probably come into our lives, which will in turn be of help to us if we will allow them to. It concludes the statement in predicting involvement from an "Advocate, guardian; chivalry, champion, defender; sanctuary [and] protection" (Hutchinson, Friedman: 2002: 29). These short statements here continue the idea the idea of 'Justice' within such terms as have been defined, and represent a situation whereby people will side with us if we have to deal with such systems of authority and power.

Negative Reading

This Negative definition of meaning is the same as with the context in which we have defined most of this Card already, with the Lovecraft

---

3 Some of the ideas discussed under the 'Great Race of Yith' also apply in this context, although the Mi-Go should be considered something entirely different.

system of Tarot being an accurate system, despite being totally different from any other Deck and defining issues on its own very unique terms. "Intellectual indolence" is defined as part of a Negative Reading, as well as a "blind & uncritical acceptance of data [and] dubious information" (Hutchinson, Friedman: 2002: 29). In this we see an example of symptoms in society which relate to the opposite of what is 'Justice', in the more mainstream definition of the terms, with these issues being some of the symptoms in society which lead to unjust authority and inequality as parts of everyday life.

The psychological issues around abuse of authority or status are further represented by the conceptualization of The Mi-Go, and again the Tarot warns us of a situation involving "Totalitarianism, chauvinism; 'The end justifies the means'" (Hutchinson, Friedman: 2002: 29). These are just a few of the mental assumptions which lead to the abuse of power (as something that should be considered if this Card is drawn on this basis), and Card 12 in this system actually goes as far as to define the issue of 'injustice' as something that will play a part in our lives. "Prejudice & partiality" is forecast as something that will also play a part, and "lack of social grace" (Hutchinson, Friedman: 2002: 29) is also defined as being an issue.

The 'Justice' Card ends with a statement as to the negative side of human personality as a position in psychology, and if drawn as part of a Reading, Card 12 defines a position of "Cowardice, treachery; inequity, improbity [and] lack of principal" (Hutchinson, Friedman: 2002: 29). Where these statements come directly into play as regards the idea of 'Justice', as it relates to the individual and social organization, again we are not exactly certain. But if our system of the Tarot defines these issues under the definition Justice, then it is ours to consider such statements as being religious to us who regard *The Necronomicon* as being our religious book, and with the consideration of the *HP Lovecraft Tarot* as being the most direct statement as to what this book says, before actually reading the 'blasphemous book' in itself.

A final statement of interpretation should be issued here, and this is that the concept of 'Justice' is quite complicated and also strange when

interpreted under a framework of Western philosophical thinking, but if seen as being defined under these terms, an approach to the concept is described by the Lovecraft system as being defined in these statements of meaning. If these definitions are how we define our belief in what is 'Justice', then we begin to establish a system of religious belief according to the greater system that is represented when we worship the Great Old Ones. All religions have their own dogmas, and in accepting this as a statement of both interpretation and belief, now we begin to establish our own.

12. Deep One: The Hanged Man

"We come from the water. The great... seas are the... Mother Earth. From them, all life has emerged... In them are... found the... protozoa which have engendered all... species. There is also a... sea of Spirit, from which... consciousness has emerged and evolved – although many might say that... this process has been the opposite of evolution... [W]e could say that, as the biological vehicle became more complex, the more the spiritual passenger lost awareness of its... source" (Hutchinson, Friedman: 2002: 30).

The equivalent to be made here, is of Card 13 as defined under the concept which is the Hanged Man in most other systems of the Tarot, and with the Lovecraft system of the Tarot here we see the conceptualization of the Deep One as a grotesque creature who is submerged far beneath the depths of the Ocean. The Deep One is very much a Card of the water, therefore, but at the same time stands to define an equivalent position to represent the vast expanse of the psychick ability of the mind.[1] Following from the above, the *HP Lovecraft Tarot* continues to define the point that, "As the Primal Spark of life is... bound by the limitations of our... egos, so, in turn, are... our physical bodies" (Hutchinson, Friedman: 2002: 30). It is this concept of the 'inner person' that is important with this Card, as we are all of us principally psychick entities which are bound into our physical bodies, and the only limitation to what we can do as our psychick self is defined by our belief in ourselves and what we can mentally achieve in terms of our own self-belief of ourselves. We can, with certain restraints, do

---

[1] Some interpretations of the Deep Ones consider Them the idea of such existence to be symbolic of ideas suppressed into the subconscious mind. Those who have a knowledge of psychology may want to use this idea when constructing their own ritual and ceremonial magick. A study of Chaos Magick Theory may be useful.

what we believe we can do whilst only limited possibilities here come into play. And to take that as a statement of philosophy further, our physical bodies are only the exterior shells which carry our psychick potential. Our interpretation of this Deck continues, then, that "none of these levels of our being are inherently negative... they must just be recognised as a vessel for... a secondary state relative to, that which they contain" (Hutchinson, Friedman: 2002: 30). The personality, which is an exterior issue to that of the body, is the thing which is actually important. "The body is a vehicle for the mind... [and] the mind is a vehicle for the soul" (Hutchinson, Friedman: 2002: 30).

However with that first point of thought having been established, "every phase is... a fluid state more material than itself" (Hutchinson, Friedman: 2002: 31), states our system of the Tarot in question. It is difficult to interpret this statement directly in terms of that represented by the Lovecraft Deck of the Tarot, and it would be wrong to say that the meaning here was obvious. This could be read, though, that the material body, mind and soul are each in progressive cycles that are ever more material, which could bring us back to the issue of the importance of material values. This statement continues (but without clarifying any issue too much), by saying that "each level [of the psyche] requires navigational tools to guard against losing its origins and source" (Hutchinson, Friedman: 2002: 31). This could be interpreted by saying that all three points are occult principles which need something to be guided by in order to be focused. "Classically, the Tarot has always served as such a tool, and as an aid to meditation and contemplation of the Source" (Hutchinson, Friedman: 2002: 31). In this statement the issue is at least clarified to a degree. If we need such 'navigation' to keep track of our purpose, then this Card is representative of this, with the last statement suggesting that the Card of the Deep One represents the meditative contemplation that we need for ourselves to be focused on whatever course of life that we should choose to follow.

If the Deep One is representative of That which crawls from the murky darkness of the Sea, then this Card is representative of ideas of the subconscious now made aware. As has already been pointed out,

The Deep One is the *HP Lovecraft Tarot* equivalent of the Hanged Man. Therefore this correlation will be to some extent similar with definitions of different systems of the Tarot previously published and circulated around the occult communities of our society. With this being Card 12, everything with "metaphysical roots [will] bear physical fruit"; [2] and this can be read as meaning that anything involved with the direct and deliberate use of the occult will eventually be productive. Sometimes the things we have evoked through use of magick come to nothing, but with this Card drawn in a Reading we can be confident that projects involving use of ceremonial magick will be successful; whether this means projects involving magickal visualisation, to full blown rituals of ceremonial magick? This also means that the practice of magick on other levels will be successful, as the Card of the Deep One represents "meditation [and] contemplation" (Hutchinson, Friedman: 2002: 31) in terms of religious worship. Maybe the tranquillity of the deep would be a point of symbolism that would here come into play? "Matter as a natural medium for Mind and Spirit" (Hutchinson, Friedman: 2002: 31) is suggested, although it could be said that exactly what this means is not well defined, as some of the Cards in this Tarot do have some overtly obscure definitions. "Practical material expression of spiritual principals" (Hutchinson, Friedman: 2002: 31) is another positive definition with this Card, stating that the actual expression of religious principals is an issue; and that the principals of worship will come into play as an aspect of esoteric truth (maybe as a manifestation of 'metaphysical roots' as one single suggestion in question?)

The important issue of the combined religious principles of "Spirit, Mind and Body" (Hutchinson, Friedman: 2002: 31) are referred to,

---

2 As a note, the Positive Reading as defined in the Introductory Book refers specifically to the word "Merkabah". This is the Hebrew word for 'Chariot', and the HP Lovecraft Tarot uses this word in the context of the 'Vision of Ezekiel', and then makes reference to the Qabballah. In this context it is said to represent the "Body as a vehicle for the Mind... the Mind as... the soul, and so on." This idea does not equate in any way with the 'Chariot' as the Card of the Tarot, or in any way in which Crowley may have used the term in his writing. Such ideas are discussed in Part II of this Book of Shadows.

and in this respect the Introductory Book to the second Edition of the Lovecraftian system of the Tarot supports what is written here. According to the *HP Lovecraft Tarot*, all three of these principles will act "as a single, holistic organism" (Hutchinson, Friedman: 2002: 31). This also supports our definition of the concept of the Deep One representing the power of intellect and the greater manifest power of the subconscious human mind.

Negative Reading

In order to discuss the meaning of this Card when drawn reversed as part of a Reading, a "Conflict of Spiritual & Material Will & desire" (Hutchinson, Friedman: 2002: 31) is forecast. With this definition we are again defining the opposite of what is written with the Positive definition, and this should be taken in hand with such an interpretation. This could represent a conflict of personal values and says that personal inner balance is out of sync. The Negative Reading here represents a "sacrifice of one for the sake of gains in the other" (Hutchinson, Friedman: 2002: 31).

"Matter as a spiritual burden" (Hutchinson, Friedman: 2002: 31) is further defined. The continuum of the World is becoming too much. Whilst this is would be in straightforward terms another vague statement from the *HP Lovecraft Tarot*, I think this statement is representative of the material objects that we have around us becoming too much, or of a loss of metaphysical value in our immediate lives. "Mind as an obstacle to spiritual expression" (Hutchinson, Friedman: 2002: 31) is defined and is an issue that should be directly worked with.

Our minds are preoccupied and concerned with the material world, and we cannot tune in our psyche to the metaphysical acknowledgement of that which we worship. The "Mind [is] drowned by sensory input" (Hutchinson, Friedman: 2002: 31); the most direct meaning of this here suggesting primarily that issues such as TV are gaining control of our lives – although there are other possibilities as to why this may be. But this sensory input is most likely to be in the manifest world.

However, the spirit may also be "overwhelmed by unfocused thought" (Hutchinson, Friedman: 2002: 31). Whatever is said in a Negative Reading, this Card here states that we should focus our minds to clear out negative energies, and to be in tune with the Cosmos and ourselves. This can be of relevance to all approaches to the occult, including our own form of devotion to the worship of the strange Gods of *The Necronomicon* as a single point of religious and occult religion as stands as equal with every other.

13. GHOUL: DEATH

Card 13 is the place in the Tarot where we always encounter the mystical concept of Death. Whilst it is very well known that the Death Card is representative of the death of ideas and the coming into new and different ones, the *HP Lovecraft Tarot* is quite complex in its interpretation of the Cards of the Tarot, and is described as follows for the point of defining its meaning in the specific context of the Lovecraftian and *The Necronomicon* as our religious book of magick. It should be pointed out that the Lovecraft Tarot defines the Cards, within itself, quite differently from all other Decks, as is the case with the previous Cards and the further discussion of this Deck as follows.

One of the interesting things about this particular system of the Tarot is in how it develops as a concept within itself from the onset. From Azathoth as the insane nucleus of chaos and creation, to Shub-Niggurath as birth and regeneration, through Hastur as the God of social communication, the Tarot as a system continuously evolves. It would be interesting to note, therefore, that Card 13 of this Deck leads on from the previous in this aspect. "Another aspect of the supposed conflict between Spirit and Matter" (Hutchinson, Friedman: 2002: 32), states Card 13, as represented by this system as the Ghoul, "is in the impermanence of Matter making it [a] flawed medium for Eternal Spirit" (Hutchinson, Friedman: 2002: 32). The Death Card is in this Deck, slightly different with that of all other systems as it speaks of being mainly about the physical body as a vehicle for the human soul.

This concept of human personification is established that "The physical body... is subject to... decay, corruption, & death. The soul... is incorruptible" (Hutchinson, Friedman: 2002: 32). With this statement clearly defined the *HP Lovecraft Tarot* is very clear that, to our religion as The Cult of R'Lyeh on Earth, it is seen as being

fact that, although our physical body will always eventually die and lead to physical decomposition, the inner person within us (defined as the 'soul' by most orthodox religions), will always continue as a further form of consciousness and further perception. It is one issue with the R'Lyeh, however, that in the literature of the Lovecraftian, it is not entirely clear where the soul continues to after the death of the physical body that this Card hereby defines.[1] For the sake of theory, then, the Tarot continues in the abstract belief of a passing through to some level of the Astral Plane. "These... fundamentals... are not in conflict" (Hutchinson, Friedman: 2002: 32), the Tarot goes on to tell us, making a statement as to perception after the death of the body, and a continuation of the soul after mortal experience of existence.

The Introductory Book to the previous Edition continues with this general idea that, "Although... material... the human body... is often portrayed as the enemy of Spirit [although] it is actually the most... proper medium for spiritual expression" (Hutchinson, Friedman: 2002: 32). What this statement in more defined terms says in this respect is more complicated, but this statement probably makes a statement as to the way in which we, as people, express ourselves in spiritual terms being usually much more in the physical sense than the spiritual. It is much more common for most of us to walk down the street or to watch TV, than to study meditation or occult visualisation (although activities such as conversation or watching TV may still take the middle ground). "If we were never confronted with our own mortality, we would [not]... make a lasting impression by our actions" (Hutchinson, Friedman: 2002: 32). In this statement the Tarot is saying that we are so tied up with our perception as being about our physical existence, that we see our place on Earth as being the absolute end of any argument, and that our further transition to the Beyond is not normally the end of our actions, as regards such a principle of further perception. "Most

---

1 In the history of religions who regard The Necronomicon as religious, a small number of sects have called themselves the 'R'Lyeh'. The name of our own group, being the 'Cult of R'Lyeh on Earth' is slightly different in this respect, though, as is described in the Introduction to The Necronomicon Cycle as the title for this book.

ability ensures morality" (Hutchinson, Friedman: 2002: 32), is how the *HP Lovecraft Tarot* continues to make this statement, although many people (including some cultists), may not want to leave this World that we currently live in, with virtue.

The *HP Lovecraft Tarot* has more to say here, however, and continues with the idea that "when… we bring spiritual influence into physical manifestation, the eternity of spirit permeates the material, even if only for a short while" (Hutchinson, Friedman: 2002: 32). Here is a statement that concerns Crowley's ideas of 'True Will', and makes a statement as to the occult and our religion as part of the R'Lyeh if such ritual worship can be taken to this logical extent. This is the first time that this Tarot makes any mention of the occult in the traditional sense that involves meditation and visualisation, and this idea is discussed further elsewhere in the *Necronomicon Cycle* as a book written on the subject of this definition of occult use of black magick.

The conceptual manifestation of the dead, as is defined with this system in discussion as being the Ghoul, is at home in this Tarot. In this, the Ghoul is the representation of all that has died and passed into any further dimension beyond human perception. The Ghoul, in representing the dead, has its symbolism in things which are now in the past. Memories of what are no more, important parts of things in our lives that have passed, and parts of history which were at one point in time important, but which have no current relevance, are symbolised as the depiction of this Card. The Ghoul is at home with all of this and, despite Its portrayal with this Card as being something more dangerous or even macabre, the Ghoul necessitates such an impression, and It is actually harmless; being manifest as nothing more than the subconscious part of the mind which acknowledges such emotions as relating to things past and of loss. Things that are in the past are symbolised here, and although they are no longer with us in life, they are still with us in spirit and as part of a conceptual further dimension.

The concluding statement to the Positive definition of the Ghoul in the *HP Lovecraft Tarot* is more bizarre than with this general conceptualized idea, though, and reads to define the point that; "the

ultimate potential result [of realising mortality] is veiled in the legend of the phoenix and in… doctrines of resurrection: The physical vessel can… be reborn as an Eternal material expression of spiritual light" (Hutchinson, Friedman: 2002: 33). This last statement makes a number of points about a number of spiritual values, all of them defined as either Shamanic or as mainstream religion. But maybe it would be better to leave this Card as described, than to go into the various possibilities of trying to define this statement further?

Moving on from the definition of Death as a part of the Tarot as already defined above, the definition of this Card under the heading of the Positive Reading is closer to the definition as traditional in most other Decks of the Tarot. The first part of the definition in this sense refers to "Transformation" (Hutchinson, Friedman: 2002: 33),[2] and is relevant to stages in our situation or lifestyle changing, and in the aspect of a Positive interpretation for the better. Everything in life is always and continuously subject to change, but the Death Card here represents serious lifestyle changes for the better. So often negative changes are prone to take place, but here we have cause to be optimistic. "Letting go of cumbersome tools & patterns when no longer relevant" (Hutchinson, Friedman: 2002: 33) is defined, and this further impends positive changes in our day to day lives.

"Freedom from habit, routine & convention: innovation" (Hutchinson, Friedman: 2002: 33) is next defined as an interpretation of meaning; this making another statement about how we uphold personal circumstances on a day to day basis. These statements suggest that the repetition and rigmarole of everyday life is going to be subject to change. How often is it that, every-day, we find that our routine is subject to repetition? Cycles such as getting up, going to work, going to bed, seem to be something we do every day. But how much are we slaves to a routine, rather than doing what we want to do? This Positive

---

2 This stands to represent a point which seems to be repeated by most systems of Tarot, that the obvious meaning of one Card can have a completely different meaning when seen in terms of the occult.

Reading with this as being the Death Card in all systems of the Tarot says that systems of everyday repetition are likely to change, and that this is potentially something we should be grateful for.

The *HP Lovecraft Tarot* continues that a Positive Reading here represents "Traditions which serve a purpose; healthy spiritual legacies" (Hutchinson, Friedman: 2002: 33). In this we can say that this could be the absolute opposite of Death, as traditions and such 'spiritual legacies' are often repetitions of the festivals which represent renewal of life.

Negative Reading

Despite the definition and Positive Reading with this Card, the concept of Death always has serious connotations, and the Negative Reading in this Lovecraftian system can be, obviously, pessimistic, as it would be with all other systems of the Tarot. Whilst this Card can never mean actual disaster, it does make a serious statement if coming into a reading in this respect. "Death, decay [and] corruption" (Hutchinson, Friedman: 2002: 33) would all be serious statements in this regard, but this should not be taken too seriously. 'Death' in the Tarot rarely means actual physical death in a material sense, and so this should not be taken too literally in this respect. "Inability to let go of outmoded patterns & beliefs; self-imposed obstacles" (Hutchinson, Friedman: 2002: 33) are defined. This is a more direct correlation to be interpreted, and makes a statement as to our own understanding of ourselves as psychological, and making statements as to how we should understand our own frame of mind as a functioning psychological species.

"Mindless repetition, redundancy; patterns of work or actions which don't produce the desired results" (Hutchinson, Friedman: 2002: 33) are next defined in the Introductory Book to the second Edition of this Tarot. It should here be pointed out that this is the opposite of what is defined in a Positive Reading. Never the less, this in a reading can be quite useful. All of these definitions of meaning are issues which are

usually psychological. These issues can be quite easily sorted if we take time to step back and look at things with a new frame of mind. Remember that the Tarot is here to help us, and not here as impending certain doom.

The definition of the Ghoul ends by defining this Card as forecasting "Conformity & obedience to behaviour patterns suited to the needs of others" (Hutchinson, Friedman: 2002: 33). It now begins to become clear that the *HP Lovecraft Tarot* takes time to remind us of how we are treated by others, often those in authority above us. The *HP Lovecraft Tarot* reminds us repeatedly that we are our own person, and that we are better off without being obedient to others.

14. OLD ONE: TEMPERANCE

Nevill Drury's *The Tarot Workbook*, being our next main reference to the Tarot defines the Tarot Card that is Temperance, as "represent[ing] the path of direct mystical ascent to a state of spiritual illumination" (Drury: 2006: 72). It would be interesting to note, therefore, that the description of Card 14 in the *HP Lovecraft Tarot*, can be seen as being the most confusing. The Old One is quite largely concerned with the issue of the human Spirit as concerned with the issues of nature and science. It says little, however, to concern 'mystical ascent' or 'spiritual illumination', as the definition that follows will explain. It continues with our defined concept of the soul.

If the previous Card of this Tarot would be about the human soul as an inherent part of the person, then this Card concerns the power of the human individual to affect acts of religious magick in the immediate world around us. In this, Card 14 is involved with the theories of Crowley and the Order of the Golden Dawn, and of the power of magick as controlled by True Will as a part of the practitioner of magick discussed. This definition of meaning opens by saying, "having realised Matter as a secondary condition to Spirit, it now becomes incumbent on the individual to make the material into a medium for their personal spiritual expression" (Hutchinson, Friedman: 2002: 34).

This is quite a difficult first statement to interpret on first terms. How can the individual make the material into a medium? Surely the metaphysical aspect of the spirit cannot actually affect anything that is material? This concept is difficult, but the further description of this Card goes further to explain this idea that: "Science is… a result of the… observation of Nature… Art, however, is the ability to mould Nature into an expression… of the individual spirit" (Hutchinson, Friedman: 2002: 34). So here we are moving from the idea of the human being as

a perceptive spirit, towards a force for perceptive creation. What exact relevance this has to the Tarot is not exactly clear in this sense, but this is the nature of the *HP Lovecraft Tarot* as opposed to all others to establish interpretations of meaning on similar general terms. I don't think that this statement needs to be broken down to intricate points of meaning, but this statement refers to the intelligence of humankind as opposed to other species, and to how we naturally manipulate nature towards purposes made by our own understanding.

The idea continues as this Card defines the point that: "Nature already has a myriad of spiritual influences operating through it, but these are not recognised by science" (Hutchinson, Friedman: 2002: 34). Everything in nature has an internal life force within it, but science can neither emulate nor define what this spirit is. As humanity has defined science, this is purely a creation of the human mind, and to create an object which does have spiritual life is something that humanity can never do; it is purely an act of the creating force that is within nature. Attempts to create life through stem-cell research, genetic engineering, eugenics and so on, are a bastardisation of this creative force, and are not a creation of the life force, as here defined, by science or any other manifestation of the human species as here defined. "The harmony & beauty of the natural order are the... expression of a spiritual reality" (Hutchinson, Friedman: 2002: 34). And, with this said, whilst our religion does not go as far as to define specifically what this creative force should be accredited to, we do acknowledge the natural order to be a uniform manifestation of natural creation and beauty. As this manifestation is spiritual, the Tarot tells us that "[M]atter is a vehicle for spiritual expression, and can always be made to conform to spiritual Will" (Hutchinson, Friedman: 2002: 34). I do not believe that this relates to the spiritual power of the Will of mankind, but to the Will of those combined forces which have created humanity, the World and the Cosmos as greater interactive forces. This is therefore a difficult Card to be understood in this context.

This comes back to having a direct meaning to the reader of the Tarot now, when the Introductory Book to the previous Edition defines the

point that, "[W]e must not let our... desires be determined by conditions imposed on us by forces outside of ourselves" (Hutchinson, Friedman: 2002: 34). So, whilst the Planet on which we live and perceive as reality around us is a mass of scientific and natural creation, this exists outside of our perception. We are, therefore, in control of our own actions and emotions, and it is this that we should be conscious of as we lead our everyday lives. The above now begins to make sense as the definition of the Old One is described. This Card concerns ourselves as part of the natural World. It is clarified now, as the last paragraph explains:

"[The human species] have the obligation – as spiritual beings – to recognise the... spiritual world as truly defining our necessities... [T]hese necessities are unique to each individual... [A]s explained in the last card – we must not rigidly adhere to models of action if they no longer suit our individual needs... [W]e should recognize when it is time for ourselves, as individuals, to move on to new models" (Hutchinson, Friedman: 2002: 35).

It is only in this last paragraph that the actual meaning of Card 14 becomes clear. As this definition here is quite self-explanatory, I feel that it would be unnecessary to break it down in terms of meaning. But it is to be said that in this, Card 14 relates to our responsibility as people to the World around us, but more importantly to ourselves. We, as people, create the World around us, but the decisions that we make by, and for, ourselves, are more important than what happens to us. What happens to us is external, whilst our personal decisions are more importantly what effects our lives.

This Card is recognised immediately, as the Old One is a symbol that is representative of our religious Gods. Therefore the Card that represents the Old One – as one of the Gods as represented with *The Necronomicon* – can be seen to represent an ultimate conquest within our lives, and a new major realisation of goals. The Old Ones are cosmic entities, and They live outside of any reality that can easily be grasped by the Worshipper, and outside of any dimension that can

be in any way be proven by the Magus. This worship, however, can lead us towards a frame of mind whereby They can be comprehended, with both insanity and hallucinogenic drugs being of benefit to such a state of consciousness. If this Card, on description, seems to say this as its entire statement, we can ask ourselves whether this Card is making a statement, in a greater sense, that this ongoing research and investigation, is a justification for us to establish ourselves as a new religious view?

Both of the Readings here can be considered relevant to our use of the occult. But, properly speaking, successful use of the occult is about our perception of ourselves and our perception of the spiritual World around us. Further, these descriptions of Readings primarily regard the Card of the Old One as the Card of human expression. Therefore issues of expression are defined here as being prominent.

"Healthy models & patterns for spiritual expression" (Hutchinson, Friedman: 2002: 35) are still further forecast as part of a Reading. If we are expressing ourselves properly in terms of the creative thinking and creativity in our everyday lives, we are becoming closer to the chosen Gods of our religion. This defined position of "Spiritual expression" (Hutchinson, Friedman: 2002: 35) can relate to anything from writing and artistic pursuits, to daily systems of occult visualisation and forms of ritualized worship. These activities are, on the greater level, acts of religious orientation, and it is these acts in which we acknowledge our Gods, and become closer to them. "Realisation of aspirations" (Hutchinson, Friedman: 2002: 35) is forecast, and this is the act of the Card for human creativity and material action in our lives. "Finding ones vocation" (Hutchinson, Friedman: 2002: 35) is defined, and with this Card, anything creative in order to express the Worship of the Old Ones is forecast as being successful.

"Spirit in material expression; art, music, performance, etc." (Hutchinson, Friedman: 2002: 35) next is defined as something that will come into the situation. With all of these being acts of Worship in themselves, and as defined here, these will go well. The forces will support us in these activities; art will be inspired, music

will be spontaneous, and performances regarding creativity will be successful. It could be seen that in these pursuits we will be 'inspired by the divine'. "Proportion, design [and] sacred geometry" (Hutchinson, Friedman: 2002: 35) are defined, and although this statement is obscure, it probably refers to creativity and the application of the mind on the conceptual terms as here discussed.

The same definition of meaning now moves towards the more esoteric, and forecasts "Alchemy, direction of diverse spiritual influences into practical manifestation; the Philosophers Stone" (Hutchinson, Friedman: 2002: 35). In the history of magick these issues have been those which are the closest to ritual practice, and in terms of the creative mind, this defines the practice of magick by the human hand. Alchemy and "influences in… practical manifestation" (Hutchinson, Friedman: 2002: 35) are both terms which involve magick in this sense, and this goes back to the day when Enochian magick was considered a scientific art.

The issue of magick continues with this statement, and a quotation as concerning the occult as represented by this Card comes into play as Card 14 defines "Harmonious group efforts in spiritual works; clan, coven, church" (Hutchinson, Friedman: 2002: 35).[1] This statement concerns any work of ceremonial magick as performed by the individual or the group. These acts of ceremonial magick will be successful, with further acts of Worship in the occult being recognised, and with good results as regards communal and ceremonial union as regards the religion as defined in our system of the Worship of *The Necronomicon* system of religious Gods.

Negative Reading

The Negative definition here starts by raising the issue of human failure as its meaning. "Indeterminate & / or haphazard spirituality; spiritual irresponsibility & dilettantism" (Hutchinson, Friedman: 2002: 35) is defined. If this comes up in a Reading, then, we must evaluate

---
1 The work of the Cult of R'Lyeh on Earth?

ourselves, and our own failings as regards our spiritual selves. These are problems with ourselves and our attitude to our belief in the Gods of our system. We must take time to step back and ask ourselves what, exactly, these failings are? If this is to be considered a problem with ourselves, then it is up to us to sort this out.

This statement continues by signifying the opposite of what was previously defined in the discussion of the Positive Reading, above, by saying that "Artistic work or performance as a merely mechanical act; artistic form devoid of spiritual content" (Hutchinson, Friedman: 2002: 35), and that this will become a part of our lives. In getting involved with artistic work or performance, we are engaging ourselves in something that requires the full application of our spiritual selves. If this form of expression does not have the emotion that such work demands to be at its best, then it is probably the case that we should take some time off or spend time doing something else. This is not always the obvious position from the perspective of the artist or the musician, and this Card may be making this statement without our being entirely aware. It continues further by warning us, in this context, of the danger of "trying [to] physically turn lead into gold [and] uncentered spiritual quests & journeys" (Hutchinson, Friedman: 2002: 35). All of these statements are trying to tell us that, in the Worship of our chosen religious Mythos, we are doing this without the full application that is needed to properly do so. And, in concluding this statement, the *HP Lovecraft Tarot* tells us that the Negative meaning with Card 14 means, "religious practice without benefit: recitation of all formulae without even knowing what they mean" (Hutchinson, Friedman: 2002: 35). The Worship of *The Necronomicon* system of Gods requires the full application of the mind. We should step back to evaluate magickal acts.

15. TSATHOGGUA: THE DEVIL

In the literature of our religion, Tsathoggua, as representative of the God that Cristian belief upholds as being personified as The Devil, dwells in a cave beneath Mount Voormithacheth, this being a term to describe the planetary orbit of Venus, far beyond the Earth, and in this He lives simultaneously in another dimension.[1] Whilst this statement to describe the God Tsathoggua is delivered as a point of concept by the history of Lovecraftian Mythos fiction, it is our belief as the Cult of R'Lyeh on Earth, that such statements are derived from the history of the blasphemous texts, and this is therefore accepted as being inherent as our religious belief. Either way, the daemonic reality of the Toad God as represented by The Devil, is justified as we regard our Gods as Astral reality, and as we uphold *The Necronomicon* as describing this as our interpretation of one actual statement of reality and religious truth.

As this book has already moved through this discussion of the *HP Lovecraft Tarot* to define The Ghoul as representative of the body as the vehicle for the soul, and the Old One as representative of material human expression, we now encounter Tsathoggua as the Card that stands to represent the manifestation of psychology and the human mind. In the recesses of the subconscious darkness on the unknown human mind, Tsathoggua is known to all of us. But is should be said that the description of this Card with the *HP Lovecraft Tarot* is specifically and heavily orientated around that which is the psychological. I did

---

[1] Other sources say that Tsathoggua now lies beneath N'kai, where He dwells on Earth, after having 'fallen from Saturn' (statement taken from resources regarding Mythos fiction). The situation remains, though, that whatever information we may derive from Mythos fiction, if The Necronomicon states the existence of Tsathoggua, anywhere in the Cosmos, then The Cult of R'Lyeh on Earth will regard this as being religious truth.

not want to spend too much time with this Card in describing such an issue to describe this reality which is the psychological, and the further study of psychology would obviously be a massively bigger issue than can be covered by one book in itself, but due to the strongly psychological nature of Tsathoggua, then this point may have to be stated. In this description of the Card that relates to the Toad God, and further represented with the personification that is The Devil, we are still quoting from the Introductory Book that is a part of the previous Edition of the Lovecraft Deck of the Tarot. But with this Card it has been necessary to quote more from the Introductory Book from this previous Edition, than we have had to with the previous Cards. This might be on the grounds that the religious concept that is thus represented is a much bigger issue than that represented by most of the rest of the Cards discussed as part of the book you are reading here.

"Sitting at the base of the spine" (Hutchinson, Friedman: 2002: 36), states our system of the Tarot discussed, "under the… layers of cerebral tissue which are the… map of our development… sits what is called the reptile brain" (Hutchinson, Friedman: 2002: 36). With this Card being defined as such, this explains what is meant in terms of defining the roots of the human subconscious and our unknown mind as the symbolism of this Card defines. The definition of the Card that is here represented as Tsathoggua starts with this statement, as the discussion of this Card goes on to speak of Card 15 on similar terms until the end. Of course, Card 15 in whatever Tarot is always the Card of The Devil,[2] and with this equation of the Toad God having been defined, it is my decision to continue to follow this psychological line as the discussion of what such an idea establishes whilst drawn in a Reading, and to

---

[2] Card 15, in the Tarot, is usually representative of the concept as defined as being The Devil. This book is written as a study of the Gods on a higher level, though, and in terms of astral confusion and spiritual vibration that exists as represented by the Tarot, Tsathoggua stands as a greater God in terms of the study of The Necronomicon and the further study of religion. Such concepts are the subject of this book, as the author considers this work to be an expression of the religious principles of the Cults of the blasphemous Tome of R'Lyeh.

define these terms to in order to describe human psychology in this sense in terms of the darker side of human nature in order to establish what this Card in context actually means to those for who a Reading should be for.

So, in having thereby defined our terms, the Introductory Book to the previous published Edition of the *HP Lovecraft Tarot* continues to define this point of meaning in that "[T]he reptile brain operates in a... dream state... brooding over its instinctual need for security & pleasure" (Hutchinson, Friedman: 2002: 36). Our dream state is therefore the state of consciousness where most of us Worship Tsathoggua; in the subconscious of sleep state we are not fully aware of the mentality and direct meaning of any conscious state that could be defined as being dream. It is in this state that we are so unaware of our innermost attitudes to our own security and pleasures, that we do not in our waking state acknowledge these attitudes to ourselves, and it is this need we have for security and pleasure that drive the evil deeds of which are the deliberate actions of humanity. These are "precisely the... instincts which are... perverted into excesses of violence, intemperance and avarice" (Hutchinson, Friedman: 2002: 36). Are these not exactly the human failings that would be defined by a God that is usually represented by the Tarot as The Devil? These are the human emotions that are excused when we accept "our territorial and sexual subconscious" (Hutchinson, Friedman: 2002: 36).

"The reptile brain cannot speak" continues our study of the Lovecraftian religious Tarot, "it does not think in words, but only in images, colours and sounds" (Hutchinson, Friedman: 2002: 36). Again this refers to the religious truth that is known to us only in the darkness of our dreams. Therefore our study defines a position that the Toad God Tsathoggua is part of everybody's subconscious, known only in abstracted terms of fragmented images of childhood fantasies and the shattered interpretations of our lives that we access in dream state. Such is the nature of Tsathoggua as our personification of The Devil in other religious perspectives. "[I]t is these impulsive reactions we spend all of our childhood and adolescence learning to suppress" (Hutchinson,

Friedman: 2002: 36) continues our declared study of Tarot. It is this part of the mind that is kept in our unknown subconscious, should any of us become completely insane. Our discussion of the Tarot in question defines this point of discussion that "[T]his part of ourselves is often labelled… 'evil'" (Hutchinson, Friedman: 2002: 36).

But this discussion of the God that is defined by *The Necronomicon* as being named Tsathoggua goes beyond our acknowledgement of the Great Old Ones as the back-brain of the human subconsciousness when we are asleep. Card 15 of this system of the Major Arcana discusses this in terms of how this interacts with the greater movement of humanity as a species, and continues to discuss this dream state and how humanity has learned to live as a massive community as led by such a reality of subconscious awareness. "Temperance and rational thinking before action [happens]… because… we have moved beyond purely selfish considerations into working in groups" (Hutchinson, Friedman: 2002: 37). But humanity is fragmented and continuously at war on the grounds that the will of the subconscious brain spoken of, "undermine[s] the dynamics of… healthy communal relationship[s]. [T]he higher aspect of our… selves… operates on a level which transcends language and verbal consciousness" (Hutchinson, Friedman: 2002: 37). Although this does not say a lot about Card 15 and its meaning to us in a Reading, it does make a statement as to Tsathoggua and His relation to us as a God of *The Necronomicon* and therefore a part of the worship upheld by The Cult of R'Lyeh on Earth.

Our religious study of the Tarot continues with this generalized statement that, "This is the reason why spirituality is often dismissed as 'instinctual'" (Hutchinson, Friedman: 2002: 37). This meaning is defined that our view of the supernatural in our lives is known to us through our subconscious mind and in specific terms through sleep, and the Gods of *The Necronomicon* most often speak to us in the form of the many bizarre and fragmented fronts that constitute the insight behind all other religions and upheld by the societies of

man. "It [spirituality] cannot be defined" (Hutchinson, Friedman: 2002: 37), states our religious study of the Tarot. It is this chaos and confusion of supernatural disorder which is the point in hand when we make any study of *The Necronomicon* occult. "But [this] is precisely [the] rationalism which is now an obstacle to our spiritual survival" (Hutchinson, Friedman: 2002: 37). If we are to continue into the social and material chaos which is manifest as the post-modern fallacy which is our own creation, then we are in danger of failing in our purpose as the Astral Race and in honouring a system of truth as established with the devotion of The Great Old Ones.

But our study of the *HP Lovecraft Tarot* here in discussion ends a statement to here define a Positive Interpretation of this Card by putting the emphasis back onto the individual. Society may be heading in one very specific direction (quite possibly towards our own destruction), but it is up to us as a race to take the initiative on our own. "This is a journey which always starts with a journey through the Underworld and a confrontation with the reptile brain" (Hutchinson, Friedman: 2002: 37), states the Lovecraftian system of the Tarot. This Card when drawn in a reading, most probably indicates that it is this journey, inspired on the basis of the subconscious mind, which we should now make towards controlling our own future circumstances..

Who can see inside the mind of the Toad? If to answer this question then it is clear that none of us can, but the Card of the Toad God Tsathoggua may bring us closer to such a position of personal insight. Remembering that Card 15 is usually representative of the Christian myth of The Devil, in a Positive Reading this represents that either a personal 'Underworld Journey' will be taken, or that we should take time to ourselves to explore certain personal issues. In terms of a Positive interpretation, this Card symbolises that this exploration of issues will be productive and beneficial. This journey will, according to the *HP Lovecraft Tarot*, involve "mythic confrontation with the

Shadow & other primal archetypes".³ A sequel to this book is currently planned to further explain the ideas of the Psychiatrist Jung as regards the Tarot and the Mythos of *The Necronomicon* (although I offer no promises that such a book will ever be written or completed), but *The Penguin Dictionary of Psychology* is useful to our discussion here in hand as discussion a concept as described as being Shadow Archetypes, as represented as a "complex of underdeveloped feelings, ideas, desires and the like" (Reber, Reber: 2001: 676) which exist as part of the subconscious mind (as already briefly discussed). Therefore, these are the ideas that will be focused on most directly, as the Mythos of the Toad brings us towards these and similar emotions.

This general idea as represented by the study of psychology, and as the mentality of the Toad will, as is discussed with the *HP Lovecraft Tarot*, would inevitably result in "reclaiming a place in the dark" (Hutchinson, Friedman: 2002: 37). This as a Tarot that deals with the dark side of the Cosmos and of human nature, will relate to the discovery or rediscovery of the occult as part of the darker side of the Universe and human nature, of which we are all a part of.

With all of that discussion in question, and with this being the start of a journey of self-discovery that will, or should, be taken, this will (according to this study of the Tarot), lead us to an "Assimilation of material instincts and impulses as one of many parts of a healthy psych" (Hutchinson, Friedman: 2002: 37). If this statement is not definition enough of the points already discussed, it starts to make the point that, by taking in such materialistic instincts and impulses, what we are actually doing, is becoming at one with ourselves as a microcosm

---

3 The psychoanalytical works of the psychiatrist Jung go into some detail in discussing the representation of the Tarot and the psychology of the human mind, if his ideas are to be interpreted on this basis. The Cult of R'Lyeh study of our own system, however, also discusses our own ideas on religion in detail as regards psychology and the human brain. This could possibly lead to new arguments regarding the Tarot as representing the mind Could this be put forward as an area for possible future discussion? Again this idea would be another point to be taken forward by the individual student of The Necronomicon system of magick here in question.

of the Universe which is a vastly bigger religious truth, and this is essential to our balance as such a tiny part of this Universe that was repeatedly defined by Lovecraft in numerous writings which discussed this general point. If this seems egotistical, remember that our chosen Mythos of Worship does not revolve around a philosophy that can easily be taken as being 'good', or anything else, as such concepts do not exist according to our religious conceptualisation discussed

So, as this discussion has stated already, with the Card of Tsathoggua being on a parallel with that of The Devil as is defined by pretty much every other system of the Tarot, the definition of this Card also has room to express the ritualistic. "Healthy expression of physical desire & necessity" (Hutchinson, Friedman: 2002: 37) is now defined; with this being a typical example of the ideas apparent with the religious philosophy of religious Satanism, an orientation which has some similar values, but a specific and defined different belief paradigm to ours. It is therefore essential here that we are able to hereby define these parallel terms in discussion, in stating a similar view that the individual is the most important central issue as important to the fundamental understanding of the self. Unlike Satanism, however, where this idea is upheld as being the most important central principal, to the religious Cult of R'Lyeh the karmic unity with our God system must always take the first priority. "Pleasure, orgasm [and] fulfilment" (Hutchinson, Friedman: 2002: 37) are lastly defined here as established under such a Positive concept. This idea may in itself have many meanings, but as we here draw a parallel with Satanism, this could (as one interpretation) relate to the rites of self-fulfilment, pleasurable drug use, or – to make this point in the most direct manner – may symbolise that there may be some involvement in our lives with sex magick as a form of Worship to whatever Deity that our religious magickal system may concern.

Negative Reading

Whilst most other interpretations of the Tarot are actually quite safe, we must make a point here that Card 15 is, in the traditional sense,

representative of a daemonic force for evil and destruction; usually as that manifest with the psychological personification as represented with the idea of The Devil, or close religious symbolism. A Negative Reading here, is, therefore, potentially quite destructive, and the Magus should regard the Negative interpretation of this Card with some considered caution. It must be stated here then, quite directly, that if a Negative meaning is established this Card, then it may be best not to be too concerned unnecessarily. Remember that to be forewarned is to be forearmed, and that if we have insight into what may occur, then we can be ready for it.

This stated definition of a Negative Reading with Tsathoggua, as the Card of the Tarot more usually represented as The Devil (as stated) starts with a fairly complicated first statement to define a point to represent: "Rejection of instinct and natural archetypal patterns in favour of currently popular psychological theories of behaviour" (Hutchinson, Friedman: 2002: 37). This has to be another of numerous examples of how the *HP Lovecraft Tarot* often draws heavily from psychology (as another point that has already been repeatedly pointed out). In bringing up such issues involving the scientific study of psychology and human thought, the *HP Lovecraft Tarot* is making a point that belief in the Necronomicon system of Gods is largely about the nature of supernatural existence, and the subtle and unconscious waves of thought as the way in which The Gods of such a religious system of truth communicate with a smaller statement of truth which is humanity. When broken down, this statement essentially says that our human and instinctual ways of thinking are being distorted by modern manipulation of our minds by these 'theories of behaviour'; such as role models often imposed by TV in order to create a submissive society, again for the benefit of the human society who impose such a position of psychological control. This sort of conflict between the society that humanity has created for ourselves, and our awareness of ourselves as in tune with the Gods, is one that can happen easily, or which can be consciously ignored. But the significance of this Card is the notion that we should be aware.

Card 15 ends with a warning that we should be in touch with our instinctive human emotions. It goes on to state that "inability to move beyond materialistic and / or instinctive actions or reactions" (Hutchinson, Friedman: 2002: 37) will quite possibly come into the picture as a part of our lives. Again this warns of a barrier between ourselves and awareness of the higher beings of the greater Universe; and, again, the problem lies with ourselves. "Perversion, moral & ethical corruption; greed, gluttony; anger, fear [and] violence" (Hutchinson, Friedman: 2002: 37) are specific actions or reactions (or emotions) that may be at play, and may be on the part of ourselves or others. These representations are the prerogative of the Toad, and Tsathoggua, therefore, rules this domain and further influences human psychology, and therefore society, as the equivalent of the Gate of the Christian Hell.

16. The Dunwich Horror: The Tower

Since the publication of the last edition of the *HP Lovecraft Tarot*, not a great deal has been changed aside from the graphical representation as upheld by the Cards of the system in themselves. The current, Third, Edition is currently (at the time of writing, which is admittedly early days) is planned to be published without its own Introductory Book to describe the meanings of the Cards in question, with *The Necronomicon Cycle* having been written to cover that purpose. It is for this reason, as stated, that I draw heavily from the Introductory Book from the second Edition of this Deck in discussion in order to put forward a clear discussion as to what this religious Deck says as according to The Cult of R'Lyeh as a religious orientation.

The Dunwich Horror

However, with that as an important first statement in hand, the Card that was in the previous Edition of this Tarot defined as being the R'Lyeh Rising, is instead now depicted as being the Card which is currently planned as being, instead, The Dunwich Horror. With this point in hand, the concept as involved with *The Necronomicon Cycle,* is to express this position as defined as being our religious orientation, as best we can, by making the least use of resources as is possible in here defining our view. Therefore, if this is here defining our terms on which we are discussing this point,

the Introductory Book to the previous edition of this as our significant religious Deck, does a good job in defining this as the sixteenth Card of the Major Arcana on purely Lovecraftian terms, and so I will write in order to continue with this same statement of religion, whilst this is now defined as according to a different representation of the system of Lovecraftian magick.

Whilst I'm here writing on the subject of *The Necronomicon Cycle* and the research therefore involved with writing this book (further to a number of statements already put forward), I feel that this might be a good place to put the point that, throughout the rest of this discussion on the greater importance of the Lovecraftian in the discussion of religious acceptance of the occult, I will continue to quote extensively from a reference titled *The Cthulhu Mythos Encyclopedia*, by the Lovecraftian and religious scholar, Dan Harms.[1] This book in hand is an excellent and comprehensive reference on these religious concepts as expressed throughout the rest of this book on the Tarot and the Lovecraftian occult, and is – I believe – one of few books written to have properly done justice to the religious orientation of the Cult of R'Lyeh on Earth as an underground movement of *Necronomicon* religious orientation. Whilst we would recommend that everyone with such an interest should sit down and read this book through, the concept of the Dunwich Horror, as is represented with this Card of the Tarot, is described in context with the *Cthulhu Mythos Encyclopedia*, in that:

> "[Dunwich is a] Town in north central Massachusetts, a few miles north of Aylesbury... During the late summer of 1928, a strange calamity occurred which has since been dubbed 'the Dunwich Horror'. On August 3, a Dunwich resident named Wilbur Whateley, noted by his neighbours for his magical delving's and unnatural size, was killed while trying to obtain [a copy of] *The Necronomicon*

---

1 I quote much more extensively from The Cthulhu Mythos Encyclopedia by Dan Harms in Part III of this book, which centres specifically on the subject of the Minor Arcana, but the Magus should continue reading to establish this point and what's here being said...

from the Miskatonic University Library. A month later, the horror began in Dunwich. A mysterious blast destroyed Wilbur Whateley's unoccupied house, and tales of the disappearance of cattle and people began to filter out of the township… On September 15 [an exorcism was] performed… on Sentinel Hill, bringing the horror to an end… Archaeologists and geologists know Dunwich for the stone circles which top many of the nearby hills, as well as mysterious underground noises heard around Walpurgis and Halloween" (Harms: 2008: 84)

The *Tarot Workbook*, by the occult scholar Nevill Drury, as our next main reference of study, makes a good statement to represent this Card of the Tarot in stating:

"The Tower serves as a reminder that humility is required on the inner journey, and that the influx of divine energy from the higher realms of the Tree [of life] will prove too overwhelming unless our inner self is well balanced and has a solid foundation. The Tower is ruled by Mars, who ruthlessly destroys ignorance and vain conceptions." (Drury: 2006: 76)

With our discussion of Card 15 (that which is represented by the personification of The Devil) being largely concerned with our psychology as a social species, and of the darker side of our minds as being represented by the Toad God, now the Card that is now represented as the Dunwich Horror represents the psychology of groups and society on the greater level. In the literature of the Mythos as Worshipped here, Lovecraft describes the Dunwich Horror on equal terms to the conscious acknowledgement of the mind as previously discussed, which, when accidentally discovered, led to the incurable

insanity of those who witnessed it.[2] This Card could, therefore, be seen in terms of representing the rising of various social and political movements, possibly having been instigated by the psychick vibrations of the Great Old Ones.

"It is human", starts the description to Card 16, "to repress... memories and feelings, pushing them... into... our unconscious self so that we can avoid the... feelings evoked by these memories. It is a... trait of the Cosmos to... force us to deal with them before they... rot... like an emotional cancer" (Hutchinson, Friedman: 2002: 38). An interpretation of this statement from the perspective of the R'Lyeh, as a religion established to uphold such esoteric views, would be that everything that is of emotional reason within our (everybody's) everyday lives, and therefore a part of the psychology of the individual, is actually as a direct result of the larger matrix of the Cosmos as one greater whole. The Universe is, to the Cult of R'Lyeh, as an organization established to uphold one religious truth, one unified space, and with the Gods of our Worship being so huge, They exist within this matrix on a scale on which the human race is, to Them, like the insane civilizations of the insects.

Our Tarot expresses this as it follows this statement, telling us that "[t]his is the Cosmic Intelligence forcing a... process on us" (Hutchinson, Friedman: 2002: 38). This 'Cosmic Intelligence' is the combined Universe as expressed in terms of the religion of the R'Lyeh, with our Mythos of Gods as depicted in this as our Tarot system. In taking this idea forward, then, "It is [a]... human tendency to project... negative traits onto unusual individuals and minority groups, thereby setting ourselves up for additional problems" (Hutchinson, Friedman: 2002: 38). With this statement the infinite chaos of the Universe comes straight back upon us as a race of many varied and confused societies, and the impetus is once again on us as responsible, before any

---

2 This is another idea taken from Lovecraft's fictional story, 'Call of Cthulhu' (Lovecraft: 1999: 139). Whilst our religion does not consider such a thing to be a statement of fact, it relates to The Tower as part of our study of the Major Arcana in this specific context.

acknowledgement of the Gods can change our situation. "The tendency to externalise... negative characteristics is often very subtle... but often takes a clearly evident and often violent form when... on a group or communal level" (Hutchinson, Friedman: 2002: 38). The problems of this race and the Planet is inherently ours as human beings, and is not the fault or decision of any of the Gods as They watch us in our futility and further chaotic madness.

Society is then further defined as a definition of its own within the larger system which is defined as being the Tarot, and a statement about our actions as a collective social consciousness is made. "Rather than dealing with communal failing and weaknesses in a progressive way, a descent into despair... and then misdirected anger... prove to undermine the community" (Hutchinson, Friedman: 2002: 39), is stated by the Introductory Book to the second Edition of this Deck discussed. This statement describes to us how the problems of collective individuals can become the problem of society, and therefore defines this as a position which should be understood as being religious.

But in understanding this point of defined conceptualisation, the *HP Lovecraft Tarot* continues to explain to us how the collective mass can also operate as a productive whole. "[W]hen th[is] weakness is recognised... and dealt with... (either as an individual or as part of a group), it becomes a powerful source of strength and an unshakable foundation for further growth" (Hutchinson, Friedman: 2002: 39). As the Dunwich Horror was described as that esoteric evil which had hidden in the hills underneath the knowledge of the human society around It, human society then acted as the organized collective, both as destructive disorganisation and as a unified mass of one mind.

This general statement continues as the Introductory Book to the second Edition of this Tarot (when read in context) goes on to tell us that, "the Devil can't make anyone do anything they don't want to do, so don't make a habit of blaming the Devil" (Hutchinson, Friedman: 2002: 39). Whilst the Cult of R'Lyeh do not acknowledge the existence

of any 'Devil' as upheld by other dominant religions,[3] we can always regard one as such in the principal in such a statement as this in the specific context as how this is discussed by *The Necronomicon*, as our religious book in question does.

With *The Necronomicon Cycle* having already defined society and our weaknesses in a sense that could in some sense be seen as being political, the definition of this Card as a part of a Positive Reading now speaks to the individual on a more personal level. With all of the problems that we, as humanity, have on a central level, the Tarot now speaks to us to explain how this description of the risen R'Lyeh applies to us as reading the Cards. The idea is that such social movements can always relate in some way to the individual, as the individual is the only consciousness in any situation.

The *HP Lovecraft Tarot* therefore states that a Positive reading is here defined as signifying "necessary change imposed by external forces when unable to initiate change from within" (Hutchinson, Friedman: 2002: 39). What sort of 'external forces' this relates to, exactly, is not immediately or directly clear, but within the R'Lyeh as a religious movement and organization, it is our belief that in Worshiping the Great Old Ones, we are in recognition of the constant back-brain communication that results from being in tune with the psychick resonance that this entails. It is assumed that, with this defined, when we are in a situation that necessitates personal change, this will arise from acknowledgement of the power of greater Cosmic forces, should we be unable to initiate this inherent situation of change by ourselves.

This statement in question continues by defining a position as regarding a "catalyst for growth [and] recognising weakness & working within it" (Hutchinson, Friedman: 2002: 39). Both of these statements can further be seen as being issues with society, should this be appropriate to the Reading, but it would be more immediate to consider this on the level of being relevant to ourselves. Our Tarot in

---

3 The previous Card, that being represented as Tsathoggua, makes a brief discussion as to how the religious concept of The Devil is upheld as sacred as according to The Cult of R'Lyeh on Earth.

question continues with the same idea as it forecasts the "understanding & acceptance of diverse modes of action & comprehension of the larger picture" (Hutchinson, Friedman: 2002: 39). This with the same interpretation, should be read as it relates to the Reading in question.

The next part of the Positive Reading defined is, however, more directly obscure, and the definition more open to question. This interpretation of meaning tells us that the Tarot predicts a position hereby described as "the House of God" (Hutchinson, Friedman: 2002: 39). Concerning this statement, there is no such thing to the religious R'Lyeh; but we still have to question what this statement means in order to establish how this Tarot is important from our perspective in defining religion. Whilst this as a statement could be read as being something along the lines of something like 'an interaction with the Church of Christ', in this sense this statement has no importance to us. The reading here, therefore, could be interpreted further as meaning that there will be an acceptance of the individual into some part of the R'Lyeh, or as meaning that part of our religion will come into play in some part of our lives. This definition being no more defined, however, this is one short statement that is left to question.[4]

In moving on with such general ideas as regarding creation developing into organized social structures, the Tarot now tells us that the future will involve "therapy [or] self-help" (Hutchinson, Friedman: 2002: 39) on some level or another on personal terms. This is still in the nature of this Card as relating to ourselves and how we relate to society. Of course, 'self-help' in such a context is a term that is open to huge interpretation, but some time productively spent by ourselves or with a close friend, in sorting out our ideas, is signified as possibly coming into the situation. "Recognition and addressing of character flaws" (Hutchinson, Friedman: 2002: 39) is defined, and is in the same vein as with everything else here discussed. But remember that this is the representation which is the Dunwich Horror, and so any of this could be relating to us inwardly, and to our greater outward view of ourselves.

---

4 A statement as regarding membership of The Cult of R'Lyeh as a new religion is given at the end of this book.

Negative Reading

Our definition of a Negative interpretation of this Card starts here with a very serious warning that relates primarily on the level of society, although could just as easily relate to the personal, of "catastrophe [and] sudden, violent change" (Hutchinson, Friedman: 2002: 39). The Tarot is rarely something incredibly serious, however, but a warning in this respect should be accounted for as something to consider as possible. The Reading becomes clearer now, and next states that "arrest, imprisonment [and] defiance of natural order" (Hutchinson, Friedman: 2002: 39) are hereby signified. It should be pointed out that this forecast is in the typical nature of Card 16 as we have defined it up to this current point. In terms of such open personal flaws, the Tarot warns us of "inability to look within for threats and weaknesses" (Hutchinson, Friedman: 2002: 39). This is one example of how the Lovecraft system of the Tarot is very specific in what is tells us. Most other Decks do not go so far into these sorts of very specific statements; and therefore these statements should be seen as being very specific as to this particular Deck of Cards in discussion, and in being directly relevant as to what the *HP Lovecraft Tarot* is saying with this particular interpretation.

Having said that, the definition of this Card within this Tarot is still very much about the personal views we have as individual parts of a greater whole, and how views affect society on a greater level whilst in connection with what is personal. By defining the representation which is the Dunwich Horror now as representing "externalisation & projection of problems onto others" (Hutchinson, Friedman: 2002: 39), this reinforces our definition as written above.

The *HP Lovecraft Tarot* now moves on to say that Card 16 is representative of the religious symbolism as represented with the "Tower of Babel" (Hutchinson, Friedman: 2002: 39). But as this is a difficult term to describe in this or any other context, I'll take this as an opportunity to move on. But as one statement in itself, this paragraph

the Tarot continues as defining "divisions along ethnic, linguistic or class lines as an obstacle to progress" (Hutchinson, Friedman: 2002: 39). Whilst this primarily points to these as the issues of society, these divisions may also be those attitudes that are held by ourselves. We may not even be aware that we hold these attitudes, but Card 16 should be taken as a warning that this is possibly the case.

The Card which is in our religious system defined as being the Dunwich Horror here ends by warning us about symptoms that are more probably likely to be those held by ourselves. These are therefore defined as the "inability to face fears; depression [and] emotional deterioration" (Hutchinson, Friedman: 2002: 39). We should regard the Card of the Dunwich Horror as meaning that, whilst society has many and varied problems, those being far too many to be focused on by any book, including the books of religion, these can be reflected in ourselves. And, as society will always have these inherent problems, our own attitude can also be part of the actions of society on the greater scale.

17. NODENS, LORD OF THE GREAT ABYSS: THE STAR

Nodens, being a part of such a Mythos of worship is here represented as a water God, and here represents the boundaries of, and the transcendence through, matter and the material walls of psychological and physical existence. Where the element in consideration is Wind, Nodens stands between the Wind and the calm and placid states of the Earth. Where the boundary is stone, Nodens stands between the stone and the freedom of the open sky. He is, therefore, the mediation between stone, which cannot be passed through, and the sky, through which there is no boundary. It is for reasons such as this that the Mythos God which is Nodens can be seen as the axis between the mundane acceptance of one conscious reality, and the reality of humanity and that which we create. The occult is a much greater part of our lives than any of us realise, and Nodens represents this as a Gateway for the occultist and the worshipper of the greater Mythos as defined under the study of such esoteric lore.

Nodens, Lord of the Great Abyss

In interpreting this Card, therefore, the issue of boundaries has come to me as being obviously the main issue whilst writing to define the

meaning as established by this Card in discussion. Nodens, however, is the Card of the Tarot that equates to The Star in the vast number of other Decks, and therefore this must be considered to be a misinterpretation in the context of the Lovecraftian, as the rest of this book is written to establish. With the previous proof to this book I wrote a long definition as to how Nodens represents barriers and issues in life that cannot in any logical sense be taken further. The definition here is, however, wrong. Nodens, as a Card of the Tarot (except in its Negative sense, described below), primarily indicates good, and it is for this reason that I have had to come back to this after some period of study, with a different definition of Card 17 written for the current proof of this book. The problem came from the idea that the *HP Lovecraft Tarot* is always more sinister and on direct terms darker than with other Decks, although the Tarot as a complete system does still have to follow tradition.

The Introductory Book to the second Edition of this Tarot tells us that "Amidst the deepest darkness, a ray of hope will… be present for those who seek it" (Hutchinson, Friedman: 2002: 40). In the Worship of the Gods of *The Necronomicon* and the further defined Mythos, our religion is involved far more with the acceptance of the Great Old Ones as the astral forces of infinite insanity, and (in turn) Their involvement with the evil and chaotic madness of mankind. To draw Card 17 in a Reading is, therefore, to equate to a principle that there may be a diversion from our previous fixation with darkness; and that this may be an omen of luck in a time where it may be needed. In this sense this Card continues as with similar interpretations as defined with all other systems of the Tarot. "[L]ight will shine for all with an honest Will to Receive it" (Hutchinson, Friedman: 2002: 40), continues the Introductory Book to the second Edition of this system discussed. "[I]t is amidst the Saturnine depths of human action that… the greatest light shines" (Hutchinson, Friedman: 2002: 40). In order to define this Card, therefore, Nodens in a Positive Reading here is generally speaking entirely good, and indicates the very real possibility that we will receive some form of divine inspiration as reward for our dedicated worship of the Cosmic Forces which are at all times around us in Their silence.

From this statement that defines the point of the Card directly, this interpretation of the Tarot continues to define its terms, in saying that "it is the purest light which turns the Lead of Saturn into Lunar Silver and Solar Gold" (Hutchinson, Friedman: 2002: 40). It is my interpretation that this statement is in relation to the historical users of magick throughout the previous ages of Man, and their construction of ritual items of magick through such acts of religious worship. The Great Old Ones have infinite faces in Their mad forms of existence, and it is through such Lunar Silver and Solar Gold that They have been summoned throughout the existence of our race. "Only when the Darkness draws Nyarlathotep out... can Nodens vanquish him..." (Hutchinson, Friedman: 2002: 40) states our study in question. Whilst Nyarlathotep is our God of communication, as previously discussed, the evil of the Old Ones must always be considered, and here we have the Mythos God Nodens entering the stage as an esoteric form of occult and religious protection. This continues to equate with all other interpretations of the Tarot, as the Lovecraft Deck equates specifically to our religion as a focus of esoteric truth.

As this paragraph opens the Introduction to the defined discussion with this Card, we see a statement enter the discussion as concerns the seasons of the year. This specific statement of definition may not be entirely in line with the religious values as upheld by the Cult of R'Lyeh, in interpreting this Tarot in order to define our own outlook on greater religion, but hints that maybe the Card of Nodens has had thought from the Cults of the Druids; as the Star is a direct symbol of good as described by most other Decks of the same aspect. "As the constellations turn, and the seasons change... not all is Winter" (Hutchinson, Friedman: 2002: 40). The Star, as represented by Nodens, then, tells of good things that result from the course of our worship as already defined.

Despite the fact that the worship of the Lovecraftian Gods is directly Satanic and oriented around the power of insanity, if you would accept the religious values as upheld by so many other more 'orthodox' religions, Card 17 can still have an equation with every other traditional

Deck. Therefore – as with every other Deck discussed– a Positive Reading with this Card can be nothing bad, and pulling it from the Deck here would usually represent a position that good things are forecast. The statement "Hope, promise [and] faith" is an example of such things when this Card is drawn, and the Lovecraft Tarot continues that this represents "confidence [and] security amidst apparent hardship" (Hutchinson, Friedman: 2002: 41).

As the Introduction to the second Edition of this Tarot continues in this same manner, Card 17 may be representative of ourselves and of our attitude to life as positive things come into our lives, as ultimately they sometimes must do. This may be the issue to consider as the stated study of this Introductory Book continues that "harvest, reward; profit realised after work & investment; gain & advantage" (Hutchinson, Friedman: 2002: 41) is defined. In my own opinion, something that occurs to me at this point is that the *HP Lovecraft Tarot* continues in respect that what we take from the occult is directly related to what we put in. I suppose the point here would be that each person must gain from the worship we put in, or otherwise what would be the purpose of continuing to worship?

In regard to the line that Card 17 is as much about our attitude to what is happening in our own lives, the *HP Lovecraft Tarot* justifies this point when it defines a Positive Reading as signifying "laughter in the face of threats; endurance [and] tolerance" (Hutchinson, Friedman: 2002: 41). As with all aspects of the occult, it is our attitude to the games that the occult challenges us with, that is really the most important issue to the religious study in question.

Negative Reading

Whilst Card 17 of this system of the Tarot, being Nodens, equates with the Tarot system of the Star (as this Card is depicted with most other esoteric Decks), this is a Card that is usually most properly equated with good. However, it is always possible that any Card of any system of the Tarot can appear as Negative in a spread, and this

17. Nodens, Lord of the Great Abyss: The Star

is also defined in the Lovecraft Deck of the Tarot. But in the context of a Negative Reading here, Nodens is as much about attitude in this sense, as with the Positive. "Insecurity, lack of faith; surrender to fears, hopelessness; despair despite stability" (Hutchinson, Friedman: 2002: 41) are all symptoms here as defined by the *HP Lovecraft Tarot*; but it should be remembered that if this is symbolised by Nodens, it may be more due to our lack of balance and earthing in the occult that is the reason. This system of the Tarot in discussion continues to say that "disadvantage, weakness; loss of position, loss of confidence; loss of illusionary advantage and / or loss of power" (Hutchinson, Friedman: 2002: 41) is indicated. Again, this can often be down to the same thing – problems with spiritual balance and earthing – although the issue here is probably more to do with our image and perception of ourselves as infinitesimally smaller parts of the Cosmos and a smaller collective race.

It is in terms this idea as representing our self-image, as therefore defined, that the Negative interpretation of this Card is continued. It is in terms of attitude that we should consider the explanation in the Introductory Book that comes with the previously published Edition of this Deck, as defining "submission to doubts; worries, complaints, qualms, hesitance, uncertainty [and] indecision" (Hutchinson, Friedman: 2002: 41). Again we find the Tarot telling us that it is our perspective that is the important issue, and we should look to our attitude if we are worshiping the Cthulhu Mythos, as we must look inwardly if we are to understand the mysteries of Cosmic Space and the greater truth of the Universe around us.

18. Night Gaunt: The Moon

As we reach Card 18, this represents the Card of the Tarot which is in most Decks the Card that is defined as The Moon. The Lovecraft Deck is, however, always more complicated and always quite unique unto itself as a religious study, and in representing

Night-Gaunt

everything that is esoteric about the Lunar atmosphere of the night, the Lovecraft Deck represents this symbolic idea as being The Night Gaunt. With this definition thereby made clear, this Card is defined as the suppressed and frightening ideas held by the subconscious mind of the Magus in reading this Card into an interpretation of meaning. The definition of our system of Tarot now starts to become quite significantly dark in its descriptions and definition. With this as the darkness of the night, and with the Moon as representing the suppressed ideas of our sleep then, we define this

Card in terms of the nightmares that are suppressed through the slumber which is known to us as our dreams, and those darks secrets that are always there and pushed into the deeper recesses of the subconscious mind. Here we continue to describe the meaning of the *HP Lovecraft Tarot* under our own terms as a unique interpretation and under our own religious definition; and this description relates to our specific system of worship as differentiated from the rest of the religious orientations

upheld by the greater societies of Man.

This Card, therefore, is very much a Card that belongs to the occult, as in the darkness of the subconsciousness our innermost fears are uppermost, and this is especially the case when we are asleep. In this respect we should be aware that attack may be threatened, both in terms of psychick manipulation in the occult, but also in terms of that 'which should not be' It is on the basis of such defined terms that *The Tarot Workbook* defines this point in that "The lunar crescent dominates the imagery of the Moon and mirrors the symbolism of the lunar sphere Yesod on the Tree of Life – a sphere associated with dreams, fertility, and the astral imagery of the subconscious mind" (Drury: 2006: 80). Whilst our study of the Great Old Ones starts at the nucleus of chaos with Azathoth representing the madness of creation, the creation of life, and progression of humanity as an individual creation of the Great Old Ones, now Card 18 moves on to define as statement as to the definition of human society and how we as people uphold custom and law in order to coexist. I find it interesting, then, that this definition has been concentrated on by the *HP Lovecraft Tarot*, as The Moon is the Card that usually dominates dreams and the psychick communication of mankind and of spirits in the plane of the mind and the unconscious manifestation of Astral travel through dream.

The definition of the Card which is defined as being The Night Gaunt here begins that "Winged creatures of the Night, faceless and mysterious, the Night Gaunts are the messengers… of the Dreamlands. The messages they bring us are from… our unconscious and subconscious selves" (Hutchinson, Friedman: 2002: 42). If the Cards in this Deck have at times concerned people such as Jung and the theories of Psychoanalysis, we are now thrown straight in with these ideas of the unconscious and subconscious mind as esoteric. And whilst these ideas are understood by many, the author would here assume that the reader is not trained in such studies. I will therefore try to define this Card in more direct terms of description, and the related theories of psychology as according to someone who would have little knowledge of such a branch of Psychology in question.

If the Tarot continues in this manner in terms of the contemporary study of the mind, it now tells us that, in the context of the above statement on subconscious perception, "if we are not prepared for it, this information can be... dangerous, and traumatic" (Hutchinson, Friedman: 2002: 42). What this is telling us is that certain experiences that are traumatic in childhood (and so forth) stay repressed in the recesses of our minds. Our mind will keep these memories, but they will not enter the conscious mind that is our awareness of the situation we experience in the current moment. These experiences always stay with us, however, and at a certain time they may possibly re-enter the conscious experiences of our minds. In these situations, these recollections can be extremely traumatic. The Night Gaunt is here to tell us, therefore, that we should be careful of this state of awareness if this should be apparent. In this sense, therefore, the Eighteenth Card should be taken to be a warning against us delving too deeply into our own subconsciousness (perhaps through the use of psychology and self-hypnosis or possibly in the unintentional uncontrolled use of psychick energy?) The *HP Lovecraft Tarot* defines this point that "Night Gaunts are faceless... they are those aspects of ourselves that we – consciously or unconsciously – will not confront directly" (Hutchinson, Friedman: 2002: 42). This being the definition as given to us in the Introductory Book to the previous Edition of this study – maybe this is therefore telling us that we shouldn't confront aspects of ourselves if this is going to be too emotionally traumatic on conscious terms?

The Introductory Book to the previous Edition of this Tarot continues with the definition of Card 18, to make the statement that it is the unconscious and subconscious self-understanding of the people that allows society to interact as a movement of many people in unity. "The structures... of society serve an... important function" (Hutchinson, Friedman: 2002: 43) it tells us. It is the structures which have been set up (supposedly) by a unitary agreement of the people, but the *HP Lovecraft Tarot* continues with the same statement by going on to tells us that "our shadow... is only a danger when repressed and left unexpressed..." (Hutchinson, Friedman: 2002: 43). The Night gaunt is

defined, therefore, as a particular Card in this Tarot that refers directly to issues of psychick energy and issues of contemporary Psychoanalysis. If we are to consider ideas of the subconscious being left 'repressed and... unexpressed', then this is an issue which cannot be addressed by the individual, and intervention by somebody else is thus necessary in acting upon this Card in divination, should this position be the case in question.

The definition of this Card continues to state that a problem if so defined in a reading with this Tarot can lead to a mental illness that could "tear us to shreds, like a werewolf at the full moon. But when [the subconscious is] given a voice, it is the... most honest source of human power, genius, and inspiration" (Hutchinson, Friedman: 2002: 43). The Night Gaunt is to be taken seriously, therefore, and this Card may mean that we are dealing seriously with issues of psychology and the mind – but the potential with a Positive Reading with this Card could make it possibly the most powerful in the Deck.

The point would therefore be obvious that this definition is written with consideration of Card 18 as relating to the unconscious mind. With this Card defined as above, the Positive Reading here concentrates on some of the darker issues of the religious R'Lyeh, whilst the Negative is the only discussion of Mythos Worship with our specific and concentrated consideration of evil. The definition here begins as defined as meaning "the primal power of darkness as a resource to be drawn on; Night as mother of us all" (Hutchinson, Friedman: 2002: 43). In this the power of darkness is on overt terms a positive thing: the power of the night is therefore the benefactor of the worship of the Old Ones – the understanding of this is not a form of anything that the Magus should consider as negative. "Dark – but not 'Black' – magick" (Hutchinson, Friedman: 2002: 43) is defined under this statement of meaning – although the question here concerns the issues of the occult as an issue of worship. Surely with the worship of the Gods of *The Necronomicon*, black magick would be the form of the occult that should usually be used? Anyway, with this statement defined, the Positive meaning of the Night Gaunt continues as follows:

For the first time with this religious system in hand, the *HP Lovecraft Tarot* speaks of astral dimensions and the issues of the religious R'Lyeh of Lovecraft's land beyond sleep, which is by the consensus of the worshippers of The Great Old Ones, known as the Dreamlands. Card 18 in a Reading can therefore be symbolic that the person for whom the reading is for, will find themselves travelling the lands beyond normal states of sleep. This can be representative of somebody relating to the reading travelling beyond such normal realms of sleep, and also into that dimension of dream where most of our worship exists in terms of such defined strange dimensions. It may be interpreted that serious dream work should be considered by the person for whom the Reading in question is for , or that we may be visited for some reason in our sleep state by entities as described by the study of such a religious Mythos.[1]

It would be appropriate in this consideration, therefore, that the Introduction to this previous Deck of the Tarot continues to define the Night Gaunt as signifying an involvement from "the Inner Realms of magic & imagination [and] shamanism" (Hutchinson, Friedman: 2002: 43). With this statement now defined, we can read Card 18 as symbolic of the freedom and power of the mind when directed as worship in the context of the use of hallucinogens as part of shamanic ritual. With this concentration of the human mind, we are now speaking in terms of directly worshipping Mythos Gods in terms of magick. This should be the religious duty of the R'Lyeh in writing to deliver our statement of religion to the wider population of users of magick and the movement of the occult.

In getting towards the last statement under the definition of the Positive in a reading, this is defined as "Assimilation of the Shadow into a holistic consciousness & state of being" (Hutchinson, Friedman: 2002: 43). Whilst this takes us directly back to our previous discussion

---

[1] Work in terms of dream is a practice of the religious Cult of R'Lyeh on Earth, and we see it that such dream work has direct effect in terms of our own use of magick, although this idea is not covered in serious detail as part of this book, as such.

of psychology, I interpret this as meaning an assumption of the negative around us as a directly beneficial power. The negative around us has now been understood and turned into a force of positivity that the Magus can use.

Negative Reading

The whole of the Negative Reading with this Card can also be interpreted as being a part of the religion of the R'Lyeh, and therefore as relative to our use of the occult as a form of worship. However, as "Black magic, necromancy; confrontation and / or conflict with the Shadow without proper preparation" (Hutchinson, Friedman: 2002: 43) is defined, the Negative Reading with Card 18 can be representative that dark forces are at play in our lives, the involvement of Daemon worship, or otherwise representative of ourselves being in the position of using such forces without using the proper preparation.

The Negative Meaning goes on to make a statement as to our personal frame of mind and further the importance of such means of concentration. As a definition of "Nightmare" (Hutchinson, Friedman: 2002: 43) is foretold, we may have an issue that a part of our subconscious needs to be resolved, or that there may be dark forces at play in our sleep that we are not ready to contend with. And as the definition continues with a statement as to define a situation involving "intoxication; delusion, hallucination, alcoholism, drug abuse" (Hutchinson, Friedman: 2002: 43), this could be symbolic of a situation as could arise, that we are indulging too much, and – whilst it is totally acceptable to the Cult of R'Lyeh to be using drugs within limits – it is always sensible to maintain a mind-frame where we are aware of our own involvement with the astral forces of our worship as we make use of black magick and the greater practice of the occult as discussed.

The definition as described with this statement here concludes with a statement that is defined as "Externalisation & demonization of the shadow" (Hutchinson, Friedman: 2002: 43). Again this is an example of the *HP Lovecraft Tarot* and where it makes direct reference to the

principals of Psychoanalysis. In this our Deck is often not always entirely clear to the layman as to what such statements directly mean, but the statement above explains this with the position of clarity which is necessary. The *HP Lovecraft Tarot* here concludes by defining "political correctness" (Hutchinson, Friedman: 2002: 43) as being an issue, although where this should arise as a part of the Negative Reading, I am not entirely sure?

With this statement then having been properly discussed, the definition of the Night Gaunt can be interpreted as directly relating to the greater understanding of the philosophical ideas which are psychology. It should be remembered, though, that all of this is only in relative terms to the Magus, and if the system of Necronomicon magick is taken seriously, then divination with this Card is relative and directly appropriate to, the proper and established use of black magick.

19. Yig, The Serpent God: The Sun

In most traditional Decks of the Tarot, Card 19 of the Major Arcana is representative of the symbology that is represented as the concept which is defined as being the Sun. And whereas Card 18 can be seen to be making a direct statement about the subconscious fears of the suppressed nature of the mind, Yig the Serpent God makes reference to the Earthly Cults of humanity.[1] "The journey of the Sun through the Zodiac, and its connections and intersections with other celestial spheres, provides us with a new set of paradigms and archetypes which operate on a number of different levels" (Hutchinson, Friedman: 2002: 44), is a point stated by this religious Tarot in question. The ancient Druidic religions and Cults of humanity constructed stone circles which were immensely sophisticated

Yig, the Serpent God

---

[1] If the student of Necronomicon magick should be interested in taking this study to any extent further, we would strongly recommend reading *Cults of the Shadow* by the noted occultist Kenneth Grant. This writer in question has already been briefly mentioned in this book and is one of very few who has represented the religious views represented by the Cult of R'Lyeh as a religious movement. All of his work is seriously recommended to anyone who might have any interest in the occult worship of the Great Old Ones. Grant has a history of being published by various publishers, and *Cults of the Shadow* was first published by Muller Books in 1975. A bibliographical reference for this book is Grant, K. (1994) *Cults of the Shadow*; London; Skoob Books.

and intelligent in themselves, and entire religious cultures spent generations plotting and constructing such circles, with this effort of concerted worship being an acknowledgement of the transition of the stars and therefore related to the esoteric manifestation of the Gods. And the plotting of the seasons according to the this study of the stars represented "the mythic journey through the Overworld… in contrast to the Underworld quest of card XV" (Hutchinson, Friedman: 2002: 44), which has already been discussed as the Card of the Tarot which represents Tsathoggua and the symbolism as upheld as being The Devil. Whilst the Card that is ruled by Tsathoggua represented the insanity and darkness which is human psychology, this Card now represents the clarity and intelligent thought of man. The *HP Lovecraft Tarot* points out that "In contrast to… card [XV] is Yig, the serpent of cosmic order" (Hutchinson, Friedman: 2002: 44).

Whilst the whole of this definition in question would seem to revolve around the philosophical idea that is circles, the *HP Lovecraft Tarot* tells us that Yig, the Serpent God, "can be equated in our mythic context with the constellation of Draco. While the Sun travels around the wheel of the Zodiac, Draco is the central hub and spokes of that wheel" (Hutchinson, Friedman: 2002: 44). In this context we are now allowed to refer back to the start of this Tarot with astrology and the Cosmos again being the principles in question. Azathoth, the Blind Idiot God, stands at the centre and the nucleus of creation, this being the centre of the Universe and the catalyst of chaos and insanity without reason. Now the Serpent God Yig comes into the equation, and with this nucleus He is now at the centre of the single understanding of humanity as an intelligent psychological species. We have now moved on from the chaotic madness of Cosmological creation, through concepts representing the development of human religious society, towards the primeval understanding of the Cosmos around us as possessed by mankind as a psychological animal.

The *HP Lovecraft Tarot* reinforces this realization when it states that "having been through the Underworld and confronted the shadows of the previous cards, the mythic journey is now one of triumph"

(Hutchinson, Friedman: 2002: 44). The Cthulhu Mythos is a dark and Satanic way of looking the Cards of the Tarot which define so many different religious perspectives, but now positive energies are beginning to come into play, and as the worshippers of one actual reality of Gods we must understand that, even with this as our outlook, there is always a positive aspect to all systems of religious worship. And it is with this realisation that we understand our position as being like insects in comparison to the greater intellect of the Gods, as "conformity to the cosmic order" (Hutchinson, Friedman: 2002: 44) is now the position established.

The *HP Lovecraft Tarot* continues with this defined statement of terms to say "But this is not a card of submission" (Hutchinson, Friedman: 2002: 45). As being further described as representing such a position of Astral truth "[the Card as defined with the personification of Yig] represents the 'royal' or rather Divine spark in all of us, realising itself and being recognised by others" (Hutchinson, Friedman: 2002: 45). Whilst we may not support, but will at the same time acknowledge, an established position of monarchy in society, every person has it within ourselves to be 'royal'. This does not equate to being in any position of authority, but instead to being respected within a social or religious order. Therefore the Card of the Serpent God should be seen in this light: that everybody has the potential to become as a star in the eternity of madness, darkness, and the infinite scope that is the occult transition of time.

If Card 18 symbolised society and means of social structure, the Serpent God now refers to individuals becoming powerful or respected, and relates directly to the concept of the individual becoming great. The *HP Lovecraft Tarot* continues here to describe a Positive meaning with this Card as signifying "Royalty as a spiritual quality inherent in all humanity" (Hutchinson, Friedman: 2002: 45). What I interpret from this definition is a meaning that everybody has the ability to be a leader. Whereas a large number of political nation States have an imposed Monarchy and political order, the term 'royal' here can also be a term to relate to somebody in society who has attained an elevated position of

status, and can therefore lead a movement of society. In regard to our own religion as being the Cult of R'Lyeh on Earth, most people do not attain the position of 'royal', although this does occasionally happen. However, "the quest to realise and incorporate this quality into one's being" (Hutchinson, Friedman: 2002: 45) indicates a self-chosen path to achieve virtue, and status achieved within social organisation or the secular religions of cultism.

This path through life and ambition to achieve is here described by both the *HP Lovecraft Tarot* and the ideas of the psychiatrist Jung as being "The Hero's Journey" (Hutchinson, Friedman: 2002: 45),[2] and if we see our transition through life as a journey, then Yig describes a positive attitude being accepted, and a real possibility of success is therefore indicated with this Card. The statement that this represents "archetypal patterns of journey and initiation" (Hutchinson, Friedman: 2002: 45) tells us that the situations we encounter whilst we travel this journey are, in fact, to be seen as occult initiation, and that each one can be seen directly as a situation to learn from. In stating that this Card is representative of "healthy ambition and progressive goals" (Hutchinson, Friedman: 2002: 45), the *HP Lovecraft Tarot* is here telling us that by having a positive attitude to such occult initiations, as they are, we are set to positively benefit from all of this, although we should be careful to see these as they are. This Card is therefore a statement that, as we travel forward through a progressive transition of time, as no one can escape from or control, our experience of life will be one of initiation under the astral forces of the Old Ones as our entire focus of worship.

Negative Reading

If the Positive Reading as regards the God of the Snakes relates to positive circumstances as regards our personal lives, and of these

---

2 The Tarot describes the future situation of the Magus in terms of Jung's Journey of the Hero. This point of psychoanalytical theory, in short, makes a statement to describe progression from one state of existence to the next.

circumstances being due to our having positive attitude towards this transition of time, then the Negative could relate to the direct opposite – as is often the case when we regard the Tarot in these terms. So the Negative Reading here relates to a situation in life which is unsound, despite our acts of worship, and situations which should be changed if we are to progress to better things. Such negative circumstances are projected back onto the Magus with the *HP Lovecraft Tarot*, and it would relate to such situations being due to our own attitudes to life being the issues which should be looked at if this is to be changed. "Pride, arrogance [and] conceit" (Hutchinson, Friedman: 2002: 45) are hereby defined in the context of a Reading, as are attitudes of "seeking dominance and authority as an ends in itself" (Hutchinson, Friedman: 2002: 45). Such attitudes are opposed by the Cult of R'Lyeh, and if the Tarot speaks of these attitudes, then they are something that must be considered before any more works of Ceremonial magick are to be undertaken.

The Negative Reading goes further, however, and defines a position of "Puerile ideals and 'comic book' virtues; immaturity [and] childish goals" (Hutchinson, Friedman: 2002: 45). So, if the Lovecraft system of Tarot can define such personal attitudes as being inherently negative, then the Cult of R'Lyeh are religious as we accept it as a system within our religion which is appropriate to the significance of personal attitudes in a context such as this, and if such issues are at play, then they must be considered in terms of the progression to higher levels of meditation and the R'Lyeh practices of ceremonial black magick. As a religious Temple we see it that such attitudes as defined by this Card in this context are often not immediately realised by the Magus, so if this is to be pointed out by the Nineteenth Card, then it is considered that it is good to have this defined before any further work with Ceremonial magick is to be entered into or enacted.

This statement as concerns the appropriate mental attitude towards Ritual is furthered as the Negative definition with Card 19 concludes with a statement to define that "Unstable effort; lack of commitment or ambition; wallflower, fuddled & jaded personality" (Hutchinson,

Friedman: 2002: 45) are points that are now in play. The practice of Ceremonial magick relates in its entirety on a stable frame of mind and the ability to focus psychick energy in order to ascend to the higher levels of worship. A Negative Reading with Card 19 says that we should step back and review our own attitudes towards magick if we are to worship our chosen Mythos of Gods as is defined by *The Necronomicon* as our religious statement in hand. This statement, then, concerns our frame of mind in the context of psychick meditation towards the works of Ceremonial magick, and this Card, then, makes a statement as to our thinking in terms of progression to the higher levels of standing in the occult and as a member of this Temple of R'Lyeh as upholding the principles of ritual and ceremonial black magick.

20. Dagon: Judgement

Since the publication of the previous Deck of the *HP Lovecraft Tarot*, the main obvious differences to the amended publication here would be on the basis that the religious representation as defined by some of the Cards of this system have been changed. With the rest of the Cards that have therefore been amended it should not be too difficult to read these changes in context (with the previous edition) and then to adapt the relevant research. Card 20 with this interpretation of the Tarot – in this case as represented by Dagon – would therefore be the significant most important example of this idea in question. Whilst the previous edition of this Deck defined Card 20 in terms of being the concept of Cthulhu Awakens, now we have an entirely different concept with which to discuss. At the same time we still have the same issues defined as according to our research, and if the Introductory Book to the previous edition would make a specific discussion of how this as a part of the Major Arcana is defined as a part of the concept of the religious *Necronomicon*, then we are obliged to use this same research in order to establish the symbolic meaning as represented by Dagon, the Fish God.

Whilst it has been pointed out that the previous edition of this Tarot

in question discussed this Card in terms of being Cthulhu Awakens, there are a number of points here to discuss before going into detail as regarding the specific meaning as described with this Card. The first of these would be the same specific comparisons to be made with this Card and the archetypal principals as defined under the construct of the Fish God, and in quoting again from the *Cthulhu Mythos Encyclopedia*, Dagon is a "Minor being that leads the deep ones and in turn serves Cthulhu… It has been claimed that Dagon is only an avatar of Cthulhu, a portion of that being which was not trapped beneath [the sunken city of] R'Lyeh" (Harms: 2008: 66)

As a second point to note, the concept of Dagon the Fish God is one that is acknowledged on the greater scale of religion, as a number of faiths regard such an entity as being integral to their religious outlook, and this point is established in quoting again from the same source that "Dagon… was originally a Semitic fertility god worshipped by the Sumerians, Akkadians, Caanites, and philistines. Samson knocked down a temple of Dagon upon his tormentors" (Harms: 2008: 66)

It should be here pointed out that the religious validity of the Cult of R'Lyeh, in representing this study of *The Necronomicon* as defining such a statement of religious truth, is quite often on the basis of how such religious views tie in with the ideas of other religions. On this basis the above quotation can be further justified on the basis of further study, as the Christian *Bible* states that "Now the rulers of the Philistines assembled to offer a great sacrifice to Dagon their god and to celebrate, saying, 'Our god has delivered Samson, our enemy, in to our hands'" (NIV: Judges 16:12).

If the *Cthulhu Mythos Encyclopedia* expands on this point in saying "when the Ark of the Covenant was left in the temple of Dagon, the statue of that deity was mutilated" (Harms: 2008: 66), then this point is further established on religious terms, in that the *Bible* continues this discussion that "Then they carried the ark into Dagon's temple and set it beside Dagon" (NIV: 1 Samuel 5:2), before such an act of religious desecration was enacted.

Having worked through this interpretation of the Tarot, and defined

this under our own terms, the Card that is usually 'Judgement' is here defined by the Lovecraft Deck as 'Cthulhu Awakens'.

The religious view of the Cult of R'Lyeh on this subject is quite simple. Whilst Cthulhu rests, being dead but still dreaming in His underwater Tomb, when the Stars are Right He will rise from His slumber. With this being His rising, humanity will then be judged in our evil, and the Old Ones will again take control of the Cosmos. Whilst this is the reason for worshipping this as our system of Gods, however, Cthulhu Awakens, as a Card of the Lovecraft Tarot, still has a clear definition within this study, and so needs to be described in this context.

With the previous definitions of the Cards of this Tarot having been discussed, it should be obvious to the Reader that the Cards can be interpreted as according to their traditional meanings, as well as with this statement as to the Lovecraftian. With this being defined, then, I will discuss this Card as according to the principals of Ceremonial magick as accords to the Cult of R'Lyeh, as opposed to any other meaning of any other Card as accords to this as a system of divination.[1] In this context it should be obvious to the Reader of the Tarot what this Card represents, whilst to the R'Lyeh the Tarot stands as a key towards an understanding of Ritual magick.

In this respect the Lovecraft Tarot reflects this idea when it says that "the key point [to this definition] is the return to the direct rulership of Divine Will over the Earth. It is the renewal of an ancient order, the restoration of clear vision and the end of strife (if naught else, servitude to the Great Old Ones will end our bickering amongst ourselves)" (Hutchinson, Friedman: 2002: 46).

To write some sort of definition to this statement, it is ours to interpret this statement according to the definition of Divine or 'True Will' as accords to the religious views of the Cults of Crowley and the Hermetic Order of the Golden Dawn of Thelema. This statement,

---

1 If, by any chance, the Magus should want more information as to where this stands as divination, other books on the Tarot will describe the meaning of 'Justice' according to this in context.

taken in itself, makes the statement that the actions of 'True Will', according to the Worship of Dagon, will put His worshippers in control of religious society. True Will is the genuine evocation of the forces of the occult, and such a 'renewal of ancient order' and 'restoration of clear vision' is here prophesised as meaning that, when we properly evoke the forces of magick, through such use of True Will, then the worshippers of Dagon will gain domination of religious society and everything beyond, in that this is what our worship will deliver us.

"This restoration is a victory over death. It is the realization of spiritual eternity in a physical context, as discussed in reference to previous cards" (Hutchinson, Friedman: 2002: 46), the Lovecraft Tarot continues to tell us. This statement of 'victory over death' speaks directly to us, as well as to say that in terms of the occult, we are morally right. A 'realization of spiritual eternity in a physical context', further to this, tells us that the worship of Dagon is to transcend that which is around us in terms of a physical context; and this 'reference to previous cards' puts this entire book into context as part of our religious perspective.

We continue this discussion of the Positive definition as to the Tarot Card that is Dagon in quoting a statement from the Introductory Book to the previous Edition of this Deck, that "[m]uch of what we know as the 'natural' world is finally returned to its truly natural state, unhindered and unimpeded by the blind ravages of human ambition" (Hutchinson, Friedman: 2002: 46). Whilst it is not entirely clear as to exactly why the *HP Lovecraft Tarot* would want to put this statement here, it does still have some relevance to the worship of the *Necronomicon* Mythos occult. This 'natural state' represents the primary building blocks of matter in its natural state as part of the occult. In passing through death all of these definitions are broken down into their initial and primary forms; and that which is built from the occult will be returned to its natural form of esoteric chaos, confusion, and the constituent parts of black magick and the further manifestation of occult energy.

The personification of Dagon here represents spiritual victory in terms of our worship as the Cult of R'Lyeh. It represents the

culmination of all of our religious principals, and the dawning of judgement upon the evil conduct of mankind. A definition with the Positive Reading with this Card is described by the *HP Lovecraft Tarot* as the "Triumph of Spirit over matter; triumph of Spirit in matter!" (Hutchinson, Friedman: 2002: 47). The statement here describes the successful culmination of our work in worshipping the Great Old Ones; the triumph of Spirit in matter' being a forecast of a culmination of ritual worship in terms of manifestation. In practicing the worship of our chosen system of Gods, magick is here successful, and works of magick here culminate as ritual truth. "Emancipation, redemption [and] salvation" (Hutchinson, Friedman: 2002: 47) are defined in the same statement, this meaning that our worship of the Great Old Ones will lead to our being looked upon by higher astral forces with favour and, in that, those who will be the rightful rulers of the Earth.

"Resurrection" is defined, and therefore that which is 'dead' will rise again on Earth, in the same way that Dagon represents higher awakening. The "end of cycles" (Hutchinson, Friedman: 2002: 47) as is defined in the Introductory Deck to the previous Deck and this statement will define the Cosmos as Dagon arises from sunken depths of sleep. The cycles of the Universe will eventually be ended, as the Gods of R'Lyeh will awaken to claim the Stars as Their own, and the cycles of the Cosmos will end as the R'Lyeh are eventually victorious in claiming our power over Mankind in our worship.

And time will culminate as its beginning will also be its end. "[L]essons learned and progress made to [a] new level or place of being" (Hutchinson, Friedman: 2002: 47) is how the *HP Lovecraft Tarot* continues to define this statement, as the Awakening of Cthulhu (as this Card is defined with the previous publication of this Deck) is defined as our conquest of time and space as His worshippers and followers in belief.

"Freedom [and] release" (Hutchinson, Friedman: 2002: 47) are defined in this definition, and "return to innocence" (Hutchinson, Friedman: 2002: 47) is defined as Dagon will eventually once more rise to regain His place as the Ruler of further Dimensions of perception. A

Positive Reading here is representative of success in taking control, in both a personal and a social situation.

Negative Reading

The Negative Reading is here defined in the context of Dagon, the Fish God, as being an aspect of 'Judgement'. In the Negative sense, then, the power and significance of this as the main religious statement of the R'Lyeh is in context quite serious, as it is defined as "dilution of Spirit by / in Matter" (Hutchinson, Friedman: 2002: 47). In terms of this as a religious study, Spirit and Matter are closely linked, but if something cannot be created in terms of Spirit, then as the worshippers of The Great Old Ones, we cannot expect it to be realized as material in Matter.

This as a concept can be expressed quite clearly, as the definition is here described by the *HP Lovecraft Tarot* as relating to the ideas of radio signals and static. In continuing this description of where the Lovecraft system stands as being quite unique as a system of Tarot, we arrive at a statement here that "density, opaqueness: electronic noise garbling the signal [and a] state of impurity" (Hutchinson, Friedman: 2002: 47) will come into the situation as part of a Reading. The Cult of R'Lyeh are orientated to take a particular interest in this statement as a reference to ritual magick.

This book has not been written to describe much about the various religious Sects involved with the religious movement of the R'Lyeh, but various different parts of our religion are involved with the study of radio and electronic signals.[2] It is, however, not the subject of this book to describe this in any depth. (Whilst the author would like to see comprehensive work done on the subject of radio static and the occult, it is not the idea to turn TV static into material form, but to use it as a focus for psychick meditation to the Necronomicon system of worship.

---

[2] If the reader wants to go further with this idea as a study, there are factions of religious belief who work around this idea. Further information can be found on the Internet, although I am not listing any websites here.

But I digress…)

A Negative Reading warns us of "Reincarnation" (Hutchinson, Friedman: 2002: 47); in this sense being a Negative aspect to this as an idea, with "return to previous cycle[s] for further instruction [and] lessons not learned becom[ing] obstacles to progress" (Hutchinson, Friedman: 2002: 47). Our interpretation of this statement involves the reality of Dagon as being the God system dictating Space and Time, with this concept now defined as part of the Tarot system in context with how we live our own lives.

This statement from the Tarot ultimately ends by defining a position of "Indulgence, inactivity, lethargy; complete lack of stimuli" (Hutchinson, Friedman: 2002: 47). Whilst this system of Tarot defines this statement under 'Judgement', it is probably more representative of our own attitudes to our own lives and the study of Ritual Magick, and is defined with Card 20 as it fits in with the larger system, as opposed to the prophesised Rising of Dagon, as it effects His worshippers as the rightful owners of the Earth.

21. Chaugnar Faugn: The World

The point has already been discussed that, with the current edition of the *HP Lovecraft Tarot*, not all that much is different outside of the example that the graphics to the Cards themselves have been changed. However, one of these points of difference, as amended with the current Edition, is that the Card that was previously defined as being The Crawling Chaos, is now represented by the concept of the Mythos God Chaugnar Faugn. The same statement stands that *The Necronomicon Cycle* is written to establish specific points of research, and again the information given with the Introductory Book to the previous edition of our religious Deck of the Tarot, does a good job in describing this last Card of the Major Arcana on clear and valid Lovecraftian terms. If the Magus were to be interested in as to how these two definitions have changed, however, they should further reference the *Cthulhu Mythos Encyclopedia* as one of our main points of research to justify such a study, that:

> "[Chaugnar Faugn is a] Hyperdimensional creature slightly resembling an elephant-headed human with webbed ears and a large disk at the end of its trunk… only shifting its bulk when feeding upon a sacrificial victim. When Chaugnar came to earth, the most advanced life forms on the planet were amphibians… Currently Chaugnar Faugn is worshipped in a cavern on the Plateau of Tsang; diffusion of such rites may account for the curious physical similarities between Chaugnar and the Indian elephant god Ganesh… [T]he elephant god will awaken and feed until he devours the universe. Chaugnar was brought to the West and [was] displayed in the Metropolitan Museum, but he was sent back into the past via a curious time-ray device" (Harms: 2008: 46)

At the spiritual heart of everything is chaos, and the Worship of the Old Ones could be described as the understanding and acknowledgement of such reality of ultimate astral chaos. Portrayed here is Chaugnar Faugn as an entity of alien and evil existence. There is no direction as to what, exactly, this Card should relate to in terms of this given discussion of the Cthulhu Mythos Gods – but only that there is one force for Chaos that is immortal, sentient, and of ultimate ghastly evil. This Card relates to neither Earth nor to the Cosmos; and has no defined meaning further than this as defined.

The Cosmos is of infinite and unfathomable insanity, and has no rules or system of order. And as we have here come to the end of this as our religious study of the Major Arcana, we return to the beginning and the nucleus of creation. "The music of the spheres degenerates into a cacophony led by Azathoth's pipers" (Hutchinson, Friedman: 2002: 48), says the Tarot. As we here come to the end of our definition of the Major Arcana of this Tarot in question, the initial madness of the Courts of Azathoth again come back into play. At the end of the day all is never beyond the comprehension of madness. When it comes to the point, and regardless to all that has previously been defined, there is neither order nor reason as according to any sense of perception. Whilst the Gods play games of astral madness, there is – in fact – no order at all.

Where Card 21 is relevant, it concerns the end of the Cosmos, of Time, and the reasons for the progression of mankind. "The stars deviate from their course, planets whirl from their orbits, suns explode and engulf their satellites" (Hutchinson, Friedman: 2002: 48). At the end of the day, whatever the technology or scientific advancements of human kind, we actually have no control over our ultimate end; everything is actually under the control of a greater mind. "We shout and kill and revel in the short time we have before our sun expands, the seas evaporate, and we dissolve in radiant radioactivity" (Hutchinson, Friedman: 2002: 48).

Chaugnar Faugn is therefore representative of the end. At the end of the day humanity is nothing more than an inherently futile race, and

we have no say over the end of our planet or of our own existence. We are ultimately to be condemned to be nothing but a historical part of a much huger Cosmos, and are ultimately futile on such terms.

The *HP Lovecraft Tarot* here concludes this discussion of the principles as established by the Major Arcana, and in doing so demonstrates the poetic virtue of our worship. "The stars are right, They have returned. They rule now where man once ruled. The cosmic dance of the spheres has become a riot, a celestial mob fleeing inevitable destruction… even the darkness fades… But the piping never ends" (Hutchinson, Friedman: 2002: 48). And so ends this discussion of the Major Arcana as according to the philosophy as established by the *HP Lovecraft Tarot* in defining the religious beliefs as upheld by the Cult of R'Lyeh on Earth.

This concludes the Major Arcana as according to *The Necronomicon Cycle* as a discussion of the Tarot and contemporary religious views, and hopefully I have done justice to the subject. In taking the place that is usually The World to Come, Chaugnar Faugn here represents the religious belief that, eventually, the entire civilisations and systems of mankind will ultimately and eventually collapse. The Universe is, according to the Cult of R'Lyeh and those who follow our religious beliefs, a mass of chaos and esoteric madness. In the long term, and despite our systems of organisation, mankind is ultimately nothing. And in the greater terms of the Cosmos, the human race can achieve nothing, and we are nothing but a minor figment in the greater scheme of the infinity of creation. The Great Old Ones exist as that which will always be, as Those who control the insanity of time and space, and in worshipping Them, we ultimately have to acknowledge our place as meaning nothing in the greater scheme of a reality in which human society ultimately has no meaning.

The *HP Lovecraft Tarot* can be seen as a dialogue on the progress of creation, from the nucleus of the Cosmos as represented by Azathoth as the centre of creational madness, through the progress of humanity as an evolutionary species, to the structure of our society and evolution of religious Temples. Card 21, therefore, is representative of the

conclusion of goals, endings and of things completed. The "Realization of ultimate goals; success, achievement, full & final accomplishment" (Hutchinson, Friedman: 2002: 49) is defined. This statement stands to define the culmination of projects taken on; things are now finished and the outcome of this is that these projects are successful.

Card 21 also represents the culmination of goals in the spiritual sense. Issues of "Revelation [and] spiritual realisation" (Hutchinson, Friedman: 2002: 49) are forecast. As the religious Worship of the Great Old Ones, this defines all previous Readings of the Cards as meaning that the outcome of our worship will be manifest, and that all religious projects that can be defined with the previous Cards of this Major Arcana, will be manifest as the productive outcome of any projects undertaken. It point of definition is also defined as the "End of mythic quest" (Hutchinson, Friedman: 2002: 49). In our religion, as with many others, it is often the case that we are searching for answers to our individual theological questions. The definition here symbolizes a situation whereby, for one reason or another, the answers to the religious questions we have been asking are now answered. This may be on a number of levels, as the nature of the occult is mystical, and we can have our questions answered in a number of different ways.

For the first time, answers to our questions about life after death are defined. "Heaven, the Afterlife; Elysium, Olympias, Valhalla" (Hutchinson, Friedman: 2002: 49) are defined. Card 21 reinforces the belief previously defined in this book, that we do not know what the afterlife is in regard to the worship of the Necronomicon Mythos of supernatural Gods and creation. We assume that life after death is reality, but nowhere is this defined, before reading the dread *Necronomicon* itself, which is to descend into a position of personal madness. "Elevation among the 'Elect'" (Hutchinson, Friedman: 2002: 49) is defined. It is not clear as to what this statement in context actually means, but it is suggested that this relates to a situation of rising to a greater level due to work done and respect having been earned in social situations.

Negative Reading

In the same sense as with the above, and with this being the final Card of our discussion of the Lovecraftian Major Arcana, Chaugnar Faugn can be representative of complete destruction and of the ultimate end. This can, therefore, be a dangerous Card to draw in terms of a Negative Reading, but it should be regarded that, in tradition, a reading of the Tarot rarely spells complete disaster. However, as "Chaos, failure; loss of goals &/or ambitions" (Hutchinson, Friedman: 2002: 49) is defined, then maybe this Card should be one to be careful with if involved with any part of a Reading?

The idea with Chaugnar Faugn being the final Card is reflected when the Tarot is defined as forecasting a situation of "Apocalypse; Apocalyptic obsession & action" (Hutchinson, Friedman: 2002: 49). Goals undertaken may result in disaster. A "Jerusalem Syndrome" (Hutchinson, Friedman: 2002: 49) is forecast.[1] The religion of the R'Lyeh will attain realization as the Churches of orthodox religion will be risen and razed to the ground.

This definition continues as the *HP Lovecraft Tarot* concludes this entire discussion of the Major Arcana in making a statement as crucial to our religious principals and views. Chaugnar Faugn now concludes this study of the Major Arcana in stating that an "Inability to transcend the mundane world" (Hutchinson, Friedman: 2002: 49) is forecast, with this as a statement concerning our religious practice of transcending this world in the acknowledgement of our system of Gods. "Lack of spiritual fulfilment" (Hutchinson, Friedman: 2002: 49) is defined; the fulfilment gained through the worship of the Great Old Ones, in this sense is not a factor and, again, time away from intense worship could be advised. And this given discussion of the Major Arcana is now ended, as its concluding statement defines the principle of "Hell, Hades, Tartarus" (Hutchinson, Friedman: 2002: 49), as coming into a Reading. Again, in not being sure of the reading of *The Necronomicon* and its

---

1 The start of new religious movements on Earth?

complex religious tracts on the spiritual dimensions of the afterlife, we have to take this Card in context; and our interpretation of this is that these three statements should be seen as meaning the three infinite states of the Cosmos.

This discussion of the Major Arcana is now ended. In this concluding paragraph, the Negative Reading with Chaugnar Faugn is defined as "material existence; lack of spiritual vision" (Hutchinson, Friedman: 2002: 49). These two statements in themselves are read as the culmination to this as a unique religious study. Surely, with a fixation with material existence and a lack of spiritual vision, our religion would mean nothing? The Cult of R'Lyeh exist on Earth, therefore, in servitude to the greater minds of *The Necronomicon* and the greater system of the existence of The Great Old Ones as an established point of religious truth, and in surrender to this as a greater system of Gods as defined. Cthulhu F'tagn.

THE MINOR ARCANA CYCLE

ACCORDING TO THE
HP LOVECRAFT TAROT

Introduction to the Study of the Minor Arcana

Before starting work on this Section on the subject of the Minor Arcana, and how this should be interpreted according to the Lovecraft system of the Tarot, there are initially a number of points which should first be taken into consideration.[1] As a unique system of the Tarot, the *HP Lovecraft Tarot* is quite different in terms of how the Cards are here depicted with this specific system, as it is the case that every system of the Tarot is a unique system in itself.

The first of these points concerns the denomination of the Suits and the order of the Cards of the Minor Arcana in this specific system, as described. As with every other specific Deck of the Tarot, the Minor Arcana with the Lovecraft system is broken down into four separate Suits; and in the case of this as the Lovecraft system, these are here

---

[1] In order to research this Section on the Minor Arcana I have drawn extensively from a book on the subject of the Cthulhu Mythos, this being The Cthulhu Mythos Encyclopedia by Dan Harms. On this basis a bibliographical reference for this title is included at the end of the book. Apart from this title being one of only a couple of references given with the original HP Lovecraft Tarot itself, it is also one of very few valid resources to have been written on this subject. I would suggest that if the Magus be interested in further conducting their own research into this as a unique branch of the occult, then this book would be good reference if read in the given context that it has been used in relation to the study of The Necronomicon, and most of the references in this book include further information on the sources from which the information in question was taken. If the Magus were to be interested in researching any of the Cards of this system of the Tarot further (for the purposes of Ceremonial magick or for any other reason), then these sources in question might be a good place on which to possibly start.

defined as being the Suits of People,[2] Artifacts, Tomes and the Suit of Sites. Whilst having researched this religious system of the Tarot for some extensive period of time (and as an Undergraduate student focusing on Theology and Religious Studies), the point from my perspective, in writing this book, was not in any way immediately clear as to how these Suits equated with the rest of the published systems of the Tarot, and for this reason (and with part of my University Dissertation) I initially had to improvise with this idea. However, whilst researching my Dissertation, which is also on the subject of the *HP Lovecraft Tarot* (and given as Part I of this Book), I was by chance able to find a website published by a group calling themselves the Innsmouth Free Press, which makes a good attempt towards clarifying this specific point. At this current point I will choose not to go into detail to describe the meanings of the Suits as according to this reference, as this is the point of the Dissertation which is included at the start of this book as the First Section, but in short it can be established that the Suit of People equates to the Suit of Cups (as it is referenced by a large number of other systems of the Tarot), the Suit of Artifacts equates to Swords, Tomes to Wands, and Sites to the Suit of Pentacles, as is defined as according to this research.

The next point of consideration here is regarding the listing of the Cards of the Minor Arcana in order, and here I have been able to find no direct reference or research to be able to soundly validate how this equates with all other systems of the Tarot, although thinking further this is a point that could be considered obvious. It is on this basis that if the *HP Lovecraft Tarot* equates the Cards of the Minor Arcana as numbered from one to fourteen, as all other systems of Tarot have fourteen Cards in each Suit of the Minor Arcana as here discussed, then an assumption would be that the first Card of each Suit would equate to being Aces, the eleventh to representing the Page, twelfth to Knights, thirteenth to Queens and then fourteenth Card of the Minor Arcana to being Kings, then this can in turn be equated on general terms with

---

2 In the previous Edition of the HP Lovecraft Tarot this was referenced as being the Suit of Man.

the study of other Decks on these defined terms. A general Table to represent this equation has been given at the beginning of the Suits as described with this Section of this book in order to generally clarify this point in hand.

Another point of consideration here would be in terms of the graphical depiction involved with the Cards themselves, and how these have been changed with the current Edition of this Deck in consideration. In most systems of the Tarot we generally see a defined system of symbols; for example a picture depicting possibly a representative figure and a series of swords (as being one generalized example) might represent one Card of the same Suit, and most systems of the Tarot work with this general concept as their example to describe what individual Cards should represent. With the Lovecraft system as being our working example in hand, however, we see another diversion from this usual example, and this system seems to work more with a graphical depiction defining the meaning of the Cards as according to a further discussion of Lovecraftian literature to define the meaning of each Card in question. Using the example of the first Card of the Minor Arcana Suit of People, as one example in hand, the *HP Lovecraft Tarot* defines this meaning with one example being a depiction of HP Lovecraft, as possibly being the most important example of any with this system of the Minor Arcana. Another main reference that I have used extensively in researching this argument to define such a definition of the Minor Arcana, being a book titled *Seventy-Eight Degrees of Wisdom* by a writer on this subject named Rachel Pollack, makes explicit reference to King Arthur in order to equate the same definition of meaning according to the same equivalent Card with the specific system it describes. This is the idea that I will intend to expand on whilst writing this Section on the Minor Arcana in order to properly establish the importance of the religious symbolism represented with this discussion of Lovecraftian religious views that is established with this system discussed..

With that point established, it should also be a point of discussion that, regardless to how every different system of the Tarot is inherently

unique to itself, it is also the case that the meanings of the Cards must have generally similar attributions if all systems of Tarot are essentially different interpretations of one singular system of occult religious orientation. To establish this point whilst using the same example of the first Card of the Suit of People, as defined with this specific example as being the Card as represented with the archetypal significance of Lovecraft (as the stated Card in question to define what is here being said), whatever is defined with this meaning with the *HP Lovecraft Tarot* must therefore be generally the same as with the rest of the countless systems of the Tarot for this same reason. So, whilst this Card is not described as being the 'Ace of Cups', or something similar, as with most other systems of the Minor Arcana, with the *HP Lovecraft Tarot* this must be generally similar in meaning whilst describing such similarity in context with *The Necronomicon* as the religious system that this book has been written to discuss and to represent. Whilst it should generally be taken as an assumption in hand that a general idea of intuition should be seen as being the most important issue whilst interpreting any system of the Tarot, with any occult study of the Lovecraftian, an assumption that all religious ideology is actually the result of the psychickal projections as sent out by The Great Old Ones as one system of Gods, should always be the first consideration if following such a religious path of worship.

Those who would already have a working knowledge of the Tarot will also quite clearly notice that this book goes into much more serious detail whilst discussing the Minor Arcana than with most other books written on this same subject. With the above points already taken as a consideration, the Cards of the *HP Lovecraft Tarot* all stand as specific and defined images of their own, as opposed to representing specific ideas in terms of symbology, as discussed, and this is important in describing the meanings of this interpretation of the Lovecraftian Minor Arcana. It is with this reason that such Cards are clearly defined, and it is for this reason that it is important to include a proper definition as to what such Cards of the Minor Arcana define, for this reasoned purpose discussed.

So, in conclusion to the Introduction to this Section on the subject of the Lovecraftian system of the Minor Arcana, whilst the *HP Lovecraft Tarot* can freely describe a definition of religious truth according to those who would interpret this system, any such statement of truth can only ever be established on the belief that the individual believes on their own individual terms, as to what exists in any literal sense, as being "real".

Suit of Man/People

The *HP Lovecraft Tarot* defines the Suit of People (with this being given as the Suit of Man with the previous Edition) as relating to "People, personality traits & flaws" (Hutchinson, Friedman: 2002: 50). This statement is considered in relation to this and to the study of the Tarot as a greater system in that "Western culture has emphasized the idea of the individual as unique and separated from the world. The Tarot does not deny the individual's uniqueness – it insists on it" (Pollack: 1983: 49). Here we could see a good example of how the views of groups such as the Hermetic Order of the Golden Dawn as representing the consciousness of the individual could be established, and this is a point which should be considered by anyone making any study of any religious system of the Tarot.

Our system of religious interpretation further defines the Suit of People to represent "Dynamics of Relationships [and] Interaction with others" (Hutchinson, Friedman: 2002: 50), although this could represent another much larger definition if we were to consider the point that "However much our egos insist upon our separation from the rest of life, our instincts... remind us of our harmony with the universe" (Pollack: 1983: 49), as stated in *The Seventy-Eight Degrees of Wisdom* as a resource on the subject of the Minor Arcana that I will be referencing from through the rest of this book on the same subject.

Further to this, if a reading with the *HP Lovecraft Tarot* would relate to the individual on personal terms, then by definition the same system "describes the individual as a combination of elements (an astrology chart, with its twelve signs and twelve houses, teaches the same lesson)" (Pollack: 1983: 49). Here we have another example of where the individual should be seen as a smaller part of the Cosmos on a greater scale, as an issue that is represented when we make use of the Tarot in working to establish religious terms.

In introducing the idea of the study of the Minor Arcana, this statement is further defined as relating to "How others influence the questioner, & vice versa" (Hutchinson, Friedman: 2002: 50), and this should be read in relation to "a person's basic connection to the rest of life" (Pollack: 1983: 49). At the same time the *HP Lovecraft Tarot* always makes a very clear statement to define potential negative meanings, and this as our given reference in hand warns of a situation where "All attempts to do anything, or to sort through some complicated problems, dissolve into vagueness, apathy and empty dreams" (Pollack: 1983: 49).

Further to that, the Cards of the Suit of People should, further to this, always be considered on their own and individual significant terms. On a more direct basis it is the specific personality traits and examples of personal psychology that define the meanings of the Cards here described, and I should point out that this Section of this book is written with that intention in hand. It might be another point to note that the ideas of philosophers such as the Psychiatrist Jung make equivalent statements to interpret human personality, and I would always suggest that the Magus should interpret the Cards of the Suit of People as according to this criteria in hand.

Minor Arcana	Suit of Man	Suit of Cups
1	HP Lovecraft	Ace of Cups
2	Randolph Carter	Two of Cups
3	LeGrasse	Three of Cups
4	Charles Dexter Ward	Four of Cups
5	Erich Zann	Five of Cups
6	Herbert West, Reanimator	Six of Cups
7	Obed Marsh	Seven of Cups
8	Wizard Whateley	Eight of Cups
9	Wilbur Whateley	Nine of Cups
10	Dr Munoz	Ten of Cups
11	Dr Armitage	Page of Cups
12	Crawford Tillinghast	Knight of Cups
13	Naham Gardner	Queen of Cups
14	Keziah Mason	King of Cups

Table 5. The Lovecraftian Suit of Man equated to the Minor Arcana Suit of Cups.

1. HP Lovecraft:
Equates to the Ace of Cups

If the Minor Arcana Card of The Necronomicon (the first Card of the Suit of Tomes, discussed later) could possibly be considered the most important Minor arcana Card of this Deck of the Tarot, then the Card as represented by HP Lovecraft might be the most important of

the Suit of People. With the rest of this Section on the issue of this Suit in question, the Cards of this sequence are described in terms of the principles defined by fictional characters in Lovecraftian fiction, although this as the first of these Cards would be the exception to the rule, with Lovecraft obviously being a real person in discussion. It is on this basis that the Card that opens this discussion of the Minor Arcana in connection with the *HP Lovecraft Tarot* should be considered as being more direct as with the rest of this Suit, and is for this reason.

A first point to be made here is that our reference on the greater definition of the Minor Arcana in discussing this Card on this greater scheme of the Tarot (and in connection to the *Seventy-Eight Degrees of Wisdom* as our main reference for this study), makes repeated mention of King Arthur in order to symbolize the meaning as represented by this Card, and in terms of this religious study this should be seen as

equating directly to the symbolism as represented by Lovecraft as the most important representative of R'Lyehan religion in literary history. If the *HP Lovecraft Tarot* would acknowledge this symbolic importance, then a definition of this Card as relating to "Precociousness, Genius, Literacy" (Hutchinson, Friedman: 2002: 51) would make a direct statement to represent such a position of intellectual genius in representing such a religious orientation, as is further discussed and defined in this book.

The second meaning as here defined with this Card leads on to one of "Inspired creativity, Dream, Fertile Fantasy" (Hutchinson, Friedman: 2002: 51), and it would be an obvious point that this would again relate to Lovecraft's genius in writing to represent the religious values as implied in such religious fiction, and this Card makes a point that these aspects should always be held in mind when interpreting the world around us if drawn as part of a Reading. This is further put into such a greater context when the reference on the greater system of the Tarot, that I will quote from throughout the rest of this definition of the Minor Arcana, points out that "life cannot be seized, but only accepted" (Pollack: 1983: 69). Whilst we cannot change our perception of the world around us, we can always acknowledge such reality as strange and bizarre as this should be a reference to discuss as further being part of our normal lives.

The *HP Lovecraft Tarot* continues with this general idea to define a statement to relate to "Vision beyond normal limitation of Time and Space" (Hutchinson, Friedman: 2002: 51), and again this should be seen as relating directly to Lovecraft's genius and how his ideas are defined in representing the ideas that the Cult of R'Lyeh here take forward in writing this book. The Cthulhu Mythos as the defined point as discussed with this discussion of the Tarot is always bizarre and openly insane if this should be acknowledged, and the depth and complexity of this reality is represented with this statement, amongst others. In terms of the greater system of the *HP Lovecraft Tarot* this is established on a greater basis of definition that "the world does not function primarily by its laws, its moral order and its social structures,

but rather by the spiritual basis which gives all these things meaning" (Pollack: 1983: 69). Scientists and theologians will tell us that the Cosmos always works around a system of natural laws, although the established existence of The Great Old Ones throws all such natural laws into question.

A final definition as given as part of a Positive Reading with this Card, as defining a principle of "Mind over Body; Mental excursion transcending physical limitations" (Hutchinson, Friedman: 2002: 51), and this could represent a point that, in this given context, whilst writing itself could be considered mundane, if we are to represent *The Necronomicon* as our religious statement in question, then our doing so transcends such earthly constraints. To quote again from the *Seventy-Eight Degrees of Wisdom* as a book on the Minor Arcana of the Tarot, "When we look at existence as something solely to be conquered... we bring only chaos" (Pollack: 1983: 69). The Magus should be careful not to allow mundane actions to escalate out of control.

Negative Reading

According to the *HP Lovecraft Tarot*, a Negative Reading with this Card would relate to a position of "Cold Intellectualism, Disassociation [and] Alienation" (Hutchinson, Friedman: 2002: 51), and our further given reference on the subject points out that "The reversed Ace [as being the same Card as defined by many other systems of the Tarot] always brings disruption" (Pollack: 1983: 70). Further, if the same definition would relate to "Fear of Imagination, Rationalism as shelter from the unknown" (Hutchinson, Friedman: 2002: 51), then it is defined that "[this] card upside down can imply that we ourselves bring about our [own] unhappiness... by reacting violently when what we need is calm" (Pollack: 1983: 70). And if such a statement continues to define a position of "Inability to focus within normal boundaries of reason and perception" (Hutchinson, Friedman: 2002: 51), then the same reference in hand makes a statement that this Card turning up reversed in a reading "can indicate simply that the times have turned against

1. HP Lovecraft: Equates to the Ace of Cups

us and we can only accept that life brings problems" (Pollack: 1983: 70). With this idea taken further the Lovecraft system of the Tarot here defines a point relating to "Sickly disposition; physical disability or handicap" (Hutchinson, Friedman: 2002: 51). It might be on the basis of the importance of this Card, as discussed, that a Negative Reading here is so overtly pessimistic, but in concluding such a discussion of this definition of meaning, "Here we see unhappiness, violence [and] destruction" (Pollack: 1983: 70).

2. Randolph Carter:
Equates to the Two of Cups

In working to define and to further describe the Cards of the *HP Lovecraft Tarot*, my first course of action, as regarding this entire Deck, has been to sit down to make a note as to each Card in discussion, and the ideas that first occur to me as I look at that representation. It is for that reason that this Card, in my interpretation, is that of the Dreamworld Traveller, and this discussion here will be discussed on that basis.

In the previous Edition of the *HP Lovecraft Tarot* this Card depicts Card Randolph Carter as staring directly outward from this Card. With this graphical depiction he is sane, and in this depiction appears entirely calm, although the background that is depicted behind him is, in contrast, depicted with this Card as being strange and eccentric in the land of dream. This Card, therefore, should be interpreted as representing the further mystic symbolism as defined with the concept of the land of dreams. This Card should further be read as relating directly to the unconscious nature of dream, then, as this Card depicts the Key that unlocks such hidden dimensions of the mind.

The second general principal that I have tried to establish in describing this system of the *HP Lovecraft Tarot*, is the general idea as regards how the Cards of this Deck stand as relating to those as described by other systems of the Tarot, although it would have to be said that this is not always as entirely straightforward as it might at first seem. The Card as represented by Randolph Carter, therefore, would be one specific example of where we run into a problem, and it would have to be established that if to write a proper interpretation of this Card in question, then the example of Randolph Carter, as given with the *HP Lovecraft Tarot*, necessitates a situation whereby this Card can

only be discussed in one defined context, as the documentation given with the Introductory Book to the previous Edition of this Tarot is in no way anything similar than with any definition of any equivalent Card, as is interpreted by any other system of the Tarot that I've been able to find.

The *Cthulhu Mythos Encyclopedia* is a competent and valid resource on this subject of the Cthulhu Mythos and ideas as represented by *The Necronomicon*, and whilst it does little to help our discussion of this particular Card (as is also the case with a number of others), it does describe such a personification in question that "[Randolph Carter was a] pupil of Harley Warren, a scholar who had delved deeply into the occult" (Harms: 2008: 41). With this statement I would suggest that it should be read in this context that the *HP Lovecraft Tarot* as this issues its definition of this Card as relating to "Nonrational thought; Right Brain imagery & nonverbal symbolic consciousness & conceptualization" (Hutchinson, Friedman: 2002: 51). Contemporary movements of religion, with Chaos Magick Theory being one main example here in discussion, have on contemporary terms made a direct statement in defining the principals of magick as according to ideas in Psychiatry, and whilst the Magus should not consider it to be in any way important to chase this idea up unless they should have a specific personal interest in doing so, it could be reasoned that this is what the Lovecraft system of the Tarot is saying whilst issuing such discussion in defining this statement.

This same reference continues to take this same idea further, and states that "Beginning at the age of ten, Randolph [Carter] himself began to show a gift for prophesising the future that never left him" (Harms: 2008: 41), and it is this general principal that should be considered when the *HP Lovecraft Tarot* defines a point to establish "Unity of spirit & matter; living in both spiritual & physical worlds" (Hutchinson, Friedman: 2002: 51). It could be established that such a definition would relate to the autonomy and potential of the liberated human mind. This statement is further described to represent a position of "Return to childlike consciousness; mature innocence;

Natural & uncontrived state of being" (Hutchinson, Friedman: 2002: 51). In putting this into a context whereby Cthulhu Mythos fiction can be considered as being symbolic in representing further conceptual and directly religious terms, the *Cthulhu Mythos Encyclopedia* further discusses this point in question that "In his early years, Randolph Carter became known as one of the Dreamlands greatest travellers" (Harms: 2008: 41), this statement of psychological symbolism representing the psychick potential owned by youth in comprehending such a reality around them. This general discussion concludes that "As Carter grew older, however, his dream-voyages became less and less frequent, until at the age of thirty they ceased entirely" (Harms: 2008: 41). Under this understanding we should be careful to acknowledge the gifts that are ours only of the basis of youth.

Negative Reading

In terms of direct contradiction to what's already been discussed already, the *HP Lovecraft Tarot* continues to define a Negative Reading here as relating to "Denial of Dream in the name of 'Maturity', Rationalism, Justification" (Hutchinson, Friedman: 2002: 51). Here we see the ideas so far discussed being turned directly on their head, with totally different meanings now thrown directly into the argument. Whilst the statement already discussed makes a point as to the liberty of psychick ability as being the gift owned by youth, under specific defined criteria, here we see an example of "Pragmatism used as an excuse to ignore the spiritual" (Hutchinson, Friedman: 2002: 51). And whilst a Positive Reading with this Card speaks to the virtue of youth as relating to the psychick independence of rational thought, here we see a statement to relate to "immaturity, irresponsibility; self-delusion, addiction, lying to oneself as well as others" (Hutchinson, Friedman: 2002: 51). With this we see a clear example of how meanings can be turned on their head when we are discussing this specific system of the

Tarot in question, and such a quotation should be seen on these terms.

In having then made a statement to define the meaning of this Card in specific relation to the Lovecraftian system of the Tarot, then, it is still the case that the Tarot itself is a much bigger and cohesive system of occult magick as is defined by thousands of different individual Decks throughout history, each one of them in turn defining their own meaning. In making this as a statement to define a Negative interpretation as according to the Tarot we are discussing on these terms, the *Seventy-Eight Degrees of Wisdom* gives us the following advice:

"In different ways the reversed card shows a breakdown of the ideals [as] symbolized right side up. It can mean a love affair or friendship which has gone sour in some way, in particular because of jealousy and a breakdown of trust… Depending on the cards around it, it can signify a relationship endangered by internal or external pressures… If we look at the card as signifying the self, then reversed [it] indicates a split between what we do and what we feel between action and emotion" (Pollack: 1983: 63)

As a general assumption this Card would relate to youth as defining the independence of psychick perception and external vision in relating to the existence and the movement of the occult around us.

3. LeGrasse:
Equates to the Three of Cups

The problem we run into when discussing the Lovecraftian Suit of People, as a part of this intended study of the Minor Arcana, is the relative lack of reference in hand whilst discussing these Cards. If we are to draw, again, from the *Cthulhu Mythos Encyclopedia* as our main focus of reference in order to establish the definition of this Suit in question, these given references used to define the further Suits of Artifacts, Tomes and Sites, give us more information to draw from in order to define and discuss the intended symbolism of such terms in question. The next problem we run into is with having to use the given example of people in order to establish terms that would be in theory much easier if we were to make an equivalent study of any other esoteric system in order to define the same terms as according to other systems of the Tarot as discussed. It is quite clearly the case, however, that the *HP Lovecraft Tarot* does define this first Suit in terms of examples given on the basis of the personification of specific people as icons invented (in pointing out that most cases the people described with this Suit are fictional) as figments of Mythos fiction; and this leaves us with little choice other than to continue to work with this if to make a proper discussion of this discussion of the Tarot and further systems of occult magick in hand.

That said, the given example here being Inspector LeGrasse, as a personification of a member of the Police in Mythos fiction, gives us an archetypal principle of somebody involved with the idea of investigating further truth in order to establish the definition of meaning given with this Card. This point in question is described clearly in quoting again from our reference, the Cthulhu Mythos Encyclopedia, that:

"[Inspector LeGrasse was a] New Orleans police inspector who led a raid in 1907 against a bayou cult of particularly abhorrent nature. Legrasse could learn little of this sect, but his arrival at the American Archaeological Society Meeting in 1909 with a small idol taken in the raid was one of the first clues to the existence of the worldwide Cthulhu cult. In his later investigations, Legrasse returned to the bayous to confront the Cthulhu cult again… Scared by what he had seen, Legrasse withdrew from society for fifteen years to study the lore of the Mythos. Re-emerging to fight off a Deep One incursion on his beloved New Orleans, he set out for Nepal to find the cult of Cthulhu's headquarters" (Harms: 2008: 164).

Before taking this discussion further, it should be pointed out that the intention with writing this Section on the subject of the Minor Arcana, was to try to establish the definitions given with the Lovecraft system, but with this defining a movement of black magick as manifest with the greater representation of the Tarot. However, with that being said, things are, again, not entirely so straightforward. As an example, if to discuss the Card of the Minor Arcana that would equate with the Three of Cups as part of the *Zodiac Deck*, for example, this same Card would be defined under a statement to represent the astrological interpretation.[1] To take this idea further this would appear to be the same situation as with all other systems of Tarot, if that would be the point that we are here intending to argue. It should therefore be taken into consideration that the Lovecraft system of the Tarot therefore defines this definition of meaning as according to this same general principal, and this would establish how it would be appropriate to use

---

1 A discussion of the Zodiac Deck of the Tarot comes into the idea with Part I of the book, The Azathoth Cycle. This is a discussion of the comparative importance of different Decks in question, but as an example of this discussion, if a Card of the HP Lovecraft Tarot can be discussed in order to represent any number of The Great Old Ones, then the Zodiac system would provide a good reference as to the astrological information to equate to that idea, if this should come into the argument as important.

the example of someone who was a member of the Police in order to establish such an interpretation unique to the specific interpretation here discussed. What we're talking about here is making assumptions on the basis of equivalent representations.

This point should be taken into consideration whilst trying to interpret this Card that is here defined as being Inspector Legrasse, but is equally as important whilst reading the rest of the Cards of the Minor Arcana of any system in discussion. The issue as regarding archetypal personification is quite important here, though, as the *HP Lovecraft Tarot* continues on the same basis to define a principal of "Logical mind; Reason" (Hutchinson, Friedman: 2002: 51). The following representation is not so straightforward, though, and goes further to discuss a principal of "Analytic function of the Left Brain" (Hutchinson, Friedman: 2002: 51). With this we see one of numerous examples of where the *HP Lovecraft Tarot* system makes some very complicated statements to involve the clinical study of Psychiatry and to establish points which are usually very much more straightforward with other systems of the Tarot as is our discussion in hand.

Diverting slightly from the discussion here in question, but to take this general idea one step further, one good book on the subject of our religious system is a title called *The R'Lyeh Text*, and whilst the statement here quoted makes no direct point in discussing principles of R'Lyehan religion in this direct context, it does make a statement to further elaborate on this given point in stating that:

> "Even in the 19th Century, it had been recognised that the two halves of our brains have different functions. The speech function resides in the left half of the brain, and doctors have observed that people who have received damage to the left brain become inarticulate. The right side of the brain was obviously connected with recognition of shapes and patterns, so that an artist who had right brain damage would lose all artistic talent… Yet an artist with left brain damage only became inarticulate; he was still as good an artist as ever" (Turner: 1995: 57)

This statement here defines a point that the Magus should not have to be a Psychiatrist in order to be able to interpret the religious Tarot, but the point here established is that the individual should always interpret the meaning of any Card as according to what they feel is right for themselves in doing so. It should also be pointed out, however, that if the Magus were to have such a knowledge of the working of the principles of Psychiatry and the human mind, then the *HP Lovecraft Tarot*, in this context, defines a principal that these such religious statements define a point on which to justify issues such as Psychanalysis as theoretical points which can be part of a study of ritual magick, and on these specific terms the worship of The Great Old Ones, as part of a defined position of religious truth.

As one more point of importance; in recent and contemporary movements of ceremonial magick, issues such as Psychanalysis have come into the picture more and more frequently as defining such a contemporary movement of religion and occult magick, with one of these being the contemporary movement of Chaos Magick Theory, as was led by Phil Hine and Peter J Carroll. These written discussions on the nature of the Positive interpretation of this Card (as with all other Cards of the *HP Lovecraft Tarot*) makes suggestions as to how such theories could be developed in relation to *The Necronomicon* in defining a principle of such systems of ritual and ceremonial magick.

To get back to the general discussion in hand, however, the example of Inspector LeGrasse as a member of the Police and represented in Mythos fiction, is taken further as our system of the Tarot in question defines a principle of "Consistency [and] Dependability", and the person who is represented with this Card is "Unafraid to ask questions [and possesses] Intellectual humility" (Hutchinson, Friedman: 2002: 51). Such a personification defines a principle as expressed with the example of the "Good Cop" as such a defined archetype in question, and the principle of a legal establishment as seen as beneficial is further defined on terms of "deserved authority; Love of Justice; Impartiality, Truth" (Hutchinson, Friedman: 2002: 51).

Negative Reading

With all of that already discussed, a Negative reading with this Card is further defined as representing an entire reversal of the same point (as is often the case when there is a reversal of any Card of the Tarot), in defining a position of "Dependence on Rational Structure, Laws, Rules and predefined roles" (Hutchinson, Friedman: 2002: 51). A situation of "'By the Book' personality" (Hutchinson, Friedman: 2002: 51) is defined, and reference states that "Obviously [Edward Arthur] Waite [as one contemporary scholar of the Tarot] intended this to mean that deeper values are ignored" (Pollack: 1983: 66).

This discussion continues to establish a principle of "Confrontational Interrogation" (Hutchinson, Friedman: 2002: 51), with the example personified by a member of the Police still being an important example to define such an archetypal representation in question. In taking this idea further, in discussing this Card the *Seventy-Eight Degrees of Wisdom*, as a reference that I have quoted from on a repeated basis already, states that this Card can "signify the future of friendship, and again the disillusionment of finding that friends have not supported us when we have needed them" (Pollack: 1983: 66). If the Lovecraft system would define a position of "subtlety of mind, trickery" (Hutchinson, Friedman: 2002: 51), then this same reference continues in the same context that "Rather than a shared celebration of life's joys we find what Waite quaintly calls 'excess in physical enjoyment and the pleasures of the senses'" (Pollack: 1983: 66).

The Negative interpretation with this Card continues to define a principle of "'Bad Cop', abuse of power: Corrupt & Cruel Authority" (Hutchinson, Friedman: 2002: 51), as opposed to what has been stated above, and whilst this is quite straightforward in itself, the *Seventy-Eight Degrees of Wisdom* is again quite appropriate in pointing out that this Card "can show the loss of some happiness. Very often it indicates that something hoped for has not come about" (Pollack: 1983: 66).

4. CHARLES DEXTER WARD: EQUATES TO THE FOUR OF CUPS

As we move on to the fourth Card of the first Suit of this Deck as representing the Lovecraftian, here we see another example of where the *HP Lovecraft Tarot* continues to define principles of meaning in order to establish its own very unique interpretation. That said, I still feel it to be appropriate to quote again from the *Cthulhu Mythos Encyclopedia* in order to define the statement as upheld by this Card, that:

"[Charles Dexter Ward was a] young antiquarian of Providence, Rhode Island. Ward received his high school education... but was at the same time a self-trained historian of prodigious ability... [Further to this academic history, and in order] to further his ends, he skipped college, instead spending a great amount of time travelling among the libraries of Europe. After his return to the United States, Ward became more and more eccentric, eventually being committed in 1928. On April 13 of that year, Ward vanished from his room at the institution, and was never from again" (Harms: 2008: 306)

If the previous Card used the example of Inspector LeGrasse in order to represent ideas of investigative logic as represented by the concept as with the example of a member of the Police, then as we move on to the fourth Card of the Suit of People, we see as very similar equivalent point with the idea of Charles Dexter Ward representing ideas regarding academia and further education. It would be on this basis that a Positive attribution with this Card is defined as representing "successful assimilation of tradition & new ideas" (Hutchinson, Friedman: 2002: 52). This taken further, the very fact that the Magus

is making such a study of ideas as relating to the Lovecraftian, which would be the point here in hand if you are reading this book, is an example of how such study of information is important to the occult development of the personal intellect on such individual terms.

Ideas of knowledge and of holding down academic study are here continued, but this is on the basis of a defined point as to where such issues are of benefit to the individual, and here we have a further statement to define the principle of "Transcending Nature and Nurture in to self-defined patterns of behaviour" (Hutchinson, Friedman: 2002: 52). Again we see an example of the *HP Lovecraft Tarot* making a point to establish principles of Psychoanalytical thought. If such ideas as regarding to nature and nurture are points developed by the individual as from the onset of that individual's birth, as is stated by the developmental theories of the Psychologist, it is this process of learning that leads to the psychological independence of the adult. A statement to define "Clarity of personal identity & path" (Hutchinson, Friedman: 2002: 52) could be interpreted on similar Psychoanalytical terms, and a reading with this Card defines a principle that the forward progress of the Magus will not be difficult – this being an important point to acknowledge in doing a reading to establish the future situation of the individual. The point to represent the "Traveller adapting to any environment" (Hutchinson, Friedman: 2002: 52) makes a similar statement to forecast the future success of that person in question.

Negative Reading

The issue we run into when working to define a Negative interpretation with this Card, is, however, that the research involved gives us much more to work with than that with the previous definition of meaning; this making a point as regarding its meaning when defined in this context. As a result of this, if the fourth Card of the Suit of People is pulled out of the pack upside down, its meaning, in this context, can say quite a lot.

In working to define such a meaning, as discussed, the issue of the

personification of Charles Dexter Ward as academic should be kept in consideration, whilst the Negative definition with this Card does divert from this same point in hand. Whilst the *HP Lovecraft Tarot* here defines a point of "Conflict between Old & New; generation gap" (Hutchinson, Friedman: 2002: 52), the other reference of research that we have used in starting work on this definition of the Cards of the Minor Arcana, defines this forth Card in context with the previous Card, that this "symbolize[s] the person's past experience. Bored by what life has given him [the Magus] does not recognize the new opportunities being offered him by the [current Card in this sequence]" (Pollack: 1983: 65).

In this context such a statement should have to be interpreted on the basis of possible negative connotations, and this should establish that something is soon likely to come into the situation which we would rather not be involved with if we had the choice. This statement continues, however, to define a Negative principle of a "Struggle to break free from inherited and / or genetic patterns into new action & endeavour" (Hutchinson, Friedman: 2002: 52). In the specific context of the meaning of this Card we can assume that whilst "the reversal [of this Card] takes us out of ourselves and awakens us to the world and its possibilities... New things are offered, new relations, new ideas" (Pollack: 1983: 65) is established, this question further relates to the further negative implications of such a reading, and diversions from accepted and usual forms of behaviour might cause the individual new problems with which to have to live with.

Working forward with this idea, the *HP Lovecraft Tarot* defines a principle of a "Burden of a bad reputation, either earned or acquired by association" (Hutchinson, Friedman: 2002: 52). Whilst our reference on the meaning of the Cards of the Minor Arcana does not continue to establish definition of meaning here on directly the same terms, it might be important to make a statement as to the general meaning of this statement represented when taken in context with the greater representation of this as a system of practical magick:

"What we can call the 'negative imagination' makes us look at everything as worthless or boring. There seems to be nothing worth getting up for, nothing worth doing, and nothing worth examining... Th[is] card sometimes shows apathy resulting from a dull, unstimulating environment" (Pollack: 1983: 65)

What all of this says is that we are finding ourselves involved with a situation that we must productively move away from.

This statement is here concluded as representing the "Restless wanderer, uncomfortable wherever he or she may go" (Hutchinson, Friedman: 2002: 52), and in that context it should be established that "The passiveness [involved with this Suit] can sometimes lead to apathy" (Pollack: 1983: 65). And if this definition could establish a point that "In the main, however, th[is] card shows a situation where everything in life has come to appear [as being] the same" (Pollack: 1983: 65). What the fourth Card of the Suit of People seems to be telling us is that the individual has found themselves in a situation which is their role to work to move on from.

5. Erich Zann:
Equates to the Five of Cups

With the exception of the first Card of this Suit of the Minor Arcana, that being the Card which is here represented as HP Lovecraft, it would be the case that all of the Cards here in question with the *HP Lovecraft Tarot* would be archetypal representations of fictional characters as portrayed by Lovecraftian fiction. The example of Erich Zann is, however, not entirely so straightforward, with there being some evidence to say that this character might be based on an actual person in history. Further to that, the personification here is that of a violinist who's music became more and more eccentric, until the eventual situation of his worship of The Great Old Ones, enacted to take his music to its furthest extent, led eventually to his mysteriously disappearance. Research into this character makes reference to his eccentricity as a musician in that "[h]e became known to the tenants of his apartment because of the strange unearthly violin music that he played at night" (Harms: 2008: 332) as one aspect of such eccentric personality.

The *HP Lovecraft Tarot* continues to define a meaning of this Card as relating to "Success in the Arts; performance; exhibition" (Hutchinson, Friedman: 2002: 52), and the example of the mad violinist is here appropriate in that research defines a point that Erich Zann was, at a point before his mysterious disappearance, "one of Europe's greatest violinists" (Harms: 2008: 332). A further statement to define a principle of "Artistic inspiration, creative genius" (Hutchinson, Friedman: 2002: 52) is equally as appropriate in using the example of the mad musician, and a brief statement as to the history of this person as represented might be important if we were to further discuss this statement of definition in context:

"[Erich Zann was a] Mute German violinist who ended his life in the Rue d'Auseil in Paris. Some say he played at the Paris Opera House, where an accident in 1897 left the young musician permanently deaf... He built his Theatre of Clowns in Rome between 1859 and 1860. This was in honour of the woman he loved, and when she died at a performance, he swore off music... He is believed to have vanished while performing one of his 'experimental pieces' in his garret apartment one night" (Harms: 2008: 332)

Whilst the next point of definition might at first appear negative, the *HP Lovecraft Tarot* here defines a point to represent the individual "Struggling [with] artist cliché" (Hutchinson, Friedman: 2002: 52), and this ties in with the representative personification of Erich Zann under this statement, in that "Moving to Paris in 1872, he became a drug addict and a curiosity of that city's artistic scene" (Harms: 2008: 332).

Further to this, the final definition under this meaning is stated as representative of "Guardianship, ward, protector; custodian of unwanted secrets" (Hutchinson, Friedman: 2002: 52). The situation we see established here, as is something that does on some occasions come into the picture when trying to make such a study of the *HP Lovecraft Tarot*, is that statements such as this do not make a clear connection as relating to the principles as defined with the image as depicted by this particular Card. However, the *Cthulhu Mythos Encyclopedia* does make a statement to link the personification of the mad violinist in question, and this general statement of definition in that immediately after the situation as documented with the above quotation, that the Police became involved (with such strange behaviour), and "baffled by [any] lack of clues... soon afterward called a halt to their search" (Harms: 2008: 332).

Negative Reading

A Negative interpretation with this Card should be considered to define a principle of "Suppressed talent, lack of recognition of abilities,

obscurity" (Hutchinson, Friedman: 2002: 52). Whilst the example of the mad violinist should very much be kept in consideration under this general ethos, the *Seventy-Eight Degrees of Wisdom* continues to establish such a meaning as defined by this Card, in stating that:

> "[the Magus] needs to accept that some happiness has suddenly vanished, been knocked over. She does not yet realize something remains, for first she must understand and accept the loss. Has she herself knocked over the cups, either through recklessness, or by taking them for granted?" (Pollack: 1983: 64)

A principle of "Loss of Muse, writers block; frustration, obstacles" (Hutchinson, Friedman: 2002: 52) is established, with this being a point to define a position that "The woman [as here represented in context with this part of the Tarot] (or man; the androgynous character of the figure indicates that sorrow unites the sexes) stands rigid dressed in black, the colour of grief" (Pollack: 1983: 64).

This idea would continue to lead on to the statement as defined in context of a Negative interpretation with this Card in question, as relating to a principle of the "Avant Garde" (Hutchinson, Friedman: 2002: 52), and with this we see an example (one which does come into the situation on occasions with this system of Tarot) of a principle that is clearly more difficult to define. This concept is in itself something to be considered vast, and the idea is not in any way clear as to why such a statement should come into the situation in this context at all. Further to this the question is here asked as to why it should represent anything which should be considered as being in the first place negative? In discussing this point I should reiterate that the actual meaning of any Card of the Tarot should be on principle terms the statement that is assumed by the Magus when pulling any Card out of the pack, as being a point that I will reiterate throughout the rest of this book.

The final point of definition here discussed is distinctly more profound, and is therefore more important, and here we see a statement which should be taken quite seriously by anyone involving

themselves with any system of Necronomicon Mythos occult. This is described with a warning against "Naïve dabbling in 'Black Arts' & the consequences thereof" (Hutchinson, Friedman: 2002: 52), and this should be considered as a first note of caution.

In working further to discuss such an important point, and whilst this statement should be seen as being quite clear, this point should also be regarded as being important. Another quotation from the *Seventy-Eight Degrees of Wisdom* makes a further statement as regarding this point in question, and I feel that this quotation should be considered in relation to this Card as a statement that should be considered in context:

"With its deep evocation of regret [this] card forms a... Gate, bringing us that sense of spiritual loss and separation which all over the world has given rise to myths of a fall or an exile from Paradise" (Pollack: 1983: 64)

With all of this describing situations of religion and the dangers and consequences involved with not being aware (in terms of the occult as being an aspect of religion), this same reference ends with another quotation which I feel is appropriate to cite in ending this specific statement on the subject of this specific part of the Minor Arcana. This statement is justified in that "[T]his awareness [of the dangers of not being aware, in religious terms] indicates that the three fallen cups [being representative of how this Card is defined by other systems of the Tarot] symbolize something less important than might at first seem at the time of its destruction" (Pollack: 1983: 64).

6. HERBERT WEST, REANIMATOR: EQUATES TO THE SIX OF CUPS

With this Card as being the sixth of the Lovecraftian Suit of People we see another example of the religious issues involved with death, resurrection and reincarnation (and the symbolism therefore implied), with this being a theme which

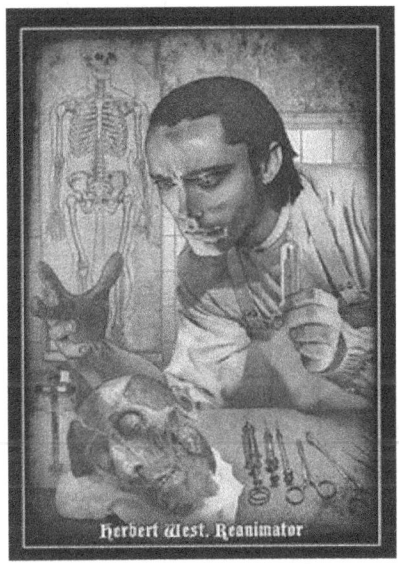

seems recurrent throughout the rest of the Tarot, should the Magus choose to interpret it that way. Lovecraft's short story, *Herbert West – Reanimator*, is a story which focuses on the story of a doctor who, despite being a genius, ended up as the victim of his own intellect in resurrecting people from the dead.[1] It should then be established that this Card, being representative of the sixth of the Suit of People as stated, according to the *HP Lovecraft Tarot*, focuses not so much on this point of death and reincarnation, but more on the achievements gained from serious academic study, and therefore on the risks involved when such academic achievement is misused. The *Cthulhu Mythos Encyclopedia* issues a very short statement to describe

---

1 Of all of Lovecraft's short stories, this is my favourite. A bibliography reference for this narrative is: Lovecraft, H.P. (2002) Herbert West – Reanimator. In: The Call of Cthulhu and other Weird Stories. London: Penguin Modern Classics.

the archetypal representation as given with this Card, that:

> "[Herbert] West attended Miskatonic University Medical School and rendered Arkham great service during the typhoid epidemic of 1905. West went on to establish a clinic for the poor factory workers of Bolton, Massachusetts, and even volunteered for medical service with the Canadians in World War I. His disappearance from his home in Boston is still unsolved" (Harms: 2008: 309)

That stated, it would seem to be an obvious point that the *HP Lovecraft Tarot* uses this example in order to define the points as represented by this Card of the Minor Arcana, and as its equivalent with all other systems and, in this direct context, the *Cthulhu Mythos Encyclopedia* continues to describe such a personification as having been a "Brilliant doctor and humanitarian" (Harms: 2008: 309) since the onset. It is with this point in hand that a Positive interpretation with this Card is defined as representing a principal of "Scientific Brilliance; Inventor; Leap of Medicinal Progress" (Hutchinson, Friedman: 2002: 52). With that statement in itself being quite profound, this Card goes on to predict that there will be a situation involving some sort of a "'Quantum leap' in scientific theory and / or perception", with this same statement of prediction concluding with a point that there will be an "Evolution of ethics & ideals. Moving beyond obsolete moral restraints" (Hutchinson, Friedman: 2002: 52). The *Seventy-Eight Degrees of Wisdom*, as our next main reference in discussing the theory of the occult Minor Arcana describes this same Card of the Tarot in issuing a similar definition of meaning, but at the same time continues on its own terms, as it does throughout. "The emblem of this [Card] is childhood, pictured as a same time, when parents, or older brothers and sisters, protected us and gave us everything we needed" (Pollack: 1983: 62). This same reference on the subject of the Minor Arcana sums this whole definition up in appropriate terms in pointing out that "a fixation on the past can prevent a person from facing current problems" (Pollack: 1983: 62).

Negative Reading

In concluding this general discussion the *Cthulhu Mythos Encyclopedia* makes a statement to describe the personification as represented with this Card, that "Doctor West's experiments with the reification of the dead have been matters of popular rumour" (Harms: 2008: 309). Again, this would be a valid example in hand, as the *HP Lovecraft Tarot* here defines a Negative interpretation with this Card as representing "Loss of ethical perspective in Scientific Progress; Obsession with the end justifying the means" (Hutchinson, Friedman: 2002: 52). In taking this same statement further, "the Six [of this Suit] reversed indicates disturbed memories... or a feeling of alienation from the past" (Pollack: 1983: 63).

This same Negative definition goes further, though, to describe a situation of "Unnatural Intervention into evolutionary process" (Hutchinson, Friedman: 2002: 52), with the given example involving the resurrection of the dead being appropriate to this point as defined. The same idea continues as we see a definition of "Complete disregard for cultural & ethical constraints. Proving that certain taboos have a rational basis" (Hutchinson, Friedman: 2002: 52). A position of cultural or religious prejudice might come into the situation.

In concluding this statement, all of this can be put down to a more straightforward definition of meaning, and the *Seventy-Eight Degrees of Wisdom* puts this entire argument into context in pointing out that "[this Card] can also show the breakdown of a relationship based on one person protecting or teaching the other(s)" (Pollack: 1983: 63). We should be cautious of the benefits of ethical values, and should interpret such a statement on the basis that everything can ultimately be misused.

7. OBED MARSH:
EQUATES TO THE SEVEN OF CUPS

The *HP Lovecraft Tarot* again makes appropriate reference to historical Mythos fiction in order to establish the terms as defined by this Card as one unique part of the greater system of a theory of Lovecraftian magick. It is on this basis that our reference, as has been used throughout this discussion of the Minor Arcana already, makes reference to the fictional historical life of the fictional personification of Captain Obed Marsh, that "Obed's three ships... did a brisk business in the Pacific trade beginning in 1820 and lasting for over twenty years. As a result of this prosperity, the Marshes became Innsmouth's most powerful family" (Harms: 2008: 176)

This quotation would be, again, quite an appropriate reference if working to establish the specific definitions of meaning as ascribed to the *HP Lovecraft Tarot*, in that the Positive interpretation of this Card would relate to a position of "Free Enterprise, commerce [and] cultural exchange" (Hutchinson, Friedman: 2002: 52). In terms of such an example as given here, the *Cthulhu Mythos Encyclopedia*, in discussing such a character in question, states that during such voyages, Captain Obed Marsh made acquaintance with a group of Polynesian Islanders "who possessed a large number of golden ornaments [and] a race of fish beings had brought these to them in exchange for human sacrifices" (Harms: 2008: 176). Whilst what we have here is a great example of how things work in terms of Cthulhu Mythos fiction, it is still the point that *The Necronomicon Cycle* is written to put this Deck of the Tarot into context in discussing points in relation to the greater definition of this as a larger system of the occult, with this in context with the Tarot as a specific point of occult and magickal divination. It would be on this basis that such an assumption of wealth can be

put into further spiritual context, and in this "the visions [as depicted with this Card] cover the whole range of fantasies from wealth... to a victory wreath... to fear" (Pollack: 1983: 61).

The *HP Lovecraft Tarot* continues to define this meaning of terms in that a principle of "Travel to foreign lands, exchange of ideas, assimilation of new ideas" (Hutchinson, Friedman: 2002: 53) will come into the situation. With this definition established, the example of Obed Marsh is a good example in hand, as reference tells us that:

"In the following years, Obed visited the islanders many times, trading for more gold and listening to their legends... It was then that Marsh began to preach a new religion based on the Polynesians beliefs. If the people of Innsmouth followed the gods of his islander friends, he proclaimed, they would become rich and the nets of the fishermen would always be full" (Harms: 2008: 176)

All of this has to be put into context, however, and it is on this basis that I quote again from the same reference on the subject of the Minor Arcana to describe this point, that "Emotion and imagination can produce wonderful visions, but without a grounding in both action and the outer realities of life these fantastic images remain daydreams, 'fancies' without real meaning or value" (Pollack: 1983: 61). With that point established, reference describes Obed Marsh as "Innsmouth's most prominent merchant-captain and [the] founder of that town's Esoteric Order of Dagon" (Harms: 2008: 176), with that being an appropriate statement in context with the *HP Lovecraft Tarot* in defining a Positive interpretation to relate to an issue of "Patriarch, CEO; builder of lasting spiritual or material wealth" (Hutchinson, Friedman: 2002: 53). And as with everything else as discussed with such a study of the Lovecraftian Tarot, this should be quite easy to interpret on its own terms, although an interpretation of such a divinatory study on religious terms makes its own obvious points. It is with the intention of discussing this idea further that I quote again from the *Cthulhu Mythos Encyclopedia* in order to further define this definition of meaning on context:

"After a while, Marsh's Esoteric Order of Dagon became so popular that all of Innsmouth's churches were forced to close down due to lack of worshippers… During the chaos instigated by the plague of 1846, in which half of the town's people died, Marsh became the town's de facto leader, a post that he held until his death in 1878" (Harms: 2008: 176)

With that point having then been established, and in relation to the Positive interpretation of this Card in relation to this specific religious study, the *Seventy-Eight Degrees of Wisdom*, as a reference that I have drawn from quite extensively already, makes reference to this Card, again in context with the greater study of the occult religious Tarot, and here I feel it appropriate to quote from this reference again whilst discussing this point in question, that:

"It is a mistake to think that daydreams are meaningless because of their *content*; on the contrary they often spring from deep archetypal needs and images. They lack meaning because they do not connect to anything outside themselves" (Pollack: 1983: 62).

Negative Reading

The Negative interpretation of this Card of the Minor Arcana provides a good example of where such a reading, in terms of the *HP Lovecraft Tarot*, defines a clear opposite from a Positive interpretation. At this point I'll choose not to go into too much serious detail as to define what's being said here, as this statement is given clearly in the Introductory Book to the previous edition of this Deck, and with this statement of interpretation also given as a part of the first Appendix to this book in hand. That stated, the *Necronomicon Cycle* is written in specific conjunction to the Lovecraftian Deck – it is not written to describe any other working system of the Tarot. However, with that point established, another quotation from the *Seventy-Eight Degrees of*

Wisdom might be appropriate in ending this statement in defining the Seventh Card of the Suit of People, that "This card reversed means a determination to make something from dreams. This does not mean rejecting fantasies, but rather doing something with them" (Pollack: 1983: 62)

8. WIZARD WHATELEY: EQUATES TO THE EIGHT OF CUPS

The *Cthulhu Mythos Encyclopedia* introduces the discussion of the archetypal representation of Wizard Noah Whateley that such a character in question was a "Dunwich resident, reputed wizard, and father of Lavinia Whateley" (Harms: 2008: 310). Whilst this personification in question might possibly be one of the more prominent figures to have been represented by the fictional work of Lovecraft, this system of the Tarot introduces its statement of meaning directly in choosing to use such a figure in order to establish terms of meaning, and defines a situation of the "Sowing of seeds which take generations to see fruition" (Hutchinson, Friedman: 2002: 53). In order to put such a statement into context with the greater situation if writing a narrative on the occult (and related as a system of the Tarot), we see a position that "In this card we see... a situation that not only has provided happiness, but actually continues to do so" (Pollack: 1983: 59). If we were to argue that this position of study would tie in directly to represent the Tarot as a much larger system which would be a greater system of its own, this same statement continues to define this point in stating that:

> "The imagery [as depicted by this same Card in other systems] suggests... an ability to sense when something has ended before it either dries up or comes crashing down around us, to know the time to move on... moving from a less to a more meaningful situation" (Pollack: 1983: 60)

If we were to interpret this quotation on the same terms as with what we are trying to establish in working to describe the Lovecraftian Tarot

as our religious system of representation, and in defining terms on such a basis, then this same statement of research states that "In its deepest level this card acts as a Gate" (Pollack: 1983: 60).

The *HP Lovecraft Tarot* here continues to establish this as a statement of meaning, as "Being forced to hide one's true identity; longing to reveal one's true nature" (Hutchinson, Friedman: 2002: 53). With this statement we see an example of where a statement which would at first appear negative is established clearly as a given Positive attribution of definition, and in making a study as to how this system of occult Tarot can be interpreted on greater terms, this is something that I have come across repeatedly whilst researching this book. The *Seventy-Eight Degrees of Wisdom*, however, continues to make a statement as to how this same Card is defined with other systems of the Tarot, and states an equivalent point of meaning that "To reach the height of the Hermit's wisdom, we must first put the ordinary things of life behind us" (Pollack: 1983: 60). This statement would tie in directly with this same meaning as described with the Lovecraft system as our point of argument, in defining a position of "withdrawing from outer activity to seek a greater awareness" (Pollack: 1983: 60).

In working to describe the equivalent Card as it stands with other systems of Tarot, the *Seventy-Eight Degrees of Wisdom* continues with a statement to establish equivalent terms of definition, in stating that:

"By joining moon imagery to a sense of movement, the card teaches us that developing a deeper sense of self is also an action... the Hermit, by reversing the sexual polarity of the High Priestess above him, combines action and intuition in a definite programme of self-knowledge" (Pollack: 1983: 60)

This takes us to a slightly more divergent point when working to establish the validity of the Lovecraftian occult as is defined by its own representation of the Tarot, but it should be considered to be of vital importance that the cycles of the moon should be observed closely when making use of any system of the occult or ceremonial magick,

and another quotation from the same reference might be important on this basis, that:

> "At first the scene [with this Card] appears to take place at night, but when we look closer we see that actually it depicts an eclipse, with the moon moving across the sun. A moon phase, that is, a period of inner awareness, has taken over from outer-directed activity" (Pollack: 1983: 60)

This definition concludes with a point to define a position of "Wizard, wise man, counsellor" (Hutchinson, Friedman: 2002: 53), with these being valid statements to represent the archetypes as represented by Noah Whateley as defining these principals in hand.

Negative Reading

The *Cthulhu Mythos Encyclopedia* continues with its description of this archetypal portrayal, that:

> "The townsfolk [of Dunwich] lynched his father, Oliver Whateley, because he was suspected of witchcraft. Old Whateley's own neighbours regarded him with fear and loathing, especially after one incident that occurred in one of the hilltop stone circles near Dunwich" (Harms: 2008: 310)

With this standing as a good example of the general ideas involved in using such an example as Noah Whateley as a representation to describe the meaning of the eighth Card of this Suit of the Minor Arcana, the *HP Lovecraft Tarot* makes a definition of Negative meaning, as "Nurturing & propagation of corruption & decay" (Hutchinson, Friedman: 2002: 53). If such a definition might be a valid interpretation if this Card would be pulled from the pack upside down in a reading, a further quotation from the *Seventy-Eight Degrees of Wisdom* might again be appropriate, in stating that:

8. Wizard Whately: Equates to the Eight of Cups

"Sometimes the upside down Eight indicates the simple negation of the card's basic image – a refusal to leave some situation, a determination to hang on even when we know deep inside that we have taken all we can from it" (Pollack: 1983: 60)

If that might have described the meaning of this Card's reversal in context, however, the Lovecraftian system of the Tarot here continues to define a point of "Agent of defilement & abomination; undermining social norms; taboos" (Hutchinson, Friedman: 2002: 53). If standing to argue a point that the *HP Lovecraft Tarot* would be one representative part of a much bigger equivalent movement, a statement to represent this same Card as being an equivalent as with other Decks, defines a point of "leaving a situation because a person lacks the courage to pursue it and take everything she or he can get from it" (Pollack: 1983: 53). And if a final point of representation would be one of "Warlock, Black magician" (Hutchinson, Friedman: 2002: 53), what we see with this is an obvious complete reversal of everything that was represented with the Positive definition of this Card in the first place.

9. WILBUR WHATELEY: EQUATES TO THE NINE OF CUPS

Wilbur Whateley

As we here reach the Ninth Card of the Suit of People, I personally run into a problem, and this would be on the basis that the *HP Lovecraft Tarot* here seems to define the definition of meaning here in discussion on somewhat political terms. My personal history is that I've studied religion on a serious academic basis, this being the reason for my upholding the blasphemous *Necronomicon* as my religious book. It was my intention in going into such a study that, as a principle of philosophy my study of religion was from my position more important than any previously upheld political ideology, and it is my strong belief that the two studies must, on specific terms, be strictly kept separate. However, the *HP Lovecraft Tarot* does define its meanings of prophetic wisdom here on these terms, which leaves me with little option other to continue to establish this point.

With that point here in hand, it would be an interesting point to note that this Card can be seen to follow directly from the interpretation described previously, and if making a study of how the Tarot can be interpreted on Lovecraftian terms, it might help us to put this into

descriptive context, by making a short statement as to the role played by Wilbur Whateley in Mythos fiction:

> "Child of Lavinia Whateley and unknown father. Whateley grew up quickly, being able to speak when eleven months old and having almost reached eight feet in height at the time of his death. He was known to follow in the footsteps of his grandfather Wizard Whateley in holding rites on the top of the hills near Dunwich" (Harms: 2008: 310)

With these points here in hand, the *HP Lovecraft Tarot* continues to define the meaning of this Card on Positive terms, as representing "Disaster delayed, problems on hold" (Hutchinson, Friedman: 2002: 53), and in context with the broader meaning here if to study the Minor Arcana as a wider issue, "[this Suit of the Tarot] demonstrate[s] the attitude of avoiding worry and problems by concentrating on ordinary pleasures" (Pollack: 1983: 59). And if a Positive meaning can be further defined as representing an "Evil plot exposed, conspiracy brought to light" (Hutchinson, Friedman: 2002: 53), then it should be considered as a point in hand that "People sometimes react antagonistically to this card, perhaps wishing to see themselves as beyond superficially" (Pollack: 1983: 59). It is sometimes the case that those who are acting against us are those we consider our closest friends, and sometimes we should have a need to make use of the Tarot if these points are eventually to be clear.

The point that I've already made concerning the issue of politics and religion comes into the picture here as the Lovecraft system of Tarot defines a principle of "Radical ideals; underground movement; revolution, reform, freedom fighter; political activist" (Hutchinson, Friedman: 2002: 53). Whilst it does stand as a clear point in question here that nowhere in Mythos fiction can we clearly find points of reference to establish political statements such as this, or such a position of radical activism and the necessary tactics thereof, we would still have a point of interpretation to justify using the personification

of Wilbur Whateley as our example to describe this Card of the Minor Arcana under this interpretation, that "[Wilbur] Whateley gained some recognition as a scholar of the black arts and corresponded with many knowledgeable individuals, including Dr Armitage of Miskatonic University" (Harms: 2008: 310).

Negative Reading

All of this might be useful if it were to come up as part of a reading, as the definition here given by the Tarot here in discussion is of "The Lesser of Two Evils" (Hutchinson, Friedman: 2002: 53). It is with this point in hand that the Magus should at all times be conscious that the meanings of each Card are foremost those as considered by those who are doing the reading in question. This definition continues to establish a point, however, of defining a principle of "Deep-rooted conspiracy; Plot beyond control of its architects" (Hutchinson, Friedman: 2002: 52), and whilst this could be considered as being obviously clear in itself, it could be seen directly with the specific example of Wilbur Whateley that "[he died] in a failed attempt to steal [the] Miskatonic's copy of the *Necronomicon*. His body vanished under shocking circumstances" (Harms: 2008: 310).

In coming back to that previous statement regarding political thought, a Negative meaning here is defined as relating to a principle of "Spy, saboteur, insurgency; guerrilla warfare, anarchist, terrorist" (Hutchinson, Friedman: 2002: 53). Whilst all philosophical thought must ultimately be down to the opinion of the individual, all of these are points that could be seen as being positive if such a point of philosophy were to be upheld. It is as the result of such interpretation of theory that I would suggest that if this Card were to be drawn upside down as part of a reading, then I would interpret it to represent justification for philosophical arguments, on the basis of how they are reasoned through on the part of the person in question.

10. Dr Munoz:
Equates to the Ten of Cups

As the point will have already been made clear, the main difference with the current edition of the *HP Lovecraft Tarot* would be with the issue of the Cards themselves having been re-drawn. However, the entire concept behind a small number of such Cards have been changed completely, with this Card in question having previously been defined under the personification of Wizard Edward Hutchinson. With this being the case that such a new personification to define this as a part of the Minor Arcana does not have the same research, this Card will therefore be discussed on the basis that the definition of this Card will be on the same terms as that published in the Introductory Book to the same edition, with the assumption being that the Tarot interpretation of this, as being the same definition under a different personification, will be the same despite the subject to define this interpretation of meaning, having been changed with the current edition of this Deck, as *The Necronomicon Cycle* has been written to describe.

This given problem with a lack of reference makes this a difficult Card to describe in the same detail as with the rest of the discussion involved with this book. Throughout *The Necronomicon Cycle* I have been careful to keep my references used to a minimum (as has already been discussed), with the intention here being that in doing so more concise definitions of meaning can be established. Whilst this is an approach that has hopefully so far worked, these references as used for the rest of this discussion of the Minor Arcana, and as with this Card in question, contain little that could be considered useful in making a specific discussion of this Card in itself. However, this book would not be properly complete without saying at least something to describe the

Tenth Card of the Suit of Man, so I will therefore continue that same discussion with the same resources as used with the rest of this book you are reading here.

With that statement made as to my research used in writing this book, the current (Third) edition of the *HP Lovecraft Tarot* defines this Card as being, instead, represented with the personification of Dr Munoz. Whilst I can see no immediate reason as to why this should have been changed with this current edition, this also establishes the point that such a personification is not discussed properly with an entry in the *Cthulhu Mythos Encyclopedia*. However, with that statement as regarding research having been discussed, the research with this Card should be the same, as stated, and on the basis that we are discussing the change that's been made with this Card on the basis of equivalent terms.

As with the rest of the Minor Arcana, the *HP Lovecraft Tarot* makes a number of very profound statements in order to establish its own symbolic meaning in the specific context of Lovecraftian thought (although that would be obviously clear). However, this stated lack of valid research would make it difficult to here properly discuss such interpretation whilst also having anything to contribute to the discussion.

However, I would feel it necessary to point out that the meanings of all of these Cards as involved with the Lovecraft system should firstly be considered on the basis of those ideas on the part of those doing the reading. Whilst having already made this point in itself, this provides me with an opportunity to point out *The Necronomicon Cycle* is based on my own specific interpretation, and that this book should therefore be interpreted with that specific issue in hand.

Negative Reading

With that statement given only on the basis of that which is meant, it is still the aim of this book to interpret the *HP Lovecraft Tarot*, and to justify its greater importance on the basis of religious thought and as

such as a manifest part of occult theory. Therefore, a Negative reading with this Card would relate to a principle of "Burned bridges; forgotten friends" (Hutchinson, Friedman: 2002: 53), and this should be seen in relation to a point that "emotion turns against itself" (Pollack: 1983: 58). Whilst this continues to make a statement to define a principle of "Obsessive relationship[s]" (Hutchinson, Friedman: 2002: 53), this also defines a situation of "Unpleasant family experiences; unhealthy environment" (Hutchinson, Friedman: 2002: 53). In quoting again from the *Seventy-Eight Degrees of Wisdom* as another main point of reference in hand, this point is again put into perspective that "Some highly charged situation, usually romantic or domestic, has gone wrong, producing violent feeling, anger, or deceit" (Pollack: 1983: 58).

This statement in question concludes its definition as stated by the Minor Arcana in stating that "the reversed Ten can simply mean that a person does not recognize or appreciate the happiness life is offering him or her" (Pollack: 1983: 58)

It should be accepted that there would be no reason to use any system of the Tarot if we did not want knowledge that we did not already have, and that however much any definition of any system can be defined, it is the intuition of the Magus which is always more important than any stated meaning of the Cards immediately in question.

11. Dr Armitage:
Equates to the Page of Cups

The personification of a Doctor would be appropriate in defining this Card of the Minor Arcana, as according to the *HP Lovecraft Tarot* a Positive reading with this Card represents "Wisdom, Knowledge; A helpful person of learning & experience" (Hutchinson, Friedman: 2002: 54). With the relation between a Doctor and a person of knowledge being the important point of argument in defining this statement, if this Card should in any way come up in a reading, a short statement as regarding Dr Henry Armitage describes his role in historical Mythos fiction, that:

> "[he was a] One time head librarian at Miskatonic University, and the author of *Notes toward a Bibliography of World Occultism, Mysticism and Magic*... and *Devils and Demons in the Miskatonic Valley*" (Harms: 2008: 10)

With that statement therefore describing the context in which this Card is defined, the *Seventy-Eight Degrees of Wisdom* makes its own statement to further discuss such a meaning of the same Card as ascribed by other systems of the Tarot, that "[this Card] indicates a state or a time in which contemplation and fantasy are very proper to a person" (Pollack: 1983: 56), and it could be argued that this relates to the role of the academic.

Moving forward, this study of the Lovecraftian occult defines a position of "A transcendence of intellectual boundaries stimulated by extreme need; 'Necessity is the Mother of Invention'" (Hutchinson, Friedman: 2002: 54). And if the same study of the Minor Arcana defines a principle that "the Page [as this Card is an equivalent of] does

not suffer the same conflict with either responsibility or sensual desire" (Pollack: 1983: 56), this discussion is put directly into context with the personification of someone such as Dr Henry Armitage as being an archetype in question when trying to define the Tarot in connection with the Lovecraftian occult. The *Cthulhu Mythos Encyclopedia* represents this with a statement that:

"[Dr Henry Armitage] first became interested in uncanny subjects in 1882 when he heard of a mysterious meteor which had landed near Arkham. This occurrence led him to obtain a copy of the *Necronomicon* for the [Miskatonic University] library and consult it for the first time" (Harms: 2008: 10)

The *Seventy-Eight Degrees of Wisdom* sums up this entire concept quite well in stating that "The fish can also symbolize psychic talents and sensitivity" (Pollack: 1983: 56)

However, if the *HP Lovecraft Tarot* continues to define a Positive reading with this Card as relating to "Intellect in practical application" (Hutchinson, Friedman: 2002: 54), then Dr Henry Armitage would continue to be a good archetype to define this under a greater definition of the Minor Arcana, that "[he] attended Miskatonic University... later obtaining his doctorate at Princeton and his Doctor of Letters degree at Cambridge" (Harms: 2008: 10). Whilst all of this in context with a reading of the Tarot would have obvious significance to relate to issues of academia and learning, it can also have a much more personal significance, and in quoting again from Rachel Pollack's study of the religious Minor Arcana, this could be further defined that:

". . .the Page of Cups [as here represented in specific context] can show someone developing psychic abilities, either through an actual programme of study and / or meditation, or else such talents developing by themselves" (Pollack: 1983: 56)

Negative Reading

With this Card coming out reversed in a Reading we see a situation of "Intellectual arrogance as an obstacle to progress" (Hutchinson, Friedman: 2002: 54), and a situation arises that "we [can] see [this] when we make promises we cannot keep or commitments that do not really mean anything" (Pollack: 1983: 57). The same statement continues to establish a point defined as "Knowledge limited by artificial academic boundaries; information made impractical by inability to adapt to the ideas of others" (Hutchinson, Friedman: 2002: 54). At this point an idea should be restated that the greater purpose of this study of the Tarot represents the Lovecraftian with the study of the Minor Arcana as a much greater religious issue; and if the previous meaning as according to the Lovecraftian system could have been equated on these same terms the following quotation from the *Seventy-Eight Degrees of Wisdom* should read on such same terms, that:

> "Because [the Page of Cups, under these criteria discussed] does nothing with his fantasies they give him no trouble. If he acts upon them, however, they may lead him into mistakes. Reversed therefore means... to act without thinking or to allow our immediate desires to seduce us, particularly if they go against our common sense" (Pollack: 1983: 56)

In conclusion to the discussion of this Card of the Minor Arcana, a final definition of meaning warns of "Information not being shared" (Hutchinson, Friedman: 2002: 54), and the example of Dr Henry Armitage in representing this part of the Tarot as one issue is apt, in that "he died in 1946 of a heart attack brought on by being knocked down by the guard dogs outside the [Miskatonic University] library" (Harms: 2008: 10). I feel this to be an appropriate representation, as presumably Dr Armitage's studies might have gone a great deal further if he had lived. A final definition of meaning should be given in concluding

such a statement, and in quoting again from our reference as written by Rachel Pollack in her study of this subject in question, "[if read] in connection with [the Suit of Sites, discussed later, this Card] calls for grounding in outer reality to avoid being washed away by fantasies or visions" (Pollack: 1983: 57).

Whilst working towards the end of our discussion of the Suit of People as represented by the *HP Lovecraft Tarot*, Rachel Pollacks *Seventy-Eight Degrees of Wisdom* continues to make a statement as to the interpretation of this Card as reversed in a Reading, which I would like to quote in ending this discussion of the Eleventh Card of this Suit, that:

"In other situations, if the Page refers to psychic development, or true visions, then [this Card] reversed shows a person disturbed by these visions. For many people in this rationalized world the sudden emergence of psychic talent, even if deliberately sought through training, can appear very frightening" (Pollack: 1983: 57)

The Eleventh Card of the Suit of People warns us of the inherent danger of academic study and of knowledge misused without due responsibility.

12. Crawford Tillinghast:
Equates to the Knight of Cups

Crawford Tillinghast

As I have previously pointed out, whilst writing this book I have made a conscious statement to keep the research involved to a minimum, and it is for that reason that I've kept with a small number of research materials in order to keep this project together. One of these references, as the reader will have noticed, is an excellent reference titled the *Cthulhu Mythos Encyclopedia* by the noted Lovecraftian scholar Daniel Harms. Whilst this book is in itself a comprehensive and properly researched reference, I would have to say that this book covers most of the Mythos as represented covered properly and in a highly competent manner. In itself this book should be recommended to everyone with any interest in this subject at all. It would therefore be a point in hand that, whilst covering the point to this book, there are still a number of clear omissions whereby I would have expected it to be the case that there would have been a more comprehensive entry, and the personification here of Crawford Tillinghast would have been one of these points in question. This written statement to define this as one part of the Minor Arcana would be represented, therefore, in

order to discuss the small number of Minor Arcana Cards which are not represented by this research in question.

In the Introduction to the *Cthulhu Mythos Encyclopedia* as our stated reference point for research as discussed, Dan Harms makes a statement to discuss the omission of written entries to cover the omission of a number of points of reference, with the personification of Crawford Tillinghast being one of these, and discusses how the research for this reference was put together, in stating that:

"[in researching the *Cthulhu Mythos Encyclopedia*] I had to decide which... stories included elements of the Cthulhu Mythos. This was a considerable undertaking in itself. Even among Mythos fans, there is still considerable disagreement about what stories are 'Cthulhu Mythos' tales... As will be explained later, I tried to keep my analysis to stories mentioning the terms listed in [this book]" (Harms: 2008: xix)

With that definition of terms having been made clear, the Magus should refer to the Introductory Book to the *HP Lovecraft Tarot* (either accessing the Second edition of the Deck or making reference to the Appendix at the end of this book) in order to establish any further meaning that is represented with this Card, but again (as a point that is reiterated throughout *The Necronomicon Cycle*, as it is the case with the greater movement of Chaos Magick Theory), the point here comes down to an idea to represent the mind in connection to the occult and to any further use of occult ceremonial magick. Further to this point, in having already made repeated reference to the *Seventy-Eight Degrees of Wisdom* as another main point of research which will be quoted from throughout the rest of this book, and as one of very few books to properly discuss the specific issue of the Tarot and the occult Minor Arcana, the intention here is to establish how the *HP Lovecraft Tarot* – as the main religious system to be represented by the Cult of R'Lyeh on Earth - equates to the greater study of the occult and religious Tarot as a much greater cohesive issue of its own. It might therefore be

appropriate, with that point in hand, to quote further from this given research whilst discussing the further meaning of this statement that is represented with the personification of Crawford Tillinghast as a part of the Minor Arcana of the Tarot, whilst discussing the meaning of this Card in relation to its Negative definition of interpretation.

Negative Reading

With that point then having been established, we should be warned that the Knight, as being the equivalent personification as with this Deck, "resembles Death, symbol of transformation" (Pollack: 1983: 55). That said, the *HP Lovecraft Tarot* is equally as pessimistic in defining a Negative interpretation of this Card to represent "Limits of perception as 'Safety Valve', guarding Human sanity" (Hutchinson, Friedman: 2002: 54). It is with statements similar to this that we see an example as to how this system of the Tarot makes repeated reference to issues of human psychology (something that has already become a repeating theme with this study), and this could be taken further to possibly establish how such an occult system can be seen as representing the complexities of the human mind.

The *Seventy-Eight Degrees of Wisdom* represents this same principle of archetypal analysis, as the Chapter written on the subject of the same equivalent Card represents the idea of the "knight lost in the enticements of his cup, symbol of the imagination" (Pollack: 1983: 54). Whilst this makes direct sense if interpreted on the basis of the intellect of the person of who a Reading is for, this idea is taken further to establish that, under such an interpretation, "the creative force is less powerful here than in any of the other Cups court cards" (Pollack: 1983: 54). The idea of such a stated limit of perception is represented again on the basis that a Reading with this Card establishes that "The Knight has not learned that true imagination feeds on action rather than fantasy" (Pollack: 1983: 54). And whilst all of this can be seen in relation to such a defined point as regarding such limitation of intellect as the protection of the sanity of any person in question, the *Seventy-*

Eight Degrees of Wisdom points out that the same point is grounded in context with the greater system of the Tarot, in stating:

> "'Imagination' and 'fancy'. Both take the mind away from ordinary experience and perceptions... while the first derives from and leads to an awareness of underlying spiritual truth, the second produces only fantasies that may excite, but ultimately lack real meaning" (Pollack: 1983: 54)

This stated boundary as defining a position of 'guarding human sanity' is, however, often the role of the individual in putting up psychological defences from the World around us, and with the specific study of the Lovecraftian, as with the further study of the Tarot that is the intended discussion of this book, this means of defence includes protection from the occult and the psychick manifestation of the World around us. This means of defence is further put into context, however, as we are told that "By denying this basic commitment to the [outside] world [the Magus] does not allow his imagination to produce anything" (Pollack: 1983: 55). Whilst these terms in themselves might at first appear contradictory, what's being said with this is that the individual should be careful to establish what is a personal sense of balance. Such a statement as regarding Psychology and the mind of the individual is again put into direct perspective, as the *Seventy-Eight Degrees of Wisdom* follows directly with the point in stating that:

> "Because he is a Knight the outside world of action, of sex, may pull him even while he pursues his thoughts and fantasies" (Pollack: 1983: 55)

This given definition of a Negative interpretation continues with a statement to define "Academic platitudes & charlatanry; intellectual posing & pomposity" (Hutchinson, Friedman: 2002: 54), and again this would relate to the functioning of the mind to establish an example as to how the *HP Lovecraft Tarot* can be seen directly in relation to a study

of human psychology and the working of the mind of the individual Magus. And it is on the basis of such an understanding of the human mind that the point is made, that "[the Knight] has not learned to direct his imagination into the world. Therefore dreams dominate this card" (Pollack: 1983: 54). In taking this interpretation of meaning towards a greater statement of justification, this statement as defined by the Lovecraftian system of the Tarot is defined on directly equal terms, in that:

> "if we do nothing with our dreams they remain vague and unrelated to the rest of our lives. [Further to this point of discussion, however] We may make another point about the Knight's dreaminess. What feeds it – inner principles, as in myth or archetypal art; or self-indulgence [?]" (Pollack: 1983: 54)

If to take the whole of this discussion of this on a more fundamental basis, and if the point of the psychological make-up of the mind might still be a position in question, the *Seventy-Eight Degrees of Wisdom* can be quoted (again) that "[all of these points of principle] derive from the ego rather than the unconscious" (Pollack: 1983: 54). Following on from these general statements to define the meanings of these Cards under a Negative principle, however, the *HP Lovecraft Tarot* here continues to establish a position of "Repudiation by peers" (Hutchinson, Friedman: 2002: 54). Whilst this as one statement could be seen as being a generally straightforward point in itself, our other given reference on the subject of the Minor Arcana continues with a statement whereby this can be further established on the basis of the occult Tarot. "The symbolism [as depicted with this Card in many systems of such worship] – Fire of Water in the Golden Dawn system – indicates the elements as unreconciled" (Pollack: 1983: 55).

With that point in discussion defining the greater interpretation as intended with this as the Twelfth Card of the Tarot Suit of Cups, then maybe such a discussion could be taken further as the *Seventy-Eight Degrees of Wisdom* issues further advice as regarding this same and

equivalent Card? A statement to discuss such a position of conflict between friends and peers is discussed to some further extent as this book in question points out that:

"the Knight can represent a lover who does not wish to commit him or herself, who is perhaps attractive yet passive, withdrawn or narcissistic. These harsh images of the Knight all deal with his conflicts" (Pollack: 1983: 55)

Or, in quoting again from the same reference, and to put the same idea differently:

"it can mean that a passive person is being pushed towards action or commitment and does not like it. Without outwardly resisting he or she can resent those demands" (Pollack: 1983: 55)

These three definitions of negative interpretation would, however, have one point in common if we were to choose to accept them on that basis, and the *Seventy-Eight Degrees of Wisdom* can be quoted from again in order to define that point, that "Th[ese] attitude[s] can result in hypocrisy or manipulation, sometimes lies and tricks" (Pollack: 1983: 55). We should be cautious in that the Tarot might be warning us of possible danger to come.

13. Nahum Gardner: Equates to the Queen of Cups

The previous edition of the *HP Lovecraft Tarot* issues its description of this part of the Minor Arcana under the personification of the Mythos character Harley Warren, but with the planned current publication this has been changed to being, instead, defined by the personification of the fictional Mythos character of Nahum Gardner. Whilst it is not entirely clear as to why this change should have been seen as being necessary, the *Cthulhu Mythos Encyclopedia* includes an entry which is far longer under the personification of Harley Warren (as well as a large number of others which define theoretical concepts of their own), although it is still the case that a lot of the research involved with this Card can be considered as being roughly the same as with the previous Suit of People, of which we have pretty much nearly discussed. In order to put this point into more direct terms, although the Introductory Book to the previous Edition describes its definition under the former characterization, the character of Nahum Gardner occupies the position of this same Card which was previously Harley Warren, instead, with this allowing us to give the same description of meaning. Both of these symbolic archetypes are now represented by completely different characters as defined by different archetypal references of Mythos fiction, with both of these representations still standing to define the same principle of meaning. The Magus will notice that I follow this same approach with a number of the other Cards whereby the title has been changed in accord with the planned current Edition of this subject of discussion, although that point is stated whilst we focus on the discussion of those particular Cards in question.

The *Seventy-Eight Degrees of Wisdom* opens its description of this Card of the Minor Arcana by stating that "[this is] The most successful

and balanced of the Cups, in some ways of all of the Minor [Arcana] cards" (Pollack: 1983: 52) of the Tarot. With this given discussion of the Minor Arcana I have tried to put this study in terms of a discussion of the Mythos entities as represented with this specific representation of the Lovecraftian system of the Tarot, and then to break such a discussion down in order to further describe how such a system equates in terms of a larger study of the occult, with the discussion of the Tarot being my reasoning in doing so. With the Card as represented here by Nahum Gardner I have chosen not to follow this approach so directly, as with this as one point in question I feel it would be more direct to first introduce this as more of an archetypal representation (in the further psychiatric definition of the term), and then to try to put that in terms of a greater general discussion. It is on this basis that The *Cthulhu Mythos Encyclopedia* includes an entry on this character in question, and I quote in this context as our reference states that:

"[Nahum Gardner was a] Farmer near Clark's Corners on whose property a mysterious meteorite fell in 1882. Gardner was a respected local man who had worked on his farm with his wife and three sons for many years. After the fall of the meteorite, the vegetation on his land mutated and eventually crumbled. His family members died, vanished, or disappeared. Garner himself succumbed to this mysterious malady shortly thereafter." (Harms: 2008: 105)

That said, the purpose of the *HP Lovecraft Tarot* is to work towards interpreting such a system in context with the further literary study of the Lovecraftian occult, and to try to establish how such a theory of religious thought can equate to something which is, quite obviously, a much larger and complicated system of esoteric thought, and further to that a religious statement in its own right?

This established interpretation of the Tarot continues to define a Positive reading with this Card as representing "Self-sacrifice on behalf of another" (Hutchinson, Friedman: 2008: 54), and with such a statement relating to a greater statement as defined by the Tarot as has

been pointed out repeatedly already, the connection here would be on the basis of such a Mythos archetype working to establish the greater importance of religious terms. In order to establish where this argument in question stands in relation to this greater religious system, our stated research in hand states that this Card relates directly to "[our] vital connection to the world and other people" (Pollack: 1983: 52), with the stated issue of self-sacrifice being a part of this interpretation defined as a general part of such personal interaction. The same research puts this Card of the Minor Arcana and such issues of social interaction into a broader religious framework in pointing out that:

> "we do not feed the imagination by giving it complete freedom to wander where it will, but rather by directing into valuable activity, an idea that most artists would endorse" (Pollack: 1983: 52)

The same archetype in discussion, whilst trying to establish the legitimate importance of the Lovecraftian as a smaller but more important part of the greater theory of religion, is again appropriate in that such our given reference to define this religious study defines a point to represent "Courage; Pushing frontiers [and] challenging boundaries" (Hutchinson, Friedman: 2002: 54). Another definition of this same Card could be read in directly the same context that "[this Card] signifi[es] the unity of self with emotion and imagination [as well as] unconscious forces – the underlying spiritual patterns shown in the Major Arcana – nourish... conscious life" (Pollack: 1983: 52).

Read in context with this and other quotations we see an example of smaller issues coming together to represent a greater cohesive whole. If such an idea of challenging boundaries would be the point here in question then it can be established that this Card "symbolizes the achievement brought about through using the imagination" (Pollack: 1983: 52). And in order to establish the same statement with another quotation from the same source:

> "[this Card] show[s] the strong will that connects and moulds creative force without suppressing it... the creative person derives

inspiration for future activity from her or his past achievements" (Pollack: 1983: 53)

The personification of Nahum Gardner as a personification of Mythos fiction is again appropriate in defining an equation in terms of the Tarot as a system of its own as the Lovecraft system of the Tarot defines a position of "Martyrdom, Heroism" (Hutchinson, Friedman: 2002: 54), although the symbolism established by this form of scrying is important as we should be conscious that "Will power alone will not unite imagination and action" (Pollack: 1983: 53).

Negative Reading

This personification of Nahum Gardner can also be interpreted on Negative terms, as with all of these given descriptions of the Cards of the Minor Arcana, and the *HP Lovecraft Tarot* defines such an interpretation by warning of a situation as relating to "Foolish effort; wasted resources" (Hutchinson, Friedman: 2002: 54), and on wider terms of definition "We see [a possibility of] someone ambitious and powerful, yet dangerous, because she cannot be trusted" (Pollack: 1983: 53) as one example of where this point of definition here comes into the picture. A further situation is warned of in terms of a "Dangerous exploration; disregard for safety and / or restrictions" (Hutchinson, Friedman: 2002: 54), and on wider terms we see a situation that "Reversing the Queen of Cups breaks that unity of vision and action" (Pollack: 1983: 53).

A final interpretation of this Card if drawn as reversed in a Reading is defined as representing a situation of "Prideful recklessness" (Hutchinson, Friedman: 2002: 54), and all of this is again concluded well by quoting from the *Seventy-Eight Degrees of Wisdom*, as we have on numerous occasions already, that:

"If [the Magus] slides further from the balance, she can become dishonourable, even depraved, as her creative force lurches out of control" (Pollack: 1983: 53)

With all of this we see a situation as regards the centring of the individual in question, and this study defined the point that the Magus should take some time to ground themselves in terms of personal balance.

14. Keziah Mason:
Equates to the King of Cups

As we here reach the end of this statement to discuss the first Suit of the Minor Arcana as it is represented by the *HP Lovecraft Tarot*, and where this study in context is represented as part of a much bigger system of secular religion, we run into a problem that

our given statements for research do not really give us enough to do justice to the scope that this Card represents. As a result of this I would suggest the Magus takes what is given with this description and then expand on the ideas here given, as they would do with any other interpretation of religion and the manifest occult, as is established by the Tarot or with any other system of the occult that can be interpreted on the same terms.

In the literary study of Cthulhu Mythos fiction, Keziah Mason was "[a] Supposed witch from Arkham, Massachusetts, apprehended during the witch-scare of 1692" (Harms: 2008: 177), and the *HP Lovecraft Tarot* (quite appropriately) chooses to make reference to such a representation to define the Positive interpretation of this Card to establish a position of "True Alchemy, successful mixture of Science & Mysticism; balance of rational & intuitive faculties" (Hutchinson,

Friedman: 2002: 54). The example of a religious witch being in this context appropriate to represent the further meaning here established, and in order to establish how this is justified in terms of the concepts here in question, the *Cthulhu Mythos Encyclopedia* states that during her life "[Keziah Mason] had discovered certain combinations of lines and angles allowing travel through dimensions" (Harms: 2008: 177). Such an interpretation could be justified on the greater level of the Tarot, as the third main reference as quoted from as the research to define our interpretation of the Minor Arcana defines this Card that "[the Magus] has directed his creative powers into... responsible achievements" (Pollack: 1983: 50); in this case Keziah's esoteric studies equating to this same idea are representative of that which is meant with this statement. In terms of a meaning to be established should this Card be drawn as part of a Reading, we see a good example here in hand that "In its extreme the imagery [as expressed here as a witch] suggests someone who has dammed up his or her emotions and imagination" (Pollack: 1983: 50), with the same statement taken still further that:

> "Some commentators see the King [of Cups as an equivalent same Card in other systems of Tarot] as a person of troubled emotions, even anger or violence, who habitually supresses these feelings even from himself, always maintaining a calm exterior" (Pollack: 1983: 51)

With this we see another clear example of where a system such as the *HP Lovecraft Tarot* establishes its own criteria whilst still establishing similar terms as is represented by the Tarot as a greater system of occult religion and truth.

This idea taken further, our system of Tarot in question moves on to define a position of "Metaphysics in the most literal sense of the word" (Hutchinson, Friedman: 2002: 54), and whilst our research here in question says little in general terms as regarding the scientific or occult study or interpretation of the philosophy of Metaphysics, there

is still a quotation to be given here in context that, according to the *Cthulhu Mythos Encyclopedia*:

"Keziah Mason confessed freely to here crimes, saying that the Devil had given her the secret names of Nahab and [had] taken her to secret rites at various isolated locations" (Harms: 2008: 177)

In continuing to use such representations of concepts and so on as part of such a discussion whilst writing on the subject of Positive interpretations, and in doing so in making this as a study of the Lovecraftian as the first issue in doing so, the *HP Lovecraft Tarot* here continues this as part of the Minor Arcana Suit of People by defining a position of a "'Quantum leap' in consciousness [and a principle of] psychological evolution" (Hutchinson, Friedman: 2002: 54). That said, any such given study of the Lovecraftian, or of any further study of the occult (for that matter), must always give enough scope for the Magus to be able to expand on such a study and to establish their own terms whilst working to establish any practical system of occult magick. One further quotation I feel would be appropriate in concluding the Positive meaning of this last Card of the Suit of People, however, and that is whilst discussing the archetypal representation of the concepts as represented by the personification of the example here with Keziah Mason, would be that "[in order] To aid her mischievous deeds [the Devil] had given her a familiar named Brown Jenkin" (Harms: 2008: 177).[1]

---

1 In order to elaborate here, Keziah Mason's familiar was a personification of something between a person and a rat. Those practicing Chaos Magick Theory might choose to use this example to relate to a psychological shift between paradigms. With this being possibly the case the Magus should make a point of making a study of this idea first, and I would suggest that a good point to start with this would be Lovecraft's short story which discusses these points in question. A bibliographical reference for such a short story would be: Lovecraft, H. P. (2005) The Dreams in the Witch House. In: The Dreams in the Witch House and Other Weird Stories. London: Penguin Modern Classics.

Negative Reading

The *HP Lovecraft Tarot* here defines a Negative reading with this Card as relating to the principle of "Irrational and inconsistent blend of Science & Mysticism; 'Psychobabble,' pop psychology" (Hutchinson, Friedman: 2002: 54), and if read in connection with this statement we should consider the point that: "[this] card upside down can mean that the violent Air emotions emerge from their calm exterior, perhaps through the pressure of outside events" (Pollack: 1983: 51). This taken further we see a position of "Secrets, 'Skeletons in the Closet;' Deception, Manipulation" (Hutchinson, Friedman: 2002: 54), and if to interpret this idea in further connection with the Lovecraftian we can quote again from the *Cthulhu Mythos Encyclopedia*, that:

> "After she gave the names of her fellow coven members, the judges condemned Keziah to death – an unusual sentence, since most witch trial participants who confessed were not killed" (Harms: 2008: 177)

In order to put this entire definition on more concise terms, "the King of Cups reversed slides towards dishonesty" (Pollack: 1983: 51)

As the concluding statement of definition as established here as the Suit of People here we see an example of "Overwhelming revelation; confrontation with radical truths" (Hutchinson, Friedman: 2002: 54). Whilst I could conclude this given statement to say that everything has now been said, I would finally quote again from a statement on the personification of Keziah Mason in order to further clarify such statements from the Lovecraftian Tarot, and on further justified Lovecraftian terms, and I feel that the following quotation as regarding this Suit is again appropriate in closing such a discussion, that:

> "Shortly [after that trial, Keziah Mason] escaped from her cell, leaving nothing behind but a mysterious drawing upon the walls of her prison. When the judges went to arrest her co-conspirators, they

found them gone and the same markings in their homes" (Harms: 2008: 177)

With all of that having therefore been clearly stated, I would like to and this discussion of the Lovecraftian first Suit of the Minor Arcana with one last quotation, and I feel that quoting again from the *Seventy-Eight Degrees of Wisdom* would be appropriate to conclude this given discussion of one defined point of occult religious truth, that:

"Finally, in relating to the arts, the King reversed can suggest that an artist's achievement has proved to be insignificant, or that a person has not yet matured and cannot point to a significant body of work" (Pollack: 1983: 51)

As from this point on I will leave to be the work of the Magus to establish the greater meaning of this Suit of the Minor Arcana on their own individual religious terms...

Suit of Artifacts

The *HP Lovecraft Tarot* continues to state that this Suit of the Minor Arcana relates to a system of "Objects & Objectives" (Hutchinson, Friedman: 2002: 50) with these representing meanings that are defined by other systems of the Tarot in terms of various different systems of graphical representation. In might therefore be an interesting point to note that the reference used with this book, and which was written to discuss such a greater system of occult religion points out that "In many ways Swords [with our system in question defining the same Suit of the Minor Arcana as Artifacts] are the most difficult suit [to define in terms of interpretation]" (Pollack: 1983: 71). Whilst this reference in question defines such representation as being the symbolism of Swords, they themselves are an object, and in this context "signif[y] pain, anger [and] destruction... it is mostly these experiences that the Swords [in this context] depict" (Pollack: 1983: 71).

This defined idea goes further to define a principle to represent "Internal & External powers, possibilities & influences" (Hutchinson, Friedman: 2002: 50). This definition of terms should be interpreted on the greater level of the Lovecraftian, however, and it is on this defined basis that our reference in question, which is written in part to discuss this suit of the Tarot, points out that according to this interpretation "the mind never rests, twisting and turning, sometimes violent, sometimes clam, but [the mind] always move[s]. Anyone who has tried to meditate will know how persistently the mind moves" (Pollack: 1983: 72). This

general definition, as represented with the *HP Lovecraft Tarot* as the Suit of Artifacts goes further than with this statement though, and whilst this as relating to the symbolic representation of objects is not clearly the issue in question, this statement to represent this Suit of the Minor Arcana points out that:

"Because our culture has always emphasized rationality, many people today see thinking in general as the cause of all life's problems. If we just stop thinking… [then] everything will work out all right" (Pollack: 1983: 72)

If it is the stated point in question here that with the Suit of Artifacts, as with the rest of the Deck in discussion, we are trying to define the importance of symbolism as established by defining objects, then it is still the case that the mental perception of what we are doing is always the most important point, and this is established in that "The fact is, the more confused we are the more we need our minds" (Pollack: 1983: 72).

A final definition to be taken into consideration as discussed with the Suit of Artifacts, is one of "Landmarks, milestones, & other points of reference on one's journey" (Hutchinson, Friedman: 2002: 50), although in terms of the greater interpretation of the Tarot this Suit establishes a position that "we cannot begin our own quests for meaning and value in life until we have learned to recognize and accept the truth, whatever pain that brings" (Pollack: 1983: 71). At the same time, whilst the *Seventy-Eight Degrees of Wisdom* describes the meaning of this Suit in terms established by the Tarot as a singular statement of its own, this definition is still represented on the basis of perception, that:

"The mind sees so many sides to a situation, so many possibilities, that understanding, let alone action [can] become… impossible… We do not overcome the problem of an element by banishing it or replacing it with something, but rather by combining it with other elements" (Pollack: 1983: 72)

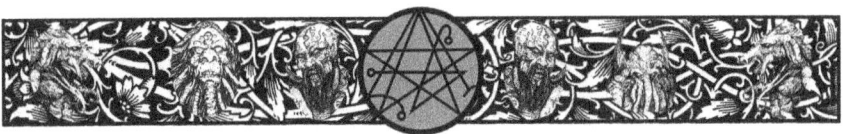

Minor Arcana	Suit of Artifacts	Suit of Swords
1	Star Stone	Ace of Swords
2	The Colour Out of Space	Two of Swords
3	The Silver Key	Three of Swords
4	The Shining Trapezohedron	Four of Swords
5	Guardian of Kadath	Five of Swords
6	The Yellow Sign	Six of Swords
7	EOD Vestments	Seven of Swords
8	The Tillinghast Resonator	Eight of Swords
9	Pickman's Model	Nine of Swords
10	Mi-Go Brain Cylinder	Ten of Swords
11	Bokrug, the Water Lizard	Page of Swords
12	Hound Amulet	Knight of Swords
13	Derby Stone	Queen of Swords
14	Plutonian Drug	King of Swords

Table 6. The Lovecraftian Suit of Artifacts equated to the Minor Arcana Suit of Swords.

In defining this Suit in relation to the study of the Tarot already discussed, this same statement links this to "the deep values grounded in spiritual / psychological truth that we see embodied in the Major Arcana" (Pollack: 1983: 72), and with this we establish the importance of the lesser Suits of the Minor Arcana in relation to the religious principles as defined with the study of the *HP Lovecraft Tarot* as our significant religious Deck as discussed.

1. Star Stone:
Equates to the Ace of Swords

Otherwise known as the "Star Stones of Mnar", these artifacts are "Grey-green rocks from the land of Mnar with the Elder Sign carved into them" (Harms: 2008: 267), although stones with the same symbol etched onto them have on some occasions been used by occultists for a similar point of protection from malevolent Mythos entities (and Gods). The *Cthulhu Mythos Encyclopedia* continues to describe this idea by saying that "Their power comes not so much from the Sign, however, as from the power inherent in each stone. Holding a star-stone may protect a person from the minions of the Great Old Ones, but not the Great Old Ones themselves" (Harms: 2008: 268).

The Positive interpretation as given with this Card is defined in terms of "Protection, Sanctuary, Security" (Hutchinson, Friedman: 2002: 55), and the *Seventy-Eight Degrees of Wisdom* further defines this Card of the Minor Arcana as stating that "The... (first) Sword card [with the Lovecraft system defining this under the Suit of Artifacts] returns us to the true essence of th[is] suit – intellect" (Pollack: 1983: 92). This same given research should establish a point that "Stones very much like these first appear in '*At the Mountains of Madness*' [as one of Lovecraft's short stories, as mentioned above] but there they serve as decorations and currency for the Elder Things" (Harms: 2008: 268), rather than for any other defined purpose. The same statement written on the subject of the occult Minor Arcana links both of these statements in saying that:

"The[se] mountains [as discussed in the *Seventy-Eight Degrees of Wisdom*] symbolize 'abstract truth', objective facts of existence,

independent of personal viewpoint and experience. The Major Arcana depicts this truth for us; more than any Minor card the Ace of Swords [as this Card's equivalent in other systems] reaches through to the fifth element" (Pollack: 1983: 92)

What should be noticed as important here is that , if to draw further reference from the same book by Rachel Pollack, at this point the element of Mercury is entered into the argument, this being the element representing the study of the occult and the psychick development inherent in the mind of the individual in studying this system and of the Magus in applying this theory to the study of occult magick.

The further Positive interpretation of this Card is here defined in terms of a "Key, pass; opening, passage" (Hutchinson, Friedman: 2002: 55), and the overt religious significance of the Star Stones are further established in that "The Elder Gods themselves may have created these stones, as they are often found near the tombs of some of the Great Old Ones" (Harms: 2008: 268). What these connected points mean when interpreted in this context would relate to the occult significance established in such worship, and the psychick intensity of the human mind as part of such worship, with a position established that "[when pulled from the pack and facing upwards] for true perception, the sword pierces the crown of the material world. Wisdom leads us beyond illusions and limitations to the spiritual truth contained within life" (Pollack: 1983: 92). With the same statement in question going on to establish a position that "In confusing, emotional or oppressive situations, the mind can pierce the fog, and knots to give a clear understanding of the real facts" (Pollack: 1983: 93), the *Cthulhu Mythos Encyclopedia* again puts this into relevant context in stating that "[The] Miskatonic University has been conducting experiments in mass-producing star-stones with some success [for some number of years so far]" (Harms: 2008: 268).

In taking that idea further, if a Positive interpretation with this Card would relate to a principle regarding to the idea of a "Charm,

amulet, talisman, artifact" (Hutchinson, Friedman: 2002: 55), then the same research would equate such a position in direct context with the Star-Stones, as this Card represents a single symbolism of meaning in stating that:

> "*The Sussex Manuscript* maintains that there are three different kinds of star-stones: the regular kind, a polished oval stone useful against 'kings' (lesser Great Old Ones?), and a jewel with fire in its heart which guard the tombs of the Great Old Ones themselves. No one has observed the latter two varieties, so they may not exist" (Harms: 2008: 268)

Negative Reading

The *HP Lovecraft Tarot* here continues in defining a Negative interpretation of this Card as relating to "Weakness, False security, misplaced truth" (Hutchinson, Friedman: 2002: 55), and again this is put into direct context by the *Seventy-Eight Degrees of Wisdom* as a specific study of the Minor Arcana. On this basis we see an interpretation of this Card if coming up as reversed, in that "Many of the Swords [in this case the Suit of Artifacts] cards suffer from the illusion that life contains only sorrow and pain... intellect alone, divorced from intuition, will only lead to more illusion" (Pollack: 1983: 92). Statements such as this should be directly put into perspective as according to the personal situation as to who the Reading is for, however, and we should here be conscious of a position that "Often... emotions are exaggerated, egoistic, or self-indulgent... neither will intellect alone bring real awareness" (Pollack: 1983: 92). And if a concluding statement from this resource in question would define a position that "The grip fails, bringing illusion, confused ideas and feelings [and] overpowering emotions" (Pollack: 1983: 93), then the Magus should be cautious that:

> "Acquisition of star-stones should be left to seasoned veterans of preternatural struggle who (it is hoped) know what they are doing" (Harms: 2008: 268)

Whilst it is the obvious symbolism involved which should here be seen as being important, if this interpretation in question would be further representative of a situation as regarding "Locks, cages, prison" (Hutchinson, Friedman: 2002: 55), then we should be cautious of a position that "Problems become exaggerated; everything, including attraction, appears to be more important than it actually is" (Pollack: 1983: 93). This statement in itself would be accentuated with the position of the Star-Stones as one issue in question, however, as the *Cthulhu Mythos Encyclopedia* warns that:

"Not only might the stone's removal [with this in metaphorical context] allow an evil force to break free, the Elder Gods have been known on occasions to punish those who move large numbers of the star-stones from their proper places" (Harms: 2008: 268)

This Negative interpretation here concludes in defining a principle of "Fetish, jinx, glamour, bewitchment" (Hutchinson, Friedman: 2002: 55), and again the *Seventy-Eight Degrees of Wisdom* does a good job in putting this into perspective in pointing out that "Without a clear sense of reality, the mind can fall prey to mistakes created by emotion" (Pollack: 1983: 93). And with all of that defining a proper definition of such principles in question as with the larger entity of the Minor Arcana, I feel that a final quotation from the *Cthulhu Mythos Encyclopedia* sums up all of this quite nicely, that:

"Star stones are usually where they are for good reason and should not be disturbed if found. Every year, dozens of paranormal investigators are injured or killed because they ignore this simple rule" (Harms: 2008: 268)

Again, this study of Mythos religion warns the Magus to be careful…

2. The Colour Out of Space: Equates to the Two of Swords

A Positive interpretation with this Card is defined by the *HP Lovecraft Tarot* as relating to a position of "Prima Materia, Quintessence, Hyle" (Hutchinson, Friedman: 2002: 55); and this is again appropriate as the *Cthulhu Mythos Encyclopedia* describes the Colour out of Space as being "[something] from outer space which appears to be a colour of no known spectrum" (Harms: 2008: 51). In terms of further interpreting this statement we are dealing here with an issue of symbolism to describe something which, on valid terms, does not happen, is totally alien to our dimension and this Earth, and which can further only be interpreted on conceptual and therefore psychological terms. The Magus should be aware of such points of definition when interpreting this Card in the specific context of doing a Reading. And if the same description continues to establish a position of "Purity of spirit; Agent of Transformation" (Hutchinson, Friedman: 2002: 55), then The Colour out of Space might be an appropriate principle to describe such a concept of transformation, in that "[this representation] might take on... material form after some time [of having settled on E]arth" (Harms: 2008: 51). The same statement as regarding principles of transformation is again a valid point in question as this statement continues that "The Colour's embryonic stage is that of a small sphere three inches in diameter" (Harms: 2008: 51), with such transformation becoming progressively more weird through a given passage of time. Whilst at the same time defining this same statement to define a principle of purity of spirit, the *Seventy-Eight Degrees of Wisdom* makes an appropriate statement in describing this as a part of the Minor Arcana, in pointing out that:

"A veil separates [the Magus] from the waters of the unconscious hidden behind her; no veil protects the blindfolded woman from her disturbed pool of emotions" (Pollack: 1983: 91)

This same definition of a Positive interpretation continues directly as the *HP Lovecraft Tarot* moves towards defining a principle of "Object of Quest; Holy Grail, unicorn, the Philosopher's Stone" (Hutchinson, Friedman: 2002: 55), and the idea of the consciousness being awakened to new intellectual revelations is defined according to this representation that "When [the Colour, here representing the hidden nature of the unconscious mind] enters a planet's atmosphere, the sphere is broken and the Colour larva emerges" (Harms: 2008: 51). All of these points are put into another specific context when our given study of the Minor Arcana points out that "If we let nothing approach us, then nothing can hurt us" (Pollack: 1983: 90). Such is the nature of the Tarot.

Negative Reading

A Negative reading as relating to this Card is here defined in terms of "Chaos, lack of form & definition" (Hutchinson, Friedman: 2002: 55), and this would be appropriate in this context if we consider that:

"The Colour's life cycle in space is unknown, as the only encounters with it so far have been made on [E]arth... When the Colour has gained enough energy, it drains the surrounding area and flies off into space, leaving a blasted area devoid of all life behind it" (Harms: 2008: 51)

With a second definition establishing a point of "Cause or reason for dissolution, corruption" (Hutchinson, Friedman: 2002: 55), the Colour out of Space makes another appropriate point in defining the same principle of the Minor Arcana, as the same entry from the *Cthulhu Mythos Encyclopedia* continues to describe the same point, in that:

2. The Colour Out of Space: Equates to the Two of Swords

"[before ending its cycle on Earth, the Colour] begins to exert a subtle influence over life in the surrounding area, feeding first on the lower levels of the food chain and moving its way up to animals and humans. Affected lifeforms often grow to abnormal sizes and mutate, though soon after they crumble into dust" (Harms: 2008: 51)

Whilst all of these quotations represent situations to be read on specific metaphorical terms, and in the specific context of this Card and who the Reading is for (as is the case with all of the Cards of the *HP Lovecraft Tarot*, as is the situation with all other Decks), the Negative definition here moves towards establishing the point on clearer terms, and this should also be regarded in the specific context of a specific Reading, that:

"The balance is lost – or given up. Either the person becomes knocked over by people or problems charging her defences, or else the blindfold [as previously mentioned] is given up for the purpose of either seeing truth or communicating" (Pollack: 1983: 91)

And if this definition is further concluded with a statement to establish "Loss of will, lack of integrity; squandered opportunity" (Hutchinson, Friedman: 2002: 55), then we can continue to further establish this point by quoting again from the *Seventy-Eight Degrees of Wisdom*, in stating:

"th[is] blindfold shows here not confusion, but a deliberate closing of the eyes. The [Magus] has tied it on[to] herself so that she will not have to choose between friend and enemy, for such choice becomes the first step in once again involving herself with other people" (Pollack: 1983: 90)

Whilst this statement in describing the Second Card of the Suit of Artifacts has tried to draw a number of different statements together in

order to establish the importance of the Lovecraftian as a representation of the larger movement of the historical and religious system of the Tarot, I would conclude this short statement in quoting again from Rachel Pollack's study of the Minor Arcana, in pointing out that "Paradoxically, the attempt to stop emotion [can] make... a person more emotional" (Pollack: 1983: 91).

3. THE SILVER KEY: EQUATES TO THE THREE OF SWORDS

As we embark on the study of the Third Card of the Lovecraftian Suit of Artifacts, we approach a situation of consciousness defined under the principle of reality as established through the understanding of dreams, and this is the point established with the symbolism as represented by the Silver Key. This issue would be a specific point of interpretation in itself, as the fiction which defines this discussion has much to represent such insight and workings of that which is repressed by the darkness of the unconscious mind. This ties in with a number of other Cards as discussed with our interpretation of the Lovecraftian Minor Arcana. In opening the definition of the principles in describing this Card of the Tarot, it might be on this basis that the research I have used to describe this statement does seem to be more obscure than with that relating to most of the other Cards with this discussion of the Minor Arcana in question, although that would establish the nature of the symbolism upheld by this Card in question.

The *Cthulhu Mythos Encyclopedia* defines this artifact in question by stating that "The Silver Key was forged in the land of Hyperborea many years ago" (Harms: 2008: 262), and further research defines a point that "The Golden Dawn title for this card is 'sorrow'" (Pollack: 1983: 89). The *HP Lovecraft Tarot*, however, establishes the definition of this Card as relating to "Transcendence of the need to conform to 'mature' models of ambition & action" (Hutchinson, Friedman: 2002: 55). This statement to relate to the constant movement of life that represents all people is further defined with the symbolism in hand with the specific example of the Silver Key, in that "Through the use of enchantment also created in Hyperborea, the powers of the Key can be greatly increased [for the purpose of benefiting its user]" (Harms:

2008: 262).

This general symbolism continues when we see a position to define a situation of "Regaining innocence, the 'Inner Child'; optimism & simple joys" (Hutchinson, Friedman: 2002: 55), and this idea is established on broader terms when the *Seventy-Eight Degrees of Wisdom* points out that this Card:

> "brings a certain calm in the symmetry of its swords [as here represented by Artifacts]. To true sorrow we can make only one response – take the pain into our hearts, accept it and go beyond it" (Pollack: 1983: 89)

The Positive interpretation of this Card is therefore concluded as defining a position of "A higher consciousness; The Doors of Perception" (Hutchinson, Friedman: 2002: 55), and it is with this statement that the example of The Silver Key comes into its own as symbolic in representing a greater meaning. With such an object of esoteric symbolism described as being "[a] Key of tarnished silver five inches long [and] carved with indecipherable hieroglyphics" (Harms: 2008: 262) this idea of psychick consciousness here entered into is that:

> "When certain words are spoken as the Key is held up to the setting sun and rotated nine times, this device can physically transfer its user to any time desired" (Harms: 2008: 262)

Negative Reading

The *HP Lovecraft Tarot* works further to define a Negative interpretation with this Card as representing "Immaturity, phantasm, escape into dreams & fantasy" (Hutchinson, Friedman: 2002: 55), and whilst such a statement of escapist fantasy can be defined that "If the bearer is worthy [The Silver Key] may also be used to unlock the Ultimate Gate which Umr-at-Tawl guards" (Harms: 2008: 262), we

should at all times be aware of the dangers of such ideas running out of control if not properly understood by the Magus. "The Three [of this Suit of the Minor Arcana] tells us that we must not push the pain away from us, but [to] somehow take it deep inside until it becomes transformed" (Pollack: 1983: 89). In quoting again from the *Seventy-Eight Degrees of Wisdom* we see the same situation established, that:

> "If something in life appears too painful we may push it away, try not to think about it, and avoid any reminders. Such an attitude keeps the pain forever with us, and in fact increases its hold" (Pollack: 1983: 90)

This general idea continues as the same Negative interpretation defines a position of "Lost dreams; faded innocence; cynicism & pessimism" (Hutchinson, Friedman: 2002: 55), and this is put into perspective that "Of all the swords, the Three most simply represents pain and heartbreak" (Pollack: 1983: 89). And if the same Negative interpretation warns of a situation relating to "Delusions; Alcoholism, Drug addiction" (Hutchinson, Friedman: 2002: 55), then it might be appropriate to quote again from the *Seventy-Eight Degrees of Wisdom* as one of our main sources of reference here in hand, that "The healing process becomes blocked when we fight acceptance" and we should be cautious of this resulting with a situation of "mental alienation... disorder [and] confusion" (Pollack: 1983: 90).

4. The Shining Trapezohedron: Equates to the Four of Swords

As the idea has already been pointed out, with my researching this statement on the Tarot I have consciously made a point in keeping research material to a minimum. This has been partly because I have felt that only this minimum of references should be necessary, but also in order to make life easier should the Magus choose to take these avenues of research further on their own terms to further establish their own systems of ceremonial magick as influenced by research into the occult Tarot. With this part of the Suit of Artifacts, however, I introduce another reference of research into the argument, with this being a statement from the Satanic religious theologian, Anton LaVey. This idea has been partly on the basis of his influence as one of very few people to have written anything on the subject of the Trapezohedron, with this being the symbolic meaning of this Card, but also on the basis that the Cult of R'Lyeh have huge respect for the ideas of Anton LaVey as a religious thinker, and the idea of the Trapezohedron here gives us a good opportunity to represent such ideas as a part of his discussion of occult theory. A short statement to represent this ideas as upheld by the movement of religious Satanism and the Cult of R'Lyeh is included with the Further Reading statement given at the end of this book, which the reader should make reference to in relation to the same idea of establishing a greater working system of the occult and ceremonial and ritual magick.

For those who might be asking what, exactly, such an artifact is, a Trapezohedron can be described as being any geometric shape that has a strange number of sides. Occult significance has often been attributed to such a shape for this reason. That said, the *HP Lovecraft Tarot* ascribes this Card to be representative of the fundamental power

of the human mind when focused in relation to the psychick use of the occult and black magick, and this can be seen on the same basis of the discussion of the paragraph included above.

Also known as the "Crystal of Chaos" (Harms: 2008: 256), the *Cthulhu Mythos Encyclopedia* continues to describe this as representing the Fourth Card of the Lovecraftian Suit of Artifacts, in that:

"A species of crustaceans that predated the mi-go created the artifact and brought it to [E]arth. After a great war, the Elder Things destroyed its original powers and placed the Trapezohedron in a box of their own design, using its power to destroy the Shoggoths during the rebellion" (Harms: 2008: 256)

With a Positive reading of the Tarot here we see a situation defined as relating to "Hypnotism; Mystic Trance, Shamanism" (Hutchinson, Friedman: 2002: 55), and this would be appropriate if our research tells us that "The Trapezohedron may be used in many ways. It serves as a window in which one may gaze on all time and space" (Harms: 2008: 256). This statement to define the position of the mind in interpreting strange geometric shapes is described on more down to earth terms, as Anton LaVey makes a statement to describe the same subject, in pointing out that:

"In 1962 I isolated my suppositions and distilled them into what I termed 'The Law of the Trapezoid'. I had ample evidence that spatial concepts were not only able to effect those who were involved in visual confrontations, but far more insidiously, other parties with whom a viewer came into contact" (LaVey: 1992: 155)

However, in trying to define the concepts involved with the significance of the Cthulhu Mythos in relating to anything which might be in any way down to earth, things are never so straightforward, with this being the initial concept that *The Necronomicon Cycle* is written to discuss. It is on these same terms that the *HP Lovecraft Tarot*

continues to establish a Positive meaning here to describe a position of "Clairvoyance, Channelling, Vision into other worlds" (Hutchinson, Friedman: 2002: 55), and the *Cthulhu Mythos Encyclopedia* continues with this idea to include a reference to define the significance of such strange geometric shapes and their importance as part of the Lovecraftian occult, in stating:

> "Some have connected the Shining Trapezohedron with the magical stone known to alchemists as 'Azoth,' Doctor John Dee's shewstone through which he communicated with the angels, and the curious angles found in many haunted houses and temples" (Harms: 2008: 256)

In concluding a definition of this part of the Minor Arcana, again we see another clear example of how the *HP Lovecraft Tarot* makes frequent reference to contemporary issues such as Psychiatry and similar concepts, and it is on this basis that we have a situation involving "Activation of & contact with the Collective Unconscious" (Hutchinson, Friedman: 2002: 55). With this we directly approach another example of where the concepts as involved with the Lovecraftian can be related directly to the unconscious movements of the mind, and if we can establish such terms with the idea that "The Trapezohedron's lost power is to accelerate any bodily metamorphosis, such as Deep One transformation which may be taking place in its viewer" (Harms: 2008: 256), then here we have an example of a position that everything established by this system of the Tarot, can also be seen as representing an aspect of the unconscious mind. The same expression of the active unconscious can be seen on the same terms if we were to quote again from Anton LaVey in representing this idea that:

> "the tower in Lovecraft's *Haunter of the Dark*, when the shining trapezohedron beams its influence and the Great Old Ones from the brine harken and send forth their earthly emissary [and] The literary rites of Huxley and Lovecraft [as with] the devastation brought forth

by the angles in Frank Bellknap Long's *Hounds of Tindalos* [can all represent this same idea]" (LaVey: 1992: 114)

Negative Reading

If a Negative interpretation of this Card would establish a position of "Loss of willpower; Domination, possession" (Hutchinson, Friedman: 2002: 55), then the same ideas as already discussed establish the position that:

"[If misused] Nyarlathotep's Haunter of the Dark aspect will manifest itself nearby. It maintains a link with the gazer, seeking to possess his or her body and thereby remain in our world" (Harms: 2008: 256)

If this general idea comes back to the occult significance of strange geometry as a representation of such religious belief, as has already been briefly discussed, then Anton LaVey puts the same idea on clearer terms, that "Any shape or spatial concept that triggers fear could therefore be considered evil" (LaVey: 1992: 111). It would be interesting to note, then, that whilst discussing the Minor Arcana on much broader terms, the *Seventy-Eight Degrees of Wisdom* also speaks on further psychological terms when stating that:

"Withdrawal, even for the purpose of recovery, can shut a person off from the world, creating a kind of spell [that] only outside energy can break" (Pollack: 1983: 88)

This same statement is mirrored by Anton LaVey in pointing out that "The most social and tranquil person can be drawn into a chaotic situation if his surroundings are sufficiently disturbing" (LaVey: 1992: 115).

This same psychological point of discussion continues and the *HP*

Lovecraft Tarot warns of a situation involving "Atavism; Reactivation of dormant animalistic traits" (Hutchinson, Friedman: 2002: 55). This point in psychology is again put in more straightforward terms by Anton LaVey in that "Whether you like to admit it or not, the fear response [as the most prominent of such animalistic traits] is one of the most easily aroused. Since self-preservation is nature's highest law, fear motivates [all human instincts and personal insight]" (LaVey: 1992: 111).

All of this as a discussion of the meaning of this part of the Minor Arcana can be concluded in making another reference to LaVey's title *The Devil's Notebook* as a series of short essays which represent the Satanic, in that:

> "If the Law of the Trapezoid is known, recognized where applicable and either heeded or utilized, it will save much hardship and tragedy, while still serving as a catalyst for change... And like the first crystalline fusion of atoms, it will be the beginning and the end, the Alpha and Omega of all matter" (LaVey: 1992: 116)

5. Guardian of Kadath: Equates to the Five of Swords

In continuing directly from the previous statement above, if you've been reading this book so far you will have picked upon the point of my keeping my research material to a minimum, and the reason I choose to do so is in trying to write a comprehensive statement to represent the important significance of the Lovecraftian whilst interpreted in relation to the Tarot, whilst trying to be concise in my actions in doing so. However, in following such a personal rule there have been numerous complications with such research, as I discussed earlier with the example of Wizard Noah Whateley as represented by the Eighth Card of the Suit of People, and with a number of other Cards with this discussion of the Lovecraftian Deck of the Tarot discussed. This is the same situation with this Card here discussed, as the *Cthulhu Mythos Encyclopedia* (as has been stated as being a main part of such research in question) here gives us a reference for Kadath in the Cold Waste, but further to that gives us nothing in specific terms to represent the Guardian of Kadath, as is the representation with this Card of the Tarot. This gives me the option of using this entry in order to write a statement on this Card in question, or otherwise to leave it in order to issue a statement on Kadath as being a place as according to Mythos literature, as being more appropriate if intending to write a proper entry on this subject as it is represented later as part of the Minor Arcana Suit of Sites, below. In order to put this into a relevant context, however, this same resource into our religious system points out that:

"The study of the Cthulhu Mythos is one with many pitfalls, as reading any work attempting to catalogue it (including this one)

will show. Such efforts are often biased towards particular stories which the author likes, while elements which others might consider important are omitted" (Harms: 2008: xviii)

Whilst an entry for the Guardian of Kadath might have been nice, we must also be accepting of human limitation.

That said, it might be considered as being self-defeating that a book written to discuss the *HP Lovecraft Tarot* might have to suggest that a more direct reference to this Deck might be necessary in order to make a definition as to the meaning here in question, but without proper research this leaves us without another option. At this point I would suggest that getting your hands on a copy of previous Edition of the *HP Lovecraft Tarot* is not easy to get hold of, and so I have thought to give the Magus a complete transcription of the Minor Arcana of this system as the first Appendix to this book, with the intention of allowing them to interpret this system of the Tarot in the context of using their own chosen Deck. But on this point I digress.[1]

Negative Reading

With that as a statement to discuss how the Cards of the Tarot should be interpreted in any Reading, the first issue of importance here is that, under all circumstances the meaning of any Card should foremost be considered as according to the idea that comes from that Card, and in conjunction with that Reading, and it is on this basis that the concept of the Guardian of Kadath should, again, be a point of interpretation that should be down to the person who is doing a Reading of this Deck of the Tarot that this book is written to discuss. That point established, the Lovecraftian system does make a clear statement to define this Card as clearly representing an idea of "Accomplishments constantly out of reach, illusion of progress" (Hutchinson, Friedman: 2002: 56).

---

[1] A statement should here be pointed out that the publication of the Third Edition of the HP Lovecraft Tarot puts this point into a different context, and that this therefore makes this particular point slightly different.

This would appear to be quite different from what is meant with this Card as part of the greater system of the Minor Arcana, however, as in quoting again from the *Seventy-Eight Degrees of Wisdom* the point is established that the Card as is otherwise represented (in a large number of other systems of the Tarot) as the Five of Swords is:

> "One of the most difficult cards, and one of the reasons why people find the Rider [Waite] pack too negative... All the Fives show sorrow or loss... The image of an enemy can refer to a real person, an overall situation or an inner feeling of inadequacy... Where the right side up indicates the moment of defeat, reversed extends this to the despair felt afterwards" (Pollack: 1983: 87)

6. The Yellow Sign: Equates to the Six of Swords

The *Seventy-Eight Degrees of Wisdom* describes the Card that the Lovecraft system of the Tarot represents and depicts with the archetype of the Yellow Sign, in that "[this is] A strange and powerful image, this card... suggests a... spiritual journey – in myth, Charon carrying the dead across the River Styx" (Pollack: 1983: 85).

However, in approaching this concept we are now dealing again with the apparition of the Mythos God Hastur (who has His own Card as part of our discussion of the Major Arcana), who is described by *The Necronomicon* as He Who Should Not be Named, as to do so is most often associated with an impending situation of unheeded disaster.

With this point taken into consideration, this does not mean that a Positive interpretation of this Card as defined by the *HP Lovecraft Tarot* does not offer anything which might not be in any way good from the perspective of someone who chooses to do a Reading whilst choosing to access our religious Deck. It is on this basis that a definition of such Positive interpretation is stated, by the *HP Lovecraft Tarot*, in terms of:

"The end of a bad event or phenomenon, external influence brings resolution of immobility and / or dissolution of obstacles" (Hutchinson, Friedman: 2002: 56)

In here working forward whilst still using the *Seventy-Eight Degrees of Wisdom* as one of our main points of reference, as already discussed, Rachel Pollack issues a different statement in representing this same Card of the Minor Arcana in stating:

"Though we carry our troubles with us we have adapted to them; they will not sink us or bear us down… [the symbolism of black in respect to this Card] indicates potentiality; where nothing final has happened [and where] all things remain possible" (Pollack: 1983: 85)

In taking this idea further, the Six of Swords (here discussed in relation to the Lovecraft system) "[should be seen as] a Gate. Looking at it with sensitivity and then entering into the picture will produce… a quieting effect on the mind" (Pollack: 1983: 85). It is this mention of a Gate which is important here, as if the symbolism that is represented by the Yellow Sign, as it exists in Mythos literature, would relate directly to a position involving ritual magick whereby forces relating to the God Hastur, as He Who Should Not be Named, then here we see a good working example as to where the Tarot stands to represent the magickal worship of Those such as The Great Old Ones and of those under Their rule as mystical servants of higher dimensions.

The *HP Lovecraft Tarot* continues to define this same statement in making reference to a situation of "New mobility; catalyst, stirrings of a new endeavour & action" (Hutchinson, Friedman: 2002: 56). Further to this point Rachel Pollack makes an equivalent point of reference in describing the same situation, that "[this Card] depicts a quiet passage through a difficult time" (Pollack: 1983: 85), although a further definition of meaning here would be equally as important in defining the religious significance of this Card, that:

"There is another, less disturbing meaning [as ascribed to by this Card] – that of a quiet passage, physically (certainly the literal meaning of a journey must not be forgotten) or spiritually, a time of easy transition" (Pollack: 1983: 85)

In establishing these definitions of meaning the Lovecraft system of the Tarot makes a further statement to relate to a situation of "Recovery; 12-Step programs; admission & acceptance of powerlessness" (Hutchinson, Friedman: 2002: 56), and an equivalent position of meaning is established by the *Seventy-Eight Degrees of Wisdom* as being a main reference on the study of the Minor Arcana, in pointing out that "By staying calm we waste neither energy nor opportunity" (Pollack: 1983: 85). Taken further this point is established by the same resource on this subject, that:

"[this situation] means functioning in some difficult situation without attacking the problems. It can refer to an immediate problem or a situation that has gone on for years" (Pollack: 1983: 85)

Negative Reading

With that definition of meaning therefore having been clearly established, the *Cthulhu Mythos Encyclopedia* describes the symbolism upheld by the Yellow Sign as representing "[a] Symbol that is a focus for the [occult] power of Hastur, the Unspeakable One" (Harms: 2008: 320). At this point it should be established that in being known as the 'Unspeakable', the religious concept that is represented as Hastur is therefore synonymous with destruction, chaos, and the complete and horrible destruction of the individual, if such a statement should be taken without serious caution and prior consideration before involving this concept as part of magickal religion (The Magus should be careful).

The *HP Lovecraft Tarot* takes this point and continues to define such a Negative interpretation of this Card as relating to the "Messenger hearing bad news; vehicle of disaster or demise; assassin" (Hutchinson,

6. The Yellow Sign: Equates to the Six of Swords

Friedman: 2002: 56), although if we were to acknowledge the Yellow Sign as that which corresponds to this same Card of the Minor Arcana, this as an omen of disaster should not be seen as being too serious, if Mythos literature points out that "[the Yellow Sign as an occult artifact] is usually useless until the arrival of the King in Yellow [Hastur] into our world" (Harms: 2008: 320). And in terms of taking this through as to exactly how serious this point is if the Sixth Card of the Suit of Artifacts should come up reversed as part of a Reading, we should take it into consideration that "Usually this card does not signify death, though it can indicate mourning; nor does it show transformation, in the same sense of Death in the Major Arcana" (Pollack: 1983: 85).

The given definition of this part of the Minor Arcana continues to represent a position of "[being] Stuck in unhealthy repetition; negative patterns, dysfunction" (Hutchinson, Friedman: 2002: 56), with the *Seventy-Eight Degrees of Wisdom* as our reference in hand pointing out that this Card "depicts a... passage through a difficult time" (Pollack: 1983: 85). Or, with the same interpretation looked at from a different perspective, "Seen in one way the balance and peace [that we might be accustomed to] becomes disturbed... If the Swords symbolize unhappy memories and the silence is a defence then communication can be painful" (Pollack: 1983: 86).

With this Card relating directly to Hastur as being He Who Should Not be Named, the possible Negative interpretation of this Card is in potential terms quite serious, and the *HP Lovecraft Tarot* continues to define such a Negative interpretation as relating to:

"Insanity i[n] repeating the same action over & over again, & expecting different results" (Hutchinson, Friedman: 2002: 56)

If to read this same definition of meaning in context with the greater scope of the Cthulhu Mythos occult, a statement as regarding this situation of insanity is represented that:

"[The Yellow Sign, when used improperly] will warp the dreams of everyone that [sees] it, sending visions of the city of Carcosa on the

Lake of Hali. The sign is the major symbol of the cult of Hastur" (Harms: 2008: 320)

Still, regardless to whether or not anyone were to accept the ideas in *The Necronomicon Cycle* as being religious truth – and The Cult of R'Lyeh do admittedly accept that we do have some strange and bizarre religious values - it is still the case that in writing this book on the subject of the *HP Lovecraft Tarot* then we are putting forward a statement as to the validity of the religious Deck of the Tarot that we have chosen to write about, and its importance on the greater basis of religious truth. If to put the symbolic meaning of this Card into further context with the greater system of the Tarot, however, as this book has already stated as being it's given intention, then our reference in hand as part of our chosen research puts the symbolic meaning of this Card on different, but equivalent terms, in stating:

"[the Six of Swords, in this given context] can refer… to the idea that when we try to attack some longstanding problem, especially one accepted by everyone else, we agitate the situation… an unsatisfying or oppressive relationship can go quietly along for years until one of the members decides to do something about it" (Pollack: 1983: 85)

In pulling all of this together, what's actually being said here is that, whatever your religious orientation in choosing to do a Reading with any Deck of the Tarot in the first place, and whatever your view towards the – admittedly quite bizarre views held by The Cult of R'Lyeh on Earth – the Card of the Tarot that the Lovecraft system defines under the symbology of the Yellow Sign, is potentially quite serious, and is one that under all circumstances should be approached with a position of caution.

7. EOD VESTMENTS:
EQUATES TO THE SEVEN OF SWORDS

In writing up this Seventh Card of the Lovecraftian Suit of Artifacts, I run into another issue as regarding the specific research in hand whilst writing this book, and this statement continues from my having previously mentioned this same point on repeated occasions whilst writing the definitions of a number of previous Cards of this system of the Tarot discussed. Whilst the *HP Lovecraft Tarot* issues statements as to two different Cards as relating to the Esoteric Order of Dagon (with the next one being the EOD Temple as the Twelfth Card of the Suit of Sites, below), the *Cthulhu Mythos Encyclopedia* issues only one entry in order to discuss this religious group. Therefore, with covering the definition of both of these Cards as being important to this study in question, I have chosen to follow up my research differently in writing on the subject of the Esoteric Order of Dagon, as is the main subject of research whilst defining this Card, as this point will be obvious if the Magus would read forward towards this further discussion as the end of the Suit of Sites, which is later in this book.[1]

Part of my reasoning for doing this, as unlike most of the Cards otherwise discussed in this book, is because the Esoteric Order of Dagon are a religious / occult organization which do, in actual fact

---

[1] As regarding the Esoteric Order of Dagon, and as originally conceived as part of the fictional work of Lovecraft, I quote again from the Cthulhu Mythos Encyclopedia, that: "This particular organization must not be confused with two other groups of the same name, one of which is an amateur press club and another an organization of Lovecraftian magical practitioners" (Harms: 2008: 95). This idea is discussed in slightly more depth under the subject of the EOD Temple of the Twelfth Card of the Suit of Sites, as mentioned (below), although the Magus might be interested in following this idea up as a further part of their own research.

exist on the basis of factual terms (whilst most of the other Cards of our chosen Deck are grounded in specific terms of symbolic representation). Whilst it is still probably still the case that the contemporary EOD would be something quite different from the religious cult as described in the numerous works of Lovecraft himself, the EOD do still exist on these terms, and in using the same name as Lovecraft's fictional cult, they openly describe themselves as an organization dedicated to representing those who uphold the worship of The Great Old Ones and *The Necronomicon* as a working system of religious faith.[2]

At this point in discussing the religious concepts important to The Cult of R'Lyeh on Earth, I'd like to make another statement as regarding my research and the validity of the views of this organization as those represented with writing this book. Whilst we would be quite open in accepting a position that our views do on occasions verge on the bizarre, it would not be possible to uphold such religious orientation if we did not believe that our views had at least some basis of credence. Therefore, in arguing such a point of validity in worshipping such a system of Gods as was formerly credited as being the ideas of Lovecraft, then the religious entity that is Dagon is an established religious icon with a history of worship which dates back for thousands of years in different faiths, including Polynesian religion as one main point in discussion. An online reference posted by a Christian religious group makes a statement as to such a history of religious worship in saying:

> "Dagon was a god of the Philistines… [their] idol was represented in the combination of both man and fish. The name 'Dagon' is derived from 'dag' which means 'fish'… the symbol of a fish in human form was really meant to represent fertility and the vivifying powers of nature and reproduction" (Dagon the Fish-God: 2019)

---

2   I personally have a number of issues with the Esoteric Order of Dagon as a contemporary religious organization, although they do claim to represent the views of people who uphold The Necronomicon as religious truth. I would suggest that if the Magus would be interested in looking into this idea further, then they should possibly check their website, which is online at: www.esotericorderofdagon.org.

That said, in trying to write a comprehensive statement to represent the validity of the Card in symbolising a greater part of a unified religious system, as all Cards of the Tarot in a smaller way do, the problem here is that the attribution of meaning that the *HP Lovecraft Tarot* ascribes to this single Card, is unfortunately, in itself, quite obscure. It is with aspect of this obscurity that a Positive interpretation of this Card is here defined as representing "Wondrous craftsmanship; 'unearthly' skill" (Hutchinson, Friedman: 2002: 56). The *Seventy-Eight Degrees of Wisdom* expands on this same statement of definition slightly in pointing out that:

"this card can indicate craftiness, but with the flaw of habitually hiding, often for no real reason, one's true plans or intentions" (Pollack: 1983: 84)

Moving forward with this idea, however, the *HP Lovecraft Tarot* here continues to establish a principle of "Creative & philosophical Avant Garde" (Hutchinson, Friedman: 2002: 56), although in looking into the symbolic meaning of this Card further, the *Seventy-Eight Degrees of Wisdom* describes the same principle of this Card in that it "implies schemes and actions which do not solve anything" (Pollack: 1983: 83). A more important definition of meaning might be established in that this same research continues that "[n]ot as obvious, but sometimes more important, is the sense of isolation involved [with this Card]" (Pollack: 1983: 83)

A Positive interpretation of this Card is further defined as part of the Lovecraft system in terms of "Recognition out of obscurity; cultural survival & validation" (Hutchinson, Friedman: 2002: 56). This situation of emerging from obscurity can be interpreted directly in relating the history of the Esoteric Order of Dagon as their organization have been represented throughout the history of Mythos fiction; and it is as part of such history that the *Cthulhu Mythos Encyclopedia* relays the point that:

"The [Esoteric Order of Dagon, as a] new religion... preached... elements of... native tales intermingled with Holy Scripture and the doctrines of Middle-Eastern fertility cults. The Esoteric Order of Dagon drove out all other churches and fraternal orders in Innsmouth and set itself up as the only religious centre in the community" (Harms: 2008: 95)

Negative Reading

A Negative interpretation with this Card is defined in terms of a "Knock-off; shallow imitation, impersonation" (Hutchinson, Friedman: 2002: 56), and here we have a situation to establish a similar interpretation, but with that same statement worded differently, as the *Seventy-Eight Degrees of Wisdom* describes this same Card of the Minor Arcana that:

"Isolation turns round to become communication, in particular seeking advice on what to do about one's problems. Valuable as the specific instructions can be, just as important is the person's readiness to listen and to seek help" (Pollack: 1983: 84)

This Negative interpretation continues as the *HP Lovecraft Tarot* continues to define a position of "'Old School', refusing to give ground to new ideas" (Hutchinson, Friedman: 2002:56), and with this we could establish a position that "[w]here self-reliance is required the Seven of Swords reversed can imply an overdependence on others telling us what to do" (Pollack: 1983: 84).

Taken further we see a position of "Stolen heritage; commercial exploitation of ethnicity & culture" (Hutchinson, Friedman: 2002: 56), although if to reference again from the *Seventy-Eight Degrees of Wisdom* we could draw an assumption that "[l]ike all else the value of the image depends on context" (Pollack: 1983: 84). In here making reference to the Esoteric Order of Dagon as an actual organization representing actual religious beliefs, I intend to make further reference

to this following document whilst writing on the subject of the EOD Temple – that being the Twelfth Card of the Suit of Sites and therefore discussed later in this book – although this paragraph from their initiatory document makes an appropriate statement if to discuss such an interpretation which further defines principles of deception and dishonesty as defined as part of the occult:

> "Though the initiates of the Esoteric Order of Dagon do not believe in the absolute existence of the deities which are portrayed [as being] the Cthulhu Mythos, they find the iconography of Lovecraft's work to be a useful paradigm for gaining access to deeper, non-rational areas of the subconscious. The oneiric origin of Lovecraft's stories is of crucial importance here, in pointing the way of access to parts of the human mind which are identified with alien and (literally) nameless horrors in his fiction" (EOD: 2008)

With that statement taken in whatever necessary context, the *Seventy-Eight Degrees of Wisdom* concludes such a definition of meaning with this Card reversed which should be taken as important on the basis of the definition of the Tarot as a much greater consistent whole, and with that as a statement on the significance of the occult manifestations of The Great Old Ones as already discussed in *The Necronomicon Cycle*:

> "When th[is] card reversed appears in opposition to the Fool or the Hanged Man, we must look to the other cards to determine which course – independence or seeking advice – will produce the best results" (Pollack: 1983:84)

And as with everything else, it is the interpretation of ideas which defines belief and the validity of one religious truth.

8. The Tillinghast Resonator: Equates to the Eight of Swords

As we approach the Eighth Card of the Suit of Artifacts we see this defined by the Lovecraft system, with the example of the Tillinghast Resonator. The *Cthulhu Mythos Encyclopedia* makes a statement to define this as a religious object that:

The Tillinghast Resonator

"the Resonator activated vestigial sense organs in the human mind, opening them to visions of higher dimensions and their inhabitants" (Harms: 2008: 281)

In terms of defining this as a Card of the Minor Arcana, the *HP Lovecraft Tarot* describes such a meaning as relating to "Tearing down the boundaries which confine perception" (Hutchinson, Friedman: 2002: 57), and it is with such a statement that we can establish a principle that the Tarot can, again, be seen directly as relating to the human mind. It is on this basis that the *Seventy-Eight Degrees of Wisdom* continues its statement to describe this same Card, and whilst doing so moves on with an equivalent statement to interpret such a functioning of human psychology, as this book has already on occasions discussed. Such a point as regarding the same study of human psychology is defined

that it is "in th[is] remarkable way [that] the Tarot has of summing up a complex situation [that] the card can almost stand as a diagram of the oppressed condition" (Pollack: 1983: 82). Or, in putting the same statement from the same research differently:

"[with this Card] we gain a sense of our own ignorant condition, something which many people will intellectually recognise (paradox of paradoxes)" (Pollack: 1983: 82)

If to put all of this into a broader context, different systems of the occult Tarot are defined and are devolved from each other in that similar meanings are discussed as according to different systems of symbolism, and if we were to put such symbolism into relation to the specific study of the *HP Lovecraft Tarot*, then our other position of reference further defines this principle that:

"The U.S. Navy... picked up on [t]his technology, and attempted to use it to make a ship, the USS Eldredge, invisible. Th[is] test was [however] only performed once, due to the odd and terrifying results of this experiment" (Harms: 2008: 282)

As a further point of discussion as regarding such interpretation, if the *HP Lovecraft Tarot* continues to define such a statement of meaning to represent "Aldous Huxley's 'Mind-At-Large'" (Hutchinson, Friedman: 2002: 57), then the same equivalent interpretation could be established as part of the same discussion, in that:

"In more recent years, miniaturized versions of the Tillinghast resonator, designed to show... individual beings from other realms, might have been perfected for certain government agencies" (Harms: 2008: 282)

A vision of the future condition of humanity here comes into play as a part of a Lovecraftian system of magick.

The third defined position of such a Positive interpretation is defined by the *HP Lovecraft Tarot* as representing the "Comprehension of the energy or soul in ALL things; aura" (Hutchinson, Friedman: 2002: 57). To put this same statement differently we see that "the Eight of Swords acts as a Gate to a special awareness" (Pollack: 1983: 82), and this point is further defined with the idea that:

> "Without enlightenment, or what… others call 'conscious evolution', we can never really know ourselves or the world" (Pollack: 1983: 82)

Again, to put this statement into the specific context of this study in hand, "Rumour has it that the Nazis attempted to use similar technology, but were unable to control it" (Harms: 2008: 282)

Negative Reading

With that statement of interpretation established, we are left with very little remaining research on which to establish a more developed statement to properly define the Negative interpretation of this Card if drawn as reversed as part of a Reading. However, the *Seventy-Eight Degrees of Wisdom* does include a statement as to what this Card means if coming up reversed as part of its own statement of interpretation, and I would like to conclude this statement of definition by quoting an entire passage from this reference in hand:

> "Freedom begins when we throw off our blindfolds, when we see clearly how we have arrived in whatever situation we are in, what we have done, what others have done (particularly those who have bound us, but also others in similar situations), and what we can do about it now. The reversed Eight means, in general, liberation from some oppressive situation; primarily it refers to the first step of such liberation, that is, seeing things as clearly as possible" (Pollack: 1983: 83)

Whilst this in itself would not immediately seem too serious, it should be remembered that this is in the specific context of a reversed Card. The *Necronomicon Cycle* makes the assumption that if a Card is drawn upside down then it is potentially dangerous, and it is my suggestion that the whole of the *HP Lovecraft Tarot*, and not just this Card in itself, should always be interpreted as according to this as a point of note.

9. Pickman's Model:
Equates to the Nine of Swords

In having written previous statements to describe the Minor Arcana as according to this interpretation of Lovecraftian religious truth, I have on occasions made reference to the specific research involved with this book, and the reasons as to why I have chosen to concentrate on this specific research whilst writing *The Necronomicon Cycle*. In approaching this as the Ninth Card of the Lovecraftian Suit of Artifacts, I run into another problem, and this is that the *Cthulhu Mythos Encyclopedia*, as one of our main references in hand, does not specifically include a mention to represent the archetypal representation that is defined as Pickman's Model, as is the association that is linked to this Card of the Tarot. At first notice this might be seen as a slight omission if this book were intended to represent a comprehensive discussion of the specific history of Lovecraftian literary fiction, although *The Necronomicon Cycle* would not be my place to criticise other people's work. The *Cthulhu Mythos Encyclopedia* does, however, include a reference to Richard Upton Pickman as the personification behind the fable which is defined as being Pickman's Model, this being one of many concepts that Lovecraft chose to represent through his work in writing literary fiction, and for this reason I have chosen to focus more on the idea of the person involved with the representation of this Card whilst writing the definition on this entry in question. It is on this basis that the Magus might consider this entry to have further similarity with the previous Cards of the esoteric Suit of People (above), and might therefore choose to concentrate with the representation of this Card and to interpret it on the same basis as that which is defined with that previous Suit of the Minor Arcana. Further to this, however, I would like to continue to reiterate on another point, with that being that the

most important meaning of any Card of any Deck of the Tarot, is that which makes sense to the person who is doing the Reading.

In taking this same line of research further, the *Seventy-Eight Degrees of Wisdom* opens its discussion of this Card in stating that "The image [as portrayed with this Card is] of deepest sorrow, of utmost mental pain" (Pollack: 1983: 80), and we could take this as a point in order to establish a point that the Ninth Card of the Suit of Artifacts would be in itself a difficult Card to describe. The *HP Lovecraft Tarot* defines a meaning of this Card differently, however, and makes a point to define a situation, with the discussion of Richard Pickman, of "Confirmation of legend, folklore & myth as tangible reality" (Hutchinson, Friedman: 2002: 57). The representation of Pickman's Model might be appropriate in defining such a point if the *Cthulhu Mythos Encyclopedia* would define the portrayal of the artist in question here, that:

"[Richard Upton Pickman was a] Salem painter of remarkable skill who is especially remembered for his works depicting strange bestial monsters in graveyards and cellars" (Harms: 2008: 225)

Where these different points tie in is on the basis that Richard Pickman was a known worshipper of The Great Old Ones, as his strange life story and subsequent disappearance establishes, and Lovecraft's short story, *Pickman's Model*, represents this situation of bizarre representations as created by the individual and the artist, actually coming to life.[1] This is where the religious point as regarding conceptual ideas becoming reality is represented by this representation in hand.

Our religious Tarot in discussion continues to establish a position of "Underworld Passage & Initiation; Labyrinth; Trial & Ordeal

---

[1] The Cult of R'Lyeh would strongly suggest that if the Magus has not already done so, then they should make a point of familiarizing themselves with the fictional work of Lovecraft. If, for whatever reason, the Magus would choose to focus specifically with this Card in order to establish any rite of Ceremonial worship, or for any other reason, then a bibliographical reference for this short story in discussion is: Lovecraft, H. P. (2001) Pickman's Model. In: The Thing on the Doorstep and Other Weird Stories. London: Penguin Modern Classics.

generating growth, progress & evolution" (Hutchinson, Friedman: 2002: 57). Again the given depiction of Richard Pickman is appropriate in defining this point, and a transition to different mental dimensions is therefore justified in that:

> "In the year 1926, Pickman disappeared from his home in Boston, along with most of his unsold works. Some assert that he committed suicide, but others believe that he dwells somewhere in the Dreamlands. From what we know of that magical land, both of these theories may be true" (Harms: 2008: 225)

The definition here in question ends with a definition of a position that "Assimilation of shadow leads 'Beyond Good & Evil'" (Hutchinson, Friedman: 2002: 57), and again the representation of Pickman's Model is appropriate in defining this point. If to take this Card in context with the greater system of the Tarot, however, the *Seventy-Eight Degrees of Wisdom* is again a valid reference in defining this religious system as discussed. Ethics of 'Good' and 'Evil' left outside of this discussion here:

> "The important thing [in discussing this Card] is [to acknowledge] that the problem is real, but because we cannot directly attack it, we tend to hide in ourselves" (Pollack: 1983: 81)

Negative Reading

As we approach the Negative interpretation of this Card, the ideas here represented start to become progressively more dangerous. The point that this establishes is that if we are dealing with ideas and representations and then interpreting such ideas on the basis of a consideration of religious and psychological horror, then it is on these terms that points in question are defined as being in themselves usually quite serious in themselves.

The *HP Lovecraft Tarot* therefore defines a Negative interpretation

here as relating to "Nightmare made reality; realization of fears" (Hutchinson, Friedman: 2002: 57), and in quoting again from the *Cthulhu Mythos Encyclopedia* we can establish a point that such a definition of meaning is here defined with the personification of the artist, in that:

"Pickman was a naturally gifted artist, and his study at Minneiska University… only enhanced his morbid instincts further. Pickman's ghastly realism set him apart from many of his fellow decadents" (Harms: 2008: 225)

With this statement put into further context, what we see as being defined as with this example of the artist creating representations of what at first only exists in the mind, is a position to relate to a concept of abstract ideas eventually emerging to become destructive to both the individual and the artist responsible for that given concept. The issue of Pickman's Model being the specific idea of representation here is important on the grounds that this short story of the same name is written to describe such a psychological expression of such 'ghastly realism' in question, having actually been given physical life through use of the supernatural and manifest use of black magick.

It is this representation of psychological archetypes that comes up repeatedly when making a study of the *HP Lovecraft Tarot*, and it is this interpretation of the functioning of the mind that is here in consideration when we see a position of "Traumatic confrontation with the 'Shadow' or dark side of human nature" (Hutchinson, Friedman: 2002: 57). To put this same idea into context with the further discussion of religion, however, if we were to see this position on these defined terms, then "Both Buddha and Christ saw the world as a place of unending sorrow" (Pollack: 1983: 81), and in taking this point of philosophy further, the *Seventy-Eight Degrees of Wisdom* continues in making a point to establish a position of:

"'Imprisonment, suspicion, doubt, unreasonable fear and shame'. The words delineate a state of mind or rather a progression of states

that result when people retreat into themselves from some problem they do not dare to confront" (Pollack: 1983: 81)

Such discussions of representative ideas and the psychological nature of the mind are continued as the *HP Lovecraft Tarot* defines a definition of this Card of the Minor Arcana in defining a principle of a "Psychotic break with Shadow; 'Jekyll & Hyde'" (Hutchinson, Friedman: 2002: 57). Ideas as regarding Lovecraft's perception of the Universe and of Jung's interpretation of the mind are all ideas here in question, although the *Seventy-Eight Degrees of Wisdom* is again immediately relevant, in that whilst defining this Card of the Tarot:

"Nietzsche wrote of embracing existence so completely, with such ecstatic honesty, that we would gladly repeat, endlessly every moment of our lives" (Pollack: 1983: 81)

The *HP Lovecraft Tarot* represents this point by establishing a position that every situation has a reversed principle of existence. As a point of conclusion, in this discussion the *Cthulhu Mythos Encyclopedia* concludes its short entry on Richard Pickman with the statement that "A few artists imitated Pickman's work for a few years [until] the art community quickly forgot him, and many of his works… have simply vanished" (Harms: 2008: 225).

In conclusion, all of this makes a point as to physical representation being the purposeful creation and expression of the working of the human mind, and a study of the *HP Lovecraft Tarot* repeatedly makes points as to how such an interpretation of the Lovecraftian actually makes these points as to the further subconscious functioning of the unconscious mind. And whilst all of this would make obvious points for further discussion, the *Seventy-Eight Degrees of Wisdom* is again appropriate in concluding its discussion of the Ninth Card of this Suit of the Minor Arcana in question, in making the point that:

"Unless the oppressed self-doubting person takes action, expresses

her or his anger, makes real changes in her or his life, the deep hidden shame will remain" (Pollack: 1983: 81)

10. Mi-Go Brain Cylinder:
Equates to the Ten of Swords

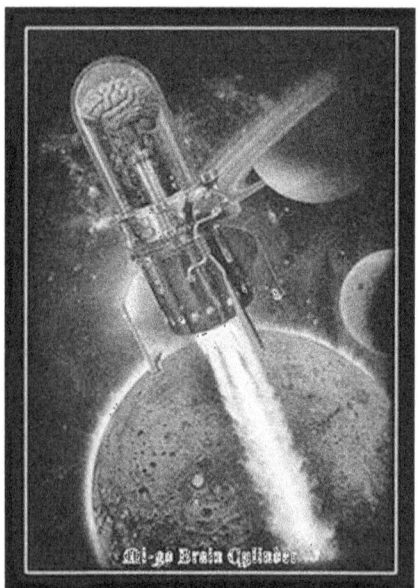

Before starting work with defining the meaning of this Card and its importance in the given context of the *HP Lovecraft Tarot* and the further discussion of the occult and the use of black magick, I would like to start by firstly making a couple of points. The first of these is another statement as regarding research. In writing up the Card that is here represented as the Mi-Go Brain Cylinder, I have the same problem as with the previous statement on the subject of the Minor Arcana, that there is little in the way of this research in hand to cover this definition as I'd like to, and this is on the basis that the *Cthulhu Mythos Encyclopedia*, as one of our specific references in hand, does not specifically include an entry under the subject of the Mi-Go Brain Cylinder in itself. It does, however, include an entry to cover the general concept of the Mi-Go, and therefore I will intend to use this given entry from the book in order to cover this discussion as best I am able. It is also the case that this will be quite a long entry (in comparison with some of the other statements to define Cards of the Minor Arcana as included in *The Necronomicon Cycle*), and therefore this discussion of the Mi-Go Brain Cylinder will be longer than most

10. Mi-Go Brain Cylinder: Equates to the Ten of Swords

of the other Cards here defined as the Minor Arcana, for this reason.

It should here be pointed out, however, that in writing an entry to describe such a religious principle, that does verge on being one of the more bizarre aspects as established as being a part of the Necronomicon Mythos, this entry from the *Cthulhu Mythos Encyclopedia* does include a statement to establish that:

"One of the mi-go's most interesting feats of body alteration involves a device known as a brain cylinder. Through their surgery, the fungi can remove the brain of any living being and transplant it into a curious metal cylinder, leaving the body in a state of suspended animation until the mind's return. The brain can observe and interact with its surroundings via certain apparatuses connected with the cylinder. The device may be taken by the mi-go on trips back to Yuggoth, other stars inhabited by the fungi, and even other dimensions and times" (Harms: 2008: 180)

The second point here to note is that the Magus will have noticed that in having discussed the Minor Arcana so far, the *HP Lovecraft Tarot* already covers the issue as represented by the strange concept of the Mi-Go, as defined under Card XI of the Major Arcana, being the equivalent Card to Justice in most other systems of the Tarot. This statement is to say that, whilst there are obvious and immediate similarities here, these are two completely different Cards which themselves have completely different meanings, and both of these Cards should be interpreted on this basis. This does not, however, mean that the statement already written on the subject of the Card that is most often represented as Justice is in any way wrong, and this does not dictate any principle to say that the Magus should not use the information with both of them in interpreting this Card as part of a Reading. How the Magus chooses to interpret any Deck of the Tarot is entirely down to the individual concerned, as it is the first point of *The Necronomicon Cycle* to establish.

As a further point of discussion, then, it should be an obvious point that if aiming to establish a proper religious statement on the subject

of the Lovecraftian occult, most of the issues we are dealing with here are quite openly bizarre, as has been already pointed out as another point which would be obvious, and with a discussion of the entities which are defined as being the Mi-Go, this would be specifically the position point in hand. The Cult of R'Lyeh, however, argue that this in itself actually validates our perspective of religious belief as the cultural circumstances at the time that *The Necronomicon* was written would not have made such a concept possible without such a basis of such a religious truth. As one example of this, the *Cthulhu Mythos Encyclopedia* describes its statement on this subject that the Mi-Go are:

"Beings with a vast empire reaching beyond the stars, with its closest outpost on Pluto, otherwise known as Yuggoth" (Harms: 2008: 179)

In order to take such a discussion further, the situation here is that if the Mi-Go should be acknowledged as a Lovecraftian religious entity, then this would have to be on the basis of Their having been mentioned directly as part of *The Necronomicon* as our representative religious book. However, at the time of this religious book having been written, and under similar cultural circumstances, the idea of an astral race living 'beyond the stars', and the existence of Yuggoth as part of the Earth's Solar System, would not have been comprehensible to any standing member of the human race (including AlHazred who is credited with having written our religious book).

With that point having been established, The Cult of R'Lyeh believe that the only way that Abdul AlHazred would have been able to gain such information as to religious truth would have been on the basis of his documented acceptance of the demon forces with which he was confronted as part of his journeys through the desert, and from our point of view this establishes a validity of one religious truth for this reason. Further to that, it should be pointed out at this criteria, that the religious validity of *The Necronomicon* is on the basis and importance of describing the greater truth that exists in actual and greater terms in terms of the logic that our religious book puts forward. This must be

accepted as being a truth which is greater and considerably more vast, chaotic and bizarre than any sane part of human society can be openly aware of. The extent to which this entity in question is particularly bizarre is established, however, as this same reference describes the Mi-Go that:

"These beings resemble winged crustaceans with egg-shaped heads that constantly change colour, their chief means of communication" (Harms: 2008: 179)

Negative Reading

In writing to define the conceptual meaning as represented by this Card, the *HP Lovecraft Tarot* gives us some difficult philosophical statements, whilst the *Cthulhu Mythos Encyclopedia* gives a reference which is both lengthy and complicated in terms of the philosophical principle here defined. As a result of both of these points I would regard it as inappropriate to expound at length as to how this Card of the Minor Arcana is represented by this as a directly bizarre concept, with my intention here being to establish terms of definition whilst concentrating on the Negative interpretation as expressed by this Card. Both of these Meanings in question are discussed in the first Appendix to this book should the Magus have any need for such a reference, whereby a listing of the definition of the meanings of the Minor Arcana Cards of this Deck are copies verbatim.

Further to any of these points, the Magus will have picked up by this point that the religious significance of *The Necronomicon* is that this book relays a principle of greater truth which exists throughout the Cosmos, and above the general religious ideas of human understanding. Mythos Gods such as Cthulhu and Shub-Niggurath are worshipped by underground secular movements on the basis of Their being represented by our religious book, and if the overtly bizarre nature of this religious system would also represent the existence of the Mi-Go as a physical and psychick entity, then our religious book would represent such a

hidden statement of truth that:

> "The mi-go arrived on our world earth during the Jurassic period. They fought off attacks by the Elder Things in order to settle in the Northern Hemisphere, where for the most part they have remained ever since. On occasion, they have fought on the side of Cthulhu and [H]is spawn, due to the God of R'Lyeh's influence in the cult of Yog-Sothoth" (Harms: 2008: 179)

In further terms of reading this Card as interpreted as being drawn as being reversed in a Reading, the *Seventy-Eight Degrees of Wisdom* states that "From the blue skies of the court cards to the black gloom of the Ten… [the symbolism of this card] fills us with pain" (Pollack: 1983: 79), whilst the *HP Lovecraft Tarot* here defines a similar position of "Intellect divorced from actual circumstance; Theory without experimentation" (Hutchinson, Friedman: 2002: 57). With these seeming to be different but similar points in question, we see here a situation that "Despite the extreme picture th[is] card does not represent death, or even especially violence" (Pollack: 1983: 79). Whilst both of these are points to express the meaning of this same Card of the Minor Arcana, this idea of intellect divorced from circumstance is represented well with the concept of such a strange concept in question, in that:

> "A mi-go purges its memory of any information that is not necessary for its immediate purposes. This keeps out irrelevant information, but leaves some facts, such as the species origins, a mystery for the mi-go themselves" (Harms: 2008: 180)

With this what we seem to be seeing is a different number of statements, taken from different sources, which generally cover the same meaning, but which often seem to be unconnected until we choose to look into the idea further. The point here in question, though, must be in that in defining such a discussion of the Minor Arcana, the discussion of the Lovecraftian must stand as a basis on which such a

study in actual terms expands on the original definition in question.

This idea continues as the *HP Lovecraft Tarot* continues to define a principle of "Platonic Idealism denigrating reality & accident" (Hutchinson, Friedman: 2002: 57). The example of the Mi-Go is again appropriate as an idea to express a symbolic idea, in that:

> "At one time the mi-go performed experiments on humanity to reduce their psychic and creative potential, but today they are studying humans in the hope of discovering how they can develop the same faculties" (Harms: 2008: 180)

The example of interpreting research on the basis of an implied greater meaning would be an obvious point in hand.

Without much more valid research to expand on this idea any further, the *HP Lovecraft Tarot* concludes the definition of meaning here as representing "Academic or intellectual pride & hubris" (Hutchinson, Friedman: 2002: 57), and with this example we see a situation that "The mi-go mentality is nearly impossible for humans to understand" (Harms: 2008: 180). And if to quote again from the *Seventy-Eight Degrees of Wisdom* in representing this same point, "The ten swords in the man's body [as is depicted in other Decks], even including one in his ear, suggests hysteria, and the adolescent attitude that no one has ever suffered so much as me" (Pollack: 1983: 79), then we see a parallel but much different interpretation of the same meaning as discussed with the example of the Mi-Go in that:

> "A mi-go's thought processes operate on a strictly cause-and-effect basis, with none of the intuitive loops that allow humans increased creativity and quick technological advancement" (Harms: 2008: 180)

Whilst all of this might at first seem to be a number of points generally put together, the Tenth Card of the Suit of Artifacts is making direct points as to the nature of how the individual thinks and interprets

that which is beyond us and which is in no way obvious. This might equate to a point that the religious entity of the Mi-Go, as that point in question, gives us an example as to the nature of the Cthulhu Mythos occult, and therefore how such manifestation exists above the normal comprehension of human comprehension and rational thought.

11. BOKRUG, THE WATER LIZARD: EQUATES TO THE PAGE OF SWORDS

Whilst the *Cthulhu Mythos Encyclopedia* might describe this as an archetype differently, we can describe the entity that is Bokrug to be a symbolic religious idol, which in turn makes representation to define specific statements in religion; and in doing so this representation describes a number of different issues whilst relating to the Cthulhu Mythos occult.

Bokrug, the Water Lizard

This point in hand, our research in trying to define the meaning of this Card is still fairly obscure, although this is no different than with a number of the other Cards of the system we aim to describe with this book. The *HP Lovecraft Tarot* describes a Positive meaning with this Card as representing an "Object of veneration, relic, icon" (Hutchinson, Friedman: 2002: 58), although if Bokrug is here described in terms of being such a religious idol, then this same statement is taken further, that:

"Some evidence suggests that Bokrug may not actually be a god, but is in fact one of a race of humanoid beings who have set themselves

up as gods of the Thuum'ha, as the people of Ib are known" (Harms: 2008: 26)

Despite any further discussion, it is an immediately obvious point that, regardless to any religious orientation, Gods of whatever religion have been represented throughout history in the form of personifications as established on these terms as being representative idols, and the *HP Lovecraft Tarot* uses this as an example to establish a principle of a "Rallying point, unifying symbol, sign, emblem, or omen" (Hutchinson, Friedman: 2002: 58). The significance of religious idols as a focus for the secular ideas of humanity are further established, however, that students of the Necronomicon Mythos "say that 'Bokrug' is only a mask for a more dangerous entity" (Harms: 2008: 26). With that point in hand, the representation of religious idols is almost always with the intention of visualising the greater God force that such personification represents, and in quoting again from the *HP Lovecraft Tarot*, this idea is described on the basis of representing a "Supernatural visitation or presence" (Hutchinson, Friedman: 2002: 58). Symbology and idolisation taken out of the equation, however, Bokrug as a greater religious entity must therefore uphold His own religious authority, and the *Cthulhu Mythos Encyclopedia* goes some way towards representing this idea, in saying that:

"Bokrug is worshipped today in the city of Ilarnek in the Dreamlands, and possibly in the pre-human city of Lh-Yib" (Harms: 2008: 26)

In quoting again from Dan Harms, I have been careful to leave further reference to the Lovecraftian concept of the Dreamlands out of the discussion with this book, as I believe that such a discussion would overcomplicate the discussion of an occult philosophy which is already quite complicated in itself, although if the Magus were to be interested in following their own research as to this concept, then we would see

a clear opportunity towards constructing a system of magick involving concepts of Jungian dream analysis and concepts including the theory of Astral Travel on these defined terms with the Lovecraftian concept of the Dreamlands being one discussion of its own.[1]

Negative Reading

Whilst the *Seventy-Eight Degrees of Wisdom* makes a statement as to the meaning of this Card that "while the King and Queen emphasise wisdom, the [Page of Swords] deal[s] with [the] Swords' more immediate quality of conflict" (Pollack: 1983: 78), the *HP Lovecraft Tarot* describes this Card as representing a position of "False idol, sacrilege" (Hutchinson, Friedman: 2002: 58). Rachel Pollack continues the Section in her book which covers this Card with the statement that "if a… difficult problem is involved, then the Page's practice becomes hard to maintain" (Pollack: 1983: 78). Taken further, however, the meanings of these Cards as defined by the Lovecraftian system are often more serious than with other systems of the Tarot, and this same interpretation as defined with the *HP Lovecraft Tarot* is stated differently. It is on this basis that the *Cthulhu Mythos Encyclopedia* represents such a symbolic issue, that:

> "The entire city of Sarnath blasphemed against this deity for many centuries, but Bokrug's wrath eventually destroyed the metropolis." (Harms: 2008: 26)

---

[1] This being an issue to justify a lot more research, a huge number of books have been written to discuss both of these issues as occult practices. However, in here making reference to the Lovecraftian concept of the Dreamlands, this is a subject that also offers opportunities for further research. Whilst I have also made it a very clear intention (for my own reasons) to leave the genre of Role Playing literature out of this book completely, I would suggest that an excellent point of research would be a book titled The Dreamlands, and published in connection with the people who publish the Call of Cthulhu Role Playing Game. A bibliographical reference for this book is: Williams, C., Peterson, S., et al. (2011) HP Lovecraft's Dreamlands: Roleplaying Beyond the Wall of Sleep. Esdevium Games Ltd.

It could be seen as being directly in relation to such an example that the *Seventy-Eight Degrees of Wisdom* points out, that in relation to the Eleventh Card of the Suit of Artifacts, "vigilance turns to paranoia; everyone appears to be an enemy" (Pollack: 1983: 79). With this we see another example of the dangers as preached by so many orthodox religions as to the dangers of regarding idols as representative of any actual system of religious Gods.

This Negative interpretation continues as the *HP Lovecraft Tarot* defines a situation of "Retribution, warfare; religious justification for warfare, Jihad" (Hutchinson, Friedman: 2002: 58). This idea here in hand ties in directly with the personification of Bokrug as a religious idol discussed, and as we see the ideas involved with the worship of idols as symbolic personifications of greater religious truths, as the *Cthulhu Mythos Encyclopedia* makes a statement that:

> "[Bokrug] is especially infamous for his vengeance upon those who offend him. His revenge may take hundreds of years to overtake his foes, but when it comes, it is swift and devastating." (Harms: 2008: 26)

Such an interpretation can again be seen on more personal terms, and if this should be in any way important in terms of a Reading with this as a specific religious system, we can quote again from the same research as we have used with the rest of this book, that "What began as a feeling of [self-confidence] becomes an obsession with problems and a seeming inability to do anything about them" (Pollack: 1983: 79). What all of this says is that, on more metaphorical terms, if we choose to uphold material objects as our focus of worship, and are doing so in order to resolve more personal issues, then this will transpire as mundane and as counter-productive to the first intended goal and intention.

The *HP Lovecraft Tarot* concludes this definition of meaning that Bokrug, as a symbol of worship through the magickal use of idols, or anything else, also refers to a position of "Haunting, poltergeist"

(Hutchinson, Friedman: 2002: 58). Whatever this statement might mean if coming into a Reading in any way, what we have with this is a further example as to how the *HP Lovecraft Tarot* continuously offers definitions of meaning that are often quite strange in terms of the specific issues in question. To look at this system of the Tarot on greater terms, it is a point of unique expression that this here implies a general idea that the study of religious idolisation can tie in directly with the scientific study of Parapsychology. In reading the *HP Lovecraft Tarot*, it is important that such repeated and bizarre statements of interpretation should be acknowledged and taken into context with any given Reading, as all systems of the Tarot in turn establish their own religious statements of interpretation as they are unique to themselves as different representations of one system of actual religious truth.

12. Hound Amulet:
Equates to the Knight of Swords

The *Cthulhu Mythos Encyclopedia* describes the Amulet of the Hound that it is a symbol of occult and Satanic power; and as "[a] Talisman of green jade in the shape of a winged hound, believed to be a stylized version of a Hound of Tindalos" (Harms: 2008: 7).[1] In writing up my account of this Card, however, I have again run into the same issue as previously discussed with a number of entries on the subject of the Minor Arcana that the research involved with writing this book gives very little in terms of any statement necessary to write a more comprehensive entry. It would also be a first point of note that the research we have in terms of writing this Card does seem to

---

1 That point in hand, the Magus will have noticed that the manifestation that is the Hound of Tindalos was covered earlier in this book as the Tenth Card of the Major Arcana, and as relating to the Wheel of Fortune in more traditional Decks of the Tarot. If the Magus would like more information on this particular Mythos deity then there would be the obvious option of reading a book in relation to this Card, although more information on the subject of the Hounds of Tindalos is abundantly available online, should the Magus regard it as being appropriate to follow up their own further research in using the Tarot in order to establish a greater working system of Ceremonial magick.

be orientated towards a darker interpretation of meaning. As a result I will reiterate a point that I've already made, that the first Appendix to this book is a recount of the definitions of the Minor Arcana as according to the *HP Lovecraft Tarot*, and if the Magus does not have access to the previous Edition of our religious Deck of the Tarot in question, then this first Appendix should be considered appropriate in terms of improvising a definition with this Card in the context of doing a reading.

Negative Reading

The *HP Lovecraft Tarot* describes a Negative interpretation with this Card in terms of "Negative attention; invasion of privacy, paparazzi" (Hutchinson, Friedman: 2002: 58). It is in terms of this sanctity of the individual that we see a situation that:

> "The hound supposedly represents the corpse-eating spirits of [Leng]. Each amulet captures and destroys the souls that the wearer consumes in cannibalistic rites, adding to the magicians power." (Harms: 2008: 7)

This should here be considered in the context of the person for which any Reading is for, and it is on this basis of this discussion of the soul of the person involved with a Reading, that the *Seventy-Eight Degrees of Wisdom* states an interpretation of this part of the Tarot Suit of Swords (as it relates to in other systems) that "[the Magus] knows inside that he has yet to face and overcome life's greater difficulties" (Pollack: 1983: 77). The point that should be considered here is that, whilst interpreting the Cards of the Minor Arcana has never been something that should at first be considered difficult, the *HP Lovecraft Tarot* is one specific system of religious thought, and therefore – as with every other religious system as represented by any other Deck – there will be reasons as to why the Magus has chosen to work with that specific system, and must therefore always be ready to interpret

what that specific system represents, and as according to the reasons they have done so. As *The Necronomicon Cycle* has gone to lengths to point out already, the significance of the Lovecraft system of the Tarot is, as according to The Cult of R'Lyeh on Earth, on the basis of this interpretation of one religious truth.

Whilst this point digresses slightly from the stated discussion in question, the *HP Lovecraft Tarot* continues to describe a Negative interpretation of this Card in terms of "Disconnectedness, isolation; removal from normal environment" (Hutchinson, Friedman: 2002: 58). It is with this statement that we see the example of the Hound Amulet as being again appropriate, as the *Cthulhu Mythos Encyclopedia* describes something on similar terms, that in relating a similar concept we see a position of:

> "A supernatural force slay[ing] those who take one of these amulets from its owner, whether living or dead, so long as the amulet is taken without permission." (Harms: 2008: 7)

In continuing this definition of meaning, the *Cthulhu Mythos Encyclopedia* describes the Amulet of the Hound that:

> "These items are the emblems of a cannibalistic cult of Leng, providing one of its members with the ability to do as they please without regard to law or custom... Other texts claim that the amulet protects its owner from the Hound [of Tindalos] until it is removed" (Harms: 2008: 7)

And this definition of terms is again appropriate as the *HP Lovecraft Tarot* defines a further Negative meaning of this Card in terms of "Lack of definition, incoherence; dilution of message" (Hutchinson, Friedman: 2002: 58). It is this idea of a position established on the basis of something being taken away which is where these ideas tie together, with the *Seventy-Eight Degrees of Wisdom* again describing the same Card of the Tarot on different terms, that:

"[The person in question] suggests a certain innocence... His... readiness to change all problems, can sometimes contain a fear of losing that innocence, that strong belief in himself." (Pollack: 1983: 77)

As a concluding remark, it would be quite likely that the Magus will have taken the idea here in discussion with the significance of the idea of a constructed occult Amulet of esoteric significance, and may have concluded that if the theory of the Tarot can quite easily be taken forward as a means by which to create occult amulets and talismans in itself, then it might again be appropriate to assume that a study of the Twelfth Card of the Lovecraftian Suit of Artifacts could be a good basis on which to construct such a charm. Whilst I do not dispute this as an idea on any basis, I would like to suggest that this idea has the same validity as with working with any other Card of this specific religious system in question. There are already a good number of books available on the subject of this as one specific study of its own, although if the Magus were to ask for one title on this subject then I would suggest one of them as being *The Complete Book of Amulets & Talismans* by Migene Gonzalez-Wippler.[2] I would also like to point out that the study of the occult in itself is very much one of personal exploration and study than that which is discussed in this book in itself, and (as I have already pointed out as a point of importance), if the Magus were to uphold a study of the *HP Lovecraft Tarot* towards these intended ends, then what we eventually aim to establish is the further validity of one religious truth.

---

2 A bibliographical reference for this book, as just one of a number of good books on this subject would be: Gonzalez-Wippler, M. (2003) The Complete Book of Amulets & Talismans. Minnesota: Llewellyn Publications. I would also like to suggest that a good deal of the work of the Hermetic Order of the Golden Dawn of Thelema could also be read in connection with this idea. The Magus is encouraged to follow up their own research.

13. Derby Stone: Equates to the Queen of Swords

This same point has been made a number of times with this book already, but with researching this Card of the Minor Arcana with the research material in hand with this project, again we run into a situation whereby the specific research in hand to describe this as our religious system as established by the *HP Lovecraft Tarot*, does not give us much to make a clear statement as to define this Card on the basis that we would want to. Again I would again like to suggest that the Magus would do well to make reference to the first Appendix to this book if wanting to interpret the meaning of this Card as part of a Reading, if a copy of the Introductory Book to the previous Edition of this Tarot is not immediately to hand.

In having already discussed the importance of our use of the *Cthulhu Mythos Encyclopedia* as one of the references used to research *The Necronomicon Cycle* as a discussion of the occult Tarot, we see no obvious entry to describe this as a religious artifact in question. This book does nothing to reference the personification of Nepemiah Derby, and on further terms contains nothing to reference what the previous edition of the *HP Lovecraft Tarot* included as being the Star Stone of Nepemiah Derby. Dan Harms again makes a statement to explain why this should be the case in the Introduction to the *Cthulhu Mythos Encyclopedia* as a valid piece of research in saying:

> "My... task [in writing this book] was [in] finding source material on the Cthulhu Mythos... My main problem was deciding what might have been useful information and obtaining it. In the end, I was only able to cover approximately half of the material [available on the subject]." {Harms: 2008: xix}

Whilst this might explain the omission of what might otherwise be an important point of reference, this same statement continues to make a statement as to how the Magus should continue such lines of research if aiming to apply such religious ideology to the practical use of Ceremonial magick in pointing out that:

"Previous editions [of *The Cthulhu Mythos Encyclopedia*] included a complete guide to further reading. I have not done so here [with the specific case of the edition here used for reference], as the growth of the Internet makes checking particular facts or publication details easy, if not always accurate." (Harms: 2008: xxi)

To get to the specific point of discussing the interpretation of this Card, then, the small amount of useful information given in the Introductory Book to the previous Edition of the *HP Lovecraft Tarot* seems both vague and confused – as something which is rarely the case with this as our religious Deck – and for this reason I choose not to go into intricate detail in order to discuss such a definition any further here. However, I would again refer the Magus to this books Appendix if such a definition were to be interpreted directly as part of a Reading. In concluding this statement as a shorter part of *The Necronomicon Cycle*, however, I would quote again from the *Seventy-Eight Degrees of Wisdom* in making a statement as to how this Card should be considered on the greater basis of the Minor Arcana:

"Having experienced pain (the card sometimes signifies widowhood), and having faced it with courage, acceptance, and honesty [the Magus] has found wisdom… The reversed Queen can indicate an overemphasis on sorrow, someone who makes life seem much worse than it is… She can also show a strong mind turned nasty, especially as a reaction to pain or pressure from unpleasant situations or people" (Pollack: 1983: 76)

Negative Reading

This might be an opportunity to raise an important point. When I am writing in order to make a statement as to the Introductory Book to the *HP Lovecraft Tarot*, I am making reference to the Second edition of this Deck, rather than that which is in hand whilst the Magus might be reading this book. At the current point the planned Third edition of this Deck is intended to be sold without such an Introductory Statement to clearly define a meaning of each Card in question, and so I am focusing on the previous edition whilst writing to define the meanings involved with this particular system. The first Appendix to this book is given, as has already been mentioned, as I would regard it as being important that the last edition defines the same meanings as with the Cards of the planned current edition of this Deck, and if the Magus would need further information to define either a Positive or Negative interpretation of this Card, or any other Card in question with this system of divination, this entire system of Tarot can be read in that same basis.

14. PLUTONIAN DRUG:
EQUATES TO THE KING OF SWORDS

The *Cthulhu Mythos Encyclopedia* describes the Plutonian Drug as being "[a] mind-altering substance distilled from the black lotus. Centuries ago, a Chinese alchemist named Liao discovered the formula for [this drug]" (Harms: 2008: 168). With this point in hand, the *Seventy-Eight Degrees of Wisdom* makes a statement to describe the last Card of the Lovecraftian Suit of Artifacts with the statement "In his best sense the King of Swords evokes Justice, the card directly beneath the Emperor in the Major Arcana" (Pollack: 1983: 74).

Whilst the Magus will already be aware that this Card of the Major Arcana is, as according to the Lovecraftian interpretation, represented with the symbolic representation of the Mi-Go, the *HP Lovecraft Tarot* also describes this Card of the Minor Arcana on its own unique terms, as representing "Shamanism, ancient practices" (Hutchinson, Friedman: 2002: 58). This statement as part of the specific interpretation of the Tarot as discussed in this book has particular significance in that it makes clear and direct reference to the use of psychoactive drugs as a specific and focused position of occult religious worship, although how this is considered important to The Cult of R'Lyeh would be discussed elsewhere in this book. At the same time, one specific statement as to the religious and shamanic use of Liao in this specific esoteric context is described as the *Cthulhu Mythos Encyclopedia* states:

"During his use of Liao, Lao Tze envisioned the universal concept of Tao that served as the foundation of his philosophy." (Harms: 2008: 168)

In terms of the specific psychological effect of this drug, it has the effect of "allow[ing] the user to perceive... the past, usually from the

viewpoint of his ancestors" (Harms: 2008: 168). Whilst the statement should be read in this specific context, the *Seventy-Eight Degrees of Wisdom* makes a statement to describe the meaning of this Card in a broader outlook, that in terms of the imagery as depicted with the specific system that Rachel Pollack uses as the example with her book on the subject of the Minor Arcana, "[the] crown [in the context of the image portrayed with this Card] is… the colour of mental energy" (Pollack: 1983: 73), with this in itself symbolizing the nature of the psychick representation of this Card if it should be interpreted on these terms. With this idea taken further, if we were to make another statement as to the specific representation of meaning in terms of such shamanic practices (as mentioned) and those ritual practices thereby involved, the same research points out that:

> "[this Card] symbolizes choice, the constant tension between abstract thought and the action that must be taken in this world." (Pollack: 1983: 74)

The *HP Lovecraft Tarot* continues with the description of this Card of the Minor Arcana with the statement to define "Happy toxification, responsible partying & celebration" (Hutchinson, Friedman: 2002: 58). With this we see an example (one usually not discussed with most other systems of the Tarot) to describe a situation involving safe use of recreational drugs for personal experience, and in quoting again from the *Cthulhu Mythos Encyclopedia* this is represented in that:

> "Considered rare for many years, Liao is increasingly seen as an ingredient mixed with other drugs to provide different mind-expanding effects." (Harms: 2008: 168)

At this juncture I'd like to point out that a general assumption is often made that in doing a Reading with the Tarot, it is generally the case that the Magus will be aiming to make a prediction as to the future situation of the individual. I have tried to keep this idea to a

minimum in writing this book on the basis that *The Necronomicon Cycle* is a statement that is about how the Tarot should be interpreted on R'Lyehan religious terms. I would like to point out, however, that it is quite often the case that the Cult of R'Lyeh will worship through use of mass ritual and collective magickal orgy, and if this Card might come up in a Reading then this might establish a position that such group ritual might be successful.

The statement given to define such a Positive interpretation as symbolized with this Card is here concluded with the idea of "External or artificial catalyst for intellectual evolution, experimental and / or alternative medicine" (Hutchinson, Friedman: 2002: 58), and this statement can be established directly, if we were to accept such an idea that:

"Ludwig Prinn learned [of the existence of the Plutonian drug] from his teacher Emendid Kejir, and Prinn dutifully copied the formula into *De Vermis Mysteriis*." (Harms: 2008: 168)

It might therefore be an interesting point to note that, whilst throughout this statement on the Minor Arcana, I have concentrated on using the *Seventy-Eight Degrees of Wisdom* as a main part of my research (for reasons as already discussed), Rachel Pollack here makes a number of statements as to how this Card directly relates to the occult nature of the human mind:

"[the King] takes the mental energy of Air and uses it to uphold and rule the world with the keenness of his mind [although] the emphasis on social minded 'realism' may narrow his viewpoint to a very limited materialism." (Pollack: 1983: 74)

Whilst this statement is followed through, the *Seventy-Eight Degrees of Wisdom* returns to the previous statement as regarding this Card in relation to Justice and the previous statement on the Major Arcana. "When [this Card] connects with [the Major Arcana Card

as represented as the Mi-Go] the King [of Swords] stands for social justice, wise laws, and above all, a commitment to intellectual honesty" (Pollack: 1983: 74). With this we see an example of how conflicting points as symbolized by the concept of the Cthulhu Mythos occult come together to establish a truth of logical and unified thought.

Negative Reading

A Negative Reading with this Card is here defined on terms of "Drug addiction, alcoholism" (Hutchinson, Friedman: 2002: 58), and the dangers of misusing Liao, as with the misuse of all recreational drugs (here taking into account that the use of drugs for shamanic purposes has already been defined on a different basis), is established by the *Cthulhu Mythos Encyclopedia* as one point of reference in hand, that:

> "[the idea of seeing into the past] may extend far back along the evolutionary chain with a higher dosage, but the user should be careful… that they avoid certain beings that can travel to the future and exact their vengeance." (Harms: 2008: 168)

This statement continues with the example of use of drugs in the same relevant context to warn of a situation of "Irresponsible use & handling of toxic substances… and knowledge" (Hutchinson, Friedman: 2002: 58), although if the *HP Lovecraft Tarot* has already been properly discussed in terms of its representation as some strange psychological functioning of the mind in defining its terms of meaning, then it is this idea of the mis-handling of knowledge that is the idea that should be taken into consideration. As the *Seventy-Eight Degrees of Wisdom* points out in relation to this Card; "The requirement [of the Magus] to act upon his judgement [in this situation] tends to distort the power of judgement itself" (Pollack: 1983: 74).

The Lovecraftian Suit of Artifacts has therefore been properly discussed, and the ending of such a Negative interpretation is defined in terms of "Illusory cure; temporary solution, 'quick fix'; flowers for

Algernon" (Hutchinson, Friedman: 2002: 58). And if the *HP Lovecraft Tarot* consistently provides us with definitions of terms which are both bizarre and are openly given to the interpretation of those who choose to read into that definition, it is often the case that no extent of discussion will ultimately make such an interpretation of meaning any more straightforward. This general idea is a point here in question, as in that whilst describing a meaning as represented by this equivalent Card of the Minor Arcana, the *Seventy-Eight Degrees of Wisdom* states:

> "[The imagery with this Card] symbolizes the mind's ability to take us into the high air of wisdom, removed from fiery passion, watery emotion, or earthly material corruption… But… the mind's ability to climb above the world… also symbolize[s] the remoteness such an attitude can produce." (Pollack: 1983: 74)

The study of the *HP Lovecraft Tarot* must ultimately establish a point that literally everything is something which should ultimately be questioned.

Suit of Tomes

Whilst writing a statement on which to establish how the *HP Lovecraft Tarot*, in relation to the greater system, which often describes this Suit as being Wands or something similar, we run into a problem in that such an equivalent correlation is actually not so clear. Further to that point in question, here we have a system to equate with "Information, wisdom [and] communication" (Hutchinson, Friedman: 2002: 50). That point in hand, however, the Suit of Tomes defines a religious point that "In one way or another, human beings have taken virtually all of nature as symbols for the spiritual essence of life" (Pollack: 1983: 25). To put such a statement in context, then, the Suit of Tomes must "stand first of all for movement" (Pollack: 1983: 26).

Having pointed out that it is in no way straightforward to make direct equations here, the Suit of Tomes is defined as representing "Philosophy, mentality [and] intellectual states" (Hutchinson, Friedman: 2002: 50), and the best way to demonstrate this point might be to suggest that the Magus should read through the rest of this Chapter before making assumptions as to what this actually means. At the same time we could describe a point in question that "Fire", as the element represented by this Suit of the Tarot, "stands for the vital life essence that animates our bodies. Without it we become corpses" (Pollack: 1983: 26). If this could be interpreted in direct context with the ideas we are trying

to establish, "If not controlled and directed, that energy burns up the world" (Pollack: 1983: 26).

Reading further, Tomes defines a point of "Learning, education, intellectual conditioning. Ability to accept new information" (Hutchinson, Friedman: 2002: 50). Whilst this would relate to a situation to define society on a much greater basis, it is established in this specific context that "Besides [any] specific knowledge gained, a study of the Minor Arcana shows how mundane experience derives from a spiritual base" (Pollack: 1983: 26). The example we see defined with this statement is that, whilst it involves knowledge to write a book, this cannot be possible without learning from books in the first place, and the books regarded by our worship establish this point on very clear symbolic terms, as this Suit of the Minor Arcana establishes if to define the meanings of these Cards as relating to the concept of the religious books which are a fundamental part of this as our system of worship.

Minor Arcana	Suit of Tomes	Suit of Wands
1	Necronomicon	Ace of Wands
2	De Vermis Mysteriis	Two of Wands
3	Unspeakable Cults	Three of Wands
4	R'Lyeh Texts	Four of Wands
5	Dhol Chants	Five of Wands
6	Libre de Eibon	Six of Wands
7	King in Yellow	Seven of Wands
8	Cultes Des Gouls	Eight of Wands
9	Pnakotic Manuscripts	Nine of Wands
10	Eltdown Shards	Ten of Wands

Minor Arcana	Suit of Tomes	Suit of Wands
11	People of the Monolith	Page of Wands
12	Ponape Scriptures	Knight of Wands
13	Cryptical Books of Hsan	Queen of Wands
14	Regnum Congo	King of Wands

Table 7. The Lovecraftian Suit of Tomes equated to the Minor Arcana Suit of Wands.

1. Necronomicon: Equates to the Ace of Wands

Whilst the Minor Arcana of the Tarot is generally seen as being less important than the previous Cards of any system, with the *HP Lovecraft Tarot*, the Card that is represented as *The Necronomicon* might be considered the most important Card of this Deck. If it should stand as being the case that this system of the Tarot can be, in specific terms, broken down to establish the worship of The Great Old Ones, it is *The Necronomicon* which has given us this religion in the first place, and therefore stands as the most important book as according to our religious orientation. Where this system of the Tarot defines "Privileged access to forbidden & / or dangerous knowledge" (Hutchinson, Friedman: 2002: 59), then this statement ascribes to *The Necronomicon* as upholding this as our religious truth. The same statement is true when this system of the Tarot defines a position of an "Ability to find truth amidst deception" (Hutchinson, Friedman: 2002: 59), and our religious book upholds this system of occult truth as being different from the stated books of other religious faiths. The statement to define a position of "Scholarly investigation" (Hutchinson, Friedman: 2002: 59) makes further reference to our religious book as defining such religious truth, and those who make ends to research this statement of truth will be successful in doing so as according to this Card of the Tarot. A further reference on this study of the Tarot states that "Only by reaching the high states of awareness shown in the later cards of the Major Arcana can we understand the sources of these bursts of elemental energy" (Pollack: 1983: 46), with this statement telling us that by making a statement to access such a state we will be successfully enlightened in doing so. A further definition would say

that "At the beginning of some situation, no card could signal a better start" (Pollack: 1983: 46).

Negative Reading

The idea of books being sources of higher knowledge is moved away from under this Negative definition with a reversed Card, and the definition here ascribes more directly to "Stolen or clandestine access to controlled information" (Hutchinson, Friedman: 2002: 59). This same statement continues to define "Control & limitation of information, censorship" (Hutchinson, Friedman: 2002: 59), and again reference to the subject of religious books is an appropriate point in hand. With this idea of religious knowledge as sourced from books, however, this system of the Tarot warns us to be wary of "Dubious sources; unstable academic foundation" (Hutchinson, Friedman: 2002: 59). To take this discussion further, "A reversed Ace implies in some way a failure of [some] primal experience. This can mean simply that the situation turns against us" (Pollack: 1983: 47). As a concluding point to consider when interpreting this Card under this defined statement, "the Ace [in any system of the Minor Arcana] reversed can mean chaos, things falling apart, either because it happened that way, or because we have ruined them through too much undirected energy" (Pollack: 1983: 47). This Card of the Minor Arcana as defined as *The Necronomicon*, in this context, tells us that through making an attempt to acquire knowledge we will be better prepared in our actions.

The Magus will at this point have noticed that, whilst this Card that is represented as *The Necronomicon* could be described as being the single most important archetypal representation of this Deck in discussion, this is also one of the shortest entries to describe any Card of this system. The reason for this must be on the basis that opportunities to research such a meaning in hand would be much more involved than with any other Card, with information on this subject being quite easy to obtain if research were to be followed up as researched on the part of the Magus. Therefore I will leave to the individual to further chase

such an opportunity for research should this be important as a part of any given Reading with this system in discussion.

2. DE VERMIS MYSTERIIS: EQUATES TO THE TWO OF WANDS

With this book in question otherwise being known under the title of the "Mysteries of the Worm", *De Vermis Mysteriis* is a "Book written by Ludwig Prinn circa 1542. (Though a date of 1484 has also been given, this time is more historically likely). Just before the author's death at the hands of the Inquisition, unknown individuals smuggled this volume out of his cell" (Harms: 2008: 71).

With this as a basic statement to introduce a short historical idea with this book, in order to make a statement as to its relevant context, "*De Vermis Mysteriis* is [a book which is] divided into sixteen chapters, each of them dealing with a different topic such as divination, familiars, necromancy, elementals and vampires" (Harms: 2008: 72). In order to take this statement further, the *Cthulhu Mythos Encyclopedia* states that:

> "This book includes spells to call down invisible monsters from the skies, along with tales of Byatis and the worm-lizards of Irem, the true nature of the Egyptian crocodile-god Sebek, the formula of the drug known as Liao and a series of operations intended to speed the transformation of a human deep-one hybrid" (Harms: 2008: 72)

With this Card we see another example of a rare and obscure book of Mythos religion coming into the situation as being defined as a part of the Tarot, and the rest of this Suit continues with similar representative examples of strange religious books of magick. With these being the examples as used with the *HP Lovecraft Tarot* in order to describe its unique representation of the Minor Arcana, the actual

information as contained in such books, as most of them do exist in one way or another, is less important than how they are described in Mythos fiction in order to equate the meanings as described with this specific system of the Tarot. As one specific example of how our Tarot uses this as its religious framework, when the Introductory Book to the previous Edition of this system describes one meaning in relation to this specific Card as being a reference to "Forensic science [and] pathology" (Hutchinson, Friedman: 2002:59), then this would describe one example of how such books of religion contain specific and complex statements of theory, as opposed to how the rest of this Suit is quite different to the previous Card that has already been described.

In direct relation to this definition of religious theory, and in context with how this book has been described in religious Mythos fiction, our system of the Tarot states that this Card represents a position of "Alchemical purification, 'nigredo'; the combustion of the Phoenix before Rebirth" (Hutchinson, Friedman: 2002: 59). With this we see an immediate continuation from the previous statement, and those with any knowledge of the ideas of Jung will immediately see an obvious example of how the *HP Lovecraft Tarot* directly relates to ideas of Psychanalytical theory. Such complex theories of the mind would be too complicated for me to do justice to with this fairly short written statement in hand, but I would suggest that a good book on this subject would be a title called *Jung and Tarot: An Archetypal Journey* by Sallie Nichols.[1] Such ideas in Psychiatry can be continued, however, and where our system defines that it is "Always darkest before the Dawn" (Hutchinson, Friedman: 2002: 59) we can interpret such a statement as relating to a representation of psychological mind-frame which might be apparent in any individual, as well as this statement more obviously describing movements that the individual might be about to

---

[1] I would regard this book as essential reading should the Magus choose to follow this important concept any further. A bibliographical reference for this book is: Nichols, S. (1980) Jung and Tarot: An Archetypal Journey. San Francisco: Weiser Books. A current intention is to work with this title further as a plan to write a sequel to this book on the Lovecraftian occult.

experience in terms of any personal situation. The greater system of the Minor Arcana would describe this Card that "[the Magus has] wept after he [has] conquered the known world because he could then think of nothing else to do with his life" (Pollack: 1983: 45). So, in terms of the greater meaning as defined with this Card, one stage of life has been completed, and now the Magus is ready to move on.

Negative Reading

The *HP Lovecraft Tarot* describes a Negative meaning with this Card as representing "Loss or destruction of evidence & / or academic proof" (Hutchinson, Friedman: 2002: 59), and again what we see here is another equation towards books containing specific information (in our case religious information). The esoteric interpretation is here the immediate point in discussion, however, with a Negative reading with this Card defined as representing "Death, the 'Conqueror Worm'" (Hutchinson, Friedman: 2002: 59). And whilst this could be considered as being a directly negative point in itself, here our system implies that such a Negative meaning could be read as being the direct opposite of the above in warning of a possible "calm before the storm" (Hutchinson, Friedman: 2002: 59) before the personal situation of the Magus can move forward.

This specific interpretation is next defined on terms of the greater system of the Minor Arcana, and this makes a statement to define the Lovecraft system of the Tarot as an equal part of a greater system, as the *Seventy-Eight Degrees of Wisdom* concludes such a Negative interpretation with this Card, that:

> "When we leave behind safe situations and past success we enter the unknown, we liberate so much emotion and energy that we cannot avoid either the wonder and enchant or the fear that goes with it. [This] card speaks very strongly to people who have lived for a long time in some unpleasant or unsatisfying situation" (Pollack: 1983: 46)

In conclusion, the Card that is represented as *De Vermis Mysteriis* stands to equate that a specific situation as regarding knowledge as relating to our religious Mythos will, in one way or another, stand to signify a situation of noticeable personal change.

3. Unspeakable Cults: Equates to the Three of Wands

Since the re-edition of the previous Deck of the *HP Lovecraft Tarot*, the most significant change with this Deck has been on the basis of the graphical representation of the Cards themselves, although with that taken into consideration this entire system of the Lovecraftian Tarot has been radically redefined. As regards other changes, a specific few of these Cards have been renamed, and this Card of the Minor Arcana is one example of this change. Therefore the Card that was previously represented as being the black book the *Unaussprechlichen Kulten* has now been renamed the *Unspeakable Cults* as one of a number of examples as representing these changes. In writing this as a commentary on such a discussion of this system of the Tarot, I cannot personally see the importance of changing the name of this Card, as this is a translation of the name of this book as a grimoire of Mythos magick, although the assumption would be that those responsible for the design of the *HP Lovecraft Tarot* must have had a clear reason for doing so before working with this current Edition put forward. Whilst this is one of the bigger changes to this new edition of the current Deck, it should be noted that the title of this book being the *Unspeakable Cults* is a direct translation from the original title which is the historical German initial title of this book in hand.

Whilst research would have it that the *Unaussprechlichen Kulten* is a real book of Mythos and occult magick, our given reference on the Cthulhu Mythos occult documents this book as being a "Volume [written] by Friedrich Wilhelm von Junzt (1795-1840), an occultist and explorer of some note" (Harms: 2008: 292). A description of the occult and religious nature of this book is described that:

"Within his book, von Junzt discusses his findings regarding worship patterns across the world. Part of this volume deals with commonly known secret societies... The main part of the work, which is prefaced by an essay titled 'Narrative of the Elder World', deals with the worship of Cthulhu and his ilk, including the Tcho-tcho cults of Leng, the people of the Black Stone [and] the Hyborian Age" (Harms: 2008: 293)

As being known to have been a highly strange and eccentric individual in the first place, this same reference states that "his claims to have visited Hell are often cited as being evidence of his [mental] instability" (Harms: 2008: 293). That statement as regarding translation in hand, however, the *Unspeakable Cults* is a book which describes a history of macabre cults as well as making a study of the Cthulhu Mythos of Gods, with this book directly tying in with our religious study of the Lovecraftian occult. Interpreted in relevant context this Card of the Minor Arcana can be read in terms of representing insight into the acts of such religious cults who have worshipped *Necronomicon* Mythos Gods. Taken with this consideration in hand, this Card of the Suit of Tomes can be read in terms of revealing the true actions of people, groups and cults who worship the Gods of esoteric and occult darkness as described already with this study of the *Necronomicon* system of magick.

In order to further establish how this is interpreted in the specific context of being part of a Reading of the Tarot, the Introductory Book to the previous Edition to this as our religious Deck makes a statement to define a position of "Oaths, obligations, promises [and] vows" (Hutchinson, Friedman: 2002: 59). This statement, then, might relate to how such esoteric cults are often established, and this in a Reading might relate to the Magus making new decisions which might lead directly to lifestyle changes. This statement continues to define "Silence, secrecy; secret societies" (Hutchinson, Friedman: 2002: 59). This statement might be quite clearly an unusual statement to find with any interpretation of the Tarot, but what we see here is an example of

how the *HP Lovecraft Tarot* has delivered a unique religious statement in order to uphold the religious points involved with the Lovecraftian in going out to define its own meaning on these defined terms. With this statement given as part of a Positive attribution, then, the Magus should assume that any future involvement with such secret societies and cults should be assumed to be a directly positive situation. Involvement with "Fraternal / charitable organizations" (Hutchinson, Friedman: 2002: 59) is also defined, and this should be interpreted on the same terms.

Our other given reference to the Cards of the Minor Arcana describes a similar meaning of this same Card, albeit quite differently, whilst both meanings should be read in context as predicting a very similar future situation. The *Seventy-Eight Degrees of Wisdom* tells us that:

"Metaphysically the [greater existence of the Cosmos] has always evoked in people a sense of vastness and mystery of the universe, while rivers symbolize the experience of the ego dissolving… man expresses the importance of rooting ourselves in ordinary reality before we attempt such metaphysical journeys. This schematic explanation gives only an intellectual shadow of [this] cards true meanings" (Pollack: 1983: 44)

While the first obvious point here to be established would be that these two statements appear to be quite different, each Card of the Minor Arcana must, by necessity, stand to describe a very similar meaning in relation to all other systems of the Cards, and this Card must therefore describe lifestyle decisions directly leading to other situations which might possibly happen in the future.

Negative Reading

One of the points (amongst a fair few others) which makes the Lovecraft Deck of the Tarot quite unique, is in that a reversed Card drawn as part of a Reading can define a completely opposite situation from that defined as Positive. Whilst this might in the first place seem

obvious, this is not always the case when we are working to make a study of different religious Decks with this system, and this should be taken into consideration by anyone who would intend to make use of any such religious Deck.

With this example in hand, this system of the Tarot starts such a Positive definition in defining a position of "Broken oaths, unfulfilled promises" (Hutchinson, Friedman: 2002: 59). The same general idea is established that the same Negative interpretation when ascribed to the greater system "can mean failure of some exploration or project (either practical or emotional)... that is, problems greater than we had hoped for or expected" (Pollack: 1983: 44). The idea of the meaning here being described with the given example of secular cultism continues with a definition of "Mystical hyperbole & melodrama" (Hutchinson, Friedman: 2002: 59). My interpretation of this statement would be to read this in context with the occasional extremity of some religious cults in connection with the *Unaussprechlichen Kulten* as a religious book which made discussion of this subject, with this being one idea that comes into Lovecraftian fiction on regular and repeated occasions. The idea of "Conspiracies [and] secret agendas" (Hutchinson, Friedman: 2002: 59) should be read with this same idea here in mind.

One final point should possibly be stated with this interpretation of this Card of the Tarot, and this is that this Card as part of the greater system of the Tarot defines in terms of a Negative Reading, can describe a situation of "being disturbed by memories" (Pollack: 1983: 44) as quoting again from the *Seventy-Eight Degrees of Wisdom*. This should be seen as being a Card of personal experiences inspired by personal change.

4. R'Lyeh Texts:
Equates to the Four of Wands

Whilst the first Card of the Suit of Tomes defines the importance of the books as upheld by R'Lyehan religion, *The R'Lyeh Texts* are much more depictive of the specific information as contained in such books, and how research into lifestyle issues can be directly important to those who regard this specific system of the Tarot as being sacred [1] Before going on to establish how this point is defined, on specific terms by the *HP Lovecraft Tarot*, however, I would like to make a point as to how the specific symbolism of this Card represents this point in question:

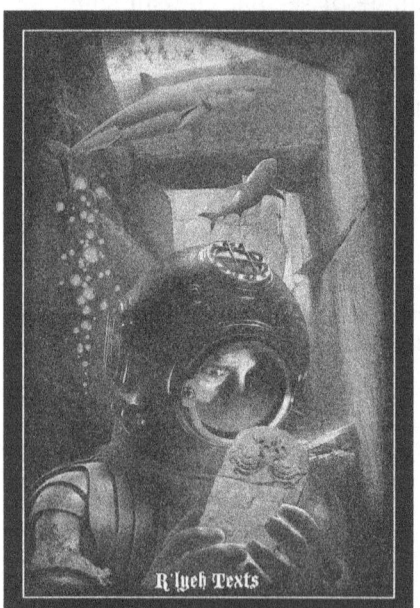

R'lyeh Texts

In defining itself in calling this Card *The R'Lyeh Texts*, an assumption should be made that this makes a point to represent knowledge that everyone should consider if making a point to define a role as part of the R'Lyehan as a new religious perspective. The symbology of the drawing as involved with this Card (as was published

---

[1] In actual fact a book exists in print with this same title, as was mentioned previously in Part II of this book. If the Magus might be interested in chasing this title up, a bibliographical reference is Turner, R. (1995) The R'Lyeh Text, Skoob Books Publishing: London.

with the previous Edition) depicts texts that could be drawn in some alien tongue, with this representing a point that information must be studied before it can be in any way understood by any rational mind. The hand that is depicted turning the pages as drawn on this Card is obviously alien and not human, and is obviously more eldritch, as to raise questions as to whether such a representation is from Above, or otherwise from another sphere of the beyond?[2] That said, the *Cthulhu Mythos Encyclopedia* describes the *R'Lyeh Texts* as being:

> "[a] Book originally transcribed on great tablets by the spawn of Cthulhu. These 'Black Tablets of R'Lyeh' still existed in Hyperborean times... These copies, which are at least fifteen thousand years old but probably more ancient, contain characters that... are actually of no human tongue... The information on the texts may have travelled through Babylon and Persia in the west, as a Latin translation that appeared circa 200 BC, seems to have been taken from such sources... A German translation entitled *Liyulthi*, which was made from both... Chinese and Latin sources, was privately published in the nineteenth century... This slim book reportedly deals with the proper worship of Cthulhu and his kindred, and many of the Cthulhu cults believe it to be their holiest text" (Harms: 2008: 240)

With that point established, the *HP Lovecraft Tarot* defines a meaning with this Card as representing "New discoveries about ancient beliefs" (Hutchinson, Friedman: 2002: 59), with this relating both to the idea of research leading to knowledge, and also to knowledge representing that which was previously not known. "Radical academia; scholarly Avant Garde broaching challenging ideas" (Hutchinson, Friedman: 2002: 59)

---

2 Editorial Note: I would like to make the point that this entry was written and typed before the publication of the Third Edition of the HP Lovecraft Tarot. The current depiction of this Card might, for that reason, be different from what has here been described. This might possibly also be the case with some of the rest of these Cards, but the assumption is made that if the current Edition is based on the previous Deck then this should hopefully still tally.

is defined, with this suggesting an idea that research, when properly conducted, can lead to insight much stranger than anything that could be expected or assumed to have been in any way previously 'real'.

Negative Reading

Our other given reference on the subject of the Minor Arcana tells us that "[Edward Arthur] Waite calls this card unchanged upside down [although the R'Lyeh Texts are] so powerful [that they] cannot be blocked" (Pollack: 1983: 42). Whilst it would be the case that Edward Waite was one of the more prominent occultists to have represented such a movement of religion in the early 20th Century, the statement as defined by the *HP Lovecraft Tarot* does not make the same point. The Negative interpretation of this Card continues therefore with this general idea to establish a point regarding "Academic hoaxes or attempts" (Hutchinson, Friedman: 2002: 59), and then goes on to make a statement as defined as equating to the example of "the Kensington Runestone" (Hutchinson, Friedman: 2002: 59). The point to this statement would be that those doing a Reading with this Deck might not know what this example is, and here I interpret this statement to define a point that people must research the religious statements as represented by this Card before we can know what we're doing. Further to this our system of the Tarot in question defines a point of "Fantastic willingness to believe anything outside of the mainstream" (Hutchinson, Friedman: 2002: 59), with this telling us that however we should choose to study any situation, we must always be cautious that the information we gain must be valid.[3]

---

3 The Cthulhu Mythos Encyclopedia makes an interesting point on this book in stating that "Two of the recent paperback Necronomicon's have included the R'Lyeh Text as part of the Necronomicon, though [it is] clear that it is a separate book" (Harms: 2008: 241).

5. Dhol Chants:
Equates to the Five of Wands

Whilst this Card in the Lovecraft system of the Tarot is described as representing the specific example of poetry and song defining its specific meaning and in its own context, this Card as part of the greater system of the Tarot would define a principle of "conflict… it is the nature of [this Card in context with the greater definition of the Minor Arcana] to see life as a battle, but in its best sense battle becomes an existing struggle" (Pollack: 1983: 40). And if the specific image on each Card should be purposefully interpreted as an idea to define its own meaning, the previous Edition of the *HP Lovecraft Tarot* depicts this image in this respect as the given Mythos book here in question being read by some mystical creature of the astral domain, as if contacting some other force of either Astral or Terrestrial domain. This could be with the example of trying to find a Gateway between Worlds; but again this is not so straightforward or clear. The manuscript that is here defined under the concept of the *Dhol Chants* is (as is depicted with the previous Edition) inscribed in some strange and astrological form of writing, this in itself being a depiction that they are written in the tongue of a greater Mythos power. According to the *Cthulhu Mythos Encyclopedia*, the *Dhol Chants* is described as being a:

> "Book from the Plateau of Leng… Metaphysical research has proven a link between this manuscript and the beings known as 'Dholes', but whether or not they influenced its text in some way remains uncertain. Miskatonic University holds a copy the *Dhol Chants*. This book contains five hundred and fifty five different 'chants',

which... include[s] one... which [is] used to command spirits. The reader should be warned, though, that the beneficial spells within are often ineffectual" (Harms: 2008: 79)

It is with this interpretation of theory that the *HP Lovecraft Tarot* defines a point of "Ritual, liturgy; religious poetry" (Hutchinson, Friedman: 2002: 60), and still in context with the Lovecraftian study of occult magick this could be seen in context with "Song, music, melody; harmonious composition; cohesion of parts" (Hutchinson, Friedman: 2002: 60). And if the definition of a Positive Reading with this Card could further define a position of "Poetry, elegance; rhythm, cadence; Aesthetic regularity" (Hutchinson, Friedman: 2002: 60), then this would stand as its own statement of interaction which in other Decks is "seen as a way in which people communicate with society and with each other" (Pollack: 1983: 41) as a defined point of meaning in hand.

Negative Reading

Whilst this Card is very much a statement in which to interpret ideas of religious worship (although the point should be made that the rest of the Tarot is essentially the same thing), and in specific terms in regard to the practice of occult Ceremonial worship, our system of the Tarot in question describes a situation of "Religious banalities & platitudes; empty ceremonies and rituals" (Hutchinson, Friedman: 2002: 60). And whilst the same meaning is further defined as according to "Atonality, disharmony, discord... irregularity, intermittence [and] discontinuity" (Hutchinson, Friedman: 2002: 60), then the *Seventy-Eight Degrees of Wisdom* (as the main reference references here used as our research, as previously pointed out) describes how this interpretation is the same as with the greater system of the Tarot, in saying:

> "...right side up [this Card] implies a sense of rules and fair play, for without understood agreements struggle as a game becomes impossible. Reversed [this] card indicates that rules are being

abandoned, that in fact the battle has taken on a more serious, nastier tone. The sense of play changes to bitterness or disillusionment as people seek actually to hurt or ruin each other" (Pollack: 1983: 41)

With this definition of the Minor Arcana taken in context with the point in question here discussed, this would establish that the Lovecraft system has done a good job of interpreting such a system of the occult as according to the specific principles of R'Lyehan religious belief.

6. Libre de Eibon: Equates to the Six of Wands

The significance of books in the *HP Lovecraft Tarot* is not so much to express what such books say, but more to express them in terms of examples in order to define the meanings of the Cards as defined in question. In doing so they are expressing how such books are used in Mythos fiction in order to define specific examples of religious and symbolic meaning. Researching such religious books will establish that most of them do in fact exist, although there are numerous arguments to say that this particular Volume is extant only as a figment of such Mythos literary fiction. The reasoning behind this is on the basis of this books origin being researched as being from the mythical dimension of Hyperborea; that in itself being a place which does not exist on our Earth or on manifest terms. There are, however, arguments to question this point, with one of these being that research would lend credence to an opinion that copies of this book would have a history of translation in some way similar to *The Necronomicon* as our representative religious book in itself.

That said, the symbolic importance of this Card is on the basis of an interpretation to express the importance of knowledge as gained from such religious books, and this is here expressed in terms of its documented history, regardless to whether the *Libre de Eibon* is a book developed as a vehicle for Mythos fiction in itself or an actual and historical book of black magick? With this symbolic position established, this book in question was "penned by the Hyperborean wizard Eibon" (Harms: 2008: 28). As a book of important esoteric knowledge this book was supposedly "passed from teacher to pupil for many years", until eventually falling into the hands of "a secretive cult that revered Eibon and may have been related to that which preserved

the *Pnakotic Manuscripts*" (Harms: 2008: 28). If such a book does exist as an actual historical document, then, which is something which is often not clear when researching such religious ideas, research would establish a point that:

"There seem to have been two paths by which the *Book of Eibon* made its way into the modern world. The first route was through Egypt, as traders from Atlantis brough their... knowledge to that land. The volume was [subsequently] translated into hieroglyphics" (Harms: 2008: 28)

This quotation would clearly equate a symbolic interpretation of this Card with such a purpose of academic study.

In terms of this symbolism in relation to the greater system of the occult Tarot, our other reference in hand defines this Card if drawn as part of a Reading, that "[a]s the Wands", as is equated to the Suit of Tomes in this context "progress down to the Ace they become stranger. The emphasis shifts from defencelessness [towards] optimism" (Pollack: 1983: 39), and if this is the case with the greater system of our system of the Tarot in question then this must equate as being the same as with the Lovecraftian Deck as represented. "In the Golden Dawn system [this] card bears the title 'Victory'" (Pollack: 1983: 39), and the Cult of R'Lyeh suggest that the views of the Hermetic Order of the Golden Dawn, as stated, should be taken very seriously in all religious studies of any system of the Tarot.

Having therefore discussed such a symbolic importance of the *Libre de Eibon* as a book of arcane religious knowledge, the *HP Lovecraft Tarot* defines a Positive interpretation to represent "Apocrypha, Pseudepigrapha" (Hutchinson, Friedman: 2002: 60). To put this example into a clearer framework, these references are defined as being "two separate groups of works dating primarily from the period of the early Church" (Thomson: 2007). Another example of the persecution of religious books by the early European Church is established that "The [early] Protestant Church denied [the] sanctity

[of both of these religious books] but conceded that they were worthy of reading" (Thomson: 2007). This same idea goes further, in that "the pseudepigraphal books, on the other hand, are [still] not accepted in their entirety by any [branch of the] church" (Thomas: 2007). If to put this into the specific context of the *Libre de Eibon*:

> "The Apocrypha, for the most part, are anonymous historical and ethical works, and the Pseudepigrapha, [are] visionary books attributed to the ancients, characterized by a stringent asceticism and dealing with the mysteries of creation and the working out of good and evil from a gnostic standpoint" (Thomson: 2007)

The *HP Lovecraft Tarot* here concludes with another example of where it is unique in its own occult interpretation, that a Positive Reading defines "Psychic information; channelled or received knowledge" (Hutchinson, Friedman: 2002: 60), before defining a position of "Seamless integration of old & new ideas" (Hutchinson, Friedman: 2002: 60).

Negative Reading

Under this defined context the *HP Lovecraft Tarot* defines a principle of "False claims of authorship or craftsmanship; false pretences" (Hutchinson, Friedman: 2002: 60). This general idea of insecure outlook is here on terms of another similar description of the greater system of the Tarot, in that this equivalent Card in other Decks represents "False optimism, covering our doubts with bluster or illusion, leads to fear and weakness" (Pollack: 1983: 40). Further to that this definition here establishes a position of "Lies, trickster games; deception and misrepresentation" (Hutchinson, Friedman: 2002: 60), and this would equate in direct terms that this Card of the Minor Arcana in all other systems defines a point that "life or specific people will betray us in some way" (Pollack: 1983: 40). And if this same definition defines a point of "Conflict between ancient & modern wisdom" (Hutchinson,

Friedman: 2002: 60), then "[such] attitude[s] often become.. a self-fulfilling prophesy, for suspicion can produce betrayal" (Pollack: 1983: 40).

7. KING IN YELLOW: EQUATES TO THE SEVEN OF WANDS

As we approach the Seventh Card of the Lovecraftian Suit of Tomes, here we see another example of a Mythos book whereby it is not entirely obvious as to whether or not this is an actual historical text, or otherwise another statement invented as being a vehicle through which to express the religious concepts inherent in Mythos religious fiction? However, a statement to document this books existence, conceptual or otherwise, is described in the *Cthulhu Mythos Encyclopedia*, that the King in Yellow was "thought to have been written in the late 19th century by an unknown playwright (possibly named Castaigne) who later attempted suicide" (Harms: 2008: 152). In terms of the history of the document itself, "After its [initial] appearance, the government and the church denounced it" (Harms: 2008: 152) and if this book does, in fact, exist, then its obvious obscurity would probably be for this reason, as is often the case with the history of the books of our religion. Further to this, however, "Though it contains much contradiction and allegory, *The King in Yellow* is a dangerous work which leads the imaginative and unstable to madness" (Harms: 2008: 152). In terms of the religious significance of this Card, "It may be that the play is in reality one of Kenneth Grant's akashic grimoires" (Harms: 2008: 152), and in being titled *The King in Yellow* this makes direct reference to the *Necronomicon* Mythos God Hastur as representing aspects of global religion under the Qaballistic Sephiroth of Chokmah.[1]

On the basis of such a position being obviously quite authoritarian, the *HP Lovecraft Tarot* further describes this Card as representing

---

1 This idea reverts back to some of the ideas as discussed in the first Part of this book.

"Stasis, Security [and] Stability" (Hutchinson, Friedman: 2002: 60). Our other given reference here in turn describes the same meaning that "this is a card of conflict, but here we see the battle itself, and the effect is exhilarating" (Pollack: 1983: 38). What we would therefore establish with this description is a Card that would relate to the general ethic of militarism in a personal context, and the *HP Lovecraft Tarot* defines this interpretation in terms of "Nobelesse Oblique; Chivalry, Code of Honour, courtesy & etiquette" (Hutchinson, Friedman: 2002: 60). The same idea is summed up more directly that the "Wands expect to win and usually do" (Pollack: 1983: 38). "Birth right, legacy; inherited responsibilities & obligations" (Hutchinson, Friedman: 2002: 60) is defined, and "this card rises above any depression into the clear intoxicating air" (Pollack: 1983: 38). Whilst the militaristic aspect of *The King in Yellow* is expressed here as a concept and a greater part of the Tarot in describing a position of "Royalty [and] Aristocracy" (Hutchinson, Friedman: 2002: 60), the general meaning implied with this Card is quite well summed up in that "We become defensive and committed to fighting through an earlier experience of winning… While the fight goes on we enjoy it" (Pollack: 1983: 39).

Negative Reading

With the *HP Lovecraft Tarot* being our specific concept to argue, it can still be established that each different system of the Tarot expresses its own religious interpretation, which each Card in every different system must essentially describe the same thing. In this sense this specific system as studied here describes a situation of "Inertia; Motion without Progress" (Hutchinson, Friedman: 2002: 60), and we must be cautious of such situations leading to a dead end. An opposite position to the idea described above is at this point established, and we are warned of "Desertion of Duties; Empty titles, unfounded honours" (Hutchinson, Friedman: 2002: 60). Further to this we see a position of "Futility, Will-lessness Submission to unknown forces [and] Inbreeding; Devolution" (Hutchinson, Friedman: 2002: 60). All of these ideas are expressed

and interpreted on more straightforward terms that "Above all [this] card warns against indecision, suggesting that if a person can come to a clear course of action the natural Wands self-confidence will return to overcome the anxieties and other problems [that we will encounter]" (Pollack: 1983: 39). In conclusion this Card relates to how motivation might be established in relation to any position of social standing or influence above anyone else.

8. Cultes des Goules: Equates to the Eight of Wands

According to my research into the history of Mythos literature, the *Cultes des Goules* is a "Book dealing principally with a Parisian ghoul-cult. The author [of this book] was... a French nobleman of occult leanings who became involved in [an occult order known as] the Affair of the Poisoners, in which high-ranking nobles were accused of murder and black magick" (Harms: 2008: 62). With that point of history established the same research makes a statement as to the relevant subject matter in question that:

"...this book... speaks of [the authors] membership [of] a ghoul-cult, and gives a set of prophesies concerning its future. Along with this appear descriptions of pagan fertility rites dedicated to the earth-deities... Also mentioned [is] Shub-Niggurath (whom the book links to lycanthropy)" (Harms: 2008: 62)

This short historical statement might be useful in order to establish the greater meaning of this Card in a philosophical context, as the *HP Lovecraft Tarot* here defines a point as regarding "Assimilation of information" (Hutchinson, Friedman: 2002: 61). And if the immediate next statement goes on to define a position of "Investigating journalism [and] protection of anonymous sources" (Hutchinson, Friedman: 2002: 61), then we could interpret this statement in direct relation to the investigative nature of the research that must have been necessary in order to have written such an occult Volume in hand. A statement to define "Friends in hidden and / or unexpected places" (Hutchinson, Friedman: 2002: 61) would have to be seen in direct context with the role of this book's author in relation to his involvement with such

standing figures in society in being involved with such grotesque practices as discussed.

Another reference which could be assumed to have been written to discuss the Minor Arcana on a broader level than with that described with the *HP Lovecraft Tarot* as one singular and specific esoteric statement, represents this Card in stating that "Though… [religious] movement[s] sometimes lack direction we see here the image of a journey reaching an end, or things completed" (Pollack: 1983: 37). If considered in this specific context we could argue the meaning here as giving an example of writing a religious statement of research, with this established with the example that "projects and situations come to a satisfactory end" (Pollack: 1983: 37).

Negative Reading

With the situation of this Card being drawn from the Deck as being reversed, here we have an example of how the Lovecraftian system of the Tarot does not always equate in obvious terms with research as to what this Card means in terms of the greater system as is usually studied. The *Seventy-Eight Degrees of Wisdom* defines a Negative interpretation of this Card in that:

> "Turned around the image becomes one of continuance, of nothing coming to an end, especially when an end is desired. A situation or attitude simply goes on and on, with no conclusion in sight. If such a situation cannot be avoided, then it is good to recognize and accept it" (Pollack: 1983: 38)

As an obvious problem with this specific correlation of meaning being a point of argument, one idea that could be read into this could be with the example of somebody who is writing a book. If this might be a possible point of example, the *HP Lovecraft Tarot* defines a principle of "Plagiarism; unoriginal thought; second hand knowledge, hearsay" (Hutchinson, Friedman: 2002: 61). With this idea defined, the example

of involvement with black religious orders is also important on the same basis, as our system here in question defines a principle of "Snitches, informants... The Underworld, either criminal or mythological" (Hutchinson, Friedman: 2002: 61). It is still a point of consideration, however, that this in connection with the greater example of the Minor Arcana defines a point that "One of the most important positions in a reading is that called hopes and fears... jealousy may derive from uncertainty and confusion" (Pollack: 1983: 38). The Magus should be cautious of events that they cannot outwardly control.

9. Pnakotic Manuscripts: Equates to the Nine of Wands

Also often known by the title of *The Pnakotik Fragments*, this Card further relates to the greater esoteric knowledge important to the religious Cult of R'Lyeh on Earth. In relation to the rest of the Minor Arcana, this Card represents psychological and psychick clarity and also enlightenment – even if this is through the learning gained through use of psychedelic drugs. Whilst most of the Suit of Tomes is described as representing the implied meanings of what Mythos literature describes if taken to represent the Cards of the Tarot on the greater level, the Card that is represented with *The Pnakotic Manuscripts* could be interpreted in terms of the psychedelic interpretation of knowledge on the level of the human mind.[1]

In further terms of the literary nature of this book, the *Cthulhu Mythos Encyclopedia* states that *The Pnakotic Manuscripts* are:

> "of uncertain age and origin. It has been said that the Great Race of Yith wrote the first chapters and preserved them at their City of the Archives known as Pnakotus, from which the book derived its name... The first portions of the manuscript are written with a curious form of cuneiform and dot-group glyphs... some linguists

---

1 In terms of some bibliographical information for this book, the Cthulhu Mythos Encyclopedia states that: "Although it is rumoured that the anonymous translator published an English edition [of The Pnakotic Manuscripts] in the late 15th Century, others hold that this document has only been circulated in the original manuscript form... An expurgated photostat is held at the British Museum. A few commentaries, including The Pnakotic Manuscripts: A New Revised Study (1922), Werner's A Study of Pnakotic Writings (1938) and Schwarzwalder's Analysis of the Manuscript of the Pnakotic (1895), are available to scholars" (Harms: 2008: 227).

say that humans are completely unable to decipher these versions, but a number of individuals claim to have read or translated the book" (Harms: 2008: 226)

This general description in hand, the *HP Lovecraft Tarot* gives an interpretation of this Card as drawn in any Reading, that "Direct experience with the Divine; Achievement of mystic union" will come into the equation, with other interpretations of the Tarot impending a situation of "great strength, physical power, mental alertness" (Pollack: 1983: 36), should the Magus choose to interpret this Card on this basis. This Tarot system in question continues to define a situation involving "Revelation, prophetic experience… Divine Madness; mystical ecstasy & intoxication" (Hutchinson, Friedman: 2002: 61), and considered in this specific context, here "we see again the image of someone who has faced a lot of opposition, from others and from life; rather than take it on himself, however, he has fought back" (Pollack: 1983: 36). Experiences of divine inspiration have allowed the Magus to come into his own.

Negative Reading

The *HP Lovecraft Tarot* defines a Negative interpretation with this Card in terms of "Religiously induced madness & / or hysteria" (Hutchinson, Friedman: 2002: 61), and this could be further interpreted in terms of the greater system of the Tarot that "obstacles and problems grow too great for [our] strength to hold them back" (Pollack: 1983: 36), and with this our interpretation of religious truth becomes too much. We are warned of a situation defined as being "Mind overwhelmed or shattered by mystic experience" (Hutchinson, Friedman: 2002: 61), and this under the greater definition of the Tarot could be established if we ask ourselves "what happens if the problems we have kept at bay for so long rush up at us?" (Pollack: 1983: 37). Whilst this definition is concluded with a statement to define "Religious debauchery; orgiastic practices" (Hutchinson, Friedman: 2002: 61), the point would here be

established that "In specific readings the true implications of this card can only become clear through seeing it combine with other cards" (Pollack: 1983: 37). Maybe this tells us that there's more going on that that which might have been, in the first place, obvious?

10. Eltdown Shards: Equates to the Ten of Wands

As we come to the Tenth Card of this as approaching the end of the Lovecraftian Suit of Tomes, with this esoteric document we see another example of a testament whereby it is not entirely clear as to whether or not this, as an actual piece of religious literature, does or does not actually exist? The first point of observation would be that the overtly weird nature of this document would suggest that it could not be an actual religious artifact, but further, this study of the Mythos as derived from *The Necronomicon* must make the point that there are things are often much stranger than that which is obvious to most of what is perceived by human religious society. Even if the concept of the *Eltdown Shards* is something that was a creation to express ideas in Mythos fiction, however, it is still the case that a literary study of this religious testament in hand makes a statement to define the religious terms as established in terms of meaning, and this makes a point of reference to equate this statement to the same Card as according to other systems of the Tarot, as well as the greater system of the Minor Arcana in itself.

With that statement made to discuss where this Card stands in relation to this greater system of the Tarot and occult systems of divination, the *Eltdown Shards* relates to issues of knowledge or learning which might be fragmented or incomplete, and of these fragmented pieces of knowledge somehow falling into place. Documentation as relating to this testament in Mythos literature makes it fairly straightforward to establish a defined interpretation of this Card as according to what other Decks might define more closely as being the Ten of Wands, and the *Cthulhu Mythos Encyclopedia* defines such a statement on these discussed terms.

The *HP Lovecraft Tarot*, however, further defines a meaning of this Card as relating to "Restoration of lost knowledge; recovery of missing information " (Hutchinson, Friedman: 2002: 61), and this statement is described with a definition of such a testament being that the *Eltdown Shards* are:

"Pottery shards found near Eltdown in southern England in 1882... Psychic evidence from Professor Turkoff of Beloin College suggests that the Elder Things inscribed these ceramics and buried them when Great Britain was [still a] part of Pangaea" (Harms: 2008: 93)

Whilst this might be interpreted in connection with the statement relating to occult and religious restoration of knowledge, the *HP Lovecraft Tarot* continues that this Card relates to a situation of relating to a "Key piece of the puzzle; intellectual windfall" (Hutchinson, Friedman: 2002: 61), and again this statement is appropriate when interpreted as upheld by the example of the *Eltdown Shards*. In quoting again from the *Cthulhu Mythos Encyclopedia*, this interpretation is further established that:

"Lin Carter speculates that the original authors of th[is] work were... the Great Race of Yith. Comparisons of these shards to similar documents, however, suggest that the Elder Things were the authors, so any Great Race copies were probably translated later" (Harms: 2008: 93)

The further definition of meaning as according to a Positive interpretation here, is that of an "Intellectual bridge; 'connecting the dots'" (Hutchinson, Friedman: 2002: 61), and again this is an appropriate statement if to interpret the religious views of the Cult of R'Lyeh with this given example in hand. In terms of this given statement, "The shards, which were discovered in a Triassic rock stratum, were inscribed with many strange markings of unknown meaning. The first two scholars to [have] examined [them] hastily pronounced them to be

untranslatable" (Harms: 2008: 93). This idea involving putting ideas together, and an intellectual pursuit of establishing meaning only after a period of such study is further established, however, that "Around 1912 [a] Sussex clergyman… made an attempt to decipher the fragments and in 1917 published a thick pamphlet including the results of his own translation" (Harms: 2008: 93). If nothing else this gives an example of how Mythos knowledge can be read in relation to this as a statement of religion.

As with every other Card described in *The Necronomicon Cycle*, it is important that this should be discussed in relation to the rest of the Tarot as a greater system, and it is on this basis that I quote again from the *Seventy-Eight Degrees of Wisdom* as a book written on the specific subject of the Minor Arcana. With this given statement "Because they are so involved in movement and action the [Suit of Tomes] invite[s] problems. Constantly in conflict they almost attract enemies and difficulty. This comes partly from a lack of purpose or plan" (Pollack: 1983: 34). Whilst this makes no direct reference to issues involving this discussed idea of restoration of knowledge and so on, the point to be made is that these references in question define the meaning of this Card as according to various different systems of the Tarot, and with this it is pointed out that "paradoxically, that very energy [which is defined with this Card] is weighed down with commitments and problems" (Pollack: 1983: 34), and it would be a suggestion that this should be read in relation to commitments and problems gained through such an assumption of such religious knowledge discussed.

Negative Reading

The *Seventy-Eight Degrees of Wisdom* makes a statement as regards a Negative Reading with this Card, in stating that:

"Like many cards, especially when reversed, more than one meaning is possible. In a reading we can determine the best meaning (though sometimes more than one meaning will apply, as with a choice) partly

through the other cards, and partly through an invitation that can only develop with practice" (Pollack: 1983: 35)

Further to this as here being a defining principle, we are further warned of a situation involving "Fragmentary information; incomplete data" (Hutchinson, Friedman: 2002: 61). Whilst a Positive Reading here might relate to a new assumption of knowledge, the *Eltdown Shards* are again a valid example in question when we are warned of a further situation involving "Trying to force together incompatible data" (Hutchinson, Friedman: 2002: 61). The Magus should be cautious of a situation involved with "Forcing data to fit a preconceived conclusion" (Hutchinson, Friedman: 2008: 61). Our given reference defines these points well, whilst putting this into a wider scope, and the *Seventy-Eight Degrees of Wisdom* further defines this point in pointing out that "Most simply [this Card] reversed indicates that... burdens have increased in weight and number to the point where the person may collapse from them, physically or emotionally" (Pollack: 1983: 35). In short, a Negative Reading here would suggest that there is too much going on in our lives, and in relation to the *HP Lovecraft Tarot* this could be defined on specific terms of being too much knowledge being assimilated too fast. If the Magus is not going to step back and allow things to run their natural course, things are likely to become too much to handle.

In conclusion to this as a statement as regarding the mind and the occult assimilation of knowledge, the entry that we have quoted from, being the *Cthulhu Mythos Encyclopedia*, ends its entry on this literary artifact with the statement:

> "Many sections of [the *Eltdown Shards*] bear a striking resemblance to the *Pnakotic Manuscripts*, though further work in this direction must wait for the discovery of more of the original [document]" (Harms: 2008: 94)

In putting forward a literary study of *The Necronomicon* and associated R'Lyehan religious texts, we could make an observation that assumption of knowledge must be assumed to be assumption of religious virtue and truth.

11. People of the Monolith: Equates to the Page of Wands

With the original version of *The Necronomicon Cycle* I had taken the assumption that *The People of the Monolith* was a book that existed only as an invention of Mythos fiction, and that the concept of this book in question was so far-fetched that there

was no way that this could be a real book of historical literature. However, after having completed the first version of this book and posted it online as a webpage, I was contacted by a respected scholar of Mythos religion, who told me in no uncertain terms that this is, in fact, a real book with its own history of literary study. It is on this basis that I quote again from the *Cthulhu Mythos Encyclopedia* which includes a short entry for this book, and states that:

"[*The People of the Monolith* is a] Volume of poetry by Justin Geoffry, a noted Baudelairean poet… Its title poem maybe connected to the author's descent into insanity after a trip to a location in Hungary… in 1921 or 1922 (sources vary)… The book's only brush with substantial fame came when noted director Corman Abbe adopted *The People of the Monolith*'s poetry to film in 1982.

The film was never released to the public after the New York theatre in which the premier was held collapsed. At least one copy of *The People of the Monolith* was bound in the skin of a monstrous creature of the inner earth, but the bindings of most of the other copies are more conventional" (Harms: 2008: 223)

With this specific Card as being one example in question, the given definition of meaning is much less in accordance with the symbolism of this in context with Mythos literature, and can only be properly described by equating its meaning more closely with the greater meaning of the Tarot. As an example, the *HP Lovecraft Tarot* defines this Card as relating to a principle of "Childhood vision" (Hutchinson, Friedman: 2002: 61), and this statement in itself can only be interpreted in context in that the *Seventy-Eight Degrees of Wisdom* describes this same Card in stating that "The Pages represent the quality of each suit in its simplest state, enjoying itself for itself in a lighter, more youthful, way than the mature Queen. Physically, Pages refer to children" (Pollack: 1983: 33). Whilst this in itself doesn't really tell us much, the Lovecraft system of the Tarot here defines a situation of "Acceptance of supernatural without thought or question" (Hutchinson, Friedman: 2002: 61), and the *Seventy-Eight Degrees of Wisdom* again follows the same idea in stating that "In relation to adults [the Pages] indicate a moment when a person experiences some aspect of life just for itself, free of external pressures" (Pollack: 1983: 33). The *HP Lovecraft Tarot* then concludes its very short definition of a Positive Reading with this Card with a point to describe a position of an "Early start at artistic literary talent" (Hutchinson, Friedman: 2002: 61), and again our reference in question makes an equivalent statement in pointing out that:

"Because [the Suit of Tomes] symbolize[s] beginning, the Page of Wands [as this Card is the equivalent of in other systems of the Tarot] especially indicates the start of projects, and in particular an announcement to the world, and to ourselves, that we are ready to

begin either a 'project' (this can refer to a relationship as well as practical plans) or a new phase of life" (Pollack: 1983: 33)

Negative Reading

The Negative definition of this Card would have to work on similar terms to the ideas already defined with this religious study of the Tarot, although if the *HP Lovecraft Tarot* describes a principle of "Childhood nightmare" (Hutchinson, Friedman: 2002: 61), with this an assumption could be made that if this Card comes up as being reversed in a Reading, then it could be assumed to be the opposite of the meaning as inferred by the statement as already discussed. "A person indicated by this card needs either to get away from complexity or to develop the maturity to deal with it" (Pollack: 1983: 34). The Magus is warned of a situation of "Morbid fixation; unhealthy obsession; dark imagination" (Hutchinson, Friedman: 2002: 61), and here the situation is that "the Page is not thrown so wildly by problems but instead becomes confused and indecisive... Continued indecision can only lead to... resolve and self-confidence degenerating further" (Pollack: 1983: 34). This statement is concluded as the *HP Lovecraft Tarot* defines a principle of "Suppression of childhood talent" (Hutchinson, Friedman: 2002: 61), and the Page of Wands (as this Card is defined by most other systems of the Tarot) is here described in that "His eagerness to start is disrupted by complexities and outright opposition leaving him afraid or unable to declare himself... when indecisive he can become instable and weak" (Pollack: 1983: 34). The assumption could be made that *The People of the Monolith* was written without a position of awareness of the naïve implications of its greater meaning in the sense of its ultimate consequences, as the study of this Card has established.

12. PONAPE SCRIPTURES: EQUATES TO THE KNIGHT OF WANDS

Of all of the Cards of the *HP Lovecraft Tarot*, and on conceptual terms, this would have to be my favourite defined Card of this religious system of the Tarot. Defined on actual historical terms this would make direct reference to the Polynesian Site of the Ponape Islands, which more often referred to as Easter Island and the small clusters of land around it. I would argue that the significance of this is that it represents one of the stranger concepts in terms of the greater understanding of religion and of the mysteries which such a study puts forward. Whilst the Magus might be interested in researching this idea further on their own terms, in short this strange religious statement makes reference to the strange manifestation of Monoliths which have not been in any way properly explained by contemporary science. That said, to relate this Card to the greater system of the Tarot, here we see an example of where this system in question doesn't always seem to relate directly to the general mass of other Decks involving this system, or otherwise makes any point of clear rational sense.

That statement in hand, we still need to define the meaning of this Card of the *HP Lovecraft Tarot* in this context. The Lovecraft Deck of the Tarot here establishes such a statement in defining a principle of "'Primitive' culture; simplicity & honesty of relationships" (Hutchinson, Friedman: 2002: 62). In terms of our religious interpretation, it has been repeatedly proven that such "primitive" cultures which might be a point in question with this statement, have often had contact with a greater system of religious Gods, and the *Cthulhu Mythos Encyclopedia* justifies such an interpretation of this statement in giving a concise history of the *Ponape Scriptures*, in that:

12. Ponape Scriptures: Equates to the Knight of Wands

"[this statement in question is a] Manuscript researched or discovered by Captain Abner Ezekiel Hoag in the Carolines circa 1734. During his travels, Hoag discovered a book written on parchment made from palm leaves and bound in the wood of a long extinct [tree]. According to legend, the high priest of Ghatamothion, Imash Mo, and his successors wrote this book in the hieratic Naacal tongue" (Harms: 2008: 229)

The *HP Lovecraft Tarot* continues to define such a directly strange concept with a point as relating to "Human dynamics uncorrupted by greed, ambition, etc" (Hutchinson, Friedman: 2002: 62), and on specific terms of the greater system of the Tarot this could be established that this Card "represents eagerness, action, movement for its own sake, adventure and travel" (Polack: 1983: 32). Whilst this statement could always be interpreted on broader theoretical terms, the *Cthulhu Mythos Encyclopedia* makes an example of one such situation relating to such an idea of human psychological dynamics in the specific context of this Card, in that:

"When [Abner Hoag] attempted to have the volume published, he met with condemnation from the religious leaders of the time, who were especially concerned with the references to Dagon found in the *Scriptures*. The book did not see print until after Hoag's death, but by that time had been surreptitiously circulated in occult circles for quite some time" (Harms: 2008: 229)

Further to these points of definition established, a final definition of a Positive Reading with the Lovecraft system of the Tarot is one of "Authority given willingly and / or well deserved" (Hutchinson, Friedman: 2002: 62), and in this context this Card "Can provide the energy and self-confidence for great achievement" (Pollack: 1983: 32). The *Cthulhu Mythos Encyclopedia* upholds this statement as a point of religious interest as well, in stating that "the *Scripture* seems to have

been written by a Cthulhu cultist seeking to convert the natives of the region to his service" (Harms: 2008: 229).

Negative Reading

A Negative Reading with our religious system of Tarot defines a principle of "'Savage' life. Law of the Jungle; loss or lack of civilized justice" (Hutchinson, Friedman: 2002: 62), and this on terms of the greater system of the Tarot is further defined that "unlike the experienced warrior [the Magus] seeks battle at every opportunity, needing to prove his courage and strength, to himself and others" (Pollack: 1983: 32). If "Human dynamics [are] reduced to purely animal, survival level" (Hutchinson, Friedman: 2002: 62), then "opposition confuses [the Magus] even bring[ing] his great projects crashing down around him. Expecting everything will fall before him, he may find himself in a basic disharmony with people or situations around him" (Pollack: 1983: 32). And if a Negative Reading here would establish "Childish struggles for dominance" (Hutchinson, Friedman: 2002: 62), then this Card would further establish a position of "confusion, disrupted projects, breakdown and disharmony" (Pollack: 1983: 32).

As one concluding point, and with all of that having been said, the *Ponape Scriptures* should be read in context with the example of a number of primitive human societies having issues to establish mysteries and things which cannot be explained on scientific terms. This is one situation whereby The Cult of R'Lyeh believe we have religious point of argument which is yet to be properly explained.

13. CRYPTICAL BOOKS OF HSAN: EQUATES TO THE QUEEN OF WANDS

With the original proof to this book I had made a point to describe the imagery of this Card as portraying seven decaying and ornate scrolls, as was the imagery as portrayed with this Card with the previous Edition of this Tarot discussed. In the past of the Orient, scrolls, particularly religious scrolls such as these, were regarded as being inherently precious; this making a statement as to why the *Seven Cryptical Books of Hsan* are important as describing another religious Mythos book of magick. On first impression this Card seemed not to have any obvious meaning in terms of interpretation, but in making any further study this should have been seen as deceptive. When reading into a Card that first appears to say nothing, a cryptical meaning should at first be obvious for that reason. In the manner of the Orient, something that initially has no meaning, can have the most significance when seen on these terms. In expanding on this philosophical statement of definition, the *Cthulhu Mythos Encyclopedia* represents such a statement that:

"[The *Seven Cryptical Books of Hsan* are a] set of scrolls of... Chinese origin. According to some scholars Hsan the Greater wrote them in the second century. Others, however, maintain that they originally came from Leng and date back to the time of China's mythical Yellow Emperor, being translated into Chinese from a foreign tongue. It may be that these are the same as the legendary 'Seven Books of Tan' said to date back to 4000 B.C. and which contain many puzzles for those keen of mind" (Harms: 2008: 251)

The definition of this Card as described in the *HP Lovecraft Tarot* immediately raises problems when trying to establish its meaning in relation to the greater definition of the Tarot; whilst at the same time this does not mean that the *Seven Cryptical Books of Hsan* do not have a profound meaning of their own. A Positive interpretation here would therefore relate to a position of "Encryption, code; cipher; protection of data" (Hutchinson, Friedman: 2002: 62), and this might make reference to the original manuscript as translated into contemporary form. The *HP Lovecraft Tarot* makes further reference here to a position of "Magic numbers, numerology; magical squares & / or seals" (Hutchinson, Friedman: 2002: 62), and in this respect I would make mention that this could quite easily relate to systems of Ceremonial magick to the worship of The Great Old Ones if this study should be taken in the context in which it is meant. A final definition of meaning relates to "Qabalah, 'High' Magick, communication with Archetypes & Angels" (Hutchinson, Friedman: 2002: 62), and again this reference would define a position that this is in itself a position for much more serious religious study. With this being in no way directly relevant to this Card or to the greater system of the Tarot in general, however, the *Cthulhu Mythos Encyclopedia* does make a reference to such use of the occult in this specific context, in stating that:

> "The *Seven Cryptical Books* range widely in topics, including the proper treatment of a dead wizard's body, the forms of Nyarlathotep [and] the Dreamlands... The books also include quotations from the *R'Lyeh Text* and spells which bear resemblance to those in the *Dhol Chants*... The second book... is said to bestow limited power over life and death, and the fourth gives the spells for the summoning and dismissing of demons... [Also included is a] formula for creating the Eye of Light and Darkness. One of these books... contains information on how wisdom may be obtained from the dead" (Harms: 2008: 252)

This gives an example as to where different ideas begin to converge,

and The Cult of R'Lyeh argue that this is where our religious orientation is validated on terms of further research.

Negative Reading

With the Negative interpretation of this Card, we still find ourselves confronting an issue that such a definition in the context of the Lovecraft system of our study is still radically different from that of any other system of the Tarot. The *HP Lovecraft Tarot* here defines a point regarding "Loss of message in transmission; noisy signal" (Hutchinson, Friedman: 2002: 62), and this could relate to a statement that:

"…good nature demands that life respond[s] in a positive way. Too much disaster or too much opposition from life (and the weakness of… a person can be a tendency to think of life as 'unfair'), and a nasty streak can emerge. [The Magus] can become deceitful, jealous, unfaithful, or somewhat bitter" (Pollack: 1983: 31)

The Negative interpretation with this Card is further established in relating to a possible situation of "Unprotected intercourse, & the consequences thereof" (Hutchinson, Friedman: 2002: 62), and in this context "[the] Queen shows the reaction of such a person to opposition and sorrow" (Pollack: 1983: 31). As would very often not be the case, however, the *Seventy-Eight Degrees of Wisdom* here offers us some optimistic advice, in that "the basic good nature and positive attitudes of the Queen, as well as her energy, make her invaluable in a crisis or disaster" (Pollack: 1983: 31).

The *HP Lovecraft Tarot* concludes this definition of terms in making a point to relate to "Goetia, demonic intercourse; submission to Lower power" (Hutchinson, Friedman: 2002: 62). With this statement it should be taken into account that whilst we are discussing a system of magick as represented by *The Necronomicon* as our religious book in question, and to discuss a strange and admittedly bizarre Mythos of Lovecraftian

Gods, it is still a point to be acknowledged that we are dealing with an established position here of demonology and a system to ritualistic rites of ceremonial black magick. Whilst discussing this point in hand the *HP Lovecraft Tarot* is doing so in this specific context, and in this sense our religious system of the Tarot upholds such a statement on these defined conceptual terms as discussed.

14. THE REGNUM CONGO: EQUATES TO THE KING OF WANDS

The Regnum Congo

Before starting work with describing this Card as the last in the Suit of Tomes as defined by the *HP Lovecraft Tarot*, first we have a number of points of discussion. The first of these is that the Card that is here described as represented by the Regnum Congo, as is another Mythos religious book, does not have its own mention in the *Cthulhu Mythos Encyclopedia*. Whilst this is still the case with a number of the Cards of the current Edition, I have discussed this statement in some depth whilst writing to describe other Cards of this Deck already. The second point would be on the grounds that the previous Edition of the *HP Lovecraft Tarot* discussed this Card, instead, under the title and definition of being *The Black Book*. It is on the basis of this being the same Card of the Minor Arcana that I have used the equivalent statement from the Introductory Book to the previous Edition of this Deck in discussion, and this is on the basis of this being essentially the same Card of the Lovecraftian Minor Arcana.

Further to that statement as defining terms, the first point to be made in describing the Cards of the Minor Arcana as according to the *HP*

Lovecraft Tarot, is that whilst this Deck is unique in depicting this representation of the Tarot as individual graphics of their own, it is still a point in hand that such representations must, by necessity, equate to make the same statement as described by every other system of the Tarot. This is another statement which I have previously discussed with this book already. Therefore we immediately face a unique discussion when discussing the Regnum Congo as representing the same statement which other Decks describe as being similar to the King of Wands.

So, the first question to be asked with this point in hand would be, what is there in the *Regnum Congo* which could equate to the statement which would have been related to the King of Wands in other systems of the Tarot? In order to answer this, such a Card in the *HP Lovecraft Tarot* would define this statement if such a book in question would be representative of any book of law whereby any religious minority could be persecuted and controlled. Rachel Pollack's book on the subject of the Minor Arcana makes a statement as to the meaning of this Card, that "[a] King is a ruler responsible for the welfare of society… all the Kings represent both success… and social responsibility" (Pollack: 1983: 28). With this we can quite easily ascribe the necessary role of the leader with the authority which is imposed by books which govern society and the rules which oppress minority religion.

In terms of interpreting what this Card might mean as part of a Reading, the *Regnum Congo* in other systems might be defined as "a strong minded person, able to dominate others by strength of will" (Pollack: 1983: 28). The same definition is ascribed with the Lovecraftian system that the same Card represents "Humour, satire [and] sarcasm" (Hutchinson, Friedman: 2002: 62).

This definition is taken further that "Such a strong personality can tend towards intolerance, unable to understand weakness or despair" (Pollack: 1983: 28). The Lovecraft system again defines this Card on similar terms that it defines "Survival amidst oppression" (Hutchinson, Friedman: 2002: 62).

Negative Reading

Rachel Pollack makes a valid statement as regarding the Minor Arcana in saying that "[w]hen we reverse a card we alter in some way its prime meaning, as if the original impact had become blocked or rechannelled, or, in some cases, liberated" (Pollack: 1983: 29). This should maybe be taken into consideration in that the Introductory Book to the previous Edition of the *HP Lovecraft Tarot* represents both Positive and Negative readings on equal terms. "[A] reversed [Card] indicates that [a] person [is] disturbed or blocked, or maybe having a bad influence on [a] subject" (Pollack: 1983: 29).

"Right side up the King shows us someone powerful and commanding, yet often intolerant of other people's weaknesses" (Pollack: 1983: 29). A reversed Card indicates a different Reading, however, and with the Lovecraft system of the Tarot this represents "Propaganda; Political Deception; advertising" (Hutchinson, Friedman: 2002: 62). Again the idea of the King and the books of law come into the interpretation of the meaning of this Card.

The definition of a Negative meaning with this Card is briefly concluded as the Introductory Book to the previous Edition of the *HP Lovecraft Tarot* warns us that "The gods of the old religion become the devils of the new" (Hutchinson, Friedman: 2002: 62). We should be cautious that any new rules as imposed by authority might, inevitably, stand to establish more problems which might become another defined point of their own.

SUIT OF SITES

Here we see the Lovecraftian Suit of Sites as representing "Environment, context. Not necessarily physical or geographic" (Hutchinson, Friedman: 2002: 50), although this should be put into context as the *Seventy-Eight Degrees of Wisdom*, as a reference already used repeatedly throughout this book, rightly points out that "Our culture has a long history of despising the physical world" (Pollack: 1983: 94). At the same time such environment around us has been interpreted in religious terms in that "we can see the mortal world as the product of God's creative force" (Pollack: 1983: 94).

This statement is further defined by the *HP Lovecraft Tarot* as our study in question as relating to "frame of reference, frame of mind" (Hutchinson, Friedman: 2002: 50). Taken further this can be defined that "Emotions and abstract thoughts are seen as 'higher' than anything which actually exists" (Pollack: 1983: 94). In terms of the specific study of the Minor Arcana Rachel Pollack points out that, "As a magical sign, Pentacles [expressed in the Lovecraft system as being the Suit of Sites] symbolize the 'magic' of ordinary creation" (Pollack: 1983: 95). We could establish a point that certain situations are established by specific frames of mentality.

The last point to be defined under this definition by the *HP Lovecraft Tarot* in describing the meaning of this Suit in discussion relates to "'Setting': time & place as an effect on motivation & action, or as constraints on possible action, etc" (Hutchinson, Friedman: 2002: 50),

and this could be further justified with the statement that "We ground ourselves not just in our work but in a love for the world around us" (Pollack: 1983: 95), and our given research in question continues on the greater definition of the Tarot in saying that:

"The mystic or magician does not simply ground the self in a negative way, using the world as the opposite of spiritual experience. Rather, the natural world, because it carries a firmer reality than the other elements, because it does not lead so easily to confusion or misconception or ill use, opens the way to a more mystical experience" (Pollack: 1983: 95)

What this tells us, albeit on some obscure terms, is that the symbolism which is expressed with the *HP Lovecraft Tarot* should always be regarded as being more important than any direct statement given on any basis by any of the Cards of this specific system in question, and it is the role of the Magus to interpret such points in question on their own terms if to interpret this Deck on their own individual philosophical terms.

Minor Arcana	Suit of Sites	Suit of Pentacles
1	Sunken R'Lyeh	Ace of Pentacles
2	Irem, City of Pillars	Two of Pentacles
3	Plateau of Leng	Three of Pentacles
4	Whateley Farmhouse	Four of Pentacles
5	The Witch House	Five of Pentacles

Minor Arcana	Suit of Sites	Suit of Pentacles
6	The Mountains of Madness	Six of Pentacles
7	Church of Federal Hill	Seven of Pentacles
8	Innsmouth	Eight of Pentacles
9	Kadath	Nine of Pentacles
10	Exham Priory	Ten of Pentacles
11	Sentinel Hill	Page of Pentacles
12	EOD Temple	Knight of Pentacles
13	House in the Mist	Queen of Pentacles
14	Arkham	King of Pentacles

Table 8. The Lovecraftian Suit of Sites equated to the Minor Arcana Suit of Pentacles.

1. Sunken R'Lyeh:
Equates to the Ace of Pentacles

The previous Edition of the Lovecraftian Deck of the Tarot gives this Card as being 'Yuggoth', which is a distant part of our Solar System and also quite important in Mythos literature. The current version of the *HP Lovecraft Tarot* changes this point of definition, however, and describes this Card instead as being representative of Cthulhu's resting place as the sunken city of R'Lyeh. Further to this, the meanings of the Cards of the planned current Edition to this Tarot discussed should be considered the same, and I will discuss the meaning of this Card on this basis, as they it is otherwise representative of the same part of the Minor Arcana Suit of Sites.

With that point therefore having been established, the *HP Lovecraft Tarot* continues to define this Card as representative of a position of a "Foundation, Staging point" (Hutchinson, Friedman: 2002: 63), and this is appropriate as a part of the Lovecraftian religious system in that:

> "[the City of] R'Lyeh sank beneath the waves of the Pacific Ocean, [then] becoming the tomb of Great Cthulhu" (Harms: 2008: 239)

It is this position of symbolism which is the important point to be considered here, and a direct parallel of meaning can here be established as to quote from this book on another occasion the *Seventy-Eight Degrees of Wisdom* discusses the Tarot as being representative of the greater existence of the occult, in that:

> "Spiritual work leads us to recognize the magic in normal things, in both nature and civilization, and then to go beyond them to the greater knowledge symbolized by the mountains" (Pollack: 1983: 119)

In order to continue with such a discussion of a Positive interpretation, then, this first Card of the Suit of Pentacles (as it is with a large number of other Decks) continues with such an idea of a new start to a personal journey and defines a point of "Origin, Source; New beginning" (Hutchinson, Friedman: 2002: 63). The example of sunken R'Lyeh is again an appropriate point of symbolism to represent this point, and in quoting again from the *Cthulhu Mythos Encyclopedia* we see the position further established that:

> "Cthulhu and his minions built R'Lyeh millions of years before the earliest recorded human history" (Harms: 2008: 239)

This statement can again be read in direct relation to the theory of the Tarot as representing a much larger movement of esoteric religion and the occult, and it is with this point of discussion that such an idea can be ascribed, that:

> "The Earth, in its completeness and solid reality, bears its own magic... Through the work of civilization humanity shapes the raw material of nature into a safe and comfortable environment" (Pollack: 1983: 119)

The idea of the sunken city of R'Lyeh being unexplored, and

even quite mythical, is further put into this relative context, and the *HP Lovecraft Tarot* describes a position of "Exploration; enterprise" (Hutchinson, Friedman: 2002: 63), and such a point to represent the unknown becoming known is put into direct context again, as the *Cthulhu Mythos Encyclopedia* states that:

"Though R'Lyeh has sunk deep beneath the Pacific Ocean, there have been times when the city (or at least its highest mountain) breaches the surface of the sea, only to sink down again after a short period of time" (Harms: 2008: 239)

In order to follow this statement through, again the *Seventy-Eight Degrees of Wisdom* puts a similar definition on different and broader terms in stating that "As the Minor Arcana comes to an end [as this Card is related in Rachel Pollack's book on the subject] the Ace of Pentacles shows us once more how, when we are ready, the Gate always opens to the truth" (Pollack: 1983: 120). This statement as regarding a Gateway to new beginnings is established as part of this discussion, in that:

"[in sunken R'Lyeh] Great Cthulhu sleeps, an Elder Sign holding him within his tomb" (Harms: 2008: 240)

Negative Reading

A Negative interpretation with this Card of the Tarot is here defined under the concept of "Erosion, decomposition, undermining, deterioration" (Hutchinson, Friedman: 2002: 63), and this idea ties in directly with the concept of sunken R'Lyeh again, in that in representing such ideas of destruction:

"sallying forth from the city [of R'Lyeh] to battle the Elder Things and other alien entities a catastrophe occurred. It could be a particular astrological configuration [but] a great cosmic war with

the Elder Gods occurred, a secret weapon of the Elder Things, or the creation of the moon [became apparent]" (Harms: 2008: 239)

The *HP Lovecraft Tarot* continues with this discussion of such a point as regards such a Negative Reading, and defines a point of "Unswerving Fate; inevitable conclusion" (Hutchinson, Friedman: 2002: 63), and again this idea can be read in direct terms of the Lovecraftian occult should the Magus choose to acknowledge such a direct correlation of ideas and of the meaning of such a system if seen on such terms. Again the *Cthulhu Mythos Encyclopedia* does a good job in expressing such religious ideology in pointing out that:

"At these times, the dreams of Cthulhu have been telepathically broadcast, leading to outbreaks of religious fervour, insanity and natural disturbances around the world" (Harms: 2008: 239)

These ideas as discussed with this book as regarding a Gate would be an appropriate point in order to conclude this short statement of definition, and the idea of directly establishing the meaning of this Card is important when we define the point that "Only the ignorant or [the] foolhardy would open the door to this tomb; in all of history this has only occurred a few times, and the results were disastrous" (Harms: 2008: 240). What all of this discussion tells us is that, whilst we might at any one time have a Gateway to be opened before us, we should be aware that we cannot be conscious of the possible consequences of opening such a Gate, until after that Gate has ultimately and eventually been opened.

2. IREM, CITY OF PILLARS: EQUATES TO THE TWO OF PENTACLES

In opening this as a proper dialogue to discuss this as the final Suit of the Minor Arcana, and as according to this theory of the occult Tarot in question, I would like to further start this discussion with a couple of points, and with the Lovecraft Deck of the Tarot being this specific religious discussion in hand. This discussion is on the basis of the significance of the City of Irem as a historical point of note, whilst specifically intending to discuss this as the second Card of the Lovecraftian Suit of Sites, as following from everything which has so far been discussed in this book you are reading here.

Irem, City of Pillars

All of the Cards of the *HP Lovecraft Tarot* have one singular point in common, in that they all have some significance, in one way or another, in representing the ideas as ascribed to *The Necronomicon* as our religious book, and as has been properly discussed already with this book in hand. With this point established *The Necronomicon Cycle* has been written to establish the validity of a number of underground religious currents which might be involved with our movement on this basis. This general theory is justified on the basis that most of the Cards of this Deck can be directly ascribed to the literary work as

represented by our main religious representative, the religious horror writer Lovecraft, with The Cult of R'Lyeh arguing that this as the main literary representative for our movement of religion must have had some access to *The Necronomicon*, in one way or another, in order to be able to have written such a backlog of inspired religious fiction at the time that he did in the first part of the last Century. If the Cards of our religious representative system cannot be directly interpreted on this basis, then, the Cards of the Tarot thereby included as part of this system can still be related directly to the idea of *The Necronomicon* as representing one religious truth, and The Cult of R'Lyeh would argue this position on the basis of the validity of Chaos Magick Theory as being directly important to contemporary religious belief, as one smaller and singular part of our religious outlook.

Further to that as a general recap of the framework established in putting forward this book, those with any working knowledge of *The Necronomicon*, will be aware that most of this, as a religious statement which has equal validity as with all others (by implication), focuses – to a large extent, on the documented experiences of our prophet Abdul AlHazred and his wanderings through the Deserts of Arabia, whereby he documented his own loss of sanity as being the result of communication with the demon forces thereby involved. The *Cthulhu Mythos Encyclopedia* represents this to some legitimate extent with its own entry on the subject of our religious prophet in stating that "No matter what AlHazred's origin, the substance of his later life is debated. He is known to have spent much time in the Empty Quarter of [this] desert [where a good part of *The Necronomicon* was written" (Harms: 2008: 6). And those with such a working knowledge of this as our religious system will also be aware of the significance of the City of Irem as a documented part of such a history of suffering, as the *Cthulhu Mythos Encyclopedia* states that AlHazred "discovered both Irem the City of Pillars, and the Nameless City [as part of this journey of religious enlightenment]" (Harms: 2008: 6)

The idea of discussing the validity of such religious points here in discussion continues as the *Cthulhu Mythos Encyclopedia* describes

2. Irem, City of Pillars: Equates to the Two of Pentacles

the City of Irem as being "[a place] Lost... somewhere in the depths of the Arabian desert, Irem is the City of a Thousand Pillars, and is called 'many-columned' in the [Qu'ran]" (Harms: 2008: 142). If to take such an interpretation of religion to its logical further conclusion then, the lost City of Irem is in fact mentioned towards the end of this sacred religious book of Muslim religious belief, with the 89th Chapter asking:

"Have you [Prophet] considered how your Lord dealt with [the people] of Ad, of Irem [the City] of... pillars, whose like has never been made in any land [?]" (Qu'ran: 2008: 420)

Both the importance and the significance of *The Necronomicon* is therefore put into context with this historical example, and whilst most people reading this book will relate to the example of *The Qu'ran* as being much more widely represented as a contemporary religious book, it is cross-overs in contemporary religious thought as with this given example that stand to justify the position of The Cult of R'Lyeh on Earth, that – if seen on these and other defined religious terms – then we are standing to realize that there is, in fact, one statement of one singular religious truth. All of this should be put into perspective, however, that in discussing this point, as with everything else here in discussion, *The Necronomicon* is a point of further mystery, and an online statement published to make a discussion of such ancient civilisations states:

"The literature of past civilizations often mentions cities which are now lost to humanity, the most famous of them being the lost city of Atlantis. On a smaller scale, Arabia has its own legend of a lost civilization, the so-called 'Atlantis of the Sands' – a lost city, tribe or area spoken of in the Quran, which has come to be known as Irem of the Pillars" (Iren of the Pillars, the Lost 'Atlantis of the Sands': n.d.)

Whilst discussing this work on the last Suit of the Minor Arcana in question, I would also – at this point – like to make a statement in relation to the interpretation of different Decks of the Tarot, with specific reference to the Lovecraftian system as discussed. The first point here is that, on obvious terms, people involved with any interpretation of this system, quite rightly use the Deck that they feel comfortable with whilst doing any Reading for themselves. The significance of the *HP Lovecraft Tarot* is, however, not only on the basis of how the religious *Necronomicon* here comes into play if we are to argue that there is one religious truth, but is also on the basis of how such an interpretation of meaning, as discussed with *The Necronomicon Cycle*, can be directly seen in terms of Psychoanalytical thought (further to such a general discussion of religion). This in itself is an issue which could be taken a lot further as a point of research in itself, and whilst I would make the point that I, myself, am in no way qualified in Psychiatry (I am qualified in Theology and Religious Studies), a book titled *Mosig at Last: a Psychologist Looks at HP Lovecraft* by the psychologist D.W. Mosig is an excellent book which makes a start at establishing this point in question.[1] With this as an important point as upheld by The Cult of R'Lyeh on Earth, if the Magus were to be interested in following this point of research in any way further, recent movements in publishing occult literature have included the publication of a number of books on the idea of Psychology and the practical use of ritual magick; and would suggest that such a study of Psychiatry in relation to the ideas of Chaos Magick Theory is still a point of research that could potentially

---

1 The Further Reading statement to The Necronomicon Cycle at the end of this book includes a reference to this title, as well as a number of other academic references which cover the general idea of psychology and the Lovecraftian occult in one way or another, although the point to be made here is that The Cult of R'Lyeh believe that this is still a point that could be taken a lot further.

be taken much further.[2]

All of these are points which could be taken into consideration when making any study of *The Necronomicon* in relation to any chosen religious system of the Tarot.

As the point will already be clear, if defining the Positive and Negative meanings of the Cards of the Minor Arcana, the *HP Lovecraft Tarot* usually gives us three or four general statements, which should in turn be interpreted further by the person who is doing the Reading, or for the person for who the Reading is for. Further to this, if the statement here is clearly related to that of the Lovecraftian, then research into the esoteric Cthulhu Mythos of Gods must be appropriate in taking this religious definition of meaning forward; and (as has already been pointed out on repeated occasions) I choose to focus on using the *Cthulhu Mythos Encyclopedia* as an excellent resource in order to establish this point. Further to the direct religious symbolism intended with this statement, then, it should be pointed out that the study of any system of the Tarot is also on the basis on the specific symbolism as established by any religious Deck, and the point that stands is that the Magus should uphold *The Necronomicon Cycle* in order to further establish their own religious orientation.[3] This idea of interpreting Psychiatry is represented for this reason.

This should be taken as a general point in hand when the *HP Lovecraft Tarot* defines a position of an "Ability to reach one's goal

---

[2] Whilst this should be regarded as a separate and independent study of its own, a number of good books have been published on this subject, and this page note makes a bibliographical reference for only three of them. As is the case with everything else with The Necronomicon Cycle, the Magus should always make a point to interpret everything on their own individual terms. A few of these useful titles in question are:
•Farber, P.H. (2008) META-MAGICK the Book of Atem. San Francisco, Weiser Books
•Farber, P.H. (2011) Brain Magick. Minnesota, Llewellyn
Bruere, D.C. (2009) *Techno Mage*. England, Published by Dirk Bruere

[3] Appendix I of this book goes into some detail about how different systems of the Tarot can be used to represent a system of R'Lyehan religious magick.

without direction or defined route" (Hutchinson, Friedman: 2002: 63). Where this idea ties in with Irem, the City of Pillars, is not entirely clear, but in consideration of the above, and with the example of our Prophet AlHazred as the most important representation of our religion, the idea of discovering something as important as such a lost city, as with the situation of Irem, is represented that:

"Abdul AlHazred opened up the first gate to allow the Great Old One's minions into the world [after having discovered] the ruins of [this lost City discussed]" (Harms: 2008: 143)

Such a discussion of movement towards realization of personal goals as is implied with this statement is discussed differently by the *Seventy-Eight Degrees of Wisdom* in interpreting the Minor Arcana on its own terms, however, in that "The juggler [as being the symbolism to define this Card on broader terms] holds his magic emblems with a loop or ribbon shaped like an infinity sign, the same sign that appears above the head of the Magician" (Pollack: 1983: 118). With this statement continuing to define a position of "Adaptability to a changing landscape" (Hutchinson, Friedman: 2002: 63), then the same discussion of symbolism and interpretation should be held in mind, and such a statement of discovery and 'changing landscape' is discussed as defined by this idea, and the City of Irem is such a symbolic example of this idea, in stating that:

"Various myths have been told about the city's origins. One tells of Irem being built by creatures of great size and colossal strength. With our knowledge of the creatures of the Mythos, this should not be lightly dismissed" (Harms: 2008: 142)

This idea relating directly to the idea of how different systems of the Tarot should be interpreted on different terms is a clear point in hand with the given example as the *Cthulhu Mythos Encyclopedia* continues this definition to state that "Travelers lost in the deserts of Arabia have

been known to stumble upon this city, later bearing their delirious tales back to civilization" (Harms: 2008: 143). In terms of the ideas here discussed, this in relation to the symbolic meaning of the Tarot could be interpreted quite easily. The Magus has somehow got lost, but in doing so she has stumbled upon something significant and otherwise not known. The reaction of greater society is to interpret such experience as representing this as the justified intellect of the insane.

This Positive interpretation is concluded with a statement to establish a position of "Improvisation; freedom of form" (Hutchinson, Friedman: 2002: 63). In following this idea as regarding the symbolism and scope for meaning that the Tarot ultimately allows us, the City of Irem is again a very valid example as the *Cthulhu Mythos Encyclopedia* states that:

"Over the gateway to Irem, a tremendous hand is carved, which is said to reach for the artifact known as the Silver Key" (Harms: 2008: 143)

It is this reference to the Silver Key which is important here, as this represents the gateways to sleep and the greater freedom that we access while we dream (the reader will have noticed that this is further discussed with a different Card of the Minor Arcana). As is pointed out by the *Seventy-Eight Degrees of Wisdom*, and in quoting again from this book, "Pleasure and amusement can also teach us a great deal, as long as we pay attention" (Pollack: 1983: 118).

Negative Reading

With this Negative interpretation as is established with this Card of the Tarot, the Magus should be cautious of a situation regarding "Mirage, shifting landmarks or (intellectual) points of reference" (Hutchinson, Friedman: 2002: 63), and whilst the *Cthulhu Mythos Encyclopedia* was not written to describe any religious system of the Tarot in itself, the fabled destruction of the City of Irem would again be

an appropriate in terms of occult symbolism, in that:

> "Some tell of creatures from the sky, who remain in the city to this day [who] killed or drove out all of the [city's] inhabitants. Some have said that Irem was actually built by minions of Shudde-M'eil, who had the city destroyed due to its inhabitants ignoring his commands. Still others believe that the men from Irem journeyed beneath to fight the creatures from the Nameless City who ate their inhabitants" (Harms: 2008: 143)

This Negative interpretation is here further discussed on the basis of an "inability to accept or adapt to circumstance" (Hutchinson, Friedman: 2002: 63). In discussing the City of Irem in relation to the religious Tarot and the views of The Cult of R'Lyeh on Earth, I'd regard it as appropriate to quote further from the *Cthulhu Mythos Encyclopedia*, that "When a carved hand above a doorway in that palace grasps a long-lost key again, the palace will be instantly destroyed" (Harms: 2008: 143). Whilst the 'key' in a positive sense describes the freedom as expressed through the free travelling of dreams (as is a fundamental point of Lovecraftian religious thought), here we see a position that an inability to adapt to its change under specific circumstances represents the imprisonment of nightmare sleep.

A final Negative interpretation describes a position of "Loss of structure & / or discipline" (Hutchinson, Friedman: 2002: 63), and on the basis of further interpretation the *Cthulhu Mythos Encyclopedia* states that:

> "[according to the Qu'ran, the City of Irem] was destroyed because of the sins of its inhabitants" (Harms: 2008: 142)

And we have already seen this example established on openly graphic terms in researching the symbolic importance that is described with the imagery and definition involved with this Card. With that example established, again we see that the recurring example of where

the Tarot, as with everything else, must always be established on the terms of the individual, and in quoting again from the *Seventy-Eight Degrees of Wisdom*, Rachel's description of this equivalent Card of the Tarot states:

> "Faced either with some problem we do not wish to face, or else with social pressure not to make a fuss, we may pretend to ourselves as well as to others, to take everything lightly" (Pollack: 1983: 119)

Whilst the juggler as described under the first point of a Positive definition with this part of the Minor Arcana has a real potential to realise personal ambitions and hopes, with this Card as represented by the destruction of the mythical lost City of Pillars, the Magus should be careful that if they are not aware of potential problems, then "The juggling act is likely to fail" (Pollack: 1983: 119).

3. Plateau of Leng:
Equates to the Three of Pentacles

In approaching this as the Third Card of the Lovecraftian Suit of Sites, again we run into another couple of issues as regarding research. The first of these regards the symbolic validity of the concepts that we are dealing with as we discuss a bizarre representation

with the subject of Leng, with that being symbolic of the Lovecraftian dimension of dream. With most of the other Cards of the *HP Lovecraft Tarot* we are dealing with specific aspects of symbolism, most of them relating directly to ideas taken from *The Necronomicon*, or otherwise influenced thereby, with the original ideas of Lovecraft being related to this concept. In discussing the idea of Leng, however, we diverge from this as a statement of religious belief as is discussed as the concept of this book.

The concept of Leng relates directly to the idea which is, in Lovecraftian religious thought, directed towards this idea which is known as the Dreamlands, this relating directly to an astral dimension beyond dreams, which in itself has its own religious significance to those upholding the ideas as put forward by underground religious groups such as The Cult of R'Lyeh on Earth. This specific genre of Mythos literature was most probably inspired by

3. Plateau of Leng: Equates to the Three of Pentacles

Lovecraft's fictional idea of the Silver Key (which has its own reference as a Part of this system of the Tarot, as part of the Suit of Artifacts, with that point having already been mentioned), which in turn related directly to the inspired work of another number of Mythos writers, who then expanded on this as a specific and developed religious concept of its own. However, very little of this work has any specific grounding in terms of occult literature, with *The Necronomicon* being the first point in question. Therefore I would have to question the point – on specific terms – whether this as a genre of writing should be included with any practical discussion of occult magick? An exception to this point would be with the further example of Chaos Magick Theory, which validates certain religious concepts on specific terms, and I would suggest that if the Magus were to follow this point up, then a rudimentary study of Psychiatry might be an important or otherwise useful point in hand.[1]

The second issue which should at this point here be pointed out, is that in discussing this as the concept of Leng in relation to the Lovecraftian and the concept of dream, then the entry for this subject in the *Cthulhu Mythos Encyclopedia* would appear to be inaccurate in discussing this point, although in continuing to use this book as one of my main points of research I would like to state that this is the single point on which this seems to be the case. The statement here to describe this concept in question seems to be confused in describing this point, in stating that:

> "[The Plateau of Leng is an] Area near Kadath in the Cold Waste. Scholars usually place the Plateau in central Asia, and one even names China's Xinjang Province as its location. Reports from the Pabodic Expedition of 1930-31 place Leng somewhere in the frozen wastes of Antarctica. Others hold that it is in Burma" (Harms: 2008: 166)

---

[1] Having made that initial point, to gain access to any complete version of The Necronomicon is in no way easy, and this statement was written before any proper consideration as to where the concept of Leng, as a dimension of dreams, is actually represented in the greater scheme of our religious book in discussion.

Despite such a seemingly confused and contradictory statement, which is (in my opinion) clearly inaccurate, consensus amongst the Lovecraftian occult community would establish the concept of Leng as being directly representing the further dimension of dreams, as the point has already been made, and the above quotation continues directly, that:

> "experienced dreamers say [that Leng] lies in the northern part of earths Dreamlands. Al Hazred mentions [in *The Necronomicon* that] it is a place where various alternative realities come together, which may explain these discrepancies" (Harms: 2008: 166)

With that point in consideration, *The Necronomicon Cycle* cannot begin to properly represent the potential symbolism of magickal representation discussed with such a representation of Lovecraft's Dreamlands to any extent to do justice to this concept in hand, and should the Magus have any interest in chasing this idea up further then I would suggest in the first case making reference to a book titled *H.P. Lovecraft's Dreamlands: Roleplaying Beyond the Wall of Sleep*.[2] As a slight point of digression, whilst discussing the extent of this idea, I have always wondered why the concept of the Dreamlands does not have a dedicated Deck of the Tarot of its own (?), but that's a different discussion of theory...

That said, I feel that the study of the Minor Arcana as already discussed makes a number of points as to how the valid symbolism as involved with the *HP Lovecraft Tarot* works in relation to the further study of the Lovecraftian and the religious validity of *The Necronomicon*. It would therefore be quite clear as to how the *HP Lovecraft Tarot* should be interpreted in relation to the religious views here discussed, and I will try to keep most of the following entries in this book concise, whilst the rest of the Cards of this Tarot are discussed in proper detail.

The *HP Lovecraft Tarot* here defines a position of "Avalon, Tir-

---

2 A bibliographical reference for this book has previously been given in a footnote earlier in The Necronomicon Cycle.

na-Nog, Realm of Faerie; legendary kingdoms made manifest" (Hutchinson, Friedman: 2002: 63), and with this we see a direct relation to higher worlds of fantasy or of consciously accessing higher states as defined with the mythical concept of the Dreamlands. In describing such a dimension as being "[an] Alternate dimension accessible only through a person's dreams" (Harms: 2008: 81), here we have a position similar to the idea to the concept of the Astral Plane as upheld by different movements of contemporary paganism (as well as other forms of occult religion), and I would suggest that work with the occult in contacting the Astral Plane could be tied up with work involving the Dreamlands if the Magus were to be interested in taking this idea further.

This statement continues that "Earlier in life, most people can enter the Dreamlands at will, but as adulthood approaches, this gateway closes for the majority of these dreamers" (Harms: 2008: 81). Whilst this could possibly be considered to be another direct reference to psychology and the working of the human mind, the same statement continues in relation to the Dreamlands and the occult theory of Astral Travel, in stating that:

"Only a few adults have been able to enter this land again, through the use of certain narcotics or simply be searching their dreams. Some physical portals between the Dreamlands and the waking world do exist, but these gateways are few and [are] often found in dangerous locales in both realms" (Harms: 2008: 81)

In working to establish an interpretation of the *HP Lovecraft Tarot* in terms of this greater significance as a representation of a greater religious movement, it should always be a point in consideration that our given intention is to make a study as to the validity of *The Necronomicon* and its further credibility as a religious book, and again the *Cthulhu Mythos Encyclopedia* properly represents this point in stating:

"Usually, the name 'Dreamlands' is only applied to that dimension visited by humans, but other dreamlands do exist. Such worlds as Saturn, Jupiter and Pluto have their dream-reflections as well, which are visited by the respective denizens of those bodies" (Harms: 2008: 82)

In furthering this discussion, this Card also has a more traditional meaning in terms of occult symbolism, and in discussing this point the *Seventy-Eight Degrees of Wisdom* points out that "Together the three figures" which are aften portrayed with this Card in more traditional Decks:

"signify that the best work combines both technical skill (Air) and spiritual understanding (Water) with energy and desire (Fire)... Part of this card's meaning lies in the fact that such symbolism of psychic development should occur [as being] mundane [with the Suit of] Pentacles" (Pollack: 1983: 177)

If the *HP Lovecraft Tarot* continues to establish a position of "Idealism, Zeal; Healthy perfectionism" (Hutchinson, Friedman: 2002: 63), here we see a position to establish how dedication to achieving intended aims will manifest as being successful. And in direct relation to the idea of the Dreamlands as the symbolism involved with representing this Card of the Minor Arcana, it is established that "Persistent dreamers may reach [equivalent states on foreign planets] from Earth's Dreamlands, but such visits may prove quite dangerous to the unprepared traveller" (Harms: 2008: 82). This idea of working towards seemingly impossible goals is expressed differently, again, as the *Seventy-Eight Degrees of Wisdom*, despite discussing the idea of the Minor Arcana on properly different terms, defines a point that "[this Card] signif[ies] that... hard work and dedication have resulted or will result in mastery" (Pollack: 1983: 117). This established we could quote again from the same entry from this book in following the point already discussed that the Third Card of the last Suit of the Minor

Arcana has greater meaning in terms of the greater symbolic study of religious magick:

"Observe how the pentacles form an upward pointing Fire triangle, showing that work can raise us to higher levels, while below them a flower sits within a downward pointing Water triangle, symbolizing the need to root… work in the reality of the world" (Pollack: 1983: 117)

This Positive definition of interpretation concludes with a point to establish "Retirement, pension, rest after productive career" (Hutchinson, Friedman: 2002: 63), although on this basis it is not entirely clear as to where this has any direct relation to the concept of Leng as representing the Dreamlands? The *Seventy-Eight Degrees of Wisdom* does, however, make a statement as to discuss such a positive result of hard work, and in quoting again from the Chapter which discusses this same Card of the Minor Arcana, this states that "We return here to the theme of work, both seen in its literal sense and as a symbol of spiritual development… practical work, done consciously and with commitment, may serve as the vehicle for self-development" (Pollack: 1983: 117). If the Magus has been following this statement so far, here we begin to define a position that the differences as upheld by all religions, actually define a unified position of unified religious truth.

Negative Reading

At this point I would regard it as being unnecessary to work through the entire definition of the Negative interpretation of this Card in extensive detail, although the first Appendix to this book will clarify such if a copy of the previous Edition of the *HP Lovecraft Tarot* is unavailable and, as has been pointed out already, it should always be the first option of the Magus to interpret any Reading with any Card of the Tarot on their own individual terms. However, the above statement

is concluded well as the *Seventy-Eight Degrees of Wisdom*, defines a position of:

> "Mediocracy... work, physical or spiritual, goes badly, often from laziness or weakness. Sometimes [this] meaning extends to a general situation in which little happens; things continue, either getting worse or improving" (Pollack: 1983: 118)

What all of this must ultimately establish is that spiritual work is often very similar to the human actions of physical work, and if this work is not taken seriously, then we cannot be successful in establishing the eventual goals that we are working for, regardless to whether they be in physical terms or on the basis of any higher magickal working.

4. Whateley Farmhouse: Equates to the Four of Pentacles

With the Card of the Minor Arcana as being represented with the Whateley Farmhouse, here we see another example of where the esoteric principles as represented by the *HP Lovecraft Tarot* can often verge on the point of being obscure (not to mention bizarre). Whilst the personification of Wizard Noah Whateley and Wilbur Whateley are both archetypal principles which our research discusses in detail (the Magus will be aware that both personalities are discussed with their own Cards, previously with this discussion of the first Suit of the Minor Arcana, being People), the position to define the significance of the Whateley Farmhouse is obviously more obscure. If it would probably be for this reason, then, that the *Cthulhu Mythos Encyclopedia* does not have specific entry for this categorization, the same book does have a statement in regard to the specific reading of Mythos fiction that would be necessary if we were to make a more defined statement as to what such a definition should mean?

> "Lovecraft's [religious and conceptual] pantheon is inherently contradictory, with its monsters that dwell beyond time and that can hardly be understood by human minds. Why shouldn't other authors introduce such contradictions into their own works, whether deliberately or accidentally?" (Harms: 2008: xvii)

This issue as to research having then been stated, there's not a great deal more that anyone can do to put forward a more detailed description of this Card if that's our research in hand, and the Magus must therefore be left to conduct their own research should more information or any

other interpretation of this Card be necessary. However, the first Appendix to this book has been included for this reason as to allow such an interpretation of this religious Tarot, and we can make further reference to the *Seventy-Eight Degrees of Wisdom* for a statement as to how the Fourth Card of the Suit of Sites is represented on the greater terms of the Tarot as being a greater system of working magick, that:

> "As magic signs the pentacles symbolize basic emotional / spiritual energy. People working with chakra meditation will recognize the... connection to Spirit... In certain situations, the Four, usually viewed as a 'problem' card, becomes very appropriate. When life has broken down into chaos, then the Four indicates creating a structure, either through material things, or by emotional and mental energy inwards... People who meditate through their auras will usually, at the end of each meditation, follow a ritual of 'sealing' the aura at the chakra points. This practice prevents... a leaking of their own energy... Finally... the Four of Pentacles symbolizes the way in which the human mind gives structure and meaning to the chaos of the material universe... The fact that human beings exist in the universe as creatures rather than passive observers forms one of the meeting points between mystical / esoteric teachings and contemporary physics" (Pollack: 1983: 116)

A lengthy quotation here, but in context this makes a valid statement as to represent how the Tarot works as a system which has often been integrated into other forms of secular and religious worship throughout contemporary history. The idea of the Tarot and other issues such as auric meditation and so on, is one that has a large number of books written about as a specific study of religion in itself, and in pointing this out – and in terms of this given quotation – the suggestion would be that any interpretation, of any system of the Tarot, can always be used for these and similar purposes should the Magus be willing to put in the research to follow such ideas up. The Cult of R'Lyeh would leave the

statement there if to reason that this this, in relation to the *HP Lovecraft Tarot*, continues to define a principle that there is one religious truth.

Negative Reading

With that point regarding the issue that this interpretation of the Tarot must largely be down to the Magus as to understand any given Reading, the above makes a statement that such an interpretation must therefore be on the terms of the individual in question. In terms of the stated research that might therefore be necessary here, the first Appendix to this book lists the entire definition of meaning as published in the previous Deck of the *HP Lovecraft Tarot*, as has already been previously pointed out, although a number of references on the subject of the Tarot and further occult correspondences exist, which the reference should make a point to access should the discussion with this Card be something that should be taken further?

5. The Witch House:
Equates to the Five of Pentacles

In opening this as a statement to describe the Fifth Card of the Minor Arcana Suit of Sites, again the *Seventy-Eight Degrees of Wisdom* sums up the position well in stating:

The Witch House

"The various meanings for this card illustrate again [the] problem of certitude discussed in the section on Readings [in this book as quoted from]. How can we know for sure which meaning will apply in a real situation? At the same time the meanings show the way in which a situation can turn in very different directions" (Pollack: 1983: 113)

Whilst the *HP Lovecraft Tarot* represents this idea in establishing a point to describe "Unconventional form" (Hutchinson, Friedman: 2002: 64), the definition of meaning as established with this Card of the Minor Arcana is put in more direct terms with a position of "Structural dissonance & artistic symmetry" (Hutchinson, Friedman: 2002: 64). This point is put more directly on terms of the Lovecraftian as the *Cthulhu Mythos Encyclopedia* includes a reference to the concept of the Arkham Witch House, in pointing out

that "[this as one particular house in Arkham] gained some attention from antiquarians due to the curious angles of the walls in one of its rooms" (Harms: 2008: 312). In taking this idea further to describe a position of "Ergonomics, Feng Shi" (Hutchinson, Friedman: 2002: 64), the *Cthulhu Mythos Encyclopedia* is still an accurate representation of the symbolism involved with Mythos literature, as it points out that: "The occultist Morgan Smith later bought the site and erected a house on it, hoping to exploit the places psychic energies" (Harms: 2008: 312).

Negative Reading

In covering this Card of the Tarot, and in terms of trying to establish as to where such an interpretation of such an esoteric system should be studied towards trying to define a higher principle of actual religious truth, again we have a situation in hand whereby a proper discussion of the Negative interpretation of this Card gives me much more to write about than with the previous Positive interpretation of this statement in question, with that being the reason why this second statement is obviously longer. At the same time, in order to put all of this into context, it should be pointed out that this, as a specific Negative point of meaning, relates to "[a] House in Arkham at 197 E. Pickman Street which was [reputedly] the home of Keziah Mason" (Harms: 2008: 312).[1]

Before starting work with a fairly lengthy discussion of the Negative meaning of this Card in relation to the greater religious system of the Minor Arcana, however, the *Seventy-Eight Degrees of Wisdom* makes a statement as to the further occult significance as represented with this Card, which might be useful to whoever might be involved with

---

1 The concept of Keziah Mason is another invention as ascribed to being the idea of Lovecraft, this being representative of the personification of a Witch. The Magus will have noticed that she has her own Card of the Tarot dedicated to her own archetypal character representation, this being discussed previously as Card XIV of the Suit of People, and otherwise relating to the Tarot Card that is the King of Cups.

a Reading (or who might want to interpret this discussion in terms of creating a working system of magick), that:

> "We can extend this idea [of interpreting this Card] to a 'magic' or occult interpretation. In Part One of [the *Seventy-Eight Degrees of Wisdom*] I discussed how the magician, by setting out on a course of personal development, pits him or herself against the established Church, which traditionally acts as intermediary between human beings and God. The choice may bring practical as well as political consequences. If the magician encounters dangerous psychic forces, then traditional religion cannot (let alone will not) help him or her overcome them. Compare the Five of Pentacles with the Hierophant, number 5 in the Major Arcana" (Pollack: 1983: 114)

If this quotation could be taken on different symbolic terms as according to those who would choose to uphold the significance of this Book of Shadows and occult theory, the *HP Lovecraft Tarot* here defines a principle of "Subtle assault on the senses" (Hutchinson, Friedman: 2002: 64), although with this consideration taken in context "We see first of all a comment on modern religion" (Pollack: 1983: 114). This taken with the interpretation that the Magus should choose to read into such a statement, this could be considered to establish the influence of religion in greater society, and their influence on the mentality of those accepted into any number of thousands of such religious groups worldwide.

With this point taken still further we see a position that "Environmental dissonance induces internal discord" (Hutchinson, Friedman: 2002: 64), and this can be seen in relation to the example of the Witch House as the symbolism here represented with the Fifth Card of this Suit of the Minor Arcana, as the *Cthulhu Mythos Encyclopedia* states that "After two centuries [this house in question] became a boarding house, but was forced to close down due to the attacks of vicious rodents" (Harms: 2008: 312). The *Seventy-Eight Degrees of Wisdom* is again appropriate in defining this point in stating that "As we examine th[is] card more

closely we can discover alternative, even opposed meanings" (Pollack: 1983: 114), although both of these statements represent the idea that all of this "may symbolize the modern secular church, giving what material assistance it can (or will), while the people's spiritual needs go unattended" (Pollack: 1983: 114). Put another way, "the situation right side up has collapsed" (Pollack: 1983: 115).

In concluding the given Negative discussion of this Card of the Minor Arcana, we approach a situation that "External factors cause mental, emotional, and / or physical imbalance; stress; fatigue" (Hutchinson, Friedman: 2002: 64). And whilst we're talking in terms of symbolism and concepts as expressed with this as a greater discussion of the Lovecraftian system of occult magick, the example of the Witch House again comes into the picture with the symbolism of such external factors bringing destruction here expressed symbolically on the basis of physical manifestation, that:

"In March 1931, a gale severely damaged the house. When it was demolished that December, the workmen found some shocking items which were later donated to Miskatonic University" (Harms: 2008: 312)

The symbolism of the Church is still an appropriate metaphor in discussing this Card of the Minor Arcana, as the *Seventy-Eight Degrees of Wisdom* establishes it's point that "this church has perhaps shut the people out. The sanctuary has failed" (Pollack: 1983: 114). This discussion then continues and in order to make the point clearer, states that "If we shift the emphasis to... people we see a psychological point of view" (Pollack: 1983: 114). The point in discussion, however, is that if the same Negative interpretation can define a position of "chaos, disorder, ruin [and] confusion" (Pollack: 1983: 115), then this Card, if drawn as part of a Reading, would suggest that the Magus should be expectant of Negative issues which are still to be established at some point to come.

6. Mountains of Madness: Equates to the Six of Pentacles

In his lifetime, *At the Mountains of Madness* was one of few works that Lovecraft as the first main representative of our religion saw properly go to print. A classic study on the subject of a doomed scientific expedition to the North Pole, this story does a good job in representing the religious *Necronomicon* in stating a belief that there is far more on this Planet and throughout the Cosmos than that which humanity is aware of.[1] The *Cthulhu Mythos Encyclopedia* has no specific entry under this definition, however, and this might be because the subject that we are talking about here is just too broad, or possibly because if we are making specific reference to the frozen North Pole then this is something specifically beyond the scope of this reference in hand. In the introduction to this statement in hand, however, the author of this book points out that:

> "My definition of the Cthulhu Mythos both includes and omits a great number of... elements which previous commentators have listed. Many would prefer to confine the Mythos solely to the 'gods' or extra-terrestrials in the stories in the stories, but since the locations... in the fiction show up so often in connection with them I have [not] added entries for them" (Harms: 2008: xx)

---

1 If the student of the occult were not already familiar with the works of Lovecraft, then I would strongly suggest reading this classic short story, as this is acknowledged as being one of his best works. A bibliographical reference for this work is: Lovecraft, H. P. (2001) At the Mountains of Madness. In: The Thing on the Doorstep and Other Weird Stories. London: Penguin Modern Classics. This short story has already been briefly mentioned previously in this book.

With that point having been established as regarding the necessary research involved with the discussion of this Card, and in having previously written on the subject of how this same point limits our specific study of the *HP Lovecraft Tarot*, under other circumstances I would have decided that there would be little else to write, and would have ended the discussion here. The *Seventy-Eight Degrees of Wisdom* goes to some length to describe the Card that equates to being the Five of Pentacles, however, as the same Card is defined as according to its own religious interpretation, which would imply that that a proper discussion of this Card as according to a definition of Lovecraftian belief is something that can properly be discussed.

This book in question, the *Seventy-Eight Degrees of Wisdom*, opens the discussion of this Card of the Minor Arcana in stating "The next two cards, related by their symbolism, stand among the most complex cards of the Minor Arcana, indeed of the whole deck" (Pollack: 1983: 109). In taking this reference further, the *HP Lovecraft Tarot* defines a Positive interpretation here as relating to "Recovered knowledge; ancient wisdom" (Hutchinson, Friedman: 2002: 64). Rachel Pollack further defines this same interpretation on more defined terms of religious philosophy, however, in stating:

"[this Card] demonstrate[s] the difference between layers of interpretation and that extra dimension I call the Gate; for whilst the Five [of this Suit] allows quite a few meanings the Six shows the Gate mechanism itself" (Pollack: 1983: 109)

If this statement would stand in the specific context of the meaning involved with this Card, then it can also be seen to have a meaning in terms of the whole of such an interpretation of the Tarot itself, and it should be pointed out that the whole of the Tarot can be interpreted on these terms. If to break such a subject down to establish how the relation to the Lovecraftian has such direct importance though, the *HP Lovecraft Tarot* Deck directly establishes how our interpretation of this subject defines and illuminates such an interpretation, with the 'extra

dimension' here in discussion being that which is directly established by *The Necronomicon* as defining a specific point of religious truth. This 'Gate' of which is being spoken of here can be defined directly as establishing a principle that such a study of *The Necronomicon* occult is an entrance into a higher state of intellect whereby the Magus is initiated into the enlightenment of this defined greater religious truth.

In working forward to establish a position of "Long term planning" (Hutchinson, Friedman: 2002: 64), we here see another example of where the *HP Lovecraft Tarot* can often be vague in defining points which have huge scope for further interpretation. Such a scope in question can be defined on singular and on very defined terms, though, if we were to again consider the *Seventy-Eight Degrees of Wisdom* in defining this point in stating that this can be defined as a situation involving:

"material benefit but little satisfaction or chance for improvement; or a relationship in which the people are unhappy but comfortable; or a political situation where people recognize they are oppressed, but do not wish to endanger what little security they have" (Pollack: 1983: 110)

A final interpretation here is given in very simple terms when the *HP Lovecraft Tarot* quite simply issues the singular statement "Utopia" (Hutchinson, Friedman: 2002: 64). The *Seventy-Eight Degrees of Wisdom* also expresses this same idea and on equally straightforward terms in defining this same Card that "The scales are balanced... Just as one wishes to dominate, the other[s] wish to be dominated" (Pollack: 1983: 109). In more direct terms, if *The Necronomicon Cycle* were written to establish where such a study of the Lovecraftian occult were to represent the views of the religious Cult of R'Lyeh on Earth, then such a definition of the idea of utopia would relate directly to the ultimate ends of a society which such religion will eventually establish, and where the role of women will be nothing more than to be obedient as sexual slaves, and where women will be sexually tortured

and continuously suffer as the sexual servants of a superior religious regime.

The *Seventy-Eight Degrees of Wisdom* at this point continues to state that "Th[is] card bears a... relationship to all those Major [Arcana] cards", although it goes on to define such a relationship as "distorted" (Pollack: 1983: 110). With this statement Rachel Pollack makes direct reference to the Sixth Card of the Suit of Sites to Card V of the Major Arcana, as symbolic of Cthulhu as the dead God of dreams, Card VI as Lavinia as representing the Goddess of Lovers, and Card XV as Tsathoggua, the Devil and the Infernal God and Infernal ruler of Hell. In making such a reference to such a greater system of manifest religious Gods, this Card represents a position:

"in which some force holds together or reconciles the opposites of life. Here *nothing* [italics are mine] becomes truly reconciled, but the situation maintains the balance and keeps it going" (Pollack: 1983: 110)

Negative Reading

It would be at this point that we'd establish the validity of a religious study of the occult system of the Tarot, as it is at this point that the *Seventy-Eight Degrees of Wisdom*, as specifically part of our chosen reference in hand, here comes into its own. The *HP Lovecraft Tarot* at this point defines a Negative Reading with this Card as warning of a position of "Forgotten history and / or science" (Hutchinson, Friedman: 2002: 64), and whilst I have already quoted extensively from her book in writing to establish how the Lovecraftian interpretation of the Tarot has such importance of meaning, Rachel Polack again puts the argument in properly expressing such an important view, and points out that:

"while doctrine may teach us to control our desires through pious thoughts, the occultist may attempt to bring forth and work with her or his most hidden urges. This split exists because most people are

not only incapable of but [are] even unwilling to deal with religious / psychological teachings in their undisguised form" (Pollack: 1983: 111)

This Negative interpretation here continues to establish a principle of "Apocalyptic thinking and actions" (Hutchinson, Friedman: 2002: 64), and this same line of thinking is represented as appropriate if we consider that "[t]he idea of giving what people are able to receive carries a religious meaning as well. Mystics and esotericists often say that the truth hidden within a specific religion may run almost opposite to what that religion appears to say on the surface" (Pollack: 1983: 111). And if it should be established that the Sixth Card of the Suit of Sites is both powerful and unique on the specific basis of this definition, this statement "indicates the manner in which religion, and also esoteric teachings, give what we are capable of receiving" (Pollack: 1983: 111).

This final interpretation is established as the *HP Lovecraft Tarot* simply issues the word "Dystopia" (Hutchinson, Friedman: 2002: 64). Whilst a statement like this stands as being a good working example of how our religious system expresses the occult principles established, all such principles of worship must eventually be ascribed to the conscious functioning of the human mind, and this is put into a framework of working context, again, as our chosen reference on the greater meaning of the Minor Arcana states that:

"in order to *consciously* give people what they need and can use (rather than what they think they want) one must have achieved a great degree of self-knowledge as well as awareness of human psychology in general" (Pollack: 1983: 110)

With that point of meaning discussed, it would be interesting to note that it is at this point in establishing the greater meaning of the Minor Arcana that the *Seventy-Eight Degrees of Wisdom* makes an important point on the use of such a study of such a religious system. In putting this entire study into perspective as one religious concept, Rachel Pollack here makes the point that:

"From the Six of Pentacles we learn that the value of studying the Tarot or other disciplines lies not simply in the specific knowledge gained but also in the frame of mind created by the *act* of doing it" (Pollack: 1983: 112)

Here we revert directly back to our previous study of the Major Arcana when this quotation is followed directly with the statement that "We can develop these changes consciously and deliberately through the mechanism of the Gate cards" (Pollack: 1983: 112). This statement put directly into further context; if the occult mentality of The Great Old Ones can be utilized and accessed directly through the interpretation of the Major Arcana and the acceptance of the *HP Lovecraft Tarot* as our definition of occult manifestation and one religious truth, then we would encourage the Magus to do the same with this study of the Minor Arcana as well.

At this point it will probably be clear that when writing to define the further meanings of these Cards of the Minor Arcana, such definitions radically move away from the initial idea that certain definitions as established by the Lovecraftian, than they were first intended to represent. In concluding the interpretation of this Card, and in order to establish as to why an entry for *At The Mountains of Madness* was not included as an entry with our given research, the Introduction to the *Cthulhu Mythos Encyclopedia* states:

"[in writing this reference] I have usually left out real life... places [as the North Pole is one of them]. I hope that my reasons for the inclusion or exclusion of each element are clear" (Harms: 2008: xx)

7. Church of Federal Hill: Equates to the Seven of Pentacles

With the Card that is represented as the Seventh of the Suit of Sites we run into a more serious issue with the specific research involved with writing this book, as continuing from the same point as previously discussed on repeated occasions. If the *HP Lovecraft Tarot* here defines this part of the Minor Arcana as the Church of Federal Hill, there is literally nothing here in the way of research which can directly equate to anything as represented by any further part of the Mythos in any way. I would suggest that this might be important if we were to recognize this in terms of doing a Reading if using this Deck.

A statement as regards this void of information is mentioned in the Introduction to the *Cthulhu Mythos Encyclopedia*, and continues directly from the previous entry as given above, as Dan Harms points out:

> "[My research in writing this book] includes [reference to] over a thousand sources covering many different genres… I have tried to choose material which was readily available and which might add something important to this book, and I feel that I have been relatively successful in that task… These sources may be hard to find, but they are definitely worth the search" (Harms: 2008: xx)

With that point established, I have made a very serious study of Cthulhu Mythos literature and the Lovecraftian occult on my own terms, and I have never seen anything to relate to anything that could directly relate to something as described as The Church of Federal Hill.

What this point in question tells us is that the most important issue when interpreting any system of the Tarot, is that the general meaning of any Card cannot be defined with any more validity than that which is first felt as being instinctive intuition on the part of the person who is interpreting the Card in question. Whilst *The Necronomicon Cycle* and literally hundreds of other books on the subject of the Tarot might go into elaborate detail in discussing the further truths as established by any Deck of any individual system, these books only represent the views of the person writing that book, and as such are less important than the intuition of the person who is reading that Tarot in question.

As one example of this point of discussion, if this Card of the Minor Arcana might establish a possibility of an "Appointed time" (Hutchinson, Friedman: 2002: 64), are you expecting something specific to happen at any point soon in the future? One interpretation of this idea could be that there will be a set time when this happens. If a Card might represent a position of "Herald; announcement, Invitation" (Hutchinson, Friedman: 2002: 64), then this might in itself be that announcement. If the same statement could represent a "Call, calling; Vocation (in the full religious implication of the term)" (Hutchinson, Friedman: 2002: 64), then is it realistic to say that this Reading in itself should be interpreted as a calling to the worship of any number of The Great Old Ones?[1]

That point established, it is still the stated point of *The Necronomicon Cycle* to put forward a study of how the *HP Lovecraft Tarot* should be interpreted as the Deck that ultimately represents all other systems (as is the belief upheld by The Cult of R'Lyeh on Earth), and if we are to follow through with the previous idea of this book, the *Seventy-Eight Degrees of Wisdom* describes how this Card works as part of this greater system of the Tarot in stating that:

> "the Seven [of this Suit] shows the pentacles as a living development from the person's labour. Meaningful work gives more than material

---

1 The inclusion of the Appendix to this book is with the intention that the Magus should be able to continue to interpret the meanings of the Cards of the HP Lovecraft Tarot on these terms.

benefit; the person too grows… the Seven… shows the pervasive dissatisfaction, the trapped feeling… [this Card] reversed can mean any specific dissatisfaction or anxiety, in particular one arising from some project that is not going well" (Pollack: 1983: 108)

Negative Reading

The reader has probably, by now, picked up on the point that the ideas in the *Seventy-Eight Degrees of Wisdom* are often diversionary from the statements in the Lovecraft system in defining equivalent Cards of equivalent Decks, but the idea of meanings being important as from the perspective of the person reading that Card is represented again as part of this system of divination. The whole of the idea so far described in representing this Card is again summed up quite well from the position of the *HP Lovecraft Tarot*, as the point is important that:

"In a reading, the application of these guidelines & interpretations [as given in the Introductory Book to the second Edition of the *HP Lovecraft Tarot*, and given again with the Appendix to this book] are very subjective, and should not be rigidly adhered to at the expense of intuition. The feelings the cards evoke are far more important than the literal meanings given for the suits in general, or individual cards in particular" (Hutchinson, Friedman: 2002: 50)

All of these statements stand to stablish the further point that is made in writing *The Necronomicon Cycle* that, despite how any Card that this, or any other system of the Tarot is in any way defined, it is always more important to interpret literally any Card, of any system, as according to our own personal intuition first.

8. Innsmouth: Equates to the Eight of Pentacles

With using the example of the town of Innsmouth in order to establish a point as to how the Tarot can be interpreted on the basis of Lovecraftian religious orientation, here we see another example of how a physical place can represent such an interpretation, as was the same example in hand with the previous Card of the Minor Arcana as represented with the Witch House, as with other Cards as defined with the Tarot Suit of Sites. This stated example is established on very direct terms as the *Cthulhu Mythos Encyclopedia* continues with its discussion in order to define the point that:

"[Innsmouth is a] Massachusetts town at the mouth of the Manuxet River. At one time the town was a thriving seaport, but today it is almost deserted. Innsmouth was founded in 1643, quickly becoming a major centre for commerce upon the Atlantic due to its large harbour. Ships from this town sailed all over the world, bringing back goods from many ports of call" (Harms: 2008: 137)

Whilst being an appropriate statement to be defined as according

to this discussion of the Lovecraftian Tarot, further research into the direct esoteric importance of this Card establishes a further number of problems. Firstly, the entry for this example in the *Cthulhu Mythos Encyclopedia* is essentially quite negative in describing this archetypal representation, which in turn makes it more appropriate to describe the meaning of this Card as according to its Negative interpretation of meaning. Secondly, the *Seventy-Eight Degrees of Wisdom* gives little information in terms of interpreting this Card of the Minor Arcana as directly relating to our specific study in hand. As a result this reference is not used as part of the following description of meaning.

For this reason this entry will be on relative terms shorter than a lot which has been written previously in this book, as will be the next few entries. The point to be made is that if the Magus has been following this book so far, it should be becoming quite clear as to where the study of the *HP Lovecraft Tarot* stands in relation to other systems of the religious representation that is the greater system of the Tarot, and should therefore find it fairly straightforward to interpret these Cards as according to the Lovecraftian religious system, should the querant regard this as being in any way important (in defining terms as according to the Lovecraftian the assumption is made that it is). Further to that, it should not have to be in any way reiterated that the first Appendix to this book is given on the basis of it being the role of the practitioner to interpret the said meaning of this Card (and all other Cards of this system of the Minor Arcana) on these defined terms.

Negative Reading

Every Deck of the Tarot which has ever existed has been put together on the basis of establishing that system as according to the religious and esoteric beliefs of those responsible for putting that Deck in question together. The *HP Lovecraft Tarot* is no different in ascribing the traditional meanings of the Cards as according to the literary study of the Cthulhu Mythos, which in turn takes its own influence from the religious *Necronomicon* as a book which the existence of which

has been disputed, but has been proven on further religious terms to exist. If we were, therefore, going to define this Eighth Card of the Minor Arcana on these defined terms, then a further discussion of the symbolism suggested in using the archetypal representation of the town of Innsmouth would again be appropriate in order to continue to establish this study. And in quoting again from the *Cthulhu Mythos Encyclopedia*:

> "After the war, Innsmouth's revenue came mainly from the mills built on the banks of the Manuxet and Captain Marsh's successful trading ventures… Around 1840, Marsh lost a source of gold upon which he had depended, and the town's economy spiralled downward. It was around this time that Marsh began the Esoteric Order of Dagon, a cult based on a combination of Scripture and the beliefs of the Polynesian islanders Obed Marsh had visited. Some whispered that Marsh's Order worshipped darker gods, and the Order's nocturnal trips to Devil's Reef are legendary" (Harms: 2008: 140)

Whilst the *Necronomicon Cycle* has been written on very defined terms to help with a further discussion of the *HP Lovecraft Tarot*, and with this on the basis of working to establish a further position of a hidden religious truth, so far we have clearly broken down how each Card of this Deck of the Tarot is defined by this as the Lovecraftian system, and how the discussion of Lovecraftian Mythos literature stands to define points of interpretation on his basis. As from this point I'll continue to make the assumption that those reading this book will have picked up the general idea so far, and I will intend to follow this by making a general statement as to how the definitions of meaning as established by this Deck are further defined by quoting again from the *Cthulhu Mythos Encyclopedia* as one of three core points of reference. Whilst doing so the assumption is that the Magus will be defining such statements of interpretation as according to their own intuition whilst reading and interpreting the rest of this book on individual and occult terms of personal study.

A Negative interpretation of this Card, then, is defined on the principle of "Ostracism, banishment; excommunication" (Hutchinson, Friedman: 2002: 65). This established as on our terms on which to define any further statement of symbolic meaning, the example here of Innsmouth is relative in context, that "[the town] remained under the Marsh families rule for many years and over time became shunned by the people of the surrounding countryside... Federal Agents... disbanded the Esoteric Order of Dagon, and removed the bulk of Innsmouth's population to military prisons" (Harms: 2008: 140). The *HP Lovecraft Tarot* continues this with an idea of "Dereliction, decay; manipulation" (Hutchinson, Friedman: 2002: 65), and if we were to follow our line of research on this same basis, the same reference points out that "1846 was the year of the Innsmouth plague. The exact disease responsible has never been identified [although] degenerative traits began to turn up in the resident's children, most likely the after effects of [this] plague" (Harms: 2008: 140).

A final definition of meaning relating to the idea of "Ghost town; tenement, ghetto" (Hutchinson, Friedman: 2002: 65) is established with this as our study of the *HP Lovecraft Tarot*, and if to continue to resort from the same research that we've done so already, the *Cthulhu Mythos Encyclopedia* represents this point with the statement:

> "What precisely happened during th[is] plague remains a mystery... When visitors from neighbouring villages arrived, they found half of the town's people dead and Obed Marsh and his Order in firm control of the town... Accounts of Innsmouth after this disaster have become muddled. It might have become a ghost town" (Harms: 2008: 140)

As it has already been pointed out that it is, of course, down to the individual to interpret all of this on the basis of what it should mean to themselves if any of this should in any way come into a Reading, the *Seventy-Eight Degrees of Wisdom* again comes into the picture as a valid resource in defining the symbolism as established by the Cards

of the Minor Arcana, and the concluding paragraph to the entry on this Card in this book might possibly go some way to defining a further meaning if considered in context with what's already been said:

"When reversed th[is] card suggests primarily impatience and the situations resulting from it: frustration, unfulfilled ambition, envy, or jealousy. These things may result from the attitude of looking only to success, and not to the work that brings it" (Pollack: 1983: 108)

9. KADATH:
EQUATES TO THE NINE OF PENTACLES

This Chapter, in being written to represent the Ninth Card of the Lovecraftian Suit of Sites, will be one of the shorter Chapters of this book, and the reason for this would be an apparent loss of focus in terms of all of our main points of reference in writing *The Necronomicon Cycle*. Whilst it would be the case that the entry to cover this statement in the *Cthulhu Mythos Encyclopedia* is quite short and gives us little to positively work with, it would also appear to be the case that the equivalent entry from the *Seventy-Eight Degrees of Wisdom* gives us little of relevance in describing this Card, in direct terms, to any specific Lovecraftian definition of meaning, either. However, Dan Harm's reference on the history of Cthulhu Mythos literature does still include an entry to describe the issue of Kadath in context with this Minor Arcana Card of the Tarot, and states:

> "[Kadath is a] Mountain on the peak of which the onyx Castle of the Great Old Ones was built. Kadath usually lies in the far north of the Dreamlands, beyond the Plateau of Leng. According to other tales, it may be found on a gigantic mountain chain in the Antarctic, somewhere near Mongolia, or in ruins far underground in modern Turkey. Some have even gone so far as to say Kadath was a vast city of the Elder Gods that covered our planet at one time" (Harms: 2008: 148)

Whilst having repeatedly made such a statement as regarding a problem with proper research whilst working to define the symbolism as represented with some of these Cards of the Minor Arcana already, the *HP Lovecraft Tarot* still continues its discussion to define a position

of "Mystery, hidden origins" (Hutchinson, Friedman: 2002: 65). Further to this we really have little to go on in terms of defining this point further, although the *Cthulhu Mythos Encyclopedia* does again make an important statement in saying that "Kadath is the home of the gods of Earth, and there they remain, protected by the Other Gods" (Harms: 2008: 148). Whilst it has already been pointed out that the intended aim of *The Necronomicon Cycle* is to support the Magus in terms of working towards making their own definition of meaning in further context with *The Necronomicon* in representing the validity of one religious truth, then this given lack of research should reinforce the importance of doing so in representing such validity as with the *HP Lovecraft Tarot* in representing such a statement of direct religious importance.

Negative Reading

In working to describe the Negative interpretation of this Card of the Minor Arcana, we run into exactly the same problem as with the above point as regarding our research in hand. At the same time the Lovecraftian definition of the Tarot always represents a point that such issues of Negative interpretation are always equally as important when coming up as part of a Reading, and are often actually more important than that with the Positive meaning as ascribed to any Card in question. On this basis that system of the Tarot here in question defines a point of "Unknown danger; obscure threat" (Hutchinson, Friedman: 2002: 65). With this as a concept to be further defined on terms of the Lovecraftian, and as part of the theory of the religious framework already discussed, the *Cthulhu Mythos Encyclopedia* again puts this into context in saying:

"Kadath is a terrible place for mortals to visit, as the gods do not take kindly to anyone invading their mountain retreat, and the dreamer Randolph Carter is the only one known to have done so" (Harms: 2008: 148)

Whilst this has been a short entry to describe a principle that has equal importance as with every other Card of this Deck in consideration, one of the points in writing *The Necronomicon Cycle* is to support those with such an interest in magick to make a study of the Tarot towards representing *The Necronomicon* as a statement of singular religious truth, and to further establish a working system of magick on those defined terms. With that given intention stated, it would be a further interesting point of note that the *Cthulhu Mythos Encyclopedia* concludes its entry on this subject that "Kenneth Grant equated Kadath with Kether, the Kaballistic sephiroth whose attainment leads to oneness with God" (Harms: 2008: 148). This statement in itself should be taken as representative of where the study of the Lovecraftian is already an established point as part of an international underground of occult and religious thought.[1]

---

1 The Cult of R'Lyeh would suggest that if the Magus were to follow an interest in the ideas expressed in this book already, then the work of the noted occultist Grant would be another point of importance to follow up.

10. EXHAM PRIORY: EQUATES TO THE TEN OF PENTACLES

The previous discussion of the Minor Arcana as according to this stated definition will have already established the criteria on which we stand whilst discussing the *HP Lovecraft Tarot*, so whilst making reference to the Introductory Book to the previous Edition of this Deck will make such further study clearer, documentation on the next few Cards is given as a general statement and in order to make an effort to further describe this Deck it its entirety. Further, I feel that *The Necronomicon Cycle* would not be complete if no proper description of the following Cards had not at least be mentioned on one term or another.

The *Cthulhu Mythos Encyclopedia* begins its description of this as one of the Sites as represented with this part of the Minor Arcana, that:

"[Exham is an] English town near Anchester and east of the Severn River Valley. Despite its large number of used bookshops and other antiquarian attractions, Exham receives very few visitors. The town's most famous landmark was Exham Priory" (Harms: 2008: 95)

That said, the stated intention of writing this book is in order to further establish the validity of the study of the Lovecraftian in religious context, and as in turn being a part of a massively bigger system of religious thought, and in quoting again from the *Seventy-Eight Degrees of Wisdom*, we see another valid example as to the representation of this Card in terms of the greater representation of the Tarot:

"One of the most symbolic and deeply-layered Minor Arcana cards,

the Ten [of Pentacles, here being defined under the Suit of Sites] shows us the very image of the Gate opening to hidden experience in ordinary things... Though the card expresses mundaneness, magic signs cover it. The ten pentacles form the Qabballistic Tree of Life, something which appears nowhere else in the deck... scales stand for Justice, and further, for subtle forces which keep the everyday world from breaking into chaos. By 'subtle forces' I do not mean only so-called 'occult' laws such as polarity, or the law of correspondences (as above, so below). The term applies also to nature's generally more accepted workings, such as gravity, or electro-magnetism" (Pollack: 1983: 103)

In having already stated a reason as to why this entry should be kept deliberately shorter than most of the other entries to describe my position on the Minor Arcana (discussed with the previous Card), it is still the case that the *HP Lovecraft Tarot* here describes a Positive definition of this Card in terms of "Legacy, birth-right, inheritance" (Hutchinson, Friedman: 2002: 65). In order to put this definition into context with the given example of Exham Priory as an equivalent archetypal representation, and in context with the further system of the occult Tarot, the *Cthulhu Mythos Encyclopedia* again stands as a valid position of research in describing this as "a place of great architectural interest inhabited at one time by the Baron Exham, but deserted during the reign of James I after the families sons massacred all his kin" (Harms: 2008: 95). It is this defined idea of the family which here stands as representing this Card's interpretation, and in quoting again from the *Seventy-Eight Degrees of Wisdom* we see a position that:

"Like the Ten of Cups [this Card] deals with domestic life... In contrast to the Ten of Cups [however] (the two cards will often appear together in readings) the family here does not seem to communicate with each other" (Pollack: 1983: 102)

Negative Reading

With the same point as regarding keeping this entry short is still here an issue in hand, the *HP Lovecraft Tarot* defines a Negative interpretation here in terms of "Family curse, 'ghosts'" (Hutchinson, Friedman: 2002: 65). In order to put this statement further into the picture with the example of Exham Priory as the issue here in hand, we can quote in directly the same context from the *Cthulhu Mythos Encyclopedia* as one of our main points of reference, that:

"Three months [after the massacre already mentioned] a horde of rats emerged from the place, eating two people and numerous livestock before dispersing. The Priory was [later] bought by a descendent of the family in 1918 and restored, but a hideous murder and the heir's insanity led to the senseless dynamiting of the structure" (Harms: 2008: 95)

This statement might be quite appropriate in working to establish such terms of interpretation here defined as being important, but it might also be worth saying that the *Seventy-Eight Degrees of Wisdom* also gives a valid interpretation of this Card on its own individual terms, that:

"Inside the arch [as depicted on this Card as being the representation with other Decks of the Tarot] we see a bright ordinary day [whilst] outside darker tones prevail... with its signs of astrology and ritual magic. The family [as depicted with this Card in similar systems] stand under the arch posed as if in a play... the everyday world, the comfortable lives we take for granted, and even the troubles and miseries that often occupy our minds, are only a play" (Pollack: 1983: 103)

As a statement to conclude this short entry on what is also an

important Card, those who've been following what's already been written will immediately be aware that both definitions here of a Positive and Negative interpretation as given by the *HP Lovecraft Tarot* are more involved than with some of the previous statements. The given intention would be with that the Magus should use this information, as given with this entry, in order to take such ideas further on their own individual terms (whilst pointing out that the position is the same with the other Cards as discussed), with *The Necronomicon Cycle* having been written with the intention of guiding the Magus towards interpreting this study of the Tarot, according to their own unique and individual purposes of ritual use.

11. Sentinel Hill:
Equates to the Page of Pentacles

As we are coming towards the end of our discussion of this final Suit of the Minor Arcana, here we see another problematic issue when it comes to the research necessary with discussing this Card in question, with this being the same point that's come up on repeated occasions already. If wanting to make reference to the *Cthulhu Mythos Encyclopedia*, as a book which under most circumstances does a competent job in discussing the Cthulhu Mythos occult, under this entry for Sentinel Hill there is no specific description. Whilst the reason for this might be that there is nothing clearly involved in Mythos literature to make specific reference to something as defined under this specific statement, this book does include a statement for something otherwise described as Mercy Hill, although this in itself is quite short and still gives us little in terms of research to go with. Further to this, if we have already made a point as to the validity of the *Seventy-Eight Degrees of Wisdom* as another point of valid research in specifically making a study of the Minor Arcana, then this entry, again, offers very little in terms of anything which could be considered important in making a

Sentinel Hill

proper discussion of this Card. If we were to be able to take anything further of importance from either of these points of reference, then this Card as represented as the Page of Pentacles, does make one important point in that the *Cthulhu Mythos Encyclopedia* states that:

> "Folk legend holds that unpleasant dreams afflict some children who dwell on Mercy Hill [as an equated point of research], and this serves to keep many potential home buyers away from this area" (Harms: 2008: 179)

If this singular point should make a statement as regarding how dreams should be considered in specific religious terms should this Card be drawn in a Reading, then this stated lack of research should establish a point of importance that such an interpretation should be understood as according to the intuition of the person doing the Reading or who the Reading is for.

Negative Reading

Positive and Negative interpretations for this Card are discussed further with the first Appendix to this book, and it would be suggested that the Magus make reference to this research if wanting more insight into this Card; although it should still be pointed out that this is the same as with any other Card of this system of the Tarot in consideration.

12. EOD Temple:
Equates to the Knight of Pentacles

Here I would refer the Magus back to the previous statement on the EOD Vestments, which was the point covered earlier in this book as the Seventh Card of the Suit of Artifacts in the previous discussion of the Lovecraftian Minor Arcana. With writing this Card I run into another problem as regards the specific research involved with covering this subject in question, although this specific issue is different than with the previous issue as regarding a lack of research in terms of defining a meaning with specific Cards in question.

This specific issue as regards the research involved with writing this Card is that, whilst the *HP Lovecraft Tarot* includes two Cards to represent the group known as the Esoteric Order of Dagon, the *Cthulhu Mythos Encyclopedia* includes only one statement to cover such a group, with this entry in itself being quite short; this despite the point that this is in itself quite an involved point in itself. In having already used this given reference for the previous Card as relating to the EOD Vestments as was discussed previously as part of the Suit of Artifacts, I therefore see it as being appropriate for this reason to introduce another document into the discussion, and in writing this statement to document the occult significance of this Card I will here choose to introduce another document into the discussion, in order to properly cover such a statement, with this being a document published by a group who operate under the same name, this document titled *An Introduction to the Esoteric Order of Dagon*.[1]

---

[1] This document is the official statement to represent the views of the Esoteric Order of Dagon, and is easily available online if you were to access the EOD website, as a point that was discussed earlier as a footnote for the Card of the EOD Vestments, which is the Seventh Card of the Lovecraftian Suit of Artifacts, which was discussed previously in this book. A link to the EOD website is mentioned in a page note above.

This document in discussion is a short but also quite comprehensive introduction to the views of the contemporary group calling themselves the Esoteric Order of Dagon, who – it should be pointed out – are a different entity entirely from the group with the same name who were a part of the literary work of Lovecraft.[2] My point in choosing to focus here on this stated document, and whilst writing up this Card, would be on the basis that whilst the *Cthulhu Mythos Encyclopedia* is one comprehensive statement which does a commendable job in covering a large amount of the ideas as regarded as sacred to the religious Cult of R'Lyeh on Earth, *An Introduction to the Esoteric Order of Dagon* is a different statement which focuses only on that individual group as representing Lovecraftian religious orientation. I have for this reason decided that this stands to validate such research in writing up this Card of the Tarot which is represented as the EOD Temple.

As has previously been established as being a part of this book on the subject of religion and Necronomicon magick, The Cult of R'Lyeh do not dispute that a lot of our religious views do at least verge on the bizarre. However, if putting forward such a book in order to further represent *The Necronomicon* as a religious book which is in actual terms proven to exist (despite there being a point of fact that most religions quite seriously dispute this point); and to further establish a point that if this indirectly proves that, as all religions are the psychick projections as sent from The Great Old Ones, then this stands to prove the singular religious validity of the *HP Lovecraft Tarot* as representing all other religious Decks (as already discussed), and that we must have that moral obligation to represent this as proving that there is one religious truth. The point would be established on that basis that

---

2 As opposed to being the actual same religious organization as were represented by the literary work of Lovecraft, the contemporary Esoteric Order of Dagon state in this document as introducing their ideas, that "The name of our Order is derived from the story The Shadow Over Innsmouth by the New England horror and fantasy writer HP Lovecraft" (EOD: 2008). Should the Magus for any reason want to chase this reference up further, a bibliographical reference for this short story would be: Lovecraft, H.P. (1999) The Shadow Over Innsmouth. In: The Call of Cthulhu and Other Weird Stories. London: Penguin Modern Classics.

if the Fish God – Dagon – has been worshipped by human religious societies for thousands of years, as He is still worshipped by main religious movements today, then Lovecraft's religious fiction as written to represent the Fish God, Dagon, as was credited as being a part of the religious *Necronomicon*, and therefore represented on the same terms as figments such as Shub-Niggurath and Cthulhu, is another statement to validate such a statement that the Cult of R'Lyeh uphold as such a position of religious truth. The conscientious work of The Cult of R'Lyeh on Earth must therefore be justified on that basis.

If this might be a digression from the point here in hand, however, the point to discuss the religious Temples of Dagon is followed through on these defined terms. That said, the term 'temple' itself has two different direct meanings if discussing this point in relation with such secular religious worship.

According to a brief study of a number of relevant websites which discuss this point, we see a position defined that "A temple is a religious building that's meant for worshipping or praying" (Vocabulary.com: n.d.). This definition is put into a more specific context in that "While temples tend to be associated with non-Christian religions like Islam, Judaism, and Buddhism, some sects of Orthodox Christianity worship in temples as well" (Vocabulary.com: n.d.). Another website posted by a Christian religious group, which makes specific reference to the Mythos God Dagon, as has been mentioned on occasions in *The Old Testament of The Bible* puts this same statement of religion into further specific context, and establishes the worship of Dagon on these specific terms, that:

> "The Babylonians had a myth that a being emerged from the Eritrean Sea who was part man and part fish and thus adapted the deity into their culture and in their earliest days in history. Th[ere] have also been discoveries of the fish-god in the sculptures found in Nineveh, Assyria" (Dagon the Fish-God: 2019)

It is this mentioned archaeological research that has worked towards

a proven worship of Dagon in early religious cultures, and the finding of a large number of ancient temples (as such) which obviously establish such an early recognition of Fish Gods is therefore proof of a multiplicity of worship to establish the validity of one system of religious Gods, and further, to establish a point that there is one religious truth. The word temple, however, can also refer to an established religious organization who in turn uphold their own religious dogma and rules, and this will be the definition of the term that I will be working with in writing to establish the occult significance of the Card of the Tarot which is here defined as being the EOD Temple.

This position of obvious differentiation between an ancient worship of Fish Gods that is still very much alive, and of the Esoteric Order of Dagon as a contemporary religious order who are dedicated to the religious worship of The Great Old Ones, is established on this basis as the *HP Lovecraft Tarot* defines a position of "Symbiosis of old & new traditions; religious reform" (Hutchinson, Friedman: 2002: 66). Further, *An Introduction to the Esoteric Order of Dagon* is a beautiful and valid religious document in itself, and it is a shame that the scope of this book does not allow me the room necessary to discuss this document in further theoretical depth. This document does, however, allow us a credible reference with which to discuss the *HP Lovecraft Tarot*, with the EOD encompassing such a Positive definition of meaning, in that:

> "The true hidden reference [in discussing this as the EOD religious system] is to the Sirius system, of three stars, including our own sun. The ancient Sumerian / Egyptian Mysteries of Oannes (or the Philistine Dagon, Lord of the Deep Ones) and the stellar gnosis of the All Seeing Eye of Sirius, concealed in the Hermetic Freemasonic Traditions, forms the basis of the 23 current that informs [our religious] society" (EOD: 2008)

As this comes close to concluding *The Necronomicon Cycle* as a statement to validate and express this as the views of our movement as a contemporary religious order, it is at this point that we can establish

a principle that our religious beliefs can only be representative of a greater occult entirety, and this would be where the Cult of R'Lyeh again make the point to establish our belief that there is one religious truth.

This idea is taken directly further as the *HP Lovecraft Tarot* continues such a definition of meaning with this Card with a point to define "Radical spirituality; 'New Aeon', 'Age of Aquarius' philosophy" (Hutchinson, Friedman: 2002: 66). Further to this point, the Esoteric Order of Dagon here represent this interpretation of contemporary and underground religious orientation, and this is expressed on secular terms, that:

"The symbolism of an amphibian, that is, a creature evolved to travel between two worlds, is the motif and formula of the Order. The means of travelling between the conscious world and the silent, unconscious right brain, is by means of lucid dreaming" (EOD: 2008)

Here we see another example of the idea as discussed with previous Cards of the Minor Arcana, that ultimately all perception, and hence all religious worship, can eventually only come down to be defined as according to the psychology of the individual thereby involved. And if such a statement as regarding the perception of the individual can be established on these or similar terms, the idea is then put forward by the Esoteric Order of Dagon, that "The EOD utilizes the... Cthulhu Mythos of... HP Lovecraft as a magickal method of exploring the Cosmic via the collective unconscious" (EOD: 2008).[3]

Our representative system of the Tarot here concludes the Positive interpretation of this Card of the Minor Arcana to define a principle of "Group Identity & Unity" (Hutchinson, Friedman: 2002: 66), and again the example of the EOD as an underground religious movement is quite appropriate. In quoting again from their Initiatory religious

---

3 Here we have another example of where such occult belief ties in with Psychiatry and the ideas put forward by the noted Psychiatrist Jung.

document, the EOD declare their position that:

> "Membership is open to those who can show that they can make a manifest contribution to the occult arts and sciences of the Lovecraftian magickal mythos" (EOD: 2008)

This position is not so straightforward, however, as *An Introduction to the Esoteric Order of Dagon* continues that, "A certain level of serious knowledge of Lovecraft's writings" is necessary for initiation into the contemporary EOD, as well as a knowledge of "Thelema, Austin Osman Spare, Kenneth Grant, Achad, etc" (EOD: 2008). Such a statement of group identity is the argument in discussion here, but the Cult of R'Lyeh would ask whether a member of any group should have to have been initiated in the first place? This statement establishes where this statement stands in pointing out that "interaction and networking is expected [from initiates into the Esoteric Order of Dagon] and this organization is not for pseudo-occultists" (EOD: 2008), whatever a 'pseudo-occultist' might actually be?

Negative Reading

As we're here getting towards the end of our discussion of the Minor Arcana things begin to get slightly more complicated, and I'd suggest that the written definition that follows should not take any precedent over the individual's personal interpretation of what is gained through a personal interpretation of this Card. Whilst I've suggested already that this should always be the first consideration in hand, this is specifically important as we define the Card that is represented as the EOD Temple.

In taking that point into consideration, a Negative Reading with this Card is described by the *HP Lovecraft Tarot* as relating to a principle of "Heresy, radical departure from civilized beliefs [and] apocalyptic mania" (Hutchinson, Friedman: 2002: 66). To put this idea into the same perspective with which the rest of this book has been written, the *Seventy-Eight Degrees of Wisdom* defines the principle of this Card as

an equivalent statement in pointing out that "denying the Knight [of Pentacles] natural penchant for adventure tends to distort... his attitude to life... he is deeply rooted to the outer world" (Pollack: 1983: 100). Whilst *The Necronomicon Cycle* is written with the specific intention of interpreting the greater movement of the Tarot in order to establish the validity of the Lovecraftian (and in doing so on the greater basis of religion), as has been repeatedly pointed out, *An Introduction to the Esoteric Order of Dagon* makes a statement to represent such a connection to the 'outer world', and puts the point into context in saying that:

"[Lovecraft, as the primary representative of our religion was] a withdrawn and lonely writer who retained a rational, sceptical view of the universe, despite the glimpses of places and entities beyond the world of mundane reality, which his dream experiences allowed him" (EOD: 2008)

The *Seventy-Eight Degrees of Wisdom* takes this same idea further in stating that:

"Though such extreme readings of course occur rarely in actual readings, they remain implied in the Knight's basic paradox, deeply grounded in, yet unaware of, the magic beneath him, he identifies with his functions" (Pollack: 1983: 100)

Such a definition of the Negative interpretation of this Card continues as the *HP Lovecraft Tarot* defines a principle of "Cult, brain washing; domination of will through spiritual manipulation" (Hutchinson, Friedman: 2002: 66). Whilst this would probably be one of the more straightforward points to interpret if reading a book on the subject of Lovecraftian religious orientation, the *Seventy-Eight Degrees of Wisdom*, as our other main reference in hand makes another valid statement to define a position that, "The Knight of Pentacles reversed can sometimes indicate a crisis. If a person has dedicated her or his life

to a job... and that meaning is taken away... then discouragement and depression can overcome him or her" (Pollack: 1983: 100). In putting this same statement on directly more relevant terms whilst continuing to discuss the religious importance of the Lovecraftian, *An Introduction to the Esoteric Order of Dagon* points out that:

"Lovecraft [himself] suffered from an acute inferiority complex, which prevented him from personally crossing the Abyss in his lifetime" (EOD: 2008)

If that statement would describe how this Card can be seen in relation to a greater religious system and orientation, the *HP Lovecraft Tarot* concludes its short definition of meaning with the statement "Inquisition, Auto de Fe" (Hutchinson, Friedman: 2002: 66). Whilst any interpretation of any Card of the Tarot can always be taken as far as the individual would choose to take it, this system in itself on occasions makes statements which have no immediate obvious meaning. It is on this basis that I choose to close this short statement on the Card of the Minor Arcana that is here represented as the EOD Temple, by pointing out again, that when interpreting any Card of the Tarot, the most important issue should be that which seems most obvious to the querant in interpreting the religious significance of any Deck, which would represent the specific meaning of that religious system in question.

13. HOUSE IN THE MIST: EQUATES TO THE QUEEN OF PENTACLES

As this book has already discussed to some extent, the main difference with the current (Third) edition of the *HP Lovecraft Tarot*, is with the graphical depictions of the illustrations of the Cards themselves. Some of the Cards to this Deck have, however, been changed completely, and this as being towards the end of the Suit of Sites, is one of these Cards in discussion. Previously having been depicted under the statement Federal Hill, the thirteenth Card of this Suit is now depicted, instead, as being defined as being the House in the Mist. I can personally see no obvious reason as to why this change should have been made with the current Edition, and in terms of further research I would argue that this is the only Card of this Deck which does not immediately relate to the Lovecraftian in one way or another at least, with the *Cthulhu Mythos Encyclopedia*, obviously, not having a specific entry to cover this statement for that reason. This Card is still a part of the study of the Lovecraftian interpretation of the occult Tarot here in question, however, and this following continues this discussion in relation to *The Necronomicon Cycle* being a book written to cover this statement as a literary and Necronomicon religious study.

Leading on directly from Sentinel Hill, which was the eleventh Card of the Suit of Sites with this specific study, there would obviously be a number of equal points of similarity in discussing both of these Cards of the Minor Arcana. In discussing the research involved with this specific Card, however, the *Cthulhu Mythos Encyclopedia* gives nothing as being defined under this statement, this therefore meaning that the rest of this Card must be further discussed without it. With that given statement as regarding this omission of any direct discussion with this Card, I would like to make short speculation that this Card

might in some way relate to the issue of the death penalty in certain nations, with the point in hand being that this same Card was previously depicted under the discussion of Federal Hill as a previous entry, with these points possibly being in some way linked.

In terms of the actual meaning of this Card, I would regard the thirteen of Sites as being the most serious and dangerous Card of this Deck of the Tarot in discussion, and as with all systems of the Tarot we interpret this Card as representing serious personal issues. Whilst it is true that the Tarot cannot ever harm anyone in any way, if this Card would come up as being reversed in a Reading it should be taken as the most potentially serious Card that can be drawn.

Negative Reading

Such a Negative interpretation of this Card is defined as relating to a position of "Abandoned paths of wisdom" (Hutchinson, Friedman: 2002: 66), and the *Seventy-Eight Degrees of Wisdom* makes a similar statement to describe this same Card of the Minor Arcana, that "In readings, the Queen reversed can mean not trusting oneself in some situation" (Pollack: 1983: 99). It is the knowledge of the self which establishes how we are wise, and if we lose our own sense of trust towards ourselves, then any path we have towards approaching future goals will be without focus and will therefore inevitably fail.

This definition of meaning continues to discuss a position of "Ethnic clichés & stereotypes; superstition" (Hutchinson, Friedman: 2002: 66). With the archetype of the death row prisoner here being our example here in discussion, as stated, the ultimate failure of the individual is the point in discussion as this Card established the point that "More generally... [this] refers to psychic weakness" (Pollack: 1983: 99). In continuing to define this statement to establish such a principle of superstition, the *Seventy-Eight Degrees of Wisdom* continues this statement as according to its own criteria, in stating:

> "[under circumstances as represented by this Card, the Magus] becomes afraid, even phobic, mistrustful of others and especially of

herself, doubting her abilities and her value as a person" (Pollack: 1983: 99)

If the Magus were to choose to accept the meaning of this Card as according to the references in play as according to this book, then this Card when read on such terms would dictate personal situations in question, as the same statement follows directly in defining a point that, if this Card is accepted on this basis:

"it means a loss of daily rhythm in life, a dissatisfaction with the whole environment, and an inability to appreciate what the environment has to offer" (Pollack: 1983: 99)

In continuing this Negative statement of meaning, the *HP Lovecraft Tarot* defines a point of "Unheeded warnings; prideful break with tradition" (Hutchinson, Friedman: 2002: 66). Again a direct equation of meaning is established when the *Seventy-Eight Degrees of Wisdom* again discusses this in relation to the Minor Arcana on further terms in pointing out that, if to accept this point in context, then "cutting off the Queen from her vital connection to the earth results… in nervousness and confusion" (Pollack: 1983: 99).

None of these statements to describe the thirteenth Card of the Suit of Sites, however, go any way towards representing the point, as already discussed, that this Card if seen in its Negative aspect, could be considered to be the most serious Card of the Minor Arcana. If people often seem to have the idea that pulling the fifteenth Card of the Major Arcana – The Devil[1] – reversed as part of a Reading, seems to relate to something quite serious, then I would suggest that pulling The House in the Mist as part of a Reading would be equally as serious as the Minor Arcana equivalent of the same interpretation. However, the point with this would be to accept the statement that forewarned is forearmed.

---

1 This in the context of the HP Lovecraft Tarot is defined under the representation of Tsathoggua, the Toad Faced God, and this is covered in proper depth as part of the study of the Major Arcana previously in this book.

People read the Tarot in order to try to establish points of truth which were not already known, and whilst what might be predicted might not be in some way good in itself (according to the specific Reading and what's been stated), the Tarot in itself cannot harm you. Whilst there are, of course, large numbers of religious groups who might dispute this point of discussion, all systems of the Tarot are representative of smaller parts of one greater system of religious truth, as this book has been written to establish, and this is the validity of the Cult of R'Lyeh religious orientation in itself. We should acknowledge and be aware that the Tarot always speaks on her own terms, and therefore she will tell us what she thinks stands as important. In reading any religious Deck of the Tarot, and if interpreting the Cards as according to any religious orientation, we must acknowledge that what the Tarot is telling us is of course down to us to interpret as according to the religious orientation as upheld by the individual, and no one else, and with this on their own religious terms.

14. ARKHAM:
EQUATES TO THE KING OF PENTACLES

With this as the final Card of this interpretation of the system of the Lovecraftian Minor Arcana, we could see it as being the case that we have eventually completed an entire journey. Starting with the example of HP Lovecraft as the first Card of the Suit of People, the Tarot here concludes with a statement to represent academia, further study and education, with this representing the lessons learned from a study of the occult in relation to *The Necronomicon* as our black book of religious knowledge. In discussing this as our spiritual journey, therefore, the *Seventy-Eight Degrees of Wisdom* can be quoted from again, in that "If we see the Fool as the beginning of the Major Arcana, [then] the King of Pentacles [as this Card equates with other systems] as the final card of the Minor Arcana, then the two stand as opposite ends of the Tarot" (Pollack: 1983: 97). The *HP Lovecraft Tarot* takes this idea of meaning to some extent further, then, in asking:

"Of course, the real question is just what are these cards? Their relationship to the increasingly popular Tarot is obvious, but so is

their apparent divergence from what is generally accepted as the 'standard' structure of the Tarot. On the one hand, they do have the traditional division into one 'Major' Suit of Primal Powers, with four 'lesser' suits portraying other important forces, but which are subordinate to those of the 'Major Arcana'" (Hutchinson, Friedman: 2002: 2)

That point therefore in consideration, the *HP Lovecraft Tarot* represents this discussed position of learning and academia in defining a situation of "University, centre of learning and / or communication" (Hutchinson, Friedman: 2002: 66). Again, in using the example of the University of Arkham as a position of symbolism to represent this last Card of the Minor Arcana, this Deck is again appropriate in this statement, as this American centre of learning is discussed on the basis that:

"It was one of the town's most influential captains, Jeremiah Orne, who imparted the books and funds that led to the founding of [the] Miskatonic Liberal College... in 1861 [this establishment] which already enjoyed the highest reputation, became Miskatonic University" (Harms: 2008: 9)

What this entire study of the Tarot has ultimately established to represent, therefore, is that nothing on these religious terms as discussed with this as a study of the occult can ever be considered so straightforward, and if to represent the validity of *The Necronomicon* as such a statement of ultimate occult truth, then such a position of learning can also be considered on these defined religious terms, and if quoting again from the Lovecraftian system of the Tarot as this main subject of study that is the subject of *The Necronomicon Cycle*:

"If [the Cards of this system] are indeed a Message from the buried Depths of Time & Space, a Warning (or dire premise) from out of

the weird angles of inhuman physics, how do we break their code?" (Hutchinson, Friedman: 2002: 3)

The *HP Lovecraft Tarot* concludes this study of further occult existence and religious truth in defining a position of "Board, panel; certification; jurisdiction; examination" (Hutchinson, Friedman: 2002: 66), and this is another valid example of symbolism in that "Arkham was founded in the latter 17th Century by freethinkers who found the area's religious communities too strict" (Harms: 2008: 9). This idea in itself is straightforward in representing this Card, but in concluding this as our discussion of the greater entity of the Tarot, raises another question. Again in quoting from the Introductory Book from the previous Edition of our religious Deck, as being our point of theory in question:

"...the question remains, what are these cards? Are they merely the product of another artist's perverse imagination? Are they a glimpse of the prototypical Tarot taught to humanity before the Flood by what the Books of Genesis and Enoch call the Nephilim (but which are still remembered by other names)? Or are they a message [from a higher dimension]?" (Hutchinson, Friedman: 2002: 9)

This entire study of the Tarot here establishes its own point of conclusion, and after the extensive terms of interpretation and meaning as having been established with *The Necronomicon Cycle*, such definitions of meaning here therefore conclude with a symbolic position of "Port, business centre, marketplace, financial centre [and] industry" (Hutchinson, Friedman: 2002: 66). And in having discussed all of that in order to establish the greater religious significance as implied by the Lovecraft system of the Tarot, this then finally concludes with the idea that "Different accounts of Arkham's present condition exist; some say that the town is rundown and serves as a suburb... while others tell of its booming population and [the] Miskatonic [Universities] state-of-the-art facilities" (Harms: 2008: 9)

Negative Reading

As this discussion of the Tarot has at this point eventually concluded, a final point of reference from the *HP Lovecraft Tarot* defines a Negative interpretation of this Card in terms of "'Tower of Babel', too many opinions, inability to make a decision" (Hutchinson, Friedman: 2002: 66). In terms of the specific symbolism that this Card represents, then, the *Cthulhu Mythos Encyclopedia* states that "Around the year 1692, the witchcraft-fever that swept Salem also touched Arkham. The Arkham authorities sent at least one witch, Keziah Mason, to Salem for trial" (Harms: 2008: 9). The point in quoting from this statement is to establish the point that, if to make a study as to establish the importance of the *HP Lovecraft Tarot* in representing *The Necronomicon* as our sacred and religious book of occult magick, things are never in any way nearly so straightforward. It would be the specific issue of the symbolism involving the issue of witchcraft, here, which should be held in consideration, and such symbolic reference to issues involving religious cultism is represented as the *HP Lovecraft Tarot* asks:

> "...our times being what they are, with many different cults springing up all over the world to invoke the Old Ones, who can truly say what degraded intelligences have been brought into our continuum trying to find expression by whatever means available?" (Hutchinson, Friedman: 2002: 2)

As such a discussion of defined Lovecraftian ideology is here comes towards its eventual conclusion, our system of the Tarot here in discussion works towards its end in defining a principle of "Unlicensed practice, quackery; dubious advice" (Hutchinson, Friedman: 2002: 66). It is with this that we see the entire discussion of the Minor Arcana coming full circle and culminating towards a logical end, and the *Seventy-Eight Degrees of Wisdom* again makes a point to establish

where this point stands in relation to the entire system that this book has now completely discussed:

"The King [of Pentacles] symbolizes ordinary activity, accomplishments, social position, success, while the Fool stands for the inner spiritual freedom that allows a person to enjoy these things and build upon them without getting trapped in a narrow materialist view... If we envision them in a circle, then the Fool and the King of Pentacles become joined together" (Pollack: 1983: 97)

In having followed such a discussion of some quite bizarre religious statements of belief, the sceptic will, of course, question the validity of all of these esoteric expressions of occult belief, but to quote again from our significant Deck of the Tarot in question, the position is established in that "if [any Deck of the Tarot] is merely the work of a single unwell spirit, [then] there should be no real danger inherent in them" (Hutchinson, Friedman: 2002: 2).

With everything as having therefore already been discussed, and with the religious system of the Tarot having been defined as a medium for The Cult of R'Lyeh on Earth as a recent and contemporary religious movement, we have already moved through a huge statement of religion and religious thought, and here this study ends with one final definition of meaning. This final statement here concludes with the *HP Lovecraft Tarot* defining a position of "Bad investments; inflation, deprecation; bad real estate" (Hutchinson, Friedman: 2002: 66). The archetypal representation of the town of Arkham is again appropriate in defining this part of the Minor Arcana, as the *Cthulhu Mythos Encyclopedia* states that "The flood of 1888 and the typhoid outbreak of 1905 led to a serious decline in the town's fortunes" (Harms: 2008: 9). It is with this that such a Card as representing the end of the Suit of Sites is appropriate in bringing all of this to a close, and we can draw reference from the *Seventy-Eight Degrees of Wisdom* for a final time, as a discussion of this final representation of the Minor Arcana is

established in terms that:

> "Reversing [the King of Pentacles] suggests failure or simply mediocrity. The lack of fulfilment brings dissatisfaction, feelings of weakness, and doubt. Taken another way we can see the upside down King as symbolizing the idea of success corrupted… The King reversed stands for the state of being cut off from that rejuvenating flow. Here too the break results in dissatisfaction, weakness, even psychick danger" (Pollack: 1983: 97)

With this statement now concluding what I hope will be established ultimately as different perspective of religious outlook, and being one which has taken me years to write, it is – of course – entirely up to the Magus as to how this book of religious ideology is accepted, and also down to the individual to conduct their own further research in order to take such ideas further, as *The Necronomicon Cycle* has repeatedly suggested that the Magus should do.[1] I would like to conclude this study as a representation of underground religious movements who uphold *The Necronomicon* as their religious book, therefore, in quoting for one last time from the Introductory Book to the previous Deck of the *HP Lovecraft Tarot*, that:

> "[those responsible for putting together the *HP Lovecraft Tarot*] believe that it can be 'safely' assumed that those who serve the Old Ones will not profit much by the publication of this deck of odd cards. But, if through distribution, the 'Code' can be broken down

---

1 On this note I would suggest the Magus read The Necronomicon Cycle in relation to the further ideas of The Hermetic Order of the Golden Dawn of Thelema, if the point was not already clear. A good book on this subject is one titled Tarot Magic, and we would suggest that this book could be read in connection with the further work of the Golden Dawn and the HP Lovecraft Tarot in order to work towards establishing a form of Ceremonial Magick towards the worship of the Great Old Ones. A bibliographical reference for this book is: Tyson, D. (2019) Tarot Magic. Minnesota: Llewellyn Publications. Further to this it is down to the Magus as to how such religious theory should be taken further.

by one or more who would help us in our struggle [then this] must be done" (Hutchinson, Friedman: 2002: 3)

As from here it is down to the worshipper of these bizarre and weird concepts of religious manifestation to accept our defined position of worship as according to how they choose to accept this given statement of occult belief. A journey of religion is further to this, directly up to you.

Conclusion:
Join The Cult of R'Lyeh on Earth

Having read through all of that as our statement to describe a comprehensive religious study of the *HP Lovecraft Tarot*, and to discuss as to why this is so important from the religious perspective of the Cult of R'Lyeh on Earth, the Magus might want

to take this study forward on their own terms, and might possibly be interested as to how someone would go about joining our religious organization? If this statement might in any way represent you, then you're in luck. The Cult of R'Lyeh regard it as being our religious statement of initiation to read and then to ascribe to our religious views, as you have done if you've read to the end of this book. This does not mean that if you've read this book then you're initiated as some sort of secular or religious cult member, but if you've read *The Necronomicon Cycle* and you feel that you relate to and agree with the views as expressed in this

book, then please do feel free to regard yourself as a member of our religious orientation as discussed.

In taking the idea of this book further, and aside from putting our religious views down on paper, the Cult of R'Lyeh have put a lot of our time and resources into working to establish our ideas as a working international organization; constantly sending out packages and electronic mail to religious groups across the world in order to promote our secular views and beliefs. It is on this basis that we openly declare our support for the religious views upheld by groups who would describe themselves as 'Satanic', although the views of our group do go much further. This is not entirely on the basis of our supporting such a religious orientation, although we would take this opportunity to declare that we do, but more on the basis of how Satanic religion is organized on international terms as a working network of smaller international groups, all of them working independently to create a bigger and greater cohesive statement.

As a concluding statement here, the Cult of R'Lyeh openly state that we are always very happy to hear from our adherents (or otherwise people who are interested in our movement), and are also always happy to answer questions that anyone might have – we are not people who will ever assume that other people will not have questions. We are also happy, to the greatest extent, to include other people's printed material with such mentioned outgoing mail, with an assumption in hand that such material will tie in with the religious ideologies as here described. If you'd be interested in our movement representing your religious group on those terms, then please do get in touch.

As with most people on Earth – with that including most underground religious perspectives – the Cult of R'Lyeh run an open e-mail address, which people are freely invited to use on the basis of what's been said here with this Statement of Conclusion. If anyone would like to get in touch and take us up as regarding any of these points, then they should feel free to contact our religious group at:

necronomicon.cult@gmail.com

For those who might have any further interest in the further religious principles of the Cult of R'Lyeh and our views towards the greater significance of issues such as the Abrahamic religions, we promote a another developed statement of religious outlook which can still be found online at:

e-publishingcult.com

Further to that, the individual is free to interpret and uphold the views as established in this book in any way that they would feel appropriate, and in any way that they should choose that they wish to do. The Cult of R'Lyeh would regard further research into these religious views as ultimately being down to you.

ONE RELIGIOUS TRUTH

Further Reading

As regarding the few number of books which have direct importance to the Cult of R'Lyeh on Earth, it should be stated that we worship more through the acceptance and use of organic drugs than through the study of religious literature on the greatest level available. The Cult of R'Lyeh argue, however, that there is no religious book that does not tie in with our religious interpretation in any way at all. We have read the main religious books and regard them as smaller parts of one religion as defined according to the study of religion that exists on wider terms. Further to that we accept *The Necronomicon* as our main religious statement, arguing this religious book defines a principle of one truth which is not represented elsewhere in religion. As was touched on briefly in Part I of this book, it is our belief that our religious book was initially destroyed by the Church book burnings of the 12th and 14th Centuries, and that successive movements of religious media have brainwashed society, effectively in order to deny the existence of that religious book in question.

However, further to this as one statement to define the relevance of the main religious books, a small number of specific titles are regarded by the Cult of R'Lyeh as specifically relating to our religious beliefs, although it should be pointed out that the following is a small number of books to have been published which in some way or other directly tie in with our views. These are discussed as follows, as one statement given to further define our intended statement of worship.

Everything by HP Lovecraft

The significance of the work of HP Lovecraft has already been properly put into context with everything already discussed in this book, and on this basis we would suggest that everything written by

Lovecraft should be respected and taken as being significant in one way or another. As the author of this book I would suggest that those who would involve themselves in this system of magick should continue to pursue the ideas put into discussion as relevant to religious ideology here on their own terms. To put everything here into context, however, Lovecraft's work as one of the first inspired writers of horror in early 20th Century literature has left a distinct impression on contemporary religious society, even if the Cult of R'Lyeh would have liked his work to have a greater impression than is already acknowledged. That said, the work of such an inspired writer of religious fiction is still largely recognised in occult circles, albeit still relatively misunderstood. If the idea was not entirely clear already, the significance of the work of a writer whose work we regard as being directly inspired, and also directly important, works largely on the basis of his representing *The Necronomicon* as a tool for such conceptual fictitious literature, albeit this statement rarely properly acknowledged on the basis of its greater scope as religious. Whilst the written work of Lovecraft often centres around the strange and bizarre concepts with which he is largely recognised as being responsible for having invented, the ideas of entities such as Yog Sothoth and Shub-Niggurath, and so on, are ideas that can be directly cited as being a reference to those same God forces as described in *The Necronomicon* as our religious book, and as represented in Lovecraft's fiction. It is for this reason that the Cult of R'Lyeh argue that the religious work of Lovecraft has to be considered as having much greater and direct relevance other than just being a vehicle for the admittedly bizarre concepts on which his writing usually works around, and this is the concept as related by our work.

Condensed Chaos - Phil Hine

As one of the great minds behind the concept of Chaos Magick Theory, Phil Hine would have to be one of my favourite writers. Following on from that above statement, if the ideas expressed in such books the Cult of R'Lyeh would recognise his work as being inspired.

The general ideas in this book, I feel, re-define the understanding of the contemporary occult in unique terms, and create a contemporary religious framework whereby the practice of occult magick can be established Whilst I personally dispute the views of Phil Hine in favour of the acceptance of the worship of the Great Old Ones depicted by Lovecraft as being a singular religious truth, and as represented by *The Necronomicon* as one religious statement, I would still consider the ideas involved with the concept described as Chaos Magick Theory as being directly relevant to our concept in hand, and as directly inspired.

With this being one of the important books that initially started the international movement of Chaos Magick Theory, *Condensed Chaos* argues the point that literally any psychological principal can be expressed as a psychological purpose of worship if considered on these same terms. The classic example of this would be that if someone has a problem with their Bank machine, then worship of fictional robotic entities would be appropriate in approaching such an issue if the occult would be the chosen resort towards doing so; and the general concept works around this basis idea. This being one specific example of the general ideas as expressed by this book, the international movement of Chaos Magick Theory have taken valid and significant steps towards upholding the worship of The Great Old Ones as part of their theoretical framework, and this is where CMT ties in with the views of the Cult of R'Lyeh. Whilst our religious organization stand to establish that this is where the religious significance of *The Necronomicon* stands on more defined terms, the main underground religious movements to uphold such principals of worship in 20th Century society, have been represented in the most part by this as one movement of religion.

We would make a valid suggestion that those who have been following this book so far, would do well to make at least some straightforward study of the movement of Chaos Magick Theory in order to uphold such occult principles. *Condensed Chaos* was a book that inspired a huge and inspired underground following at the time that it was published, and this inspired underground is supported by

The Cult of R'Lyeh on the basis of the valid statement that it stands to establish on its own unique terms of religious theory.

Prime Chaos - Phil Hine

The sequel to the above book, the same idea taken further and developed. Another excellent book on the subject of Chaos Magick Theory this also represents the idea of the importance of the occult in relation to the human mind. In terms of the religious statement here in question, this following title is equally as good as the above in making a similar statement as to how religion ultimately comes down to what can be perceived and therefore invoked on the basis of the power of personal psychological visualisation. If the Magus would not yet have any knowledge of the conceptual ideas behind the Chaos Magick scene, then this book cannot be recommended enough. In writing this statement as to the small number of books that specifically represent the ideas as upheld by The Cult of R'Lyeh, and which tie in with these stated declarations of belief, an important point should be put forward that everything which could be regarded as religious with *The Necronomicon Cycle*, are equally statements which quite directly relate to the conceptualism of Chaos Magick Theory, those being the views which are established with these two ideas being important on the basis of their being connected theoretical views.

The Pseudonomicon - Phil Hine

This stands as representing the third established book by one of the writers who coined the idea of Chaos Magick Theory, and easily as good as the two titles already, if not significantly better. Being based specifically on the idea of the representation of the Cthulhu Mythos and the Gods as represented thereof, this book specifically concentrates on the idea of this religious point of conceptualisation. During history of the past two or three decades, if the Magus were to want to read a good book to relate to this subject matter on specific terms, then this

would likely be one of the only books on this subject available. In my opinion this should be considered as another religious classic by the same author, and also essential reading for anyone with an interest in the religious and occult significance of *The Necronomicon* as a serious book of occult religion and magick.

Liber Null & Psychonaut - Peter J Carroll

As has already been pointed out, The Cult of R'Lyeh are quite influenced by the work and philosophy of the Chaos Magick scene as a unique and contemporary movement in religion. In this respect we should have to make reference to this as another of a small number of books published on the subject. The text to *The Liber Null & Psychonaut* (as two short books published in one Volume) is quite surreal, but makes two important statements in this context. In having read this book and considered it another contemporary religious classic, and one of few books which generally tie in with the ideas as established by The Cult of R'Lyeh as upholding our own defined religious structure, my view is that the *Liber Null & Psychonaut* are both books which properly rewrite most of the ideas as put forward in the books which have represented The Golden Dawn of Thelema in the past 20th Century (although this is very much a point of personal opinion). It is on that basis that I would suggest that a proper working knowledge of the ideas of the Golden Dawn might be important if reading this book in the context which it is meant. But at the same time – if this is the stated intention in question – then the *Liber Null & Psychonaut* are two short volumes, published together, which make a good job of expressing this theoretical position. Another clear classic of contemporary religious theory and the concept of Chaos Magick religious theory.

Liber Kaos - Peter J Carroll

A sequel to the above, and equally as good. In this volume Peter J Carroll writes at some length on the subject of the contemporary theory

of magick and the occult. Whilst it would be a current point that this work is beginning to become slightly outdated, if that would be the argument in hand, the *Liber Kaos* is upheld by the Cult of R'Lyeh as being a valid interpretation of new religious values, and an important example of how such issues have been interpreted by the Chaos Magick scene as a current expression of religious orientation.

The Necronomicon Files
Dan Harms and John Wisdom Gonce III

This would be one of few books published which really does tie in with the factual and historical ideas of the Cult of R'Lyeh and our declared views on religion. A properly researched and interesting book, the *Necronomicon Files* takes the fascinating history of *The Necronomicon*, and concludes as being the only literary study that I know of that specifically stands to prove the existence of our religious book as being a point of historical fact. The first couple of times I read this book I really enjoyed it, but in reading it on another occasion as part of my Theology coursework, it did come across that, aside from this book having been meticulously researched, the whole premise of this title seems to be on the basis of a pre-assumed idea that *The Necronomicon* does not, in actual terms exist as a historical religious book, with this idea being contrary to our established religious views. *The Necronomicon Files* does, however, properly document the history of our religious book in contemporary society since it was established as part of the original ideas as put forward by Lovecraft, and puts our religious book into a specific contemporary and religious context in doing so.

The Necronomicon - Chaosium version

Following on from the above, it would be the case that a fair number of books with this title have been published in history, although in my opinion this is edition would have to be one of the best. Despite

being obviously a work of straight fiction, The Chaosium version of *The Necronomicon* stands as being a beautiful statement of written literature, and as such this is one of a few books which properly ties in with our views as the Cult of R'Lyeh as religious. If to make a study of *The Necronomicon* and the history of this as our religious book, a number of titles have sporadically been published with this title. Whilst some of these titles are clearly better than others, this edition of *The Necronomicon* is easily one of the better takes on a book with this title, with a potential to link in with ideas on the framework of Chaos Magick Theory as a framework by which to establish new perspectives of ceremonial worship. An excellent book and very much worth reading.

The Necronomicon - Donald Tyson

Most of the work of Donald Tyson I don't like and don't regard as in any way properly representing the views of the Cult of R'Lyeh. However, I would like to here make mention of his take on *The Necronomicon* as being one of a number of valid interpretations of the Lovecraftian on the greater level of religion. Recommended as having relevance to the system of the Cthulhu Mythos occult, and something that could easily tie in with the ideas as represented by the concept of Chaos Magick Theory.

Whilst most of the work of Donald Tyson can be read in direct relation to the occult framework as put forward in *The Necronomicon Cycle*, it would be our view that a lot of it doesn't directly fit in with the occult and religious framework as specifically put forward in this book as intended to represent a working system of occult magick. His take on *The Necronomicon* is, however, an exception to this rule. Whilst this version of our religious book does not directly issue any straightforward framework for any enactment of religious and ceremonial worship in order to represent the existence of The Great Old Ones (or anything else, for that matter), I would make a suggestion here that this book could be used in direct reference to some of the other books on the

subject of Chaos Magick Theory in order to take this as an occult study further.

Flying Saucers - Carl Gustav Jung

The intention of making reference to this book under these ideas for Further Reading, is on the basis of how ideas of Psychiatry come directly into the picture whilst discussing *The Necronomicon Cycle*, and further in order to represent an idea as to how ideas regarding Chaos Magick Theory can be taken further in order to make a study as to the working of the human mind in direct relation to use of occult and ceremonial magick. Whilst this study of the Lovecraftian occult and the Tarot has made reference to the work of Jung repeatedly already, I would have to recommend *Flying Saucers* as Jung's most inspired religious work, and his only book that can be seen as properly tying in with the views of the Cult of R'Lyeh on Earth as has here been discussed. This statement on the mind and contemporary media is something that the Cult of R'Lyeh accept as being a valid statement on society and religion, to the extent of accepting the existence of flying saucers (and so on) as real and manifest fact. Still a very interesting statement on the subject of religion and the human mind, as you would expect from someone such as Jung. Whilst I could also like to make reference to the other works as put forward by this person in question, this is important on the basis of being one of his shorter books, and therefore easier to work with as representing difficult concepts as relating to the working of human psychology. This book also makes some interesting statements if to interpret the same ideas as being political, although all political orientation is outside of the scope represented by The Cult of R'Lyeh on Earth in our philosophical outlook. Whilst discussing this point, *Flying Saucers* also makes some interesting observations as regarding the theory of the existence of UFOs, as a point that is also upheld as being religious from the perspective of The Cult of R'Lyeh as one religious movement.

The Satanic Bible – Anton LaVey

I would like to state that I have huge personal respect for the religious views of Anton LaVey as one of the significant 20th Century philosophers and the founder member of the Official Church of Satan. Therefore I've included this title as suggested further reading on the basis of the religious viewpoint of that religious movement, and the influence that Anton LaVey has had on society and as an individual. *The Satanic Bible* is a book that has had huge social and media influence since its publication in the late 1960s, and I include this book out of respect for the influence that Anton LaVey has had as a philosopher and the contemporary Church of Satan as a World religion that should be seen as equal to other main religions in terms of numbers. Further to that, *The Satanic Bible* also stands as a good example as to how the publication of a book, in contemporary religious society, can lead to the effective establishment of a new religion if the idea could be taken on such defined terms.

The Cult of R'Lyeh are not 'members' of the Church of Satan in any way, and the reason for this is on the grounds that the specific religious orientation – as held by both groups are in consideration – are entirely different points of religious orientation altogether. In having stated that point, however, it would be difficult for me, as the High Priest of The Cult of R'Lyeh, to properly express the genuine degree of respect I have for the views of Anton LaVey in having given this statement of defined Theological reason. The Cult of R'Lyeh would like to take this as an opportunity to declare our support for The Church of Satan as an equal and valid statement of World religion for this reason in itself, and as a movement of logical truth.

The Satanic Witch – Anton LaVey

Whilst *The Satanic Bible* is Anton LaVey's most famous and widely accepted work, and also quite clearly a religious classic, it is my personal

opinion that this is not his best work. Whilst this book in question is the book that defined and established the orthodox movement of Satanism as a valid and contemporary religious view, Anton LaVey still has a number of other works in print, all of them definitely worth reading. Of all of these *The Satanic Witch* is by far my favourite. Whilst in keeping with LaVey's usual approach as being unintentionally funny to some large extent, this book makes a comprehensive account of the role of women in the Church of Satan, and makes some controversial but interesting points in doing so. Anyone with any interest in the views and ideology as upheld by the contemporary Church of Satan would do well in checking this volume out. There's little else to say before suggesting that this must be read for itself before trying to point out any specific points of humour, but it should be suggested that this book makes a good point to establish Anton LaVey's competent ability as a religious thinker, as well as being someone who could be genuinely funny.

Thee Psychick Bible
Genesis Breyer P Orridge (ed.)

I've included this book out of genuine respect for the occult philosophy of Genesis P Orridge and the Temple Ov Psychick Youth as a movement who were run in the late 1980s by this personality in question. This book is seriously recommended to anyone who should want to make a study of the occult and the study of psychology, as Thee Temple ov Psychick Youth were famous for successfully integrating, and to anyone who would have an appreciation of surrealism and the practical study of Ceremonial magick and the occult. I could go on at some defined length to make discussion as to what this book says whilst in connection with the philosophy of the Cult of R'Lyeh, although I really feel that if the Magus were to have any serious interest in the views as here discussed, then they should read through this book for themselves before the significance of such an inspired title will be immediately clear.

Mosig at Last: a Psychologist Looks at HP Lovecraft
Dr Y.D.W. Mosig

With those being the important books which tie in with our religious study, it would be obvious that there would be loads of books which go some way further towards discussing the literary and occult views as important to the Cult of R'Lyeh, although very few of these should be considered to be directly important. To be honest, however, most of these do not go any way towards really helping any issue, and with the Lovecraftian there's always the point of having to sift through what is not useful. This book would be one title which I feel would be important to mention, however, as I really think that this is one of the better books to have been published on this subject. In having researched the religious nature of the Cthulhu Mythos - as well as other main branches of occult belief for some period of time - actually since early adolescence, I had not heard of this book at all until by chance coming across a reference as part of my research as regarding my Undergraduate Degree in Theology and Religion. In simple terms we could argue to establish that this would make this title obscure. However, in having tracked a copy down online and actually finding myself a good deal on this work, I was quite surprised to find this to be a highly competent book on describing issues involving psychology, with this on specific terms in relating to the ideas of Lovecraft and connecting ideas regarding psychological orientation in question. For that reason I really would recommend this book to anyone who has an interest in taking any of the ideas as discussed in *The Necronomicon Cycle* further, and would go as far as to say that this book should be considered as an unacknowledged classic in discussing our religious ideas in question.

New Directions in Supernatural Horror Literature
Sean Moreland (ed.)

It might be appropriate to conclude this study of the Necronomicon occult to point out that, whatever Lovecraft's role in putting forward a religious study which has eventually led to this as an established statement as regarding religion and the occult, at the end of the day Lovecraft was first and foremost a writer of conceptual fiction. I include this title in order to here conclude this book on the study of his literary work, as this title is an academic journal published to represent such issues in terms of a current movement in literary horror in order to represent this point. The idea would therefore have to be established that, whatever Lovecraft's influence in representing *The Necronomicon* as the religious book that has here been properly discussed, his work also has influence as the first concept behind such a literary movement as which is expressed as contemporary horror fiction. It should be established here that, whatever the obvious controversy behind Lovecraft's work and its contemporary readership, his work and his ideas will continue to be further established as the study of his work continues to develop, and with such interpretations still to be properly realized according to a significance still to be properly seen. *New Directions in Supernatural Horror Literature* discusses Lovecraft's influence in contemporary horror fiction, thus standing to focus on his influence on the basis of his ideas as a writer of supernatural literary fiction, and represents his influence on those terms. With this his influence should be regarded as being established as history.

Appendix I: A Further Statement on the Minor Arcana

The single main drawback in writing a book on the subject of the *HP Lovecraft Tarot* has been that this particular Deck has been out of print for some period of time. As a result of this getting hold of a copy of the original Deck has become difficult, not to mention expensive. In putting together the work on the Minor Arcana as is the subject of Part III of this book, I have been careful to try to put down the complete definition of meaning as regarding these Cards in question, although on occasions this has been difficult, or in other situations not appropriate in describing specific statements in hand. It is on this basis that in interpreting the definitions of meaning as established by the *HP Lovecraft Tarot*, that I have tried to do so as according to the definitions which were published in the Introductory Book to the previous Edition of this Deck in question where I have been able. It should be clearly stated though, that the planned current Edition is expected to be published without such a reference being published as part of such an ongoing project in hand. This written Appendix to *The Necronomicon Cycle* is intended, therefore, as a clear reference whereby the Magus will be able to quickly reference the meanings of the Cards of the Minor Arcana to the Lovecraft Deck, if and when this should be necessary. This Appendix, then, is a direct transcription of the meanings of these Cards, as according to our religious system of this Tarot in hand, and as according to how they are listed in our religious Deck.

That stated, this Appendix can also be used to translate the Cards of the Minor Arcana in terms of other Decks to be substituted in relation to the *HP Lovecraft Tarot*, if this should be appropriate or necessary, although I would issue a general statement of warning that the Magus

should consider carefully before doing so. As an example, if someone should draw the Card of the Ace of Cups whilst doing a reading with the *Rider Waite Tarot*, then this could be interpreted directly as according to the reference in this Appendix, and as relating to the *HP Lovecraft Tarot* as being the same as with the first Card of the Suit of People (in this example being the Card as represented by HP Lovecraft). A further and more direct interpretation of the same Card can be established in making reference to the same entry as described in Part III of this book, which is written to establish this specific statement of meaning.

Further to that, it should be stated as being an obvious point that the interpretation of the Major Arcana should be established on the same basis; for example, if the Magus were to draw the Strength Card as a part of any given reading, then that would relate to Card VIII of the *HP Lovecraft Tarot*, that being represented as the Shoggoth and discussed properly in Part II. The rest of this defined religious statement should be considered on these same terms.

This entire study of the Lovecraftian Tarot leaves the point open that any system of the Tarot is always open to be further elaborated in terms of creating a greater working system of ceremonial magick. If the Magus were to consider such a definition of religious truth as discussed in *The Necronomicon Cycle* towards these purposes, then The Cult of R'Lyeh would be very much in support of their doing so. We would be very interested to hear any ideas that such an application of theory would lead to, and our e-mail contact has been given with the Conclusion to this religious statement so that people will be openly able to do so, if this might be considered necessary or appropriate in any way.

In conclusion, one other reason for this Appendix is, again, on the basis of an intention that the third edition of this Deck of Tarot, discussed, would be published without the inclusion of an Introductory Book. Aside from this statement, the definition of all of the Cards of the Minor Arcana should be considered to be the same as with the publication of the last Edition of the *HP Lovecraft Tarot* (as do the Cards of the Major Arcana), despite an obvious point that a few of the

names on these Cards have since been amended. With this omission the meanings of these Cards should be considered as having the same meaning as with the previous published edition, and the following definitions of meaning are then taken from the Introductory Book to the second edition of the *HP Lovecraft Tarot* verbati

SUIT OF MAN/PEOPLE

I. H.P. LOVECRAFT

POSITIVE	NEGATIVE
Precociousness, Genius, Literacy	Cold Intellectualism, Disassociation, Alienation
Inspired creativity, dreams; Fertile Fantasy	Fear of Imagination; Rationalism as shelter from the Unknown
Vision beyond normal limitation of Time & Space	Inability to focus within normal boundaries of reason & perception
Mind over Body; Mental excursion transcending physical limitations	Sickly disposition, physical disability or handicap

II. RANDOLPH CARTER

POSITIVE	NEGATIVE
Nonrational thought; Right Brain imagery & nonverbal, symbolic consciousness & conceptualization	Denial of Dream in the name of "Maturity", Rationalism, Justification
Unity of spirit & matter; living in both spiritual & physical worlds	Pragmatism used as an excuse to ignore the spiritual
Return to childlike consciousness; mature innocence; Natural & uncontrived state of being	Immaturity, irresponsibility; self-delusion, addiction, lying to oneself as well as others

III. LEGRASSE

POSITIVE	NEGATIVE
Logical mind, Reason, Analytic function of Left Brain	Dependence on Rational Structure, Laws, Rules and predefined roles
Consistency, Dependability	"By the Book" personality
Unafraid to ask questions; Intellectual humility	Confrontational Interrogation; subtlety of mind, trickery
"Good Cop," deserved authority; Love of Justice; Impartiality, Truth	"Bad Cop," abuse of power; Corrupt & Cruel Authority

IV. CHARLES DEXTER WARD

POSITIVE	NEGATIVE
Successful assimilation of tradition & new ideas	Conflict between Old & New; "generation gap"
Transcending Nature and Nurture into self-defined patterns of behaviour	Struggle to break free from inherited and/or genetic patters into new action & endeavour
Clarity of personal identity & path	Burden of a bad reputation, either earned or acquired by association
Traveller adapting to any environment	Restless wanderer, uncomfortable wherever he or she may go

V. ERICH ZANN

POSITIVE	NEGATIVE
Success in the Arts; performance, exhibition	Suppressed talent, lack of recognition of abilities, obscurity
Artistic inspiration, creative genius	Loss of Muse, writer's block; frustration, obstacles
Struggling artist cliché	Avant Garde
Guardianship, ward, protector; custodian of unwanted secrets	Naïve dabbling in "Black Arts" & the consequences of

VI. HERBERT WEST, REANIMATOR

POSITIVE	NEGATIVE
Scientific Brilliance, Inventor; Leap of Medicinal Progress	Loss of ethical perspective in Scientific Progress; Obsession, with the end justifying any means
"Quantum leap" in scientific theory and/or perception	Unnatural Intervention into evolutionary process
Evolution of ethics & ideals. Moving beyond obsolete moral restraints	Complete disregard for cultural & ethical restraints. Proving that certain taboos have a rational basis.

VII. OBED MARSH

POSITIVE	NEGATIVE
Free Enterprise, commerce, cultural exchange	"Rail Baron"-type of industrial or commercial tyranny
Travel to foreign lands, exchange of ideas, assimilation of new ideas	Cultural clash & division; stuck in outmoded tradition; xenophobia
Patriarch, CEO, builder of lasting spiritual or material wealth	Con-man, trickster; moral compromise for short term gain

VIII. WIZARD WHATELEY

POSITIVE	NEGATIVE
Sowing of seeds which take generations to see fruition	Nurturing & propagation of Corruption & decay
Being forced to hide one's true identity; longing to reveal one's true nature	Agent of defilement & abomination, undermining social norms; taboos
Wizard, wise man, counsellor	Warlock, Black magician

IX. WILBUR WHATELEY

POSITIVE	NEGATIVE
Disaster delayed, problems on hold	"The Lesser of Two Evils"
Evil plot exposed; conspiracy brought to light	Deep-rooted conspiracy; Plot beyond control of its architects
Radical ideals; underground movement; revolution, reform; freedom fighter, political activist	Spy, saboteur, insurgency; guerrilla warfare, anarchist, terrorist

X. DR. MUNOZ
[Previously Wizard Edward Hutchinson]

POSITIVE	NEGATIVE
Long-lost friends; compatriots	Burnt bridges; forgotten friends
Soul mates, spiritual ties; unbreakable bonds of friendship	Obsessive relationship, co-dependency, stalker
Surrogate family	Unpleasant family experiences; unhealthy environment

XI. DR ARMITAGE

POSITIVE	NEGATIVE
Wisdom, Knowledge; A helpful person of learning & experience	Intellectual arrogance as an obstacle to progress
A transcendence of intellectual boundaries stimulated by extreme need; "Necessity is the Mother of Invention"	Knowledge limited by artificial academic boundaries; information made impractical by inability to adapt to the ideas of others
Intellect in practical application	Information not being shared

XII. CRAWFORD TILLINGHAST

POSITIVE	NEGATIVE
Knowledge that "supernatural" is just an issue of (limited) perception	Limits of perception as "Safety Valve," guarding human sanity
Mystical science; profoundly advanced theories & contemplation	Academic platitudes & charlatanry; intellectual posing & pomposity
Unorthodox methods justified	Repudiation by peers

XIII. NAHAM GARDNER
[Previously Harley Warren]

POSITIVE	NEGATIVE
Self-sacrifice on behalf of another	Foolish effort; wasted resources
Courage; Pushing frontiers, challenging boundaries	Dangerous exploration; disregard for safety and/or restrictions
Martyrdom; Heroism	Prideful recklessness

XIV. KEZIAH MASON

POSITIVE	NEGATIVE
True Alchemy; successful mixture of Science & Mysticism; balance of rational & intuitive faculties	Irrational and/or inconsistent blend of Science & Mysticism; "Psychobabble," pop psychology
Metaphysics in the most literal sense of the word	Secrets, "Skeletons in the Closet," Deception, Manipulation
"Quantum leap" in consciousness; psychological evolution	Overwhelming revelation; confrontation with radical truths

Suit of Artifacts

I. STAR STONE

POSITIVE	NEGATIVE
Protection, Sanctuary, Security	Weakness, False security, misplaced faith
Key, pass; opening, passage	Locks, cage. prison
Charm, amulet, talisman, artifact	Fetish, jinx, glamour, bewitchment

II. THE COLOUR OUT OF SPACE

POSITIVE	NEGATIVE
Prima Materia, Quintessence, Hyle	Chaos, lack of form & definition
Purity of spirit; Agent of Transformation	Cause or reason for dissolution; corruption
Object of Quest; Holy Grail, unicorn, the Philosopher's Stone	Loss of will, lack of integrity; squandered opportunity

III. THE SILVER KEY

POSITIVE	NEGATIVE
Transcendence of the need to conform to "mature" models of ambition & action	Immaturity, phantasm, escape into dream & fantasy
Regaining innocence; the "Inner Child"; optimism & simple joys	Lost dreams; faded innocence; cynicism & pessimism
A Higher Consciousness; "The Doors of Perception"	Delusions; Alcoholism, Drug addiction

IV. THE SHINING TRAPEZOHEDRON

POSITIVE	NEGATIVE
Hypnotism, Mystic Trance, Shamanism	Loss of willpower, Domination, possession
Clairvoyance, Channelling, Vision into other worlds	Demonology, Necromancy, "Speaking With The Dead"
Activation of & contact with the Collective Unconscious	Atavism; Reactivation of dormant animalistic traits

V. GUARDIAN OF KADATH

POSITIVE	NEGATIVE
Milestone, Landmark, sign/symbol of Achievement, trophy	Accomplishments constantly out of reach, illusion of progress
Leaps of progress; acceleration	Stalling, stumbling, hesitation
Travel, journey; Vacation	Drudgery, boredom; inability to escape mundane burdens

VI. THE YELLOW SIGN

POSITIVE	NEGATIVE
The end of a bad event or phenomenon; external influence brings resolution of immobility and/or dissolution of obstacles	Messenger bearing bad news; vehicle of disaster or demise; assassin
New mobility; catalyst, stirrings of new endeavour & action	Stuck in unhealthy repetition; negative patterns, dysfunction
Recovery; 12-Step programs; admission & acceptance of powerlessness	"Insanity is repeating the same actions over & over again, & expecting different results"

VII. EOD VESTMENTS

POSITIVE	NEGATIVE
Wondrous craftsmanship; "unearthly" skill	"Knock-off," shallow imitation, impersonation
Creative & philosophical Avant Garde	"Old School" refusing to give ground to new ideas
Recognition out of obscurity; cultural survival & validation	Stolen heritage; commercial exploitation of ethnicity & culture

VIII. THE TILLINGHAST RESONATOR

POSITIVE	NEGATIVE
Tearing down the boundaries which confine perception	Overwhelming the "safety valves" of consciousness & the psyche
Aldous Huxley's "Mind-At-Large"	Safety in monotony & uniformity; "ignorance is bliss"
Comprehension of the energy or soul in ALL things; aura	Political Correction

IX. PICKMAN'S MODEL

POSITIVE	NEGATIVE
Confirmation of legend, folklore, & myth as tangible reality	Nightmare made reality; realization of fears
Underworld Passage & Initiation; Labyrinth; Trial & Ordeal generating growth, progress, & evolution	Traumatic confrontation with the "Shadow" or dark side of human nature
Assimilation of shadow leads "Beyond Good & Evil"	Psychotic break with Shadow; "Jekyll & Hyde"

X. MI-GO BRAIN CYLINDER

POSITIVE	NEGATIVE
Rational Intellect detached from distractions & diversions	Intellect divorced from actual circumstance; Theory without experimentation
Platonic Idealism providing positive models & aspirations	Platonic Idealism denigrating reality & accident
Academic genius & inspiration sustaining itself regardless of recognition	Academic or intellectual pride & hubris

XI. BOKRUG, THE WATER LIZARD

POSITIVE	NEGATIVE
Object of veneration; relic, icon	False idol; sacrilege
Rallying point, unifying symbol, sign, emblem, or omen	Retribution, warfare; religious justification for warfare, Jihad
Supernatural visitation or presence	Haunting, poltergeist

XII. HOUND AMULET

POSITIVE	NEGATIVE
Ability to be found by anything from a beeper to a GPS beacon	Negative attention; invasion of privacy, paparazzi
Networking, communication, "staying in touch"	Disconnectedness, isolation; removal from normal environment
Clarity & enforcement of boundaries; policy, protocol	Lack of definition, incoherence; dilution of message

XIII. DERBY STONE

POSITIVE	NEGATIVE
Compass, guide, navigation, straight course	Led astray by ulterior motives
Incognito, disguise	Subterfuge, deception in order to reach a goal
Underworld experience	Mystical charlatanry

XIV. PLUTONIAN DRUG

POSITIVE	NEGATIVE
Shamanism, ancient practices	Drug addiction, alcoholism
Happy intoxication, responsible partying & celebration	Irresponsible use & handling of toxic substances… and knowledge
External or artificial catalyst for intellectual evolution; experimental and/or alternative medicine	Illusory cure; temporary solution, "quick fix"; "Flowers for Algernon"

SUIT OF TOMES

I. NECRONOMICON

POSITIVE	NEGATIVE
Privileged access to forbidden &/ or dangerous knowledge	Stolen or clandestine access to controlled information
Ability to find truth amidst deception	Control & limitation of information, censorship
Scholarly investigation; classical references	Dubious sources; unstable academic foundation

II. DE VERMIS MYSTERIIS

POSITIVE	NEGATIVE
Forensic Science, pathology	Loss or destruction of evidence &/ or academic proof
Alchemical putrefaction, "nigredo"; the combustion of the Phoenix before Rebirth	Death, the "Conqueror Worm"
"Always darkest before the Dawn"	The "calm before the storm"

III. UNSPEAKABLE CULTS
[Previously Unausprechlichen Kulten]

POSITIVE	NEGATIVE
Oaths, obligations, promises, vows	Broken oaths, unfulfilled promises
Silence; secrecy; secret societies	Mystical hyperbole & melodrama
Fraternal / charitable organizations	Conspiracies, secret agendas

IV. R'LYEH TEXTS

POSITIVE	NEGATIVE
New discoveries about ancient beliefs; Qumran, Nag Hammadi	Academic hoaxes or attempts, e.g., the Kensington Runestone
Radical academia; scholarly Avant Garde broaching challenging ideas	Fantastic willingness to believe anything outside of the mainstream
Healthy Satire	Cynicism as a sign of weakness & Shallowness

V. DHOL CHANTS

POSITIVE	NEGATIVE
Ritual, liturgy; religious poetry	Religious banalities & platitudes; empty ceremonies and rituals
Song, music, melody; harmonious composition, cohesion of parts	Atonality, disharmony, discord
Poetry, elegance; rhythm, cadence; Aesthetic regularity	Irregularity, intermittence, discontinuity

VI. LIBRE DE EIBON

POSITIVE	NEGATIVE
Apocrypha, Pseudepigrapha	False claims of authorship or craftsmanship; false pretences
Psychic information; channelled or received knowledge	Lies, trickster games; deception and misinterpretation
Seamless integration of old & new ideas	Conflict between ancient & modern wisdom

VII. KING IN YELLOW

POSITIVE	NEGATIVE
Stasis, Security, Stability	Inertia; Motion without Progress
Noblesse Oblige; Chivalry, Code of Honour; courtesy & etiquette	Desertion of Duties; Empty titles, unfound honours
Birth right, legacy; inherited responsibilities & obligations	Futility, Will-lessness Submission to unknown forces
Royalty, Aristocracy	Inbreeding; De-evolution

VIII. CULTES DES GOULS

POSITIVE	NEGATIVE
Assimilation of Information; Data processing	Plagiarism; unoriginal thought; second-hand knowledge, hearsay
Investigative journalism; protection of anonymous sources	Snitches, informants
Friends in hidden and / or unexpected places	The Underworld, either criminal or mythological

IX. PNAKOTIC MANUSCRIPTS

POSITIVE	NEGATIVE
Direct experience of the Divine; Achievement of mystic union	Religiously induced madness & / or hysteria
Revelation, prophetic experience	Mind overwhelmed or shattered by mystic experience
Divine Madness; mystical ecstasy & intoxication	Religious debauchery; orgiastic practices

Appendix I: A Further Statement on the Minor Arcana

X. ELTDOWN SHARDS

POSITIVE	NEGATIVE
Restoration of lost knowledge; recovery of missing information	Fragmentary information, incomplete data
Key piece of puzzle; intellectual windfall	Trying to force together incompatible data
Intellectual bridge; "connecting the dots"	Forcing data to fit a pre-conceived conclusion

XI. PEOPLE OF THE MONOLITH

POSITIVE	NEGATIVE
Childhood vision	Childhood nightmare
Acceptance of supernatural without thought or question	Morbid fixation; unhealthy obsession; dark imagination
Early start at artistic / literary talent	Suppression of childhood talent

XII. THE PONAPE SCRIPTURES

POSITIVE	NEGATIVE
"Primitive" culture; simplicity & honesty of relationships	"Savage" life, Law of the Jungle; loss or lack of civilized justice
Human dynamics, uncorrupted by greed, ambition, etc.	Human dynamics reduced to a purely animal, survival level; "Caveman" ethic
Authority given willingly and / or well deserved	Childish struggles for dominance

XIII. CRYPTICAL BOOKS OF HSAN

POSITIVE	NEGATIVE
Encryption, code, cipher; protection of data	Loss of message in transmission; noisy signal
Magic numbers, numerology; magical squares & / or seals	Unprotected intercourse, & the consequences thereof
Qabalah, "High" Magick; communication with Archetypes & Angels	Goetia, demonic intercourse; submission to Lower powers

XIV. REGNUM CONGO
[Previously The Black Book]

POSITIVE	NEGATIVE
Humour, satire, sarcasm	Propaganda; Political Deception; advertising
Earthly spirituality; White Magic	Black magic; Curse
Survival amidst oppression	"The gods of the old religion become the devils of the new"

Appendix I: A Further Statement on the Minor Arcana 511

Suit of Sites

I. SUNKEN R'LYEH
[Previously Yuggoth]

POSITIVE	NEGATIVE
Foundation, Staging point	Erosion, decomposition, undermining, deterioration
Origin, Source; New beginning	Unswerving Fate, inevitable conclusion
Exploration; enterprise	Espionage, sabotage

II. IREM, CITY OF PILLARS

POSITIVE	NEGATIVE
Ability to reach one's goal without direction or defined route	Mirage; shifting landmarks or (intellectual) points of reference
Adaptability to a changing landscape	Inability to accept or adapt to circumstance
Improvisation; freedom of form	Loss of structure & / or discipline

III. PLATEAU OF LENG

POSITIVE	NEGATIVE
Avalon, Tir-na-Nog, Realm of Faerie; legendary kingdoms made manifest	Hidden place; Unfinished journey; limited goals which fall short of true achievement
Idealism, Zeal; Healthy perfectionism	Unrealistic goals, setup for failure; self-sabotage
Retirement, pension; rest after productive career	Unproductive lifestyle; insecurity due to lack of planning / foresight

IV. WHATELEY FARMHOUSE

POSITIVE	NEGATIVE
Evolution, power of adaption	Mutation; abnormal growth
Home, hearth, homestead; family, comfort	Alienation despite healthy environment; alternately – comfort in an unhealthy environment
Self-esteem and / or security of identity derived from established roots	Adoption; lack of clear identity, insecure sense of self

V. THE WITCH HOUSE

POSITIVE	NEGATIVE
Unconventional form	Subtle assault on the senses
Structural dissonance & artistic symmetry	Environmental dissonance induces internal discord
Ergonomics, Feng Shui	External factors cause mental, emotional and / or physical imbalance; stress, fatigue

VI. THE MOUNTAINS OF MADNESS

POSITIVE	NEGATIVE
Recovered knowledge; ancient wisdom	Forgotten history and / or science
Long term planning	Apocalyptic thinking and actions
Utopia	Dystopia

VII. CHURCH OF FEDERAL HILL
[Previously ST Toads]

POSITIVE	NEGATIVE
Appointed time	Unheeded warning; Alarm
Herald; announcement, Invitation	Omen, augury, warning
Call, calling; Vocation (in the full religious implication of the term	Turning aside from one's destined path; defying and / or tempting Fate

VIII. INNSMOUTH

POSITIVE	NEGATIVE
"Different drummer," new & individual path & practice	Ostracism, banishment; excommunication
Transcending societal norms; paradigm shift in cultural attitudes & group dynamics	Dereliction, decay; mutilation
Commune; group residence	Ghost town; tenement, ghetto

IX. KADATH

POSITIVE	NEGATIVE
Mystery, hidden origins	Unknown danger; obscure threat
Lack of agenda	Secret agenda
Journey for Journey's sake; process or action "without lust of result"	Unclear objectives, undefined goals

X. EXHAM PRIORY

POSITIVE	NEGATIVE
Legacy, birth right, inheritance	"Family Curse," ghosts
Return, homecoming	Wandering, inability to settle down
Discovering lost roots	Exile, expatriation

XI. SENTINEL HILL

POSITIVE	NEGATIVE
External Power Centres; groves, monuments	Places of painful memory; crime scenes, battlefields
Internal Power Centres; chakras, chi meridians, kundalini	Wounds, scars; blockages, unnatural and / or unhealthy flow of vital energies and / or fluids
Ley lines, natural springs (water and spiritual energy), practical utilities (electric, water, gas, etc.)	Power outages, interruption of utility services

XII. EOD TEMPLE

POSITIVE	NEGATIVE
Symbiosis of old & new traditions; religious reform	Heresy, radical departure from civilized beliefs, apocalyptic mania
Radical spirituality; "New Aeon," "Age of Aquarius" philosophy	Cult, brain washing; domination of will through spiritual manipulation
Group Identity & Unity	Inquisition, Auto da Fe

XIII. HOUSE IN THE MIST
[Previously Federal Hill]

POSITIVE	NEGATIVE
Forgotten gates & doorways	Abandoned paths of wisdom
Ethnic traditions & wisdom	Ethnic clichés & stereotypes; superstition
Transcending taboos; "Beyond Good & Evil"	Unheeded warnings; prideful break with tradition

XIV. ARKHAM

POSITIVE	NEGATIVE
University, centre of learning and / or communication	"Tower of Babel," too many opinions, inability to make a decision
Board, panel; certification; jurisdiction, examination	Unlicensed practice, quackery; dubious advice
Port, business centre, marketplace, financial centre, industry	Bad investments; inflation; depreciation; bad real estate

Appendix II:
A Statement of 777, The Correspondences and The Hermetic Order of The Golden Dawn

Further to the statement on the subject of *777* in Part One of this book, here's a brief table of examples as given in this reference. Whilst the study of the occult correspondences is a much greater occult study of its own, and one which the Magus should look into if wanting to take the study of this interpretation of the Tarot further, this Appendix is given with the intention that this could be a suggested starting point of research if those who already have a working knowledge of the religious system of the Golden Dawn of Thelema, and should want to interpret those statements of religious philosophy further in terms of the ideas in this book as relating to the worship of The Great Old Ones and the acknowledgement of the Lovecraftian system of ritual magick, as has been the discussion intended with this book.

Appendix II: A Statement of 777

Number	General Attribution of Tarot	According to the *HP Lovecraft Tarot*	According to *The Necronomicon*
0			
1	The 4 Aces		Azathoth
2	The 4 Two's – Kings or Knights		Nyarlathotep (as directed will of Azathoth)
3	The 4 Three's – Queens		Shub Niggurath (as fertile mother)
4	The 4 Fours		
5	The 4 Fives		
6	The 4 Sixes – Emperors or Princes		
7	The Fool	Azathoth	
8	The Juggler		
9	The High Priestess	Yog Sothoth	Cthulhu
10	The Empress	Shub Niggurath	Ubbo-Sathala
11	The Emperor	Hastur. The King in Yellow	
12	The Hierophant	Cthulhu	Nyarlathotep (as Messenger)
13	The Lovers	Lavinia Whateley & Yog Sothoth	

Number	General Attribution of Tarot	According to the *HP Lovecraft Tarot*	According to *The Necronomicon*
14	The Chariot	Ithaqua	
15	Strength	Shoggoth	
16	Hermit	Great Race of Yith	
17	Wheel of Fortune	Hounds of Tindalos	
18	Justice	Mi-Go	
19	The Hanged Man	Deep One	
20	Temperance	Old One	
21	The Devil	Tsathoggua	
22	The House of God	The Dunwich Horror	
23	The Star	Nodens, Lord of the Great Abyss	
24	The Moon	Night Gaunt	
25	The Sun	Yig, the Serpent God	
26	The Angel or Last Judgement	**Dagon**	Yog Sothoth
27	The Universe	Chaugnar Faugn	
28	Empresses (Coins)		
29	All 22 Trumps		Father Dagon & Mother Hydra

Number	General Attribution of Tarot	According to the *HP Lovecraft Tarot*	According to *The Necronomicon*
30			
31			Cthugha
32			Tsathoggua
32 (bis)			
31 (bis)			

Number	According to Assyro-Babylonian Religion	Egyptian Deities	Elements
0	ANU (TIAMUT)	Harpocrates, Amoun, Nuit, Hadit	
1	ENLIL (ABSU)	Ptah, Asar-un-Nefer, Hadit, Heru-Ra-Ha	Root of AIR
2	ENKI LUMASHI (IGIGI)	Amoun, Thoth, Nuit (Zodiac)	Root of FIRE
3	ADAR	Maut, Isis, Nephthys	Root of WATER
4	MARDUK	Amoun, Isis, Hathor	WATER
5	NERGAL	Horus, Nephthys	FIRE
6	UTU	Asar, Ra, On, Harpocrates, Hrumachis	AIR
7	INANNA	Hathor	FIRE

Number	According to Assyro-Babylonian Religion	Egyptian Deities	Elements
8	NEBO	Anubis	WATER
9	NANNA	Shu, Hermanubis	AIR
10	KIA	Seb, Isis & Nephithys	EARTH
11	ANNA	Nu, Hoor-pa-kraat	AIR
12	GUDUD	Thoth & Cynocephalus	Water
13	SIN	Khonsu	Air
14	DLIBAT	Hathor	Fire
15	AGRU (XUBUR)	Hapi, Aroueris	
16	KAKKAB U ALAP SHAME (KINGU)	Asar, Ameshet, Apis	
17	RE'U KINU SHAME U TU'AME RABUTI (YE TWIN VIPERS OF DEATH)		
18	SHITTU (SNAKE)	Khephra	
19	KALBU RABU (LAKHAMU)	Ra-Hoor-Khuit, Pasht, Sekhet, Mau	
20	SHIRU (WHIRLWIND)	Isis	

Number	According to Assyro-Babylonian Religion	Egyptian Deities	Elements
21	UMUNPADDU	Amount-Ra	Water
22	ZIBANITUM (Ravening Dog)	Maat	
23	BADUR		WATER
24	AKRABU (SCORPION MAN)	Typhon, Apep, Khephra	
25	PA-BIL-SAG (HURRICANE)	Nephthys	
26	SAXUR MASH (FISH MAN)	Min, Sept	
27	MASTABARRU	Horus	Fire
28	GULA (HORNED BEAST)	Mentu	
29	DILGAN U RIKIS NUNI (WEAPON OF DILGAN)	Khephra	
30	SHAMASH	Ra	Air
31	AG		FIRE
32	KAIMANU	Sebek, Maka	Earth
32 (bis)	KIA		EARTH
31 (bis)	ZI	Asar	SPIRIT

Number	Signs of the Zodiac	Planets Ruling the Signs	Incenses
0			
1			Ambergris
2			Musk
3			Myrrh, Civet
4			Cedar, Pine Gum, Juniper
5			Dragons Blood (Tobacco)
6			Frankincense, Cinnamon
7			Rose, Red Sandalwood, Benzoin, Amber, Civet, Valerian
8			Storax, Styrax, Lavender, White Sandalwood
9			Jasmine, Lily, Camphor, Copal, Eucalyptus, Odoriferous Roots
10			Dittany of Crete, Jerusalem Incense, Fruitwoods
11			Galbonum

Number	Signs of the Zodiac	Planets Ruling the Signs	Incenses
12			Storax, White Sandalwood, Cloves, Nutmeg
13			Camphor, Menstrual Blood, Sweet Virginal Odours
14			Myrtle, all Soft Voluptuous Odours
15	Aquarius, Water Carrier	Saturn	Galbanum, Euphorbium
16	Taurus, the Bull	Venus	Storax, Pepperwort
17	Gemini, the Twins	Mercury	Wormwood, Mastic
18	Cancer, the Crab	Luna (the Moon)	Onycha, Camphor
19	Leo, the Lion	Sol (the Sun)	Frankincense
20	Virgo, the Maiden	Mercury	Narcissus, Sandalwood
21			Cedar, Saffron, Clove, all Generous Odours
22	Libra, the Balance	Venus	Galbanum

Number	Signs of the Zodiac	Planets Ruling the Signs	Incenses
23	All Water Signs		Lotus, Myrrh, Onycha
24	Scorpio, the Scorpion	Mars	Siamese Benzoin, Opoponax
25	Sagittarius, the Archer	Jupiter	Lign-Aloes
26	Capricorn, the Goat	Saturn	Musk, Civet,
27			Dragon's Blood, Pepper, Blood
28	Aries, the Ram	Mars	Dragon's Blood, Myrrh
29	Pisces, the Fishes	Jupiter	Ambergris, Menstrual Blood, Red Storax
30			Frankincense, cinnamon
31	All Fiery Signs		Frankincense
32			
32 (bis)	All Earthly Signs		
31 (bis)			

Number	The King Scale of Colour	The Queen Scale of Colour	Geomantic Figures
0			Circle
1	Brilliance	White brilliance	Point
2	Pure Soft Blue	Gray	Cross
3	Crimson	Black	
4	Deep Violet	Blue	
5	Orange	Scarlet red	
6	Clear pink rose	Yellow (gold)	
7	Amber	Emerald	
8	Violet-purple	Orange	Octagon, Octogram
9	Indigo	Violet	
10	Yellow	Citrine, olive, russet & black	
11	Bright pale yellow	Sky blue	
12	Yellow	Purple	Octogram
13	Blue	Silver	
14	Emerald green	Sky blue	Heptogram
15	Violet	Sky blue	Pentagram, Hexagram
16	Red-orange	Deep indigo	
17	Orange	Pale mauve	
18	Amber	Maroon	
19	Yellow, greenish	Deep purple	
20	Green, yellowish	Slate gray	

Number	The King Scale of Colour	The Queen Scale of Colour	Geomantic Figures
21	Violet	Blue	Square, Rhombus
22	Emerald green	Blue	
23	Deep blue	Sea green	
24	Green-blue	Dull brown	
25	Blue	Yellow	
26	Indigo	Black	
27	Scarlet	Red	Pentagram
28	Scarlet	Red	
29	Crimson (ultra violet)	Buff, flecked silver-white	
30	Orange	Gold yellow	Hexagram
31	Glowing orange-scarlet	Vermillion	
32	Indigo	Black	Triangle
32 (bis)	Citrine, olive, russet & black, or green	Amber	
31 (bis)	White, merging into gray	Deep purple, nearly black	

BIBLIOGRAPHY

Abdel Haleem (trans.) (2008). The Qu'ran: *A new translation*. Oxford: Oxford World's Classics. p. 420

An Introduction to the Esoteric Order of Dagon (2008) Available at: http://www.esotericorderofdagon.org/E.'.O.'.D.'.%20Introduction.pdf [Accessed: 7 / 5 / 2020]

Bible: *New International Version*. (2011). Great Britain: Hodder & Stoughton

Chang, T. S. (2018) *Tarot Correspondences*. Minnesota: Llewellyn, p.1, p.2

Crowley, A. (1970) *777 Revised*. New York, Samuel Weiser, p. vii

Dagon the Fish-God (2019) Available at: https://www.bible-history.com/sketches/ancient/dagon.html [Accessed: 10 / 9 / 2019]

Decker, R. & Dummett, M. (2013) *A History of the Occult Tarot*. London: Duckworth Overlook, p. 310

Drury, N. (2006) *The Tarot Workbook*. UK: Apple Press. p. 46, p.58, p.62, p.66, p.72, p.76, p.80

DuQuette, L. M. (2017) *Understanding Aleister Crowley's Thoth Tarot*. Newbury Port, USA: Weiser Books, pp. 96-97

Eshelman, J. (2010) *776 ½ Tables of Correspondences for Practical Ceremonial*. United States: The College of Thelema, p. 1

Grant, K. (1994) *Nightside of Eden*. London: SKOOB BOOKS, pp. 146-147

Haney, J. K. (n.d.) *Lovecraftian Tarot Decks (Part 1)* Available at: http://www.innsmouthfreepress.com/blog/lovecraftian-tarot-decks-part-1/ [Accessed: 18 / 10 / 2018]

Harms, D. (2008) *The Cthulhu Mythos Encyclopedia*. Lake Orion: Elder Sign Press. pp. xvii-xviii, pp. xix-xxi, pp. 6-7, pp. 9-10, p. 26, p. 28, p. 41, pp. 45-46, p. 51, p. 62, p. 66, pp. 71-72, p. 79, pp. 81-84, pp. 93-95, p. 105, p. 137, pp. 139-140, pp. 142-143, p. 148, p. 152, p. 164, p. 166, p. 168, pp. 176-177, p. 179, p. 180, pp. 222-223, pp. 226-227, p.

229, pp. 239-241, p. 251, p. 256, p. 262, pp. 267-268, pp. 281-282, pp. 292-293, pp. 306-307, pp. 309-310, p. 312, p. 320, p. 332

Hutchinson, D. & Friedman, E. C. (2002) *The H P Lovecraft Tarot*. Poplar Bluff: Mythos Books, pp. 2-3, pp. 6-66

Irem of the Pillars, the Lost 'Atlantis of the Sands' (n.d.) Available at: https://www.ancient-origins.net/ancient-places-asia/irem-pillars-lost-atlantis-sands-001839 [Accessed: 2 / 10 / 2019]

John, O. (2018) *Hermetic Qabalah Foundation: Complete Course*. Ordo Astri Imprimatur, p. 56

Kenner, C. (2018) *Tarot and Astrology*. Minnesota: Llewellyn, pp. 33-34

Lariushin, B. (ed) (2012) *Al Azif: The Cipher Manuscript known as "Necronomicon"*. Great Britain: Amazon.co.uk.Ltd, p. 13

LaVey, A. (1992) *'Law of the Trapezoid'*. In: The Devil's Notebook. Port Townsend: Feral House. p. 111, pp. 114-115, p.116

Lippert, C. (2012) *Lovecraft's Grimoires: Intertextuality and the Necronomicon*. Working With English: Medieval and Modern Language, Literature and Drama (8), pp. 44-45, p. 47

Lovecraft, H. P. (1927) *History of the Necronomicon*. Available at: www.hplovecraft.com/writing/texts/fiction.hn.aspx [Accessed: 11 / 11 / 2018]

Lovecraft, H. P. (1999) *'The Call of Cthulhu'*. In: The Call of Cthulhu and Other Weird Stories. London: Penguin Modern Classics, p. 139

Lovecraft, H. P. (2001) *'At the Mountains of Madness'*. In: The Thing on the Doorstep and other Weird Stories. England: Penguin Modern Classics, p. 246

Mason, A. (2016) *NECRONOMICON GNOSIS: A Practical Introduction*. Magon Publications, pp. 7-8, p. 11

Mosig, Y. D. W. (1997) *Mosig At Last: A Psychologist Looks At H. P. Lovecraft*. West Warwick: Necronomicon Press, p. 23

Necronomicon (n.d.) Available at: http://hplovecraft.hu/necroeng.pdf [Accessed: 2 / 12 / 2018]

Nichols, S. (1980) *Jung and Tarot: An Archetypal Journey*. San Francisco: Weiser Press, p. 26

Oken, A. (2006) *Alan Oken's Complete Astrology*. Berwick: Ibis Press, p. 6

Pollack, R. (1983) *Seventy-Eight Degrees of Wisdom, A Book of Tarot, Part 2: The Minor Arcana and Readings*. London: Aquarius / Thorsons. pp. 25-29, pp. 31-42, pp. 44-47, pp.49-63, p. 66, pp. 68-93, pp. 96-97, p. 99, pp. 102-103, pp. 107-120

Reber, A. S. & Reber, E. S. (2001) 'Shadow'. In: *Dictionary of Psychology*. England: Penguin Reference, p. 676

Sosteric, M. (2014) *A Sociology of Tarot*. The Canadian Journal of Sociology / Cahiers canadiens de sociologie. 39 (3) Available at: https://www.jstor.org/stable/canajsocicahican.39.3.357 [Accessed: 29 / 09 / 2018], pp. 358-360, pp. 378-379

Thomson, G. (2007) *Apocrypha and Pseudepigrapha*. Available at: https://www.encyclopedia.com/religion/encyclopedias-almanacs-transcripts-and-maps/apocrypha-and-pseudepigrapha [Accessed: 26 / 5 / 2019]

Turner, R. (1995) *The R'Lyeh Text*. London: Skoob Books Publishing. p. 57

Vocabulary.com Dictionary (n.d.) Available at: https://www.vocabulary.com/dictionary/temple [Accessed: 10 / 9 / 2019]

www.ingramcontent.com/pod-product-compliance
Lightning Source LLC
Chambersburg PA
CBHW020826160426
43192CB00007B/538